THESAURUS OF AMERICAN SLANG

D0167650

Thesaurus
of
American
Slang

Edited by

Robert L. Chapman, Ph.D.

WITHDRAWN

Rock Valley College
Educational Resources
Center

Harper Perennial
A Division of HarperCollins*Publishers*

THESAURUS OF AMERICAN SLANG. Copyright © 1989 by Harper & Row Publishers. All rights reserved. Printed in the United States of America. No part of this book may be used or reproduced in any manner whatsoever without written permission except in the case of brief quotations embodied in critical articles and reviews. For information address HarperCollins Publishers, 10 East 53rd Street, New York, N.Y. 10022

First HARPERPERENNIAL edition published 1991

Designed by Karen Savary

Library of Congress has catalogued the hardcover edition of this title as follows:

Chapman, Robert L.
   Thesaurus of American slang / edited by Robert L. Chapman.
      p.   cm.
   Includes index.
   1. English language—United States—Slang—Dictionaries. 2. English language—United States—Synonyms and antonyms. 3. Americanisms—Dictionaries. I. Title.
PE2846.C465 1989
427′.973′03—dc20
   ISBN 0-06-016140-X

ISBN 0-06-272010-4 (pbk.)

91 92 93 94 95 CC/FG 10 9 8 7 6 5 4 3 2 1

Ref
PE
2846
C465
1991
C.2

THESAURUS OF AMERICAN SLANG

A

AC-DC
adj Erotically attracted to both sexes

ambidextrous, bi, double-gaited, swinging both ways

ace
1 *n An expert, as in "She's a computer ace"*

[chiefly Brit] boffin, crack hand, [chiefly Brit] dab hand, flash, heavyweight, hotshot, hot stuff, mavin, mean bean, no slouch, the one that wrote the book, piss-cutter, pisser, pistol, powerhouse, pundit, star, whiz, whiz-kid, wiz, wizard

2 *n A one-year prison sentence*

boffo, book, boppo, one-spot

3 *v To execute perfectly; do a superior job, as in "He aced the entrance exam"*

ace it, cream, cream up, do a grand, go great guns, hit it, max, max out, take care of business, TCB, whale

4 SEE **JOINT**
5 SEE **PAL**

acid
n LSD (lysergic acid diethylamide), a hallucinogen

A, ad, animal, beast, big D, black tabs, blotter, blue acid, blue chair, blue cheer, blue dot, blue flag, blue heaven, blue mist, blue Owsley, blue splash, brown dots, California sunshine, candy, cherry top, chief, clear light, coffee, cracker, cubes, cupcakes, D, deeda, delysid, domes, dot, electric Kool Aid, flake acid, flash, flat blues, flats, four-way hit, gelatin, ghost, grape parfait, green dragon, green swirls, green wedge, Hawaiian sunshine, hawk, haze, instant Zen, L, LBJ, Love Saves, Lucy in the sky with diamonds, Mary Owsley, microdots, mighty Quinn, mind detergent, one-way hit, orange cubes, orange micro, orange mushroom, orange Owsley, orange sunshine, orange wedges, outer, Owsley, Owsley's acid, Owsley's blue dot, peace, peace tablets, pink Owsley, pink swirl, pink wedge, pure love, purple barrels, purple flats, purple haze, purple microdots, purple ozoline, Raggedy Ann, royal blues, Sandoz, squirrel, strawberries, strawberry fields, sugar, sugar cube, sugar lumps, sunshine, Swiss purple, tabs, travel agent, trips, twenty-five, two-way hit, vials, wedding bells, wedding bells acid, wedges, white lightning, white Owsley's, white Sandoz, yellow dimples, yellow fever, yellows, yellow sunshine, Zen

☞ *The great number of slang terms for narcotics probably reflects both a need for coded reference to an illegal substance and a desire to be chic and up-to-date, in addition to the need to distinguish varieties.*

act
n A dramatic mimicking, as in "He did his Clint Eastwood act"

bit, number, riff, routine, shtick, takeoff

Afro
n A frizzy hairstyle
worn by blacks

fro, 'fro

ages
n A long time

an age, a blue moon, a coon's age, a dog's age, [esp Brit] donkey's years, a month of Sundays, since God knows when, since Hector was a pup, a smart spell

angel
1 *n A financial*
supporter of any
enterprise; a patron;
a backer
2 SEE GAY

bankroll, butter-and-egg man, cash cow, grub-staker, meal ticket, staker, sugar daddy

angel dust
n phr PCP
(phencyclidine)
inhaled or smoked
as a narcotic

ace, ad, amoeba, angel hair, angel mist, angel puke, animal, Aurora Borealis, black whack, busy bee, Cadillac, cigarrode, CJ, Columbo, cozmos, cristal, crystal, cyclones, Detroit pink, devil dust, dime of buzz, dipper, D O A, dummy dust, dust, earth, elephant, embalming fluid, flake, fuel, goon, goon dust, gorilla tab, green, green tea, heaven and hell, herms, heroin buzz, hog, the hog, jet fuel, juice, K, Kaps, K-blast, killerweed, Kools, lovely magic, magic, magic dust, mean green, mintweed, mist, monkey dust, new magic, orange cryst, peace, peace pill, peaceweed, Peter Pan, pig killer, puffy, rocket fuel, scaffle, sheets, star dust, super grass, super Kools, surfer, whack wack, wobble, wobble weed, wolf, worm, zombie buzz, zoom

☞ *The great number of slang terms for narcotics probably reflects both a need for coded reference to an illegal substance and a desire to be chic and up-to-date, in addition to the need to distinguish varieties.*

Annie Oakley
n phr A
complimentary
ticket

Chinee, Chinee ducket, Chinese ducket, comp, freebie, Oakley, paper

antsy
1 *adj Eagerly*
desirous; excited and
tense, as in "He was
antsy over the idea"

aching, all atwitter, bursting, busting, gung ho, hepped up, het up, hitchy, honked up, hopped up, horked, hot, hot-eyed, hot to trot, hurting, hyped-up, hyper, in a dither, in a doodah, in a flutter, in a lather, in a state, in a sweat, in a tizzy, itching, itchy, keen, keyed up, perishing, psyched, psyched up, ranged, rarin' to go, red-hot, spoiling, steamed up, wild, wired, worked up, yantsy

2 SEE JITTERY

ass
1 *n The buttocks;*
the posterior

[Brit, pronounced "ahs"] arse, back porch, back seat, backside, behind, bibby, bippy, boogie, bottom, botty, bucket, [chiefly Brit] bum, buns, butt, butt end, caboose, cakes, can, cheeks, cupcakes, derriere, duff, duster, fanny, gazonga, gazoo, gazool, heinie, hind end, hindside, kazoo, keister, loaves, oil bags, part that goes over the fence last, patoot, patootie, poop, popo, prat, pratt, rear, rear end, rolls, rump, rusty-dusty, seat, seat of the pants, south side, stern, tail, tail bone, tail end, tokus, tush, tushy, wazoo

2 *n Sexual activity;*
sexual gratification,
as in "I'm going to
get myself a little
ass tonight"

boff, boom-boom, booty, bop, bouncy-bouncy, butt, cat, chunk, cooz, crack, cunt, diddling, frig, frigging, fuck, fucking, gash, ginch, ground rations, hard breathing, heavy breathing, hole, hooch, hootchie-cootchie, hump, humpery, hunk, in-and-out, in-out, jazz, jellyroll, jig-jig, a lay, a make, meat, nooky, notch, party, phutzing, piece, piece of ass, piece of butt, piece of tail, pom-pom, (with a black woman) poontang, pop, push-

push, pussy, quim, ride, roll, roll in the hay, screw, screwing, shtup, stuff, tail, trade, trim, twat, zig-zig

☞ *Of course, many more such terms may be made by adding the "ing" gerund suffix to any appropriate verb at "fuck."*

3 *n The whole person; one's self, as in "Get your ass out of here!"*

backside, behind, bottom, buns, butt, can, duff, fanny, keister, patoot, rump, tail, tokus

4 SEE **ASSHOLE**

5 SEE **JERK**

as shit
adv phr
Exceedingly; to a great degree or extent, as in "That place is dirty as shit"

as all creation, as all get-out, as blazes, as can be, as hell, no end, to the max

☞ *These terms always follow the adjective being modified.*

asshole
1 *n The anus; the rectum*

A-hole, ass, back door, back way, behind, bibby, bippy, bottom, brown, brownie, bucket, [chiefly Brit] bum, bumhole, bung, bunghole, butt, butthole, cornhole, dirt chute, dirt road, exhaust pipe, gazoo, gazool, gig, giggy, heinie, hole, kazoo, keister, poop chute, poophole, poo-poo, porthole, rosebud, round brown, shitter, slop chute, wazoo, where the sun doesn't shine, wing-wang, winkie, ying-yang, yin-yang

2 *n A despicable person; a vile and filthy wretch*

A-hole, badass, bad baby, bad egg, bad job, bad lot, bastard, birdturd, blue meany, bugger, bum, bummer, cocksucker, crumb, cuntface, cunthead, dick, dickhead, dip, dipshit, dipstick, dirtbag, dirty bum, dirty rat, double-clutcher, fink, four-letter man, fuck, fucker, fuckhead, heel, heeler, horse's ass, hound, hound-dog, hyena, jerk, junkyard dog, louse, mama-eater, mama-fucker, mama-grabber, mama-jumper, mama-kisser, mama-lover, mama-nudger, mama-rammer, mammy-eater, mammy-fucker, mammy-grabber, mammy-jumper, mammy-kisser, mammy-lover, mammy-nudger, mammy-rammer, MF, momzer, mother, mother-eater, motherfucker, mothergrabber, mother-jumper, motherkisser, motherlover, mothernudger, motherrammer, mucker, muhfuh, peckerhead, piece of shit, pigfucker, pissant, pisshead, prick, punk, putz, rat, rat-fink, rat-fuck, rat's asshole, RF, ringtail, rotten egg, rotter, sao, schmuck, scum, scumbag, scum of the earth, scumsucker, scurve, scuzz, scuzzbag, scuzzo, shit, shitass, shitface, shithead, shitheel, shithook, shit-stick, shtoonk, shyster, skunk, sleazebag, sleazeball, so-and-so, S O B, son of a bitch, son of a whore, stinker, sumbitch, turd, worm

☞ *Even though most of these terms are felt to specify a male referent, some of them are increasingly used of women. Many of them are nearly synonymous with those listed under "jerk." The distinction is that while one detests an asshole, one despises a jerk. One both detests and despises a sleazebag.*

the axe
n phr Dismissal; discharge, as in "I had no idea my boss was dissatisfied until I got the axe"

the air, the boot, the bum's rush, the chop, the chuck, the gate, a hatchet job, the heave-ho, the hook, the kiss-off, the old heave-ho, the pink slip, the sack, the sackeroo, one's walking papers, one's walking ticket

☞ *These terms are almost always used after "give" or "get."*

B

back
v To give one's
support to an effort,
team, person, etc, as
in "She has an
uncanny knack for
backing the
eventual winner"

back up, bet on, boost, cheer for, get behind, give a leg up, go to bat for, go to the mat for, like, plug for, put one's money on, root for, stand behind, stick up for

back-breaker
n A very hard task;
a Herculean labor

ball-buster, bastard, bitch, bitch-kitty, bone-breaker, brute, bugger, bun-buster, butt-buster, grind, gut-buster, hard row to hoe, heavy sledding, killer, large order, pisser, son of a bitch, sumbitch, tough grind, whiz-bitch

back out
1 *v phr To cancel*
or renege on an
arrangement;
withdraw
2 SEE COP OUT

back down, chicken out, cop out, crab, crawdad, crawfish, fink out, funk out, rat out, weasel out, welsh, wiggle out, worm out

bad man

n phr A villain or scoundrel, esp in a play or movie

bad actor, badass, bad baby, baddie, bad hat, bad hombre, black hat, bugger, hard-boiled egg, heavy, meanie, Mister Bad Guy, rat, rotten egg, varmint, wrong number, wrongo, wrong 'un

bad-mouth

1 *v To denigrate; belittle, as in "He bad-mouthed her all over town"*

dump on, give a roasting, knock, pan, poor-mouth, rap, rip, roast, run down, slag, slam, take a dig at, take a swipe at

2 SEE **KNOCK**

bad news

1 *n phr Difficulty; trouble, as in "Cross the street when you see him coming, he's bad news"*

bad medicine, bad scene, bad shit, deep doo-doo, deep shit, deep trouble, diffyewculty, double-trouble, headache, hot grease, hot water, hurrah's nest, mind-fucker, murder, Old Man Trouble, pain in the ass, pain in the neck, poison, sticky wicket, tough shit, tough stuff, tsuris

2 SEE the **DAMAGE**

a bad scene

n phr A misfortune; an unhappy situation or event, as in "Our vacation turned out to be a bad scene"

bad trip, bitch, bitch-kitty, bummer, bum trip, disaster, downer, down trip, fake-out, mind-fucker, pain in the ass, pain in the neck

bad trip

n phr An unpleasant drug experience, esp with a hallucinogen; any unpleasant experience

acid funk, bad head, bum bend, bummer, bum trip, downer, down trip, drag, flip, flip-out, freak-out, low

bag

1 n A quantity or package of narcotics

bale of hay, balloon, bar, big hog, bindle, bird's eye, biz, block box, bottle, brick, can, cap, card, cargo, cube, deck, deuce, deuce bag, dime bag, elbow, feed bag, finger, foil, full moon, gang, gram, half, half bundle, half load, half piece, hunk, jug, kee, keg, key, ki, kite, ky, lid, load, long, match, matchbox, matchhead, microgram, milligram, moon, nickel, nickel bag, O, Ohio bag, O Z, paper, piece pillow, quarter bag, quarter ounce, sack, short, short piece, sixteenth, spoon, stash, tens, tin

2 n That which one prefers or is doing currently; one's specialty, as in "Looks like fun, but windsurfing's not my bag"

bit, cup of tea, dish, dish of tea, flash, gimmick, groove, joint, kick, [Brit] line of country, meat, scene, shot, thing, turf

3 SEE **CHUCK**
4 SEE **FIRE**
5 SEE **RUBBER**
6 SEE **TITS**

baldie

n A bald person

cueball, skinhead, suedehead

a ball
n phr *A very good time* — a blast, a gas, Gas City, a groove, a picnic, a supergroove

ball-buster
1 *n Someone who saps or destroys masculinity* — ball-wracker, bitch, nut-cruncher
2 SEE **BACK-BREAKER**

balls
1 *n The testicles* — ballocks, cojones, diamonds, the family jewels, jingleberries, nuts, rocks
2 SEE **BULLSHIT**
3 SEE **GUTS**

banger
1 *n A cylinder in a car engine, as in "One of its bangers only fires when it feels like it"* — barrel, bucket, hole, lung, squirrel
2 SEE **JALOPY**

bare-ass
adj *Nude; unclad* — as nature made one, b a, bare-assed, buck naked, buff, in one's birthday suit, in the altogether, in the buff, in the raw, in the state of nature, naked as a jaybird, naked as the day one was born, [esp Brit] starkers, without a stitch

barf
v *To vomit; regurgitate* — [esp Brit] be sick, blow grits, boff, call Earl's, cheese, chuck, do a Technicolor yawn, drive the big bus, dump,

feed the fish, flash, flash one's hash, have the pukes, heave, oops, oops up, ork, pray to the porcelain god, puke, ralph, ralph up, rolf, shoot one's cookies, shoot one's lunch, [Brit] sick up, snap one's cookies, talk to the big white phone, talk to the seals, toss one's cookies, upchuck, urp, whoops

barrel

v To go very fast; speed, as in "He barrels around corners with his eyes closed"

ball the jack, barrel along, barrel ass, bat, blast, bucket, burn, burn rubber, burn the breeze, burn the road, burn up the highway, carry the mail, chogie, clip, cut, dust, floor, floorboard, floor it, fly, fly low, fog, fog it, go full blast, go hell-bent, go hell-bent for election, go hell for leather, go hell to split, go lickety-cut, go lickety-split, go like a bat out of hell, go like a blue streak, go like a streak, go like Billy Hell, go like blazes, go like blue blazes, go like greased lightning, go like nobody's business, go like sixty, go like the deuce, go like the devil, go to beat the band, go to beat the Dutch, go to town, haul ass, haul the mail, hell, hell along, highball, hightail, hightail it, honk, hotfoot, hump, let her rip, make tracks, nail it, pack the mail, pour it on, pour on the coal, put it to the wood, put the hammer down, put the pedal to the metal, rip-ass, run wide open, scat, scoot, scorch, skin along, smoke, step on it, step on the gas, storm, streak, swoop, tear, tool, turn on the afterburners, varoom, vroom, zing, zing along, zip, zoom, zoomaty

basket

n The male genitals, as in "Check out the basket on that body builder"

apparatus, balls and bat, belongings, business, equipment, jewelry, meat, nasty bits, private parts, privates, works

bat around
v phr To discuss, as in "We'll bat around the idea a little before we decide"

chew over, go over, hash, hash over, kick around, knock around, toss around

bean
n The head; the skull

attic, belfry, biscuit, block, brainbox, chump, coco, coconut, conk, crown, crumpet, dome, dreambox, gourd, headpiece, knob, knuckle, noddle, noggin, noodle, nut, onion, pate, pimple, potato, pumpkin, sconce, top story, upper story, wetware

bean counter
n phr A statistician or arithmetical clerk in government or business

gnome, number cruncher, numbers cruncher

bean-eater
n A person of Spanish-American background, esp a Chicano

bean, bean-bandit, beaner, bravo, chili-chomper, chucke, chuey, greaseball, grease-gut, greaser, Mescin, oiler, pachuco, pepper-belly, pinto bean, taco, taco-bender

beanpole
n A tall, thin person

beanstalk, broomstick, clothes pole, daddy longlegs, gangleshanks, hatrack, highpockets, long drink of water, stick, string bean

beat
1 v To surpass; outdo

beat all, beat all hollow, beat one's time, burn, clobber, come out on top, have it all over, lick, outpoint, put in the shade, run circles around, show up, skin, skunk, smear, sweep, take it all, take the cake

2 SEE MOOCHER

beat-up
adj Battered and damaged, esp by age and use, as in "Our beat-up car still gets us around town"

broken-down, clapped-out, dog-eared, ramshackle, ratty, seedy

beaver
n The pubic hair, esp female

beard, brillo, bush, muff, pubes

beef
1 *n A complaint; a grievance*

belch, bellyache, big stink, bitch, gripe, grouse, holler, howl, kick, squawk, stink, tale of woe

2 *v To complain; utter a grievance, as in "She beefed about the umpire's call"*

belch, bellow, bellyache, bitch, blow up a storm, cop an attitude, crab, cut a beef, give heat, gripe, grouch, grouse, growl, have an attitude, holler, howl, kick, kick up a fuss, kick up a storm, kvetch, make a fuss, make a stink, make a big stink, moan, piss, piss up a storm, put up a squawk, raise a fuss, raise a ruckus, raise Cain, raise sand, raise the roof, squawk, squeal like a stuck pig, yammer, yap, yell bloody murder, yell blue murder, yell one's head off

3 SEE COCK
4 SEE the DAMAGE
5 SEE HASSLE

a bee in one's bonnet

n phr A particular idea or notion, esp an eccentric one; an obsession, as in "He's had a bee in his bonnet ever since he went to that preacher's lecture"

a bee, a bug, a flea in one's nose, a maggot, a maggot in one's brain, a thing

beer bust

n phr A party where beer is the featured drink

beer blast, beerfest, brew-out, hopfest, kegger, keg party

belly

n The stomach

basket, bread basket, gut, kishkes, kitchen, labonza, middle, pantry, solar plexus, tum, tummy, tummy-tum-tum, tum-tum

belly laugh

n phr A very loud and hearty laugh; a guffaw

belly-buster, bellytickler, belly-whopper, belly-wow, big yuck, boff, boffo, boffola, button buster, gut-buster, horselaugh, knee-slapper, side-splitter

belly-whopper

1 n A dive in which one strikes the water stomach first
2 SEE BELLY LAUGH

belly-buster, belly-flop, belly-flopper, belly-smacker, chewallop, chewalloper, gut-buster

bennies
n Any
amphetamine pills

A, aimies, amp, amt, amy, B-29s, bam, bambita, bams, bean, beans, benz, black beauties, black bombers, black bottle, blue angel, bombita, bottles, box of L, brain ticklers, brownies, browns, bumble bees, businessman's lunch, cartwheels, chalk, Christinas, Christmas trees, coast-to-coasts, copilot, crank, crink, cris, cross-countries, crosses, crossroads, cross-tops, crystal, dexies, dexo, dominoes, double cross, drivers, dynamite stocks, eye-opener, fives, football, forwards, glass, goies, grads, green dragon, greenies, hearts, horseheads, in-betweens, jam, jam Cecil, jelly-babies, jelly beans, jolly beans, joy pellet, L A turnabouts, leapers, lid poppers, lightning, lip proppers, nuggets, orange peaches, pep-em-ups, pep pills, pixies, purple hearts, rhythms, rippers, road dope, roses, sky rockets, sparkle plenties, sparklers, speckled birds, speed, splach, splash, splivins, STP, stuka, tabs, thrusters, truck drivers, turnabouts, uppers, uppie, ups, wake-ups, West Coast turnabouts, whites

☞ *The great number of slang terms for narcotics probably reflects both a need for coded reference to an illegal substance and a desire to be chic and up-to-date, in addition to the need to distinguish varieties.*

best shot
n phr One's
maximum effort; the
best one can do

one's all, all one's got, all-out try, all one's worth, one's damndest, full court press, the works

bet one's ass
*v phr To be
absolutely sure of
something; be
confident, as in "I'd
bet my ass he knew
it all the time"*

bet one's bippy, bet one's boots, bet one's bottom dollar, bet dollars to doughnuts, bet one's last nickel, bet one's life, bet one's neck, bet one's shirt, bet one's sweet ass, bet one's sweet life, bet the farm, bet the ranch, bet the rent, bet one's whiskers, make book

bet your ass
*affirmation Abso-
lutely; definitely, as
in "Bet your ass he's
the next winner"*

bet the house, bet the rent, bet your bippy, bet your boots, bet your bottom dollar, bet your life, bet your shirt, bet your sweet ass, bet your whiskers, fucking ay, fucking ay right, fucking well told, I'll drink to that, I'll tell the world, natch, right on, seguro que, shitsure, sure as shit, U B B, word, yeah, yep, you ain't just flapping your gums, you ain't just whistling Dixie, you bet, you betcha, you better believe it, you're damn tootin', you're telling me, you said a mouthful, you said it

Bible-banger
*n A strict
religionist, esp a
Protestant
fundamentalist*

amen snorter, Bible pounder, Bible-puncher, Bible-thumper, Christer, Holy Joe, knee-bender
☞ *This list is close to the one at "goody-goody."*

big deal
*1 n phr Something
very important*
2 SEE **BIG SHOT**

BFD, biggie

big-league
adj Serious;
important;
professional, as in
"This is a big-league
deal we're putting
together"

big, big-bore, big-time, double-barrel, four-star, front-page, hardball, heavy, heavyweight, hefty, high-power, large, major-league

the big leagues
n phr The more
serious reaches of a
profession, business,
etc, as in "For
accountants, the Big
8 firms are the big
leagues"

the bigs, the big time, hardball, the major leagues

bigmouth
n A pretentious and
deceitful talker; a
know-it-all

armchair general, armchair strategist, bag of wind, big wind, blower, blowhard, bull artist, bullshit artist, bullshitter, bullshooter, bull-thrower, crapper, gasbag, gasman, gatemouth, ho-dad, ho-daddy, hot-air artist, loudmouth, Monday morning quarterback, paper tiger, popoff, satchel mouth, Spanish athlete, windbag, windjammer

big O
n phr Opium

auntie, black pill, black snake, black stuff, brew units, brick gum, brown hash, brown stuff, bunk, button, chicory, Chinese molasses, chocolate, cookie mud, cream, cutered pill, dopium, dream, dream beads, dream wax, elevation, fire-plug, foon, fun, ghow, glad stuff, goma, gow, gow crust, goynk, grease, green ashes, green mud, green powder, gum, hop, lemkee, lightning smoke, mahogany juice, midnight oil, molasses, munsh, O, Op, pan juice, pekoe, pen yen, piki, pill pillow, plack shit, poppy, poppy rain, poppy train, pox, puff, rooster brand, root tonic, sam how, san lo, sealing wax, son lo tar, yen chee, yen chiang, yen pock, yen shee suey

☞ *The great number of slang terms for narcotics probably reflects both a need for coded reference to an illegal substance and a desire to be chic and up-to-date, in addition to the need to distinguish varieties.*

big shot
1 *n phr A very important or self-important person; an influential person*

the berries, big bean, big bloke, big boy, big bug, big cheese, big deal, big do, big doolie, big enchilada, big fish, big frog, big gee, biggie, big gun, big guy, big hombre, big macher, big man, big noise, big squeeze, big stuff, big timer, big wheel, boss, boss man, brass hat, the cheese, face card, the great one, heavy, heavy-weight, higher-up, high muckety-muck, high-up, himself, his nibs, honcho, hoohaw, hotshot, macher, magoo, muck, mucky-muck, nabob, panjandrum, pooh-bah, shot, topsider, VIP, wheel

2 SEE **WHEELER-DEALER**

bike
n A motorcycle

hog, iron, sled

a bill
n phr A hundred dollars

C, century, C-note, C-spot, yard

billy club
n phr A police officer's nightstick

billy, hickory, rosewood, shill

bind
n A predicament

box, clutch, crunch, fine kettle of fish, fix, hell of a mess, hell of a note, hell to pay, hell to pay and no pitch hot,

hobble, hole, hot spot, hot water, how-de-do, jam, mell of a hess, mess, pickle, pinch, pretty pickle, spot, [Brit] sticky wicket, tight spot, tough spot, unholy mess
☞ *This word is very often used in the expression "in a bind."*

binders
n The brakes of a car

anchors, cinchers

binge
n A spree; a carousal

bat, bender, booze-up, brannigan, bust, caper, guzzle, hell-bender, hooley, jag, randan, rip, shindy, soak, stew, tear, toot, twister, whooper-dooper, wingding

bingle
n A base hit in baseball

ace, B, bagger, base knock, dinger, tater

the **bird**
1 *n phr A rude flatulatory noise made in derision*

Bronx cheer, raspberry, razoo, the razz

2 *n phr An obscene, insulting gesture made with the middle finger*

the finger
☞ *This term is usually used after "get" or "give."*

bit
1 *n A prison sentence*

hitch, jolt, lag, piece, spot, stretch, time, trick

2 SEE **ACT**
3 SEE **BAG**

bitch

1 *n* A woman one dislikes or disapproves of

broad, cunt, witch

☞ *Female equivalents of the contemptuous terms for men, listed in this book under "asshole," are relatively rare. Contempt for females, in slang, stresses their putative sexual promiscuity and weakness rather than moral vileness and general odiousness. Some terms under "asshole," though, are increasingly used of women.*

2 SEE **BEEF**
3 SEE **HUMDINGER**

a bitch

1 *n phr* An unhappy occurrence; a wretched circumstance, as in "Isn't it a bitch, his dying so young?"

hell, a hell of a note, hell on wheels

2 *n* Anything arduous or very disagreeable

an all-nighter, a back-breaker, a bastard, a killer, no picnic, no tea party, a son of a bitch

3 SEE **BALL-BUSTER**

bitch box

n phr A public address system or loudspeaker

growler, squawk box

bite

1 *v* To accept a deception as truth; be gullible, as in "He bit when I told him he'd won the lottery"

be an easy mark, be a patsy, be a sucker, be easy, be green, eat up, fall for, gobble down, go for, gulp down, lap up, swallow; swallow hook, line, and sinker; swallow whole, take the bait

2 *n One's share of a sum*
cut, divvy, end, look-in, percentage, piece, rake-off, score, slice, split, takeout, taste, whack

3 SEE the DAMAGE

bite the bullet
v phr To accept the cost of a course of action, though it be painful
face the music, [Brit] grasp the nettle, pay the piper, stand up and take it, take it, take one's medicine, take the rap

blabbermouth
n A person who talks too much; a logorrheic person
babblemouth, babbler, bag of wind, barber, big breeze, bigmouth, big noise, big wind, blabber, blabberer, blabmouth, blah-blaher, blatter, blowhard, chatterbox, chatterer, chinwagger, ear-bender, flapjaw, gabber, gabblemouth, gabbler, gasbag, gatemouth, gibble-gabble, gum-beater, hot-air artist, jabberer, jawsmith, load of wind, loudmouth, motor-mouth, ratchet-jaw, ratchet-mouth, rattletongue, satch, satchelmouth, spieler, spouter, spouter-offer, tongue-wagger, windbag, windjammer, woofer, word-slinger, yapper, yenta

blackball
v To hold in strong disfavor; ostracize; reject
black, blacklist, put on the crap list, put on the ditch list, put on the shit list, shit-list, stink-list, thumb down, tin-can, turn thumbs down on

black eye
n phr An eye surrounded with darkened areas of contusion
goog, mouse, shiner

Black Maria
n phr A police van
blue liz, go-long, milk wagon, paddy wagon, pie wagon

blank check
n phr General freedom of action; carte blanche

free ticket

blankety-blank
adj or n A generalized euphemism substituted for a taboo or vulgar term, as in "Get your blankety-blank car out of my way"

bleep, bleeping, bliggey, so-and-so, you-know-what

blast
1 v To attack, esp with strong verbal condemnation; excoriate

crack down on, lambaste, lay into, let fly at, let have it, let loose on, light into, pile into, pitch into, plow into, rip into, roast, sail into, scorch, skin alive, sock, sock it to, tear into, tie into, wade into, whale, whale into

2 SEE **BALL**
3 SEE **BARREL**
4 SEE **CLOBBER**
5 SEE **FIX**
6 SEE **KICK**
7 SEE **PLUG**
8 SEE **WINGDING**

blind pig
n phr A saloon or club that operates illegally

after-hours club, blind tiger, bootleg joint, social club, speakeasy

☞ *Many of these terms were more current during the prohibition era than they are now.*

blind-side
v To attack by surprise; fool an opponent

blind-pop, bushwhack, sucker-punch

Blind Tom
n phr A sports official

guesser, hizzoner, ref, ump, whistle tooter, zebra

blood
n A black person

blood brother, blood sister, bro', brother, mamber, sister, soul brother, soul sister, youngblood
☞ *These terms are not per se offensive, unlike the terms under "nigger."*

blow
1 v To do fellatio

bite, dick-lick, eat, eat it, give cap, give cone, give good head, give head, gobble, go down and do tricks, go down on, hoover, lick, play the skin flute, suck, suck off

2 v To do cunnilingus

do it the French way, eat, eat furburger, eat fur pie, eat hair pie, eat it, eat seafood, French, go down and do tricks, go down on, have a box lunch, lick, slurp

3 v To spend money, esp extravagantly or foolishly, as in "He had a nice nest egg, but he blew it gambling at the track"

blow in, diddle away, dish out, drop, fool away, fork out, fork over, fribble away, fritter away, frivol away, lay out, piddle away, piss away, pour down the drain, pour down the rathole, shell out, shoot, throw away

4 *v To expose something secret; bare, esp a scandal, as in "He threatened to blow the whole nasty story unless they paid him"*

blow sky-high, blow the lid off, blow the whistle, blow wide open, give away, let it all hang out, show up, spill, spill one's guts, tattle, tell all

5 SEE **BLOW GRASS**
6 SEE **BLOW OFF**
7 SEE **FLUFF**
8 SEE **FUCK UP**
9 SEE **SNORT**
10 SEE **SPLIT**
11 SEE **SQUEAL**

blow grass
v phr To smoke marijuana

bang, beat the weeds, be in weeds, bend the head, bite one's lip, blast, blow, blow a stick, blow smoke, blow one's top, bounce the goof balls, break a stick, burn an Indian, burn the hay, bust, do, do a joint, do up, do your business, drag, drink Texas tea, drop a joint, fire up, get down, get it on, get off, get on, go loco, goof, hit, hit the hay, hoka toka, hump the sage, kiss Mary Jane, light up, pick up, poke, pot out, power hit, pull, send, send up, sip, smoke rings, straighten out, taste, tighten one's wig, toke, toke up, torch up, tote, trigger, turkey, turn on, waste

blow it with someone
v phr To make someone hostile or estranged; antagonize

blot one's copybook, break one's shovel, get on someone's list, get on someone's shit list, miss the boat, queer it

blow job
n phr An act of fellatio or cunnilingus

cap, French job, good head, hair pie, head, head job, hose job, job, knob job, lipstick on a dipstick, suck, suction, tongue job

blow off
1 *v phr To boast; brag*

big-mouth, big-talk, blow, blow one's bazoo, blow hard, blow off one's mouth, blow off one's trap, blow off one's yap, blow one's own horn, blow one's own trumpet, blow smoke, brag oneself up, bullshit, crack one's jaw, lay it on thick, loudmouth, loud-talk, mouth off, pat oneself on the back, pop off, pop off at the mouth, run off at the mouth, shoot off one's mouth, shoot the bull, shoot the crap, shoot the shit, sling it, sling the bull, spout, spout off, talk big, throw the bull, toot one's own horn, woof

2 SEE COP OUT

blow one's top
1 *v phr To become angry; fly into a fit*

become livid, blow a fuse, blow a gasket, blow one's cool, blow one's cork, blow one's stack, blow one's stopper, blow one's topper, blow up, blow one's wig, burn, burn up, cast a kitten, climb the wall, fall apart, flip, flip one's lid, flip out, flip one's raspberry, flip one's wig, fly off the handle, get one's back up, get one's dander up, get one's gauge up, get one's hair up, get hot under the collar, get in a swivet, [Brit] get in a wax, get into a lather, get into a snit, get into a state, get into a stew, get into a sweat, get one's Irish up, get mad, get pissed off, get one's shit hot, get sore, get the red ass, get the wind up, go ape, go off the deep end, go out of one's skull, go up the wall, have a bird, have a blowoff, have a blowup, have a catfit, have a conniption fit, have a cow, have a duckfit, have a fit, have a shit fit, have kittens, have pups, have steam coming out of one's ears,

Rock Valley College - ERC

hit the ceiling, jump salty, lose one's cool, lose one's wig, pop one's cork, see red, shit a brick, shit bricks, simmer, sizzle, smoke, smolder, spit tacks, steam, stew, sweat, throw a fit, throw a hyper, turn purple

☞ *These terms share semantic territory with "make a scene," which should also be considered.*

2 SEE **FREAK OUT**

blowup
n A fit of anger; a rage

blowoff, catfit, conniption, conniption fit, duckfit, flare-up, hemorrhage, lather, stew, sweat, tantrum, tizzy, [Brit] wax

blow up
v phr To exaggerate the importance of; overemphasize, as in "They blew the thing up into a major scandal"

make a big deal, make a big production, make a big stink, make a federal case, pump up, run into the ground, work into the ground

☞ *These terms share semantic territory with "nit-pick," which should also be considered.*

blubber
n Body fat

avoirdupois, beef, flab

blue movie
n phr A pornographic movie

adult movie, beaver, blue flick, dirty movie, flesh flick, fuck film, skin flick

the blues
n phr Depression; low spirits

blahs, [Brit] blue funk, doldrums, dumps, [Brit] funk, grumps, mulligrubs, the pip, red ass

bluff
v To use confident deception as a means of winning or succeeding, as in "He bluffed a throw to first to keep the runner from taking a large lead"

cheek it, fake it, shuck, vamp, wing, wing it

bobtail
n A dishonorable discharge from the armed forces

bob, DD, kick, yellow ticket

bone factory
1 *n phr A hospital*
2 SEE **BONEYARD**

bonehouse, butcher shop, croaker joint

boner
1 *n A blunder; an egregious mistake*

[Brit] balls-up, bitch-up, bloomer, bloop, blooper, bobble, bonehead play, bonehead trick, boo-boo, boot, clam, clinker, cross-up, dumbo, flub, flubdub, flub-up, flummox, foozle, foulup, fuck-up, goof, goof-up, howler, louse-up, miscue, muck-up, muff, screw-up, slip-up, snafu, whoops

2 SEE **GRIND**
3 SEE **HARD-ON**

boneyard
n A cemetery

bone factory, bone orchard, marble city, marble orchard

booby hatch
n phr A mental hospital

the bin, bughouse, cackle factory, cracker factory, crazy house, funny farm, funny house, laughing academy, loony bin, nut academy, nut box, nut college, nut factory, nut farm, nut foundry, nut hatch, nut house, rubber room

the book
n phr Figures and other materials concerning past performance, as in "The book on this guy is he'll take the easiest way out"

chart, dope, dope sheet, form, numbers, stats, track record

boondockers
n Heavy and sturdy shoes or boots

clodhoppers, shitkickers, stompers, wafflestompers

the boondocks
n phr Remote places; rural regions

the back country, the backwoods, the Bible Belt, the boonies, the brush, the bush, hickdom, the middle of nowhere, [Australian] the outback, the provinces, the rhubarbs, stick country, the sticks, the tall timbers, yokeldom

booze
n Any alcoholic drink, esp whiskey and other spirits; liquor

alky, the bottle, the cup that cheers, the demon rum, firewater, grog, hard stuff, hooch, John Barleycorn, joy-juice, juice, laughing soup, rum, the sauce, stuff

boss
1 *n The leader; the highest authority*

big boy, big cheese, big chief, big enchilada, big gee, big guy, big shot, boss man, chief cook and bottle-washer, godfather, governor, head cheese, himself, his highness, his nibs, honcho, kingfish, kingpin, main squeeze, the Man, man in the front office, man upstairs, Mister Big, number one, number-one boy, numero uno, old man, pooh-bah, skipper, top dog, top sawyer, topsider

2 *v To control; manage, as in "She bosses a Fortune 500 firm"*

be at the helm, be in the driver's seat, call the shots, crack the whip, handle the reins, have the last word, have the say-so, head up, mastermind, rule the roost, run, wear the pants

both hands
n phr A ten-year prison sentence

couple of fives back to back, double finn, sawbuck, tenner, ten-spot

the bottom line
n phr The decisive essentials; the grim reality, as in "Sales are the bottom line here"

the ball game, the clincher, the meat, the meat and potatoes, the name of the game, the nitty-gritty, the payoff, the score, the story, where the rubber meets the road

bounce
1 *v To eject by force; expel*

boot out, bum-rush, chuck, give the bum's rush, give one the gate, give the hook, give the old heave-ho, give the one-two-three, kick out, put the skids to, throw out on one's ass, throw out on one's ear, turn out

2 SEE **PIZZAZZ**

bracelets
n A pair of handcuffs

braces, clamps, cuffs, darbies, mitts, nippers, wristlets

brain wave
n phr A sudden, useful idea, as in "I thought for hours, then wham, a brain wave struck"

brainstorm, hot notion, idear, idee

the brass
n phr High officials; chiefs

big boys, big brass, biggies, the big money, brass hats, execs, front office, gold braid, honchos, lords of creation, muckety-mucks, our betters, people upstairs, power, powers that be, power structure, top brass

break out
1 v phr To escape from prison or some other confining situation

absquatulate, beat it, blow, blow town, breeze, broom, bust out, cheese it, clear out, crash out, crush out, duck out, dust, fly the coop, go over the wall, hightail, hit the hump, lam, make a break for it, make oneself scarce, powder, run out, [Brit] scarper, scram, skedaddle, skin out, skip, skip out, split, take a powder, take a runout powder, take it on the lam, vamoose

2 SEE RUSTLE UP

break up
v phr To laugh uproariously

bust a gut, cackle, crack up, die laughing, [Brit] fall about, fall out, har-har, pee one's pants, piss one's pants, split a gut, split a gut laughing, split one's sides, yuk

break someone up
v phr To cause laughter; amuse enormously

bowl over, convulse, fracture, kill, knock dead, lay in the aisles, lay low, mow down, panic, put in stitches, slaughter, slay, wow

brew
n Beer

the amber brew, barley broth, brewskie, froth, suds

brick-top
n A red-headed
person

carrothead, carrot-top

briefed
adj Informed;
prepared by
instruction

brought up to speed, clued, clued in, filled in, pooped up, prepped, primed, put in the picture

broad
1 *n A woman*

babe, baby, baby doll, biddy, bim, bimbo, [Brit] bint, [esp Brit] bird, bit of fluff, bozette, bundle, bunny, butt, canary, chick, chickabiddy, chicken, chicky, chippy, cooz, cow, crack, cunt, cunt meat, cutie, dame, dearie, dish, doll, dollop, dolly, fem, femme, filly, fluff, frail, frau, gal, ginch, girlie, hammer, heifer, hen, hide, honey, honey-bun, honey-bunny, jane, jenny, job, klooch, lady, lassie, leg, mama, mare, mat, miss, missie, missis, missiz, moll, momma, mouse, pet, piece, pussy, pussycat, quail, rag and a bone and a hank of hair, rib, shemale, she-she, shouter, sis, sissy, sister, skeezer, skirt, slash, snatch, squab, squaw, stuff, sweet baby, sweetheart, sweet momma, sweet patootie, sweet stuff, sweet thing, tail, tart, tomato, toots, tootsie, twist, wench, witch, wool, wren

☞ *The semantic boundaries between "broad," "dish," and "floozy" are not easy to set. All three terms should be considered.*

☞ *Many women find many of these terms offensively sexist.*

2 SEE **DISH**

broke
adj Penniless;
destitute

beat, bust, busted, clean, cleaned out, cold in hand, dead broke, dingy, down and out, down for the count, flat, flat-ass, flat broke, flat on one's ass, melted out, on one's ass, on one's ear, on the hog, on the rims, on the rocks, on one's uppers, O O F, oofless, piss-poor, shatting on one's uppers, short, [Brit] skint, stone broke, stony, stony cold broke, strapped, tap, Tap City, tapped, tapped out, thin, tight, wasted, wiped out, without a pot to piss in, without a red cent, without a sou, without one dollar to rub against another

brown-nose

1 *v To curry favor; toady*

apple-polish, back-scratch, back-slap, blow smoke, bootlick, brown, get in solid with, get next to, get on the right side of, honey up to, kiss ass, lick ass, play up to, polish apples, shine up to, suck, suck around, suck ass, suck up to, sweeten up, wipe someone's ass

2 *n A toady; a sycophant*

apple-polisher, ass-kisser, ass-licker, ass-sucker, asswiper, back-patter, back-scratcher, back-slapper, bootlicker, browner, brown-noser, bucker, earbanger, eggsucker, A K, kiss-ass, kiss-butt, stooge, suck-ass, suck-off, TL, TLer, tokus-licker, yes man

bruiser

n A big, strong man

big beef, big bozo, big bruiser, big horse, big hunk, big hunk of beef, big tuna, brute, heavy, heavyweight, hulk, jumbo, man mountain, moose, whale

brush up

v phr To improve, review, or perfect one's mastery, as in "You'd better brush up your math before you try for that job"

bone up, bone up on, brush up on, check up on, cram, cram up, fresh up, get up, get up on, polish up, sharpen up, shine up, smarten up

buck

1 *n A US dollar*

berry, bone, buckeroo, cartwheel, case note, cent, clanker, copeck, ducat, fish, frogskin, iron man, one-spot, peso, plaster, plunk, potato, rock, rutabaga, scoot, scrip, simoleon, single, skin, slab, smacker, snuff, toad skin

2 *v* *To resist; defy,*
as in "Be very
careful if you
intend to buck the
mayor"

fight, go up against, take on

buck private
n phr An Army
private; a common
soldier

buckass private, bullet bait, cannon fodder, dough, doughboy, doughfoot, GI, GI Joe, Joe, Joe Blow, Joe Shit the Ragman, Joe Snuffy, Joe Tentpeg, John Dogface, Private Slipinshits

buddy up
v phr To become
friends

be buddy-buddy, be palsy-walsy, chum up, click, get chummy, hit it off, pal together, pal up, play footsie, team up

bug
1 *v* *To annoy,*
anger, pester, or
harry

aggravate, be in one's face, be on one's back, be on one's case, break chops, burn, chivvy, discombobulate, dog, drug, flake off, get, get someone down, get down on, get someone's goat, get in one's face, get in one's hair, get someone's nanny, get on someone's back, get on someone's case, get on someone's nerves, get to, get to someone, get under one's skin, get up someone's nose, give someone a bad time, give someone a hard time, give someone grief, give someone the needle, gravel, gripe, gripe one's ass, gripe one's balls, gripe one's butt, gripe one's cookies, gripe one's left nut, gripe one's middle kidney, gripe one's soul, hassle, hock, hound, jerk someone around, jerk someone's chain, jerk someone's strings, miff, needle, nudge, nudzh, peeve, pick on, push, push someone's button, rank, rank out, rattle someone's cage, rib, ride, rile, roust, shag, sound, yank someone's chain

2 *n A horse that has never won a race* maiden

3 SEE **FAN**

4 SEE **HOT ROD**

5 SEE **NUT**

bugger

1 *v To do anal intercourse; sodomize* assfuck, BF, boogie, brown, brownhole, bumfuck, bunghole, buttbang, buttfuck, cornhole, dick, do it the Greek way, Greek, pack fudge, pack some mud, part cheeks, pitch, punk, ream, split some buns, stretch some jeans

2 SEE **BACK-BREAKER**

3 SEE **BAD MAN**

4 SEE **SUCKER**

build

n One's physique, esp one's figure bod, shape

built

adj Physically well-developed, esp in a sexually attractive way built for comfort, built like a brick shithouse, constructed, curvaceous, hunky, stacked, well-built, well-upholstered

bulldoze

v To intimidate; overcome by force bogart, buffalo, bullyrag, get tough with, gorilla, lean on, manhandle, railroad, roust, sandbag, snowball, steamroller, strong-arm

bullheaded
adj Obstinate

feisty, hardheaded, hardnosed, hardshell, hardshelled, mulish, pigheaded, set in one's ways, stiffnecked, stubborn as a bobtail mule, stubborn as an ox

bullshit
1 *n Nonsense; absurdities; pretentious or deceitful talk*

all that jazz, apple butter, applesauce, [Brit] balls, baloney, banana oil, beans, bilge, blah, blah-blah, blahs, blarney, blather, borax, bosh, BS, bull, bulldink, bullrag, bullshine, bunk, bushwah, cheese, claptrap, cowflap, cowplop, crap, crapola, crock, crock of shit, crud, dogshit, eyewash, fiddle-faddle, flamdoodle, flapdoodle, flubdubbery, flummadiddle, garbage, gas, gash, guff, gum-beating, hockey, hogwash, hoke, hokey-poke, hokey-pokey, hokum, holly-golly, hooey, hop, horsefeathers, horseshit, hot air, hully-gully, jabberjack, jazz, jiggerypokery, jive, jive-ass, kafooster, malarkey, marmalade, monkeydoodle, moonshine, mumbo-jumbo, mush, oil, phony-baloney, phonus-balonus, piece of shit, piffle, pile of shit, poppycock, rot, rubbish, schmegeggy, shit, shit for the birds, smoke, spinach, tommyrot, [Brit] tosh, trash, tripe, twiddle-twaddle, yack, yackety-yack, yap

2 *v To talk nonsense, esp with an intent to deceive*

blow off, blow off one's mouth, blow off one's trap, blow off one's yap, con, crap, fast-talk, fatmouth, guff, horseshit, jive, lay it on, lay it on with a trowel, mouth off, pile it up, pop off, run off at the mouth, shit, shoot the breeze, shovel the shit, shuck, shuck and jive, sling it, sling the bull, spread it, spread it on thick, spread it thick, sweet-talk, talk big, talk through one's hat, throw the bull, woof

3 SEE **BLOW OFF**
4 SEE **GAB**

bum

1 *n A vagrant; a derelict*

bag lady, bag woman, barrelhouse bum, bindle stiff, bo, bottle baby, Bowery bum, bummer, busthead, dock rat, drifter, floater, grifter, hobo, low-life, moocher, shopping bag lady, shopping cart lady, skell, Skid Row bum, speck bum, stewbum, stiff, stumblebum, vag, weary Willy, wino

2 *v To beg; cadge, as in "Where can I bum a cigarette?"*

chisel, dog it, drop the lug on, freeload, hit up, make a touch for, mooch, put the arm on, put the lug on, put the touch on, scrounge, scrounge up, shake down, sleaze, stick for, touch, touch up

3 SEE ASS
4 SEE ASSHOLE
5 SEE CON
6 SEE CRUMMY
7 SEE GREEN AROUND THE GILLS
8 SEE HOOKER

bum rap

n phr An unjustified condemnation or punishment

bad deal, bad rap, bum beef, bum deal, bum finger, frame, frame-up, lousy deal, phony rap, raw deal, RF, rotten deal, royal fucking, the shaft

bundle

1 *n A large amount of money, as in "That car must have cost a bundle"*

bale of hay, bankroll, barrel of money, big bankroll, big bucks, big money, bunch, bundle of dough, carload, chunk of cash, chunk of dough, cool million, deep pockets, gobs, hard coin, heaps of cash, heavy chips, heavy coin, heavy jack, heavy lettuce, heavy money, heavy sugar, important money, king's ransom, megabucks, mint, mintful, mucho dinero, nice hunk of change, nice hunk of jack, nice piece of change, nice piece of jack, package, [Brit] packet, piece of cash, piles, pretty penny, raft, rafts, real money, scads, serious money, tidy sum, wad, wads

2 SEE BROAD

bush
1 adj *Mediocre;*
second-rate

bush-league, cut-rate, dime-a-dozen, fair-to-middling, garden variety, low-rent, narrow-gauge, of a sort, of sorts, one-horse, piddling, pissy-ass, the poor man's, run-of-the-mill, run-of-the-mine, scrub, small-beer, small-bore, small-potato, small-time, softball, a sort of a, so-so, tacky, tatty, tinhorn, two-bit

2 SEE PIDDLY

the bush leagues
n phr *The mediocre*
and inferior reaches
of business,
entertainment,
sports, etc

the minor leagues, the small time

bust
1 v *To arrest; take*
prisoner

bag, claw, clip, collar, cop, flag, flake, grab, haul in, jab, knock, make a pinch, nab, nail, nick, pick up, pinch, pull in, put the arm on, put the claw on, put the collar on, put the sleeve on, roust, run in, sidetrack, stiff collar, gotcha, grab, pickup, pinch

2 n *An arrest*
3 SEE BROKE
4 SEE CLOBBER
5 SEE SOCK

bust one's ass
v phr To strive; make one's best effort, as in "She didn't exactly bust her ass to make me feel welcome"

bend over backwards, break a hamstring, break one's neck, buckle down, bust a gut, bust one's balls, bust one's buns, bust one's butt, bust one's chops, bust one's conk, bust one's cork, bust hump, bust one's hump, bust one's nuts, bust one's sweet ass, do one's damndest, give it one's all, give it one's best, give it one's best shot, go all the way, go for all the marbles, go for broke, go for it, go out of one's way, go the extra mile, go the full yard, go the limit, go the whole hog, go the whole nine yards, go to the wall, haul off, knock oneself out, knuckle down, lay oneself out, make a full-court press, put one's back into it, rare back, reach back, rupture oneself, shoot the works, split a gut, spread oneself, suck it up

butt
1 n A cigarette

cig, cigareete, cigaroot, ciggy, coffin nail, coffin tack, dope, dope stick, drag, fag, gasper, grette, grit, joint, pimp stick, root, skag, slim, smoke, square joint, straight, tailormade, toke, weed

2 n The remainder of a smoked cigarette or cigar

dinch, dincher, maggot, Navy, roach, seed, skag, snipe

3 SEE ASS

butterfingers
n A clumsy, unhandy person; a fumbler

bull in a china shop, clunker, duffer, flub, flubdub, flubup, foozler, fumble-fist, goof-up, hacker, klutz, lobster, lubber, lummox, muffer, schlep, schloomp, slob

butt in
v phr To intrude; meddle

barge in, burst in, bust in, charge in, check in, chime in, chisel in, come barging in, come busting in, crowd someone's act, cut in, elbow in, get into the act, horn in, jimmy in, kibitz, muscle in, nose in, poke one's face in, poke one's nose into, put one's oar in, put one's two cents in, put one's two cents' worth in, stick one's nose into, weigh in

button man
n phr A low-ranking member of the Mafia

button player, button soldier, soldier

buy
1 v To believe; accept

buy into, buy off on, down, eat up, fall for, go for, kid oneself, lap up, sign off on, stand still for, swallow; swallow hook, line, and sinker; take, tumble for

2 v To approve; acquiesce in

drink to, give one's OK to, go along with, OK, say amen to, shake hands on, sign off on, sit still for, stand still for, string along with, throw in with

buzz
n A telephone call

jingle, ring, tinkle

by ear
adv phr By instincts and feelings rather than calculation and thought

by guess and by God, by the seat of one's pants

C

Caddy
n A Cadillac car

boat, Cad, Jew canoe, Kitty

camel-jammer
n An Arab or other
Eastern or Middle
Eastern person

raghead

can
1 *n A toilet, as in*
"No visit to this bar
is complete without
a trip to the can"

[esp Canadian] biffy, bog house, bog shop, commode, convenience, crap can, crapper, donicker, flusher, head, jakes, jane, john, johnny, kazoo, latrine, lav, [Brit] loo, pot, potty, shitcan, shithouse, shitter, throne, throne room

2 SEE ASS
3 SEE FIRE

can of worms
n phr A complex
situation; a
rigmarole

bad scene, bag of worms, mess, mish-mash, perplex, rigmatick, ringding-do

caper
n A crime, esp a
robbery

frolic, job, touch, trick

card sharp
n phr An expert card player, esp a dishonest one in gambling

card shark, crimp, dildock, mechanic, pasteboard shark, shark, sharp, sharpie, sharpster
☞ *This list does not distinguish the modes or types of such card players.*

carry
v To be armed, as in "Don't mess with her, she carries"

be heeled, be rodded, be rodded up, carry the difference, pack, pack heat

carry a lot of weight
v phr To have power and influence, as in "The clergy carry a lot of weight around here"

draw a lot of water, have clout, walk heavy
☞ *These terms share semantic territory with "boss," which should also be considered.*

cart
v To transport; take; carry

drag, hump, lug, pack, schlep, tote

carved in stone
adj phr Fixed; immutable

in cement, set in concrete

case dough
n phr Money set aside for emergencies, "just in case"

ace in the hole, backlog, holdout, mad money, nest egg, something in the sock, stake

catch

n A hidden cost, qualification, defect, etc, as in "Any time you see a car advertised at such a low price, you know there's a catch"

clinker, hitch, joker, kicker, snag, stinger

catch hell

v phr To be severely reprimanded or punished

catch hail Columbia, catch holy hell, catch it, catch it in the neck, catch merry hell, catch the devil, get it

catch redhanded

v phr To find or seize someone in the act of doing something forbidden; catch in flagrante delicto

catch cold, catch on the hop, catch with a smoking gun, catch with a smoking pistol, catch with one's hand in the cookie jar, catch with one's hand in the till, catch with one's pants down, catch with the goods, catch with the merchandise, have bang to rights, have cold, have dead to rights, land, nail

catch-22

n A situation with contradictory requirements, as in "I'm caught in the catch-22 of needing a job to gain experience and needing experience to get a job"

lose-lose situation, no-win situation

cauliflower ear
n phr A boxer's or wrestler's ear deformed by injuries and accumulated scar tissue

pretty ear

the chair
n phr The electric chair

hot seat, hot squat, Old Smoky, Old Sparky, the smoky seat

chapter
n A division of a sports contest, esp an inning of baseball

canto, chukker, stanza, waltz

cheat
v To be sexually unfaithful

bad time, chippy, get a little on the side, nosh, play around, step out on someone, two-time, yard

check out
v phr To examine; scrutinize; inspect

check, cop a gander at, dig, double-O, eye, eyeball, gander, get a load of, give a look at, give the once-over, give with the eye, glim, glom, grab a look at, have a gander at, have a looksee, kick the tires, make, once-over, pick up, pin, pipe, put the eye on, scope on, scope out, size up, [Brit] take a dekko at, take a gander at, take a hinge at, take a reading, take a squint at, [Brit] vet

check the plumbing
v phr To go to the toilet

answer a call of nature, go powder the face, go to the little boys' (or girls') room, go to the powder room, go to the throne room, see a man about a dog

☞ *This sort of euphemism was once a rich source of wit, including the classic "go to Cannes [the famous watering place]."*

cheeky
adj Impudent; impertinent; rude

bold as brass, cocky, flip, fresh, gutty, lippy, nervy, sassy, smart-alecky, smart-ass, snotty, wise-ass, wise-guy

cheesecake
1 *n Photography and performance featuring womens' legs, breasts, hips, etc*

calendar art, gow, jiggle, jiggly, leg art, pinup, T A, T and A, tit art, tits and ass

2 *adj Showing the semiclad female body*

calendar, flesh, girlie, jiggle, pinup, skin, T A, T and A, tits-and-ass

cherry
n A virgin, of either sex

canned goods

chestnut
n A trite old story, joke, song, etc

bromide, corny joke, Joe Millerism, oldie, old turkey, old wheeze, warmed-over cabbage, yawner

chew out
v phr To reprimand; scold

bawl out, bear down on, bite someone's head off, boil in oil, call down, call on the carpet, chew someone's ass out, climb, climb someone's frame, climb someone's hump, come down hard on, come down on, crack down on, crawl, cuss out, cut someone a new asshole, dress down, eat out, give a good talking to, give a piece of one's mind, [Brit] give a rocket, give hail Columbia, give hell, give holy hell, give it in the neck, give merry hell, give the business, give the deuce, give the devil, give the dickens, give the works, give what-for, go at, go up in someone's face, haul over the coals, jack up, jump all over, jump down someone's throat, jump on, jump on someone's meat, land on, lay down the law, lay into, let have it, light into, make it hot for, pile into, pin someone's ears back, pitch into, plow into, put on the rack, put the fear of God into, put the gakk on, put through the wringer, rack out, raise hell with, raise the dickens with, rake over the coals, rake up one side and down the other, read the riot act, ream, ream out, rip into, roast, sail into, tear into, tear off a strip, tee off on, tell a thing or two, tell off, wade into

chicken

1 *n A coward; a poltroon* — candy-ass, chicken-liver, fraidy-cat, jellyfish, lilyliver, Milquetoast, pucker-ass, scaredy-cat, sissy, weak sister, wimp, yellow-belly

2 *adj Cowardly; craven* — chicken-hearted, chicken-livered, gutless, lily-livered, milk-livered, mousy, pucker-assed, rabbity, sissified, sissy, weak-kneed, yellow

3 SEE **BROAD**

4 SEE **CHICKENSHIT**

chicken feed

n phr A small amount of money — buttons, chicken money, coffee and cakes, crumbs, hay, nickels and dimes, peanuts, small beer, small bread, small change, small potatoes, tin

chicken out

v phr To cancel or withdraw from an action because of fear; be intimidated — back out, chicken, funk, funk out, get cold feet, turn chicken, turn yellow

chickenshit
n Pettiness and meanness, esp in a bureaucracy, as in "The new tax law is mostly chickenshit"

birdshit, chicken, horseshit, Mickey Mouse, shit for the birds, small beer, small change, small potatoes, turkey-shit

chiller
n A horror film

chiller-diller, slash-and-gash film, slasher, slice-and-dice film, snuff film

Chink
n A Chinese or person of Chinese extraction

Buddhahead, Chinee, Chino, pong, rice-belly, slant-eyes

☞ *These terms are all offensive.*

chintzy
adj Stingy; parsimonious

cheap, chinching, chinchy, close, Scotch, skinflint, tight, tight as a drum, tight as Kelsey's nuts, tight as O'Reilly's balls, tight as Reilly's balls

chitchat
n Talk, esp relaxed and idle conversation

bibble-babble, blah-blah, blat, buzz, chin, chin-chin, chin music, chitter-chatter, gab, gabble, gas, gibble-gabble, guff, hot air, jaw, jive, [Brit] natter, prittle-prattle, tittle-tattle, yack, yackety-yack

choke up
v phr To become tense and ineffective under pressure, as in "Their team choked up when the pennant race heated up"

choke, clutch up, swallow the apple, swallow the olive, take the pipe, tense up

choppers
n The teeth

china, crockery, fangs, grinders, ivories, pearlies, snappers, tusks

chow
1 *n Food*

eats, feed, grits, groceries, grub, the nosebag, prog, ribs, scarf, scoff, scoffings, tuck, vittles

2 SEE SCARF

Christer
n A straitlaced person, esp a very pious one

Bibleback, bluenose, goody-goody, holier-than-thou, Holy Joe, Nice Nelly, plaster saint

chuck
v To discard; rid oneself of

axe, bag, boot, can, deep-six, ditch, dump, eighty-six, get shut of, give the deep six, give the heave-ho, junk, kiss goodbye, put the skids to, scarf, scrap, scrap-heap, shitcan, shuck, toss overboard, unload
☞ *These terms share semantic territory with "nix," which should also be considered.*

chummy
adj Very friendly

buddy-buddy, palsy-walsy

chutzpa
n Extreme brashness; arrogant presumption, as in "Telling off your boss takes a lot of chutzpa"

brass, cheek, cheekiness, cockiness, crust, face, freshness, gall, guts, innards, moxie, nerve, snottiness

cinch

1 *n An easy task; anything easy*

blowoff, breeze, cake, cakewalk, cherry pie, clay pigeon, duck soup, easy digging, easy meat, gravy, jelly, kid stuff, picnic, pie, piece of cake, pipe, pushover, setup, shoo-in, slope-out, snap, sure thing, tea party, turkey-shoot, walkaway, walkover, waltz

2 *n A certainty; something sure to happen, as in "It's a cinch he'll be there, if he knows what's good for him"*

cold pack, dead certainty, dead cinch, dead-sure thing, fuzzy, lead-pipe cinch, lock, mortal lock, natural, open-and-shut case, shoo-in, sure bet, sure shot, sure thing

cinched

adj Certain; sure; assured, as in "He had the race cinched minutes before it ended"

cold, dead cinched, in the bag, knocked, nailed down, on ice, open-and-shut, racked, sewed up, taped, wired, wired up

the circular file

n phr The wastebasket

the can, file 13, file 17, memory hole

clamp down

v phr To enforce laws and rules rigorously

read the riot act, throw the book at

classy

1 *adj Having or showing prestige; typical of high society*

cushy, dicty, fancy-Dan, fancy-schmancy, flossy, high-class, highfalutin', high-grade, high-hat, high-hatty, high-rent, high-tone, high-toned, high-tony, hoity-toity, la-de-da, luxo, plush, plushy, posh, red-carpet, ritzy, silk-stocking, snazzy, snitzy, spiffy, swank, swanky, swish, top-drawer, top-shelf, [Brit] upmarket, upper-crusty, upscale, zazz, zazzy

2 SEE **GREAT**

clean
1 *adj Free of drug use, as in "She's been clean for three years, ever since she was in rehab"*

off the habit, off the needle, turned off

2 *adj Innocent; unincriminated*

clean as a hound's tooth, clean as a whistle, clear, in the clear, lily white, off the hook, squeaky clean

clean up
v phr To earn or acquire much money; make a large profit, as in "They cleaned up when the two companies merged"

cash in, coin money, hit it big, line one's pockets, make a bundle, make a killing, make a mint, make big money, make megabucks, milk the cash cow, rake it in, shake the money tree

clean up one's act
v phr To correct one's behavior or attitude; act properly

act one's age, clean up one's shit, cut the comedy, cut the crap, cut the funny business, get one's act together, get it together, get on the ball, get one's shit together, get straight, get with it, pull up one's socks, shape up, shape up or ship out, slipper, sprout wings, straighten up and fly right, suck it up, take a brace, tie one's shoes, toe the mark

cliffhanger
n Something very suspenseful

close shave, narrow squeak, near shave, near thing, squeaker, white knuckle

clinch

1 *v* To determine conclusively; finish definitively; win

cinch, ice, make official, nail down, put away, put in the bag, put in the can, put on ice, sew up, wrap, wrap up

2 *n* An embrace

bear hug, bunny hug, clutch

a clip

n Each one; each occasion, as in "His friends' weddings cost him a few hundred dollars a clip"

a crack, a go, a per-each, a pop, a shot, a slug, a smack, a throw, a toss, a whack

clit

n The clitoris

button, little boy in the boat, man in the boat

clobber

1 *v* To defeat, esp to defeat decisively; trounce

banjax, beat all hollow, beat the bejesus out of, beat the daylights out of, beat the hell out of, beat the kishkes out of, beat the living shit out of, beat the shit out of, beat the socks off of, beat the stuffing out of, beat the tar out of, blank, blast, blitz, blow away, blow someone's door off, blow out of the water, bulldoze, bury, bushwhack, bust, butcher, catch someone's lunch, clean someone's clock, clean someone's plow, clean up on, clean up the floor with, coldcock, conk, cook someone's goose, crawl someone's hump, cream, crock, do a job on, do a number on, do for, do in, doughpop, do up, drub, dry-gulch, dump, dust off, eat for breakfast, eat someone's lunch, finish, finish off, fix, fix someone's hash, flatten, give the business to, give the works to, give someone what for, gorilla, go upside one's face, go upside one's head, hand someone his (or her) head, hang one on, have for breakfast, have someone's lunch, hit someone where he (or she) lives, ice, jack up, jolt, kayo, kick the shit out of, knock someone's block off, knock for a loop, knock someone galley west, knock someone into the middle of next week, knock someone's lights out, knock off, knock out, knock someone sky west, knock the daylights out of, lambaste, lather, lay out, let someone have it, lick, lick to a frazzle, liquidate, make hamburger of, make hash of, make mincemeat of, make someone say uncle, make short work of, massacre, massage, maul, meat-axe, mess up, mop up on, mop up the floor with, mow down, murder, nuke, paste, polish off, powder, pulverize, punch someone's lights out, punch someone out, put away, put the blocks to, put the skids to, roll over, romp over, rough up, rub out, run a game on, run a number on, sack, sandbag, scalp, schmear, schneider, scrag, scraunch, settle someone's hash, shellac, shoot down, shoot down in flames, shut out, sink, skin, skin alive, skunk, slaughter, slay, slug, smear, smoke, smother, snuff, snuff out, sock, steamroller, stomp, swallow with a glass of water, swamp, take, take downtown, take into camp, take out, take to the cleaners, tie one on, topple, trash, trim, trip, vamp, vamp on, waffle, wallop, waste, wax, whale, whipsaw, whitewash, whomp, whop, whup, wipe out, wipe up the floor with, work over, wreck, zap, zonk, zonk out

☞ *These terms share semantic territory with "sock," which should also be considered.*

2 SEE BEAT

clout
n Power; effective force; impact

bang, biff, drag, the goods, grease, jazz, jism, jolt, juice, kick, kick-ass, mohoska, moxie, muscle, oof, oomph, pizzazz, poop, pow, pull, punch, push, snap, sock, spunk, starch, steam, the stuff, suck, suction, umph, wallop, what it takes

cock
n The penis

apparatus, banana, bayonet, beef, belongings, [Latino] bicho, bone, business, club, creamstick, dang, dibble, dick, dicky, ding-dong, dink, dong, doodle, dork, dummy, flute, hairsplitter, hammer, hang-down, hog, horn, hose, hunk of meat, jang, jigger, jock, John, Johnny, johnson, John Thomas, joint, jones, joy knob, joy stick, knob, love-muscle, meat, member, middle leg, pecker, peenie, peter, pinga, poker, pole, pork, prick, prong, pud, putz, ramrod, reamer, reltney, rod, root, sausage, schmuck, shlang, shlong, short arm, shvantz, skin flute, sugar stick, third leg, tool, wang, weener, weenie, weinie, wiener, wienie, works, yang, yard, ying-yang

☞ *"Dingbat," "dingus," "doodad," "dofunny," "dojigger," "thingy," or any other of the numerous terms for something one does not know the name of or does not wish to name may be used as a euphemism for penis.*

☞ *"Penis" is one of the more prolific of slang concepts. Farmer and Henley's* Slang and Its Analogues *(1888–1904) lists about 200 English terms under the heading "cream-stick."*

cockeyed
1 *adj Askew; crooked, as in "His hat was cockeyed, his clothes disheveled"*

agee, agee-jawed, all anyhow, all nohow, antigodlin, askewgee, catawampus, crooked as a dog's hind leg, every which way, galley-west, haywire, lopper-jawed, popeyed, screwy, sigoggling, six ways to Sunday, skew-gee, skew-jawed, skygodlin, slonchways, slonchwise, wamper-jawed, weewaw, whopper-jawed, [Brit] wonky, yaw-ways

2 SEE CRAZY

cocksucker

1 *n A person who does fellatio, esp a male homosexual*

come-freak, come-queen, dick-licker, eater, gobbler, goopgobbler, peter-eater, piccolo player, scumsucker, skin-diver

2 SEE **ASSHOLE**

cock-teaser

n A person who arouses a man sexually and then denies the sex act

dick-teaser, prick-teaser, PT

☞ *Plausible compounds may be made by appending "teaser" to any term for penis.*

coke

n Cocaine

base, bernice, bernies flake, big bloke, big C, Billie Hoke, birdie powder, blinkie, bloke, blort, bounce powder, brute, burese, burnies, C, caballo, Cadillac, candy cee, Carrie Nation, Carry, Cecil, cee, chalk, Charley, cheese, chick, Cholly, c-jam, coca, coca paste, coconut, cola, cookie, Corine, crack, Doctor White, duct, dust, dynamite, flake, Florida snow, foo-foo dust, foolish powder, freebase, frisking powder, gin, girl, glad, gold, golden girl, goofy dust, H and C, happy dust, heaven dust, her, hocus, hot and cold, ice, incentive, jam, joy dust, joy flakes, joy powder, the Lady, Lady Snow, Lady White, the leaf, mayo, med mojo, monkey cocaine, mosquito, nose, nose candy, nose powder, nose stuff, number three, old Madge, old slave, paradise, perico, piece, pimp dust, pogo pogo, poison, powder, powder diamonds, racehorse, rane, rock, sleep, snort, snow, snowball, snow bird, snow caine, snow flakes, speedball, stuff, sugar, super blow, toot, tootonium, turkcy, uptown, whiff, white, white cross, white death, white girl, white horse, white lady, white mosquito, white paste, white powder, white stuff, white tape, white tornado, wings, witch

☞ *The great number of slang terms for narcotics probably reflects both a need for coded reference to an illegal substance and a desire to be chic and up-to-date, in addition to the need to distinguish varieties.*

cold as hell
adj phr Very cold

cold as a bastard, cold as a bitch, cold as a welldigger's ass, cold as a welldigger's ass in the Klondike, cold as a witch's tit, cold as charity, cold as Kelsey's ass, cold enough to freeze the balls off a brass monkey, colder than hell

cold fish
n phr A person who lacks emotional warmth, compassion, sociability, etc

chilly mo, iceberg, ice maiden

the cold shoulder
n phr A snub; a contemptuous dismissal, as in "She tried to make it up to him, but he just gave her the cold shoulder"

the beady eye, the brush, the brush-off, the chill, the cold stare, the cut direct, the dead cut, the fish-eye, the freeze, the frost, the go-by, the hairy eyeball, the ice

collitch
n A college; a university

alma mammy, brainery, coll, U, varsity

come
1 *v To have an*
orgasm; ejaculate
semen or secrete
other sexual fluids
2 SEE CUM

blow off, come off, drop one's load, get it off, get one's nuts, get one's nuts cracked, get one's nuts off, get one's rocks, get one's rocks off, go off, pop one's cookies, shoot, shoot one's load, shoot one's wad, spunk, spurt

come again
sentence Please
repeat what you
said

how's that?, let's have it again, run it by again, says which, say what

come down a peg
v phr To be
humiliated; stop
behaving in a
haughty manner

climb down, come off one's perch, crawl in a hole and pull it in after, eat crow, eat dirt, eat humble pie, eat shit, get off one's high horse, land with a dull thud, pull in one's horns, sing another tune, take off one's high hat, tuck one's tail

come off
1 *v phr To occur;*
happen, as in
"What's coming off
here?"
2 SEE COME

come down, cook, go, go down, go on

come on strong
v phr To begin and
proceed vigorously;
succeed brilliantly

be on a roll, come on, come on like gangbusters, hit the jackpot, make out like a bandit, pour it on, ring the bell, set the world on fire, turn on the heat

come out
v phr To become an acknowledged homosexual

come out of the closet, debut

come unglued
v phr To go out of control; deteriorate to chaos, as in "I couldn't keep the situation from coming unglued"

come unstuck, come unwrapped, go on the rocks, go to the dogs, go to hell, go to pieces, go to pot, go to smash ☞ *The term is often used of a person who has a traumatic emotional crisis, as in "I'm afraid Ruth came unglued after the cat got killed."*

con
1 v To cheat; swindle; deceive

bamboozle, beat, bite, blind-pop, blind-side, bum, bunco, burn, chisel, clip, cold haul, cream, curve, deke, diddle, dipsy-doodle, do a number on, doodle, do out, do over, doublecross, euchre, fake out, fast-talk, fiddle, fleece, flimflam, four-flush, fox, frig, fuck, futz, give someone a line, give someone the business, gouge, gyp, gyppo, hand someone a lemon, have, hook, hornswoggle, hose, hustle, hype, jerk someone's chain, jerk someone's string, make a patsy of, milk, murphy, phutz, play for a sucker, play the dozens on, pluck, pull a fast one, pull someone's chain, pull someone's string, pull the wool over someone's eyes, rattle someone's chain, ream, rip off, roll, rook, rope, rope in, run a game on, run a number on, scam, screw, sell, sell a bill of goods, shake down, shuck, skin, skunk out of, slicker, smuck, snooker, stick, stiff, sting, sucker, take, take someone downtown, take someone for a ride, take someone into camp, take someone to the cleaners, throw someone a curve, throw the hooks into someone, trim, yentz ☞ *This term is very often followed by "out of," as in "I conned him out of a couple of new tires."* ☞ *The distinction between "con" and "fuck" in its metaphorical sense is sometimes hard to draw, and both terms should be considered; "con" also shares semantic territory with "snow," which should be considered.*

2 SEE SCAM

con
n A convict; a jail or prison inmate

jailbird, lagger, loser, stir bird, vic, yardbird

con man
n phr A confidence man; a swindler

biter, bunco, bunco artist, bunco steerer, burn artist, burner, chiseler, clip artist, cold decker, con artist, crook, diddler, dipsy-doodle, double-crosser, fiddler, flammer, fleecer, flimflam man, flimflammer, four-flusher, gouger, grifter, gyp, gyp artist, hoser, hustler, jackleg, rooker, scammer, shark, sharp, sharper, sharp-ie, shuffler, shyster, skinner, slicker, stinger, two-timer, yentzer

cookie
n A person of either sex; an individual, as in "He's not the cookie I'd pick for that assignment"

apple, article, baby, bird, breed of cat, cats, character, citizen, clown, cluck, critter, cuss, customer, dish, duck, egg, face, fart, fish, gent, gink, guy, head, hoot, item, jasper, job, jobbie, joker, number, party, piece of cheese, specimen

cook up
v phr To devise; fabricate

fudge, hoke up, hype up, put together, whomp up, work up

cool
1 adj Going well; in good condition, as in "I told the host we thought the party was cool"

all there, A-OK, cooking, copacetic, ducky, fonky, funky, grad, groovy, having one's stuff wired, hitting on all six, hotsy-dandy, hotsy-totsy, hunky, hunky-dory, in good shape, in great shape, in kelter, in kilter, in town, in whack, mellow, neat, OK, okey-dokey, rosy, sharp, toast, together, up to scratch, up to snuff, up to the mark

2 *adj Aloof and uninvolved; deliberately disengaged; totally relaxed*
beat, blip, chill, cooled-out, down, far out, fresh, gone, groovy, heavy, hep, hip, ice, illen, loose, loose as a goose, looseygoosey, mellow, nervous, out, pretty scary, rat-fuck, turned on, way out, weird, wiggy, wild, zero cool

3 SEE **GREAT**

4 SEE **LAID-BACK**

cooler

1 *n A solitary-confinement cell*
bing, hole, icebox, iso, oven, sol

2 SEE the **SLAMMER**

cool it

v phr To moderate one's behavior; to calm oneself
back off, chill out, cool out, give it a rest, go easy, hang it easy, hang loose, hold one's horses, hold it, hold one's water, keep one's pants on, keep one's shirt on, not blow a fuse, not blow a gasket, not get one's balls in an uproar, play it cool, pull in one's ears, pull in one's horns, pull one's punches, simmer down, stay loose, take a chill spill, take it easy, take the heat off

cop

1 *n A police officer; a constable*
arm, azul, big John, blue, bluebelly, bluebird, blueboy, bluecoat, blue man, [Brit] bobby, bull, cinder bull, cinder dick, copper, county mounty, dick, Dogberry, elbow, finest, finger, flatfoot, flathead, flatty, flic, fly ball, fly bob, fly bull, fly cop, fly dick, fly mug, fuzz, fuzzy, gazer, gendarme, goms, gumboot, gumfoot, gumheel, gumshoe, harness bull, harness cop, harness dick, jake, John Law, lajara, the law, the Man, muzzler, nab, nabs, narc, narco, oink, orange crush, ossifer, paddy, [Brit] peeler, pig, rubber heel, sam, screw, shamus, shoe,

Smokey Bear, Smokey the Bear, Smoky, stick man, uncle, yard bull

☞ *This list does not discriminate the various sorts of law enforcement officers, and hence should be used carefully. Several items share semantic territory with "dick."*

2 SEE **BUST**
3 SEE **SCORE**

cop out
1 *v phr To evade; intentionally fail to cope or act*

back out, blow it off, blow off, bog, chicken out, flick it in, fold, punk out, punt, rat out, shake, shine, tap dance, throw in the sponge, throw in the towel, waffle, weasel out, worm out

2 SEE **BACK OUT**

the cops
n phr The police; law enforcers in general

the finest, the fuzz, the heat, the Man

☞ *More such terms may of course be made by making plural expressions with "the" of the terms under "cop."*

corn
1 *n Sentimentality; maudlin emotionalism*

corn on the cob, drool, flapdoodle, glop, goo, hearts and flowers, mush, schmaltz, slobber, slop, slush, sob stuff

2 *n Old-fashioned and sentimental music*

Mickey Mouse, razzmatazz, ricky-tick, rooty-toot

corny
adj Sentimental; banal; pathetic

beery, cornball, corn-fed, drippy, gloppy, gluey, glutinous, gooey, goopy, gummy, gushy, hicksville, icky, moony, mushy, off the cob, on the cob, ricky-tick, rinky-dink, sappy, schmaltzy, sloppy, slushy, soppy, soupy, squishy, sticky, teary

cough up
v phr To pay; hand over

ante up, come across with, come through with, cough over, dig down for, dig up, dish out, dish up, fork out, fork over, fork up, kick in, lay down, plank down, plunk down, pony out, pony up, shell, shell out

one couldn't care less
sentence One simply does not care; one is sublimely indifferent

one could care less, one doesn't give a damn, one doesn't give a shit, ishkabibble, it makes one no difference, it's no skin off one's ass, it's no skin off one's butt, it's no skin off one's nose, mox nix aus, one should worry, tough shit, what do you want from me

a country mile
n phr A long distance

far piece, from hell to breakfast, good way, long chalk, smart piece, way to hell and gone

cowboy
n A violent and reckless criminal; a thug

dropper, gorilla, hood, hoodlum, lobo, plug-ugly, ugly customer, yegg
☞ *These terms share semantic territory with "goon" and "hit man," which should also be considered.*

cow college
n phr An agricultural college thought to be of humble distinction

cow tech, East Jesus State, old Siwash, Siwash

crack
1 n A joke, as in "That was a pretty dumb crack"
2 SEE COKE

gag, one-liner, rib-tickler, wisecrack

a crack
n phr An attempt, as in "I'll have a crack at the job"

a bash, a belt, a cut, a fling, a go, a hack, a hit, a kick at the cat, a lick, a riffle, a rip, a ripple, a shot, a smack, a stab, a try, a whack, a whop

cracker
n A rural Southerner

Arky, clay eater, good old boy, hillbilly, Okie, peck, peckerwood, redneck, white trash, wood, woodchuck, woolhat

crack up
v phr To suffer an emotional or mental breakdown; go into hysteria, depression, etc

blow one's cork, blow one's mind, blow one's stack, blow one's top, chase butterflies, crack, flip, flip one's lid, flip one's wig, freak out, go ape, go balmy, go bananas, go batty, go crackers, go off one's bean, go off one's chump, go off one's head, go off one's nut, go off one's rocker, go off the deep end, go off the track, go off the trolley, go out of one's gourd, go out of one's skull, go out of one's tree, go to pieces, lose one's marbles, slip a cog, wig out

☞ *These terms may be greatly multiplied by using "go" with many of the other terms for "crazy"; "schiz out" should also be considered.*

crap
1 *n Anything of shoddy quality; rubbish; trash*

bilge, borax, cruft, dogshit, doodle, dreck, El Cheapo, garbage, gook, junk, khazeray, a lemon, Mickey Mouse, piece of crap, piece of shit, poot, rinky-dink, rummage, schlock, shit, sleaze, spinach, tripe, truck, unkjay

2 SEE **BULLSHIT**
3 SEE **SHIT**

crash

1 *v To fail; suffer a disaster; become inoperative, as in "I was doing fine until the computer crashed"*

crash and burn, fry, go belly up, go down, go down in flames, go south, melt down, shut down

2 *n A disaster; a debacle, as in "His wife's leaving him precipitated an emotional crash"*

blowup, bust, cat's astrophe, crack-up, meltdown, smash, smashup, wash-up

3 SEE SNOOZE

crazy

1 *adj Insane; demented*

ape, apeshit, [Brit] around the bend, balmy, bananas, barmy, bats, batty, bent, [Brit] bonkers, bonzo, buggy, bughouse, bugs, bugsy, cockamamie, cockeyed, crack-brained, cracked, [Brit] crackers, crackpot, crackpotty, crazy as a bedbug, crazy as a coot, crazy as a loon, crazy as catshit, cuckoo, daffy, dick-brained, ding-dong, dippy, dopey, dotty, dumdum, a few cards short of a full deck, food for squirrels, fruitcakey, fruity, funny, ga-ga, gonzo, Gonzo City, goofy, goo-goo, half-baked, half there, having a screw loose, haywire, kooky, loco, loony, loony-tune, loopy, loose in the bean, loose in the upper story, lunch, lunching, lunchy, [Brit] mental, meshugah, nerts, nertsy, nobody home, not all there, not tightly wrapped, nuts, nutso, nutsy, nutty, nutty as a fruitcake, off, off one's bird, off one's chump, off one's head, off one's noodle, off one's nut, off one's onion, off one's rocker, off the wall, off one's trolley, out of one's gourd, out of one's head, out of one's skull, out of one's tree, out to lunch, pixilated, potty, psycho, queer, queer in the head, [Brit] round the bend, rowing with one oar in the water, rum-dum, sappy, scatty, schizo, schizoid, schizy, screwball, screwy, sick, sick in the head, sicko, sicksicksick, spaced out, squirrely, tetched, tetched in the head, tetchy, tomfool, up the wall, wacko, wacky, weird, wild-ass

2 SEE **GREAT**

creepy
1 *adj Frightening;*   furry, hairy, scary, shivery
terrifying
2 SEE **WEIRD**

croak
v To die, as in "One   belly up, bite the dust, bow out, buy it, buy the farm,
minute she was   buy the ranch, cash in one's checks, cash in one's chips,
sitting there talking   check out, conk off, conk out, cop it, exit, farm, give out,
to us, the next   give up the ghost, go belly up, go home feet first, go
minute she croaked"   home in a box, go to glory, go west, kick in, kick off, kick
the bucket, pass out, peg out, pop off, push up daisies,
slip one's cable, turn up one's toes

crooked dice
n phr Dice that   bevels, bricks, busters, bust-outs, despatchers, door
have been altered so   pops, flat passers, flats, fullams, hits, horses, low-fullams,
as not to roll true to   misses, odds splitter, passers, phonies, pigs, repeaters,
the mathematical   rollers, tats, uphills
odds   ☞ *The terms are mostly specific to a certain kind of alteration, and not generic "crooked dice."*

crowd
v phr To press or   get on someone's back, get on someone's case, lean on,
importune   press, push, put the heat on, put the screws to, put the
squeeze on

cruise

v To go about seeking sexual encounters, esp in bars or along streets

cat around, trade, troll

crummy

adj Of inferior quality; shoddy

awful, badass, bash, beastly, bum, bush-league, cheap, cheesy, cotton-pickin', crappy, cruddy, crumbun, dinky, dipshit, dog-ass, doggo, doggy, dud, for the birds, from hunger, gnarly, godawful, gross, grungy, half-assed, half-baked, hanky-pank, junk, junky, lousy, low-down, low-rent, low-ride, mangy, measly, Mickey Mouse, mouldy, no-account, no-good, piss, piss-poor, pissy, punk, putrid, raggedy-ass, raggedy-pants, rank, rat-ass, ratty, raunchy, rinky-dink, rotten, sad, scanky, schlock, schlocky, [esp Brit] scruffy, shitty, stinking, stinko, tacky, tatty, tickytacky, tinhorn, trashy, two-bit, ungodly, X-double-minus, yucky

cum

n Semen

come, cream, gism, goo, hockey, jism, jizz, juice, love juice, man oil, scum, spunk

cunt

n The vulva; the vagina

bearded clam, beaver, booty, box, cake, cat, chink, chocha, chooch, clam, cooch, couze, crack, cunny, doodle, [Brit] fanny, furburger, fur pie, futy, gash, gig, giggy, ginch, hair pie, hole, honeypot, hotbox, jam, jelly, jellyroll, man-hole, meat, muff, nooky, notch, pit, poontang, pussy, quim, slit, slot, snatch, squirrel, stuff, trim, tuna, tuna fish, twat

☞ *"Dingbat," "dingus," "doodad," "dofunny," "dojigger," "thingy," or any other of the numerous terms for something one does not know the name of or does not wish to name may be used as a euphemism for vulva.*

☞ *"Vulva, vagina" is one of the most prolific of slang concepts. Farmer and Henley's* Slang and Its Analogues *(1888–1904) lists about 700 terms under the heading "the monosyllable."*

cunt-lapper
n A person who does cunnilingus

clit-licker, muff-diver

curtains
n Death; disaster; the bitter end

bye-bye, the end of the line, hips, last roundup, lights out, the payoff, taps

cut
1 v To choose not to attend a class, examination, etc, as in "She decided to cut Econ that day"

bag, blitz, flush, shine, skip

2 v To treat with deliberate hauteur; snub

brush, brush off, chill, cold-shoulder, cut dead, freeze, freeze out, give the beady eye, give the brush, give the brush-off, give the chill, give the cold shoulder, give the fish-eye, give the fluff, give the go-by, give the hairy eyeball, high-hat, ice, ice out, kiss off, put on the frost, put on the high hat, put the chill on, put the freeze on, snoot, turn the cold shoulder

3 SEE **BITE**
4 SEE **CRACK**
5 SEE **DIVVY**
6 SEE **SPLIT**

cut a deal

v phr To make or conclude an arrangement; transact an agreement

crack a deal, deal, [Brit] do a deal, make a deal

cut no ice

v phr To have no influence or effect; make no difference

butter no parsnips, cut no shit, cut no smoke, make no diff, make no never-mind, not make a diff of bitterence

cut one's own throat

v phr To ruin or injure oneself, usu unintentionally, as in "A politician who argues in favor of legalizing drugs is just cutting his or her own throat"

commit suicide, cut oneself off at the knees, shoot one-self in the foot, snatch defeat from the jaws of victory

D

the damage

n A customer's bill or check, as in "You bought the theater tickets, so let me pay the damage at the restaurant"

the ante, the bad news, the beef, the bite, the grunt, the knock, the score, the tab, the tariff

damn

adj Cursed; accursed; wretched, as in "Give me the damn thing and I'll try to make it work"

all-fired, blame, blamed, blanked, blankety, blankety-blank, blasted, bleeding, bleep, bleeping, blessed, blinkety, blinkety-blink, blinking, [Brit] bloody, blooming, consarned, cotton-pickin', cussed, dadblame, dadblamed, dadblasted, dadburned, daddratted, dadgasted, dadgum, dadgummed, dagnabbed, damnationed, damned, dang, danged, darn, darned, dashed, dern, derned, deuce, diddle-damn, diddledamned, dingbusted, dinged, dingswizzled, doggone, doggoned, double-clutching, doubledamned, dratted, effing, flipping, forking, frapping, freaking, frigging, frogging, fucking, gee-dee, godawful, goddamn, goddamned, goddarn, goddarned, goldamn, goldang, goldanged, goldarn, goldarned, goldern, goshawful, goshdamn, goshdamned, goshdang, goshdarn, goshdarned, goshdern, goshderned, goshganded, hell-fired, mother, motherfucking, mothering, pesky, [Brit] ruddy, stinking

☞ *These terms represent the most numerous and systematic euphemisms in slang. Damning someone's soul to hell, or asking God to do that, must never be uttered outright, perhaps for fear it might actually take place.*

dead to rights
adv phr With no possibility of escape or evasion; in flagrante delicto

cold, redhanded, with a smoking gun, with one's hand in the cookie jar, with one's hand in the till, with one's pants down, with the goods, with the merchandise

dealer
n A person who peddles drugs

bagman, big man, broker, 'cainer, candy man, connection, connector, cop man, cowboy, dope booster, dope peddler, dope pimp, dope runner, feed and grain man, fixer, good-time man, grog merchant, holder, hype, ice cream man, jobber, juggler, junker, junk peddler, missionary, mother, ounce man, peddler, push, pusher, righteous dealer, swing man, tambourine man, travel agent, viper

deck
1 *n A package or portion of narcotics*

bag, bale of hay, balloon, bar, big hog, bindle, bird's eye, biz, block box, bottle, brick, can, cap, card, cargo cube, deuce, deuce bag, dime bag, elbow, feed bag, finger, foil, full moon, gang, gram, half, half bundle, half load, half piece, hunk, jug, kee, keg, kite, lid, load, long, match, matchbox, matchhead, moon, nickel, nickel bag, O, Ohio bag, O Z, paper, piece, pillow, quarter bag, sack, short, short piece, spoon, tin, z

2 *v To knock someone down, esp with the fist*

belt over, bowl over, down, drop, flatten, floor, lay flat, lay out, lay out in lavender

desk jockey
n phr An office worker

paperweight, pencil driver, pencil pusher, pencil shover, pen pusher

dick
1 *n A detective*

bloodhound, D, deek, eagle-eye, eye, flatfoot, flattie, fuzz, gazer, gumshoe, gumshoe man, hawkshaw, house dick, narc, op, private eye, rubber-heel, Sherlock, Sherlock Holmes, sleuthhound, tec, undercover man
☞ *The list includes private detectives and specialized agents as well as police detectives. Several items share semantic territory with "cop."*

2 SEE COCK

dig
1 *v To understand; comprehend*

ace in, be with it, catch on, collar the jive, colly, flash on, get, get it straight, get the drift, get the hang of, get the idea, get the message, get the picture, get wise, get with it, grok, have it down, have it down pat, have it pegged, latch on, make, nail, pick up on, read, savvy, see where one is coming from, suss out, [Brit] tumble to, twig

2 *v To like; admire; prefer*

eat up, get a bang out of, get a boot out of, get a charge out of, get a kick out of, get a lift out of, get down with, get off on, go for, groove, groove on, wig

dirt
n Gossip; intimate or scandalous intelligence

buzz, D, jazz, juicy morsel, the latest, load of dirt, the lowdown, scuttlebutt, tittle-tattle

dirty
1 *adj Dishonest; shady, as in "That was a dirty trick"*

below the belt, crooked, crummy, dirty pool, foul, not cricket, raw, salty, shabby, sleazy

2 *adj Lewd;*
obscene

blue, filthy, gamy, gully-low, hot, juicy, naughty, off-color, off-tone, racy, raunchy, raw, ripe, rough, spicy, steamy, X-rated

3 *adj Possessing*
narcotics

carrying, holding

4 SEE **HOOKED**
5 SEE **LOADED**

dirty tricks
n phr Dishonest or
underhanded
practices; malicious
tactics

dirty pool, dirty work, funny business, jiggery-pokery, monkey business, rough stuff, shady business, skullduggery

disc jockey
n phr A radio
performer who plays
and comments on
phonograph records;
also, the person who
plays records at a
discotheque

dee-jay, DJ, jock, pancake turner

dish
n A particularly
attractive woman,
esp one who is
sexually attractive

angel, angelcake, angelface, babe, bathing beauty, beaut, beauty queen, beddy, [Brit] bird, bit of jam, broad, bunny, cack, cake, centerfold, charmer, cheesecake, chick, chiquita, cover girl, crack, [Brit] crumpet, cuddle-bunny, cupcake, cute chick, cutie, cutie-pants, cutie-pie, date bait, dazzler, dog, doll, dollface, dolly, dose, dreamboat, dream girl, eating pussy, eatin' stuff, eyeful, fetcher, fine hammer, flavor, fox, frail eel, frail job, furburger, fur pie, glamor girl, glamor puss, good-looker, hammer, head, honey, hot dish, hot number, hot patootie, hot sketch, knockout, looker, lovely, lulu, mink, morsel, nifty number, oomph girl, package, patootie, peach, peacharooney, peacherino, pin-up, pin-up girl, poppet, poundcake, quail, raving beauty, sex bunny, sex goddess, sex job, sex kitten, sex pot, sex queen, slash, slick chick, snapper, snugette, snuggy, stallion, stone fox, stunner, sweet patootie, table grade, ten, tomato

☞ *The semantic boundaries between "dish," "broad," and "floozy" are not easy to set. All three terms should be considered.*

ditsy
adj Silly; scatterbrained

addled, airbrained, airheaded, brack-brained, daffy, dippy, dipsy, dizzy, dopey, fluffheaded, ga-ga, giddy, goofy, goo-goo, kooky, loopy, potty, rattlebrained, scatty, zerking

ditz
n A silly person; a scatterbrain

addlebrain, addlehead, addlepate, airbrain, airhead, diddlehead, dizzy Lizzie, dumb Dora, fluffhead, giddy-brain, giddy Gertie, giddyhead, giddypate, jingle-brains, muddlehead, ninny, rattlebrain, Silly Billy, spoony

☞ *"Ditz" shares some semantic territory with "dope." The distinction is that one feels affection for a ditz and primarily contempt for a dope.*

dive
n Any disgusting or disreputable place, esp a cheap bar, nightclub, lodging house, or dance hall

barrel house, booze joint, boozer, boozery, bottleshop, crib, doggery, dramshop, dump, firetrap, gargle factory, gin dive, gin mill, grogshop, hellhole, hole, honkytonk, hooch house, joint, juice-joint, layout, place, pothouse, rathole, shebang, spot, waterhole, watering hole, watering place

divvy

v To divide and share out receipts, profits, loot, etc

cut, cut the take, cut up, cut up the jackpots, cut up the melon, cut up the pie, cut up the pipes, cut up the touches, divvy out, divvy up, piece up, razor

do

1 *v To take or inject narcotics*

do up, slam, use

2 SEE **SHIT**

3 SEE **WINGDING**

doctor

v To alter or tamper with something dishonestly

do creative accounting, doctor up, fiddle, fiddle with, fuck with, fudge, juggle, juggle with, mess with

does a bear shit in the woods

question That was a stupid question; isn't the answer very obvious, as in "Do I feel rotten about losing my job? Does a bear shit in the woods?"

does a wooden horse have a hickory dick, does Howdy-Doody have wooden balls, is the pope Catholic, is the pope Polish

doll

1 *n Any notably decent, pleasant, generous person*

ace, fuzzy one, honey, light, living doll, Mr Nice Guy, one-way guy, prince, pussycat, sugar pants, sweetheart, sweetie

2 *n A capsule of a barbiturate drug*

amy, backward, bank bandit, barb, black beauty, black molly, blockbuster, blue, blunt, brain tickler, candy, Christmas roll, Christmas tree, courage pill, dolly, downer, gangster pill, GB, goofball, goofer, gorilla pill, green dragon, joy pellet, King Kong, King Kong pill, mighty Joe Young, nebbie, nemish, nemmie, nimby, peanut, pill, purple heart, Red, Red Devil, sleeper, softball, stum, stumbler, stupper, thrill pill, tooie, toole, truck driver, yellow jacket

☞ *The great number of slang terms for narcotics probably reflects both a need for coded reference to an illegal substance and a desire to be chic and up-to-date, in addition to the need to distinguish varieties.*

doll up
v phr To dress fancily and in one's best clothes

deck out, deck up, dog out, dog up, doll out, dress to kill, dress to the nines, dress to the teeth, dress up, dude up, dud up, fancy up, fig out, fig up, get up, gussy up, prank, primp, prink, put on one's best bib and tucker, put on one's glad rags, put on one's Sunday clothes, put on one's Sunday-go-to-meeting clothes, put on the dog, put on the style, rag out, rag up, rig out, rig up, ritz up, slick up, snazz up, spiff up, spruce up, swank it, swank up, [Brit] tart up, titivate, tog out, tog up, trick out, trick up

donnybrook
n A riotous scene, esp a general brawl

battle royal, brannigan, ding-dong, foofooraw, gin, hitfest, hoedown, hoo-ha, kick-up, knock-down-drag-out, rhubarb, riot, row, row-de-dow, ruckus, ruction, rumble, rumpus, shemozzle, shindy, slugfest

☞ *Consider "free-for-all" also, and see the note there.*

dope
1 n A stupid or foolish person; an idiot

addlebrain, airbrain, airhead, applehead, bakehead, balloonhead, bananahead, basket case, beefwit, beetlebrain, birdbrain, blithering idiot, blockhead, blubberbrain, blubberhead, bohunk, bonehead, boob, booby, bozo, brack-brain, bubble-brain, bubblehead, buckethead, bulb, bunhead, cabbagehead, cheesehead, chickenhead, chowderhead, chucklehead, chump, clod, cluck, cluckhead, clunk, clunkhead, cokehead, coot, cretinoid, deadhead, dim bulb, dimwit, dingbat, dingding, ding-dong, dip, dipshit, dittybop, dodo, doo-doo head, dough-head, drop case, drop kick, drop shot, dufus, dufus-ass, dumbard, dumb bastard, dumbbell, dumb bunny, dumb cluck, dumb dodo, dumb Dora, dumb fuck, dumbhead, dumb jerk, dumbkopf, dumbo, dumb ox, dumbshit, dumdum, dummy, farmer, fart blossom, fatbrain, fathead, feeb, feeblo, flake, flathead, flub, flubdub, flub-up, four-letter man, gearbox, gearhead, gnatbrain, goney, goof, goofball, goofer, goofus, goofy, gooney, goop, gump, hummer, ivory-dome, jackass, jarhead, jellybean, jiggins, juggins, jughead, kluck, klutz, knothead, knucklehead, lamebrain, lardhead, lip mover, loogan, lummox, lump, lunch box, lunk, lunkhead, marble-dome, meatball, meathead, melonhead, Mickey Mouse, modoc, mope, mouthbreather, mullethead, musclehead, mush-head, mutt, mutthead, muttonhead, nincompoop, ninny, nitwit, noddy, noodle, noodlehead, nougat, numbhead, numbskull, oofus, peabrain, peahead, pinhead, pod person, pointed head, pointhead, pointy-head, poop, potatohead, puddinghead, pumpkinhead, putty-head, reject, retard, retardo, ring-ding, rockhead, rum-dum, sap, saphead, sapperoo, sappo, sausage, schlemiel, schlep, schloomp, schmegeggy, schmendrick, schmo, semolia, shit-for-brains, shovelhead, simp, slow coach, spastic, spazz, stupe, stupido, tackhead, tard, thickbrain, thickhead, thicko, thickskull, thickwit, troll, turkey, twimble, vegetable, watermelonhead, woodenhead, woodhead, yahoo, yap, yo-yo, zerk, zombie

☞ *"Dope" shares some semantic territory with "ditz." The distinction is that one feels primarily contempt for a dope, but some affection for a ditz.*

2 *n Any narcotic drug*

bang, bingle, birdie powder, birdie stuff, blanks, candy, caronotics, cotics, dizzy-wizzy, dreams, dry booze, dry grog, dummy, easing powder, fairy powder, feed, flea powder, fun medicine, ganger, garbage, geez, geezer, God's medicine, goods, gosneaks, grog, happy dust, happy flakes, happy powder, happy stuff, hash, heesh, hokus, hot stuff, ice cream, Lady White, leather dew, lemon, lemonade, locus, mahoska, merchandise, mojo, mooch, needle candy, nocks, nose candy, pot, powdered joy, reefer, shit, smoke, stuff, turkey

3 SEE POOP

dope den
n phr A place or party where marijuana is smoked

balloon room, ballroom, beat pad, blasting party, blast party, club, crash pad, dopatorium, doperie, pot

do the Dutch
v phr To commit suicide

do the Dutch act, take a D

double
n A person or thing that strongly or exactly resembles another; a duplicate

clone, dead ringer, living picture, look-alike, ringer, spit and image, spitting image

double cross
n phr A betrayal or cheating of one's own colleagues; an act of treachery and deceit

cross, cross-up, dipsy-doodle, double deal, double shuffle, double-time, double X, fast shuffle, sell-out, two-time, Wichita, XX

double-talk

n Language that cannot be understood, esp overly technical jargon

double Dutch, gobbledygook, Greek, jibber-jabber, monkey talk, mumbo-jumbo

dough

n Money; currency; wealth

beans, berries, billies, bit of change, bone, boodle, [chiefly Brit] brass, bread, bucks, cabbage, change, chips, clams, coin, coin of the realm, cold cash, cush, dib, dibs, dinero, do-re-mi, doubloons, ducats, feed, the filthy, filthy lucre, folding, folding cabbage, folding green, folding lettuce, folding money, frogskin, gee, geets, geetus, gelt, gold, gravy, green, greenbacks, green folding, green money, green stuff, happy-cabbage, hard cash, hunk of change, hunk of jack, jack, kale, kale-seed, kopecks, lean green, lettuce, long green, loot, lucre, mazuma, mean green, mezonny, mon, moo, moolah, mopus, the necessary, the needful, nuggets, ooftish, oofus, ooks, ookus, palm oil, pesos, piece of change, piece of jack, poke, potatoes, the ready, rivets, salve, scratch, shekels, simoleons, skins, spondulics, the stuff, sugar, tin, wampum, wherewithal, the wherewithal, whip-out

down

1 *adj Depressed; melancholy*

blah, blue, bummed, bummed out, down, down in the dumps, down in the mouth, dumpish, in a funk, in the doldrums, in the dumps, low-down, mopey, mopish, singing the blues

2 SEE **COOL**
3 SEE **GREAT**

drag
1 *n A dull, boring person*

crashing bore, deadass, deadfanny, deadneck, dead one, drip, dull tool, flat tire, headache, jerk, pain in the ass, pain in the neck, pill, wet blanket

2 SEE **BUTT**
3 SEE **CLOUT**
4 SEE **TOKE**

duck-squeezer
n An environ-mentalist; a conservationist

eagle freak, ecofreak, econut, greenie, tree-hugger, web-foot

dude
1 *n A dapper man, esp one who is ostentatiously dressed; a dandy*

alligator, Beau Brummel, buck, cake-eater, cat, city slicker, clothes horse, drugstore cowboy, fancy Dan, fancypants, fashion plate, flash-sport, gay-cat, hard-legs, hepcat, hotshot, jazz-bo, la-de-da, lady-killer, plate, sharpie, sheik, slicker, smooth article, smoothie, sport, stud, swell

2 SEE **GUY**
3 SEE **LADIES' MAN**

duffer
n A mediocre or downright poor performer, athlete, etc

dub, hacker, muffer, scrub, second-rater

dullsville
adj Boring; tedious

beige, blah, boh-ring, dead, deadsville, dragass, draggy, dragsville, dull as dishwater, hicksville, ho-hum, oofless, yawny

dumb
adj Stupid;
mentally sluggish

beanheaded, beef-witted, beetleheaded, blockheaded, blubberbrained, blubberheaded, blunderheaded, blunt-witted, boneheaded, boobish, brainless, cabbage-headed, chowderheaded, chuckleheaded, clodpated, [Brit] clottish, clunkish, clunky, cretinoid, dead between the ears, dead from the neck up, dense, dim, dim-witted, dingy, dizzy, doodle-brained, dopey, dorky, down a quart, dufus, dufus-assed, dumb as a box of rocks, dumbbell, dumb-cluck, dumbheaded, dumdum, dunderheaded, fatbrained, fatheaded, fat-witted, feather-brained, feather-headed, feeble in the head, fizz, flatheaded, flubdubbed, fool-headed, goofy, gormless, gunga, half-assed, half-baked, half-boiled, halfbrained, half-there, jingle-brained, [Brit] joltheaded, jugheaded, klutzish, klutzy, knuckleheaded, lackbrained, lackwitted, lame, lamebrained, light upstairs, lumpish, lunch, lunching, lunchy, lunkheaded, lunky, meatheaded, missing some marbles, muddle-headed, mulletheaded, mushheaded, muttheaded, muttonheaded, nitwitted, not all there, not right bright, numb, numb-brained, numbheaded, numbskulled, ossified, peabrained, peaheaded, peanut-brained, pie-faced, pinheaded, pointy-headed, puddingheaded, pumpkinheaded, rum-dum, rummy, sapheaded, sappy, schleppy, scramble-brained, shady, shallow-brained, shallow-pated, shallow-witted, shitheaded, short-witted, soft, softheaded, soft in the head, sorry-ass, spastic, spazz, spazzy, swift, thick, thick-headed, thickskulled, thick-witted, thin in the upper crust, three bricks shy of a load, weak in the head, weak in the upper story, without all one's oars in the water, without all one's switches on, without brain one, with rocks in the head, woodenheaded

dump

1 *n Any unpleasant place; a repulsive venue*

firetrap, hellhole, hole, joint, rathole, shithole, shithouse

2 SEE **DIVE**

dust bunny

n phr A tuft of dust that accumulates under beds, tables, etc

beggar's velvet, dust kitty, ghost turd, house moss, kitten, slut's wool

Dutch rub

n phr The trick or torment of holding someone's head and rubbing very hard and painfully at a small area of scalp with the fist

barbershop quartet, noogie

dyke

n A lesbian

Amy-John, boondagger, bull, bulldagger, bulldyke, bulldyker, butch, diesel-dyke, fairy lady, fem, femme, lesbo, lez, lezzie, man, Mary, top sergeant

☞ *No distinction is made in this list between active and passive, aggressive and "feminine" lesbians.*

eager beaver
n phr An active, ambitious person

ball of fire, big-time operator, buster, bustler, cage rattler, fireball, flamer, go-getter, heller, holy terror, hot shot, human dynamo, hummer hustler, live wire, operator, piss-cutter, pisser, pistol, powerhouse, self-starter, spark plug, springbutt, stemwinder, striker, take-charge guy, young Turk

eagle day
n phr Pay day

when the eagle flies, when the eagle shits

easy as pie
adj phr Very easy

duck-soup, easy as can be, easy as could be, easy as falling off a log, easy as hell, easy as rolling off a log, like a turkey-shoot, like falling off a log, like shooting fish in a barrel, like stealing candy from a baby, no sweat, simple as ABC, soft

eat dirt
v phr To accept rebuke or harassment meekly; swallow one's pride, as in "Marine Corps recruits soon learn to eat dirt"

eat it, eat shit, lump it, pocket one's pride, take it, take shit

eat high on the hog
v phr To live well and happily; prosper, as in "Once we win the lottery, we'll eat high on the hog"

be fat dumb and happy, be in clover, be in fat city, be in hog heaven, be like pigs in shit, be sitting pretty, be up tight, eat high off the hog, eat high on the joint, have egg in one's beer, have it good, have it made, have the world by the balls, have the world by the curlies, have the world by the nuts, have the world by the short hairs, live high on the hog, live off the tit, piss on ice, shit in high cotton, sit fat, sit in the catbird seat, sit pretty

eat up
1 v phr To accept; believe, esp something a bit dubious

buy, eat, fall for, gobble up, stand still for, swallow

2 SEE FLIP

egghead
n An intellectual; a thinker

brain, conehead, conk-buster, double-dome, egg, high-brow, ivory-dome, longhair, pointed head, pointhead, pointy-head

excess baggage
n phr A person or thing regarded as unnecessary and likely to impede

[esp Brit] odd man out, one too many, square peg, third wheel

excuse me all to hell
sentence I apologize; please forgive me

pardon me all to hell, pardon me for living

☞ *Always used ironically, when one believes an attack or accusation is unjustified.*

fall
v To be arrested; be
imprisoned

break into jail, drop, fall out, take a fall, trip, tumble

falsies
n A pair of pads
worn to give the
appearance of large
breasts

gay deceivers, props

fan
n A devotee or
enthusiast, esp of a
sport, team, etc

aficionado, booster, buff, bug, fiend, freak, groupie, hondo, junkie, nut, rooter

fart
1 *v To expel gas*
from the anus;
flatulate
2 SEE COOKIE
3 SEE GUY
4 SEE ZILCH

break wind, buck snort, cut a fart, cut the cheese, lay a fart, lay one, let a fart, let wind

a fat chance
n phr No chance at all a Chinaman's chance, a snowball's chance in hell, not an earthly chance, not a prayer

fat city
n phr An ideal situation; paradise cloud nine, cloud seven, Fiddler's Green, hog heaven, pig heaven

fatty
n An obese person biggie, blimp, blubberpot, butterball, chub, chubbette, Crisco, elephant, fat, fat-ass, fat-guts, fats, fatso, fat stuff, five-by-five, heavyweight, hippo, jelly-belly, jumbo, lard-ass, lard-bucket, plumpie, porky, pudge, pudgy-wudgy, pus-gut, pustle-gut, tub, tubby, tub of guts, tub of lard, walrus, whale

fed-up
adj Satiated; surfeited brassed off, browned off, crammed, fed to the gills, fed to the teeth, full up, have a bellyful, have a snootful, sick of, stuffed, turned off, up to here

a feed
n phr food eats, grub, a hot, spread

feel
v To touch or caress sexually; fondle, as in "She slapped him hard when he felt her" cop a feel, feel up, grope, handle, honk, mouse, paw, pet, play grab-ass, [Brit] play slap and tickle, rub

feisty
adj Truculent; irascible cantankerous, crabby, crusty, cussed, dukes-up, fire-eating, grouchy, hardnosed, huffish, huffy, mean, miffy,

ornery, salty, scrappy, [Brit] shirty, snarky, soreheaded, tetchy

figure
v To make sense; be plausible and reasonable, as in "It just doesn't figure that she would leave town"

compute, hang together, hold together, hold up, hold water, stack up, wash

fill someone in
v phr To inform; instruct, esp beforehand

brief, bring up to speed, clue, clue in, give the dope, give the info, give the lowdown, give the poop, give the scoop, keep posted, lay on, let in on, poop up, post, put in the picture, put someone wise, slip the info, smarten, smarten up, wise up

filthy with
adj phr Having much of; much endowed with, as in "She's filthy with talent"

loaded with, stinking with, up to here with, up to the ass with, up to the eyeballs with

fin
n A five-dollar bill; five dollars, as in "Lend me a fin till payday"

finiff, fiver, five-spot

fingerfuck
v To insert a finger into the vulva

diddle, finger, frig, play stink-finger, play stinky-pink, play stinky-pinky

finished

adj Ruined, esp occupationally; no longer able to function or compete

canned, dead, deep sixed, done for, had it, kaput, kicked out, out in the cold, out of it, out on one's ass, out on one's ear, sent to the showers, shot down

☞ *This list may be extended by using the participial form of verbs under "fire."*

☞ *These terms share semantic territory with "kaput," which should also be considered.*

fink

1 *n A traitor to one's race, class, sex, etc, as in "We elected him to represent us, and he turned out to be a fink"*

2 SEE ASSHOLE

3 SEE SCAB

4 SEE SNITCH

[all black] Afro-Saxon, Aunt Jane, Aunt Sally, fade, handkerchief-head, h n, house nigger, Mister Tom, Oreo, Tom, Uncle Tom; [both Native American] apple, Uncle Tomahawk; [Latino] Tio Taco; [sex] Aunt Tom

fire

v To discharge from a job; dismiss, as in "I was fired for coming in late every day for a month"

axe, bag, boot, bounce, bump, can, drop, give someone his (or her) running shoes, give someone his (or her) walking papers, give someone his (or her) walking ticket, give the axe, give the boot, give the bum's rush, give the chop, give the door, give the gate, give the hook, give the kissoff, give the old heave-ho, give the pink slip, [chiefly Brit] give the sack, kick, kiss off, pay off, pink-slip, [chiefly Brit] sack, send to the showers, show someone the door, show the gate, tie a can to, toss out

fish or cut bait

sentence Do one thing or another, but stop dithering; take action

get your finger out of your ass, piss or get off the pot, shit or get off the pot

a fix

1 *n phr A dose or injection of a narcotic*

bag, ball, bang, bing, blast, cushion, do-up, fix-up, goof-ball, hit, hype, jab, joy pop, joy prick, keek, knife in the arm, line, line shot, mainline, muscle, ping in the wing, ping-wing, pin shot, pop, prod, prop, set, short order, shot, skin pop, skin pump, ski-trip, tab, taste

☞ *This list does not distinguish among the various kinds of dose or method of dosage.*

2 *n phr A situation; a state of affairs, esp a tricky one, as in "Ollie certainly got us into quite a fix"*

a how-de-do, a how-do-you-do, a kettle of fish

fix someone

v phr To punish, esp in a spirit of retaliation, as in "He swore he'd fix her for sabotaging his project"

attend to, come down on, crack down on, do for, finish, fix someone's hash, fix someone's wagon, give it to someone in the neck, give someone the business, give someone the works, jump all over, let someone have it, lower the boom on, make it hot for, settle someone's hash, skin alive, sock it to, stick it to, take care of, wipe out, wreck

☞ *These terms share semantic territory with "clobber," which should also be considered.*

fix up

v phr To set in order

do up, neaten up, police up, red up, set to rights, [esp Brit] sort out

flack

1 *n Advertising or promotion; blatant publicity, as in "Most campaign information is little more than flack"*

bally, ballyhoo, buildup, bunk, crap, eyewash, flackery, flak, hoke, hokey-pokey, hokum, hoopla, hornblowing, hot air, hype, jive, moonshine, pitch, plugging, PR, promo, pub, puff, puffery, song and dance, spiel, whoopla

2 *n A publicity person or press agent*

drum-beater, flacker, gasman, hype artist, hyper, puff artist, shill, space bandit, tout

flak

1 *n Trouble; fuss; agitation*

botheration, fireworks, [esp Brit] flap, grief, heat, hollygolly, hoopla, how-de-do, pucker, racket, rhubarb, ruckus, rumpus, [Brit] shemozzle, static, stew, stink, tizzy, to-do

2 *n Severe criticism; angry blame*

agony, flack, grief, heat, static

flaky

adj Eccentric; unconventional, as in "My flaky uncle likes to do his gardening in the nude"

birdy, cracked, cranky, flake, funny, goofus, goofy, half-cracked, half-nuts, haywire, kinky, loopy, nutty, pixilated, queer, screwy, sproutsy, squirrely, wacked, wacko, wacky, weird, zerking

flat-out

1 *adv Unrestrainedly; without reservation, as in "She flat-out told him to go away"*

all-out, all the way, one's ass off, ass over tincups, balls-out, balls to the wall, one's brains out, one's buns off, but good, clear to hell, for all one's worth, forty ways to Sunday, from hell to breakfast, from soup to nuts, from the ground up, full blast, hammer down, one's head off, head over heels, hell-bent-for-leather, hell-for-leather, hell-to-split, in spades, knock-down-drag-out, lickety-cut, lickety-split, like a dose of salts, like shit through a tin horn, six ways to Sunday, something awful, something fierce, till one is blue in the face, to a fare-thee-well, to beat the band, to beat the Dutch, to hell, to hell and gone, to the max, the whole hog, the whole nine yards, wide open

2 SEE LICKETY-SPLIT

flip

1 v To respond enthusiastically; feel great excitement and pleasure, as in "Very few readers flipped over his first book"

be bugs about, be ga-ga over, be turned on, eat up, flip out, freak, freak out, get a bang out of, get a rush out of, get high on, go ape over, go ape-shit over, go bananas over, gobble up, go for, go nuts over, go overboard for, rave about, wig, wig out

☞ *Many of these terms coincide with those for the effects of narcotics and for the onset of insanity.*

2 SEE FREAK OUT

the flip side

n phr The opposite side of a question, issue, matter, etc, as in "But the flip side is that such freedom becomes anarchy"

the B-side, the other side of the coin, the other side of the picture

floor it

1 v phr To drive at full speed
go flat-out, goose it, nail it, put the hammer down, put the pedal to the metal

2 SEE BARREL

floozy

1 n A sexually promiscuous woman
alley cat, bag, baggage, bar-girl, B-girl, bike, bimbo, broad, bum, chippy, cooz, demi-rep, dirtyleg, easy lay, easy make, easy ride, fast chick, fish, fox, gash, grass-

back, low rent, nice girl, nympho, piece, piece of ass, piece of tail, pig, pleaser, punchboard, push, pushover, puta, quickie, quick push, quiff, roundheel, roundheels, sex job, shack, shack job, shackup, snake, sweat hog, swinger, town bike, town pump, tramp, tube, whore
☞ *The semantic boundaries between "floozy," "broad," and "dish" are not always easy to set. All three terms should be considered.*

2 SEE **HOOKER**

flop
1 *n A failure, esp a total one*

blast, bomb, brodie, bust, clinker, clunker, [Brit] damp squib, dog, dud, Edsel, el foldo, fizz, fizzle, fliv, flivver, flopperoo, floppola, flukum, flummox, frost, gas, gasser, hurtburger, lead balloon, lemon, loser, stiff, turkey, washout

2 *v To fail*

bomb, bust, crap out, fall down on the job, fall flat on one's ass, fall on one's ass, fall on one's face, fizz, fizzle, flummox, fold, frost, go belly up, go down for the count, go kerplunk, go over like a lead balloon, go over like a turd in the punchbowl, go pfft, go south, lay an egg, pfft, pull an el foldo, run on empty, take a dive, tank, tap out, wash out
☞ *This list may be increased by using the negative form of terms under "hack it."*

3 SEE **SNOOZE**

flophouse
n A cheap and sordid rooming house or hotel

bughouse, cathouse, chinch pad, crib, crumb house, crumb jopint, doss house, fleabag, fleabox, fleahouse, fleatrap, flop joint, scratch house

fluff
1 *v To forget one's lines on stage*

ascend, balloon, blow, blow up, dry up, flub, go up in one's line, go up in the air, make an ascension

2 SEE **GOOF**

flunk

v To fail an examination, course, etc

bust, flag it, flush, flush it, tube it

fly right

v phr To be honest, dependable, etc

be on the level, be on the up and up, go legit, go straight, keep one's nose clean, pull up one's socks, straighten out, straighten up, straighten up and fly right, tie one's shoes, toe the mark, wipe one's nose

fogy

1 n An old person; a senior citizen

alter kocker, antique, dodo, foozle, fossil, geezer, mossback, oldster, old-timer

2 n A conservative person

die-hard, fud, fuddy-duddy, hardshell, stick, stick in the mud

fold

v To lose energy and effect; wilt; be defeated, as in "When he saw who they had as witnesses, he folded"

back down, bite the dust, burn out, call it a day, call it quits, cave, cave in, chuck it, conk out, crap out, expire, give in, give out, holler quits, knuckle under, peter out, poo out, poop out, pull an el foldo, run out of gas, run out of steam, say uncle, throw in one's cards, throw in the sponge, throw in the towel, toss in the sponge, toss in the towel

☞ *These terms share semantic territory with "go ker-flooey," which should also be considered.*

fool around with
v phr To handle or tamper with; have to do with, as in "I wouldn't fool around with that red switch if I were you"; also, to engage in sexual activity with, as in "He said he'd kill me if he caught me fooling around with his sister"

dick around with, dick with, diddle around with, diddle with, fart around with, fart with, fiddle around with, fiddle with, fool with, fuck around with, fuck with, futz around with, futz with, jack around with, mess around with, mess with, monkey around with, monkey with, muck around with, muck with, potchkie around with, potchkie with, putz around with, putz with, screw around with, screw with

forget it
interj An exclamation of pardon; a token of forgiveness

don't give it a second thought, it's nothing, makes no never mind, mox nix aus, no big deal, no biggie, no problem, no sweat

for keeps
adv phr Forever; permanently

forever and amen, for good, for good and all, till hell freezes over, till the cows come home

for kicks
adv phr For no definite or useful reason; for mere pleasure

for fun, for the hell of it, just for the hell of it

for openers
adv phr As a beginning; as a first move or suggestion

first off, for starters

for sure

adv phr Definitely; certainly; really, as in "We are beaten for sure"

but good, dead sure, for a fact, for certain, for real, no buts about it; no ifs, ands, or buts; no two ways about it, shitsure, sure as God made little green apples, sure as hell, sure as I live and breathe, sure as shit, sure as shootin', sure as the devil, sure as you're a foot high, sure-nuff, sure thing

frame

v To prepare and maneuver someone for swindling, tricking, incriminating, etc, as in "He insisted that they had framed him with a few accidental and trivial circumstances"

build, bum-beef, frame up, set up

freak out

v phr To have an unpleasant experience with a narcotic, esp a hallucinogen; to have a similar experience not due to drug use

blow one's top, flip, flip out, freak, go on a bad trip, have a bad trip

freebie
n Anything given or enjoyed free of charge, as in "My friend at the box office is usually good for a freebie"

comp, free lunch, free-o, giveaway

free-for-all
n A riotous scene, esp a general fight

barncy, battlc royal, brannigan, brawl, broil, dogfight, donnybrook, fracas, gin, knock-down-drag-out, melee, mix-up, rhubarb, riot, row, ruckus, ruction, rumble, rumpus, run-in, scrap, scrimmage, scuffle, set-to, shindy, tussle

☞ *Consider "donnybrook" also. The distinction may be only fanciful, but "donnybrook" seems to designate a boisterous scene, whereas "free-for-all" stresses the fighting.*

free gratis
adj phr Free of charge; nonpaying

[Brit] buckshee, cufferoo, cuffo, for free, for nothing, freebie, free gratis for nothing, on the arm, on the cuff, on the house

freeze up
v phr To panic; be paralyzed by fear

choke up, clank, clank up, funk, swallow the apple, take the pipe

French kiss
n phr A kiss in which the tongue of one person explores the oral cavity of another, and vice versa

soul kiss

frisk
v To search a person for weapons or contraband

body-shake, fan, frisk down, pad down, prat-prowl, prowl, shake, shake down, skin-search, strip-search, toss

Frog
n A French person or a person of French extraction

Frenchy, frog-eater, Froggy
☞ *These terms are likely to give offense.*

from scratch
adv phr From the very beginning

from square one, from the git-go, from the ground up, from the top, from the word go

front runner
n phr The leader and one most likely to win a contest, election, race, etc

best bet, favorite, hot favorite, hot horse, odds-on favorite

fruit salad
n phr A group of stroke victims or otherwise totally disabled patients

potato patch, rose garden, vegetable garden

fry
v To put or be put to death in the electric chair

burn, cook, jump, ride old Smoky, ride old Sparky, ride the lightning, roast, sizzle, squat hot, toast

fuck
1 v To do the sex act with or to; copulate

ball, bang, boff, [Brit] bonk, boogie, boom-boom, bop, buzz the brillo, crawl, dick, diddle, dip one's wick, do it, do the thing, eff, fork, frig, futy, futz, get one's ashes hauled, get one's banana peeled, get into someone's drawers, get into someone's pants, get it off with, get laid, get one's nuts cracked, get one's nuts off with, get one's nuts with, get off with, get over, get one's rocks off with, get one's rocks with, get some nookie, [Brit] get stuffed, give out, give someone the shaft, go all the way, go at it, go the limit, go to bed with someone, go to it, go to town, have someone, have a party, have one's end off, [Brit] have it off, horse, hose, hump, jam, jazz, jump, jump someone's bones, knock off, knock off a piece, lay, lay pipe, lay tube, make, make it, make out with, nail, off, party, perform, phutz, plank, play bouncy-bouncy, play hide-the-weenie, plow, pluck, poke, pop, pork, pound, prong, pump, put, put it to, put out, put the blocks to, raunch, ream, ride, roll, score, score with, scrag, screw, scrog, scrump, shaft, shag, shtup, sleep with someone, spread, spread for someone, [Brit] stuff, swing, tear off a piece, tear off a piece of ass, throw a fuck into, trick, trick out, work out, yentz

2 *v* To maltreat; victimize, as in "If he's not careful to get everything in writing, those guys will fuck him"

diddle, file, fork, frig, fuck over, fuck up, give the finger, give the shaft, grunge, hose, mess someone around, mess someone over, ream, screw, screw over, sell down the river, sell out, shaft, smuck, stiff, yank

a fuck
n An instance of the sex act

bang, boff, bop, frig, futz, horizontal bop, hump, jazz, lay, parallel parking, party, phutz, piece, piece of ass, piece of tail, poke, ride, roll, roll in the hay, screw, shag, some couze, some cunt, some jellyroll, some nookie, some twat

fuck book

n phr A porno-graphic book or magazine

stroke book

fucked-up

1 *adj Confused; chaotic*

all anyhow, all nohow, arsy-varsy, ass backwards, assed-up, balled-up, bassackwards, bollixed-up, bugged-up, buggered-up, cockeyed, every which way, flummoxed, fouled-up, fried, fubar, fubb, fucked-up like a Chinese fire call, fumtu, futzed-up, galley-west, gummed-up, gummixed-up, helter-skelter, higgledy-piggledy, hug-ger-mugger, kerflummoxed, messed-up, messy, mocus, mommixed-up, mucked-up, mussed-up, out in left field, ramble-scramble, screwed-up, screwy, skewgee, skim-ble-skamble, sky-west, sloppy, snafu, snafued, susfu, tarfu, untogether, up gefucked

2 SEE ON THE BLINK

fucking

1 *adj Utter; total, as in "Ain't it a fucking shame?"*

blinking, bloody, blooming, crying, damn, dern, frig-ging, plum, plumb, regular, stone

2 *adv Extremely; utterly, as in "Isn't that a fucking stupid thing to say?"*

bloody, damn, frigging, God-awful, goshawful, mighty, plum

fuck up

v phr To fail, esp by blundering; ruin one's prospects

be a loser, be shot down in flames, be thrown for a loss, bilge, bite the dust, blow, blow it, bomb, cave in, [Brit] come a cropper, crap out, crash, crash and burn, do an el foldo, drop the ball, fall flat on one's ass, fizzle, flop,

fold, fold up, foozle, foul up, go belly up, go down the
drain, go down the tube, goof, go under, go up the
spout, gum up, keel over, lay an egg, lose out, miss the
boat, muff, not cut it, not cut the mustard, not get to
first base, not hack it, not make it, not make the grade,
peg out, peter out, poop out, screw up, step on one's
dick, step on it, step on one's schvantz, strike out, suck
wind, take a bath, take the gas, take the pipe, whiff,
wipe out

fuck-up
1 *n A bungler, esp*
a chronic one
2 SEE SNAFU

bobbler, bonehead, dub, foozler, fumble-fist, goof,
goofer, goof-up, goofus, screw-up, slob

fuck you
interj An
exclamation of very
strong defiance and
contempt

bite moose; chuck you, Farley; chuck you, Farley, and
your whole famn damily; cram it, drop dead, eat it, eat
this, eff you, fork you, fubis, fuck you and the horse you
rode in on, get lost, [Brit] get stuffed, go fly a kite, go
fuck yourself, go impale yourself, go piss up a rope, go
pound salt, go pound salt up your ass, go pound sand,
go pound sand up your ass, go screw yourself, go shit in
your hat, go soak your head, go suck eggs, go to hell,
[Brit] I'm all right Jack, kiss my ass, piss on you, put it
in your ear, ram it, read my lips, screw you, shit in your
hat, shit on you, shove it, [Brit] sod you, so's your old
man, stick it, stick it in your ear, stick it up your ass, stick
it where the sun doesn't shine, stow it, stuff it, take a
flying fuck, take a flying fuck at a rolling doughnut, take
a flying fuck at a rubber duck, take it in the ear, up
against the wall, up thine with turpentine, up your ass,
up your butt, up your gazool, up your gig, up your
giggy, up yours, you know what you can do with it, you
know where you can stick it

☞ *These, along with "kiss my ass," constitute the most abusive and provocative nonethnic rejections available in US slang. The distinction between the two verbal assaults is not easy to draw, and both should be considered.*

full of piss and vinegar
adj phr Brimming with energy; very lively

chipper, feeling one's oats, feisty, full of beans, full of go, full of pep, full of prunes, full of steam, go-go, gung ho, hopped up, peppy, rambunctious, rarin' to go, snappy, starchy, tearing up the pea patch, zappy, zingy, zippy

full of shit
adj phr Wrong; mistaken; not to be credited, as in "Politicians are full of shit"

all wet, dead wrong, full of baloney, full of beans, full of bull, full of crap, full of prunes, full of shit as a Christmas goose, haywire, in the right church but the wrong pew

fur pie
n phr Cunnilingus

box lunch, French, the French way, furburger, hair pie, head

G

gab

1 *n* *Talk; speech*

blab, blat, buzz, chin, chin music, chinning, flapjaw, gas, gibble-gabble, guff, jabber, jawing, jibber-jabber, lip, noise, palaver, patter, prattle, rag-chewing, rap, rapping, talk-talk, talky-talk, tongue-wagging, yackety-yack, yacking, yap, yapping

2 *v* *To talk, esp idly or frivolously; chatter*

bat one's chops, bat one's gums, bat one's jaws, bat one's jowls, bat one's lip, bat the breeze, beat one's chops, beat one's gums, beat one's jaws, beat one's jowls, beat one's lip, blab, blat, breeze, bullshit, buzz, chin, fan, fat-mouth, flap one's chops, flap one's gums, flap one's jaw, flap one's jowls, flap one's lip, flip one's lip, gabble, gas, gibble-gabble, gum, hump one's chops, hump one's gums, hump one's jaw, hump one's jowls, hump one's lip, jabber, jaw, jibber-jabber, mouth off, [chiefly Brit] natter, palaver, pop off, rap, rattle, run off at the mouth, shoot off one's face, shoot off one's mouth, shoot the breeze, shoot the bull, shoot the shit, sound off, spiel, spout off, talk someone's ear off, talk up a storm, throw the bull, wag one's chin, warm someone's ear, woof, yack, yackety-yack, yack it up, yack-yack, yack-yack-yack, yammer, yap, yatata, yatter, yip

☞ *The many "yack" forms have "yak" spelling variants and variants in "yock" and "yuck."*

☞ *"Gab" shares semantic territory with "blow off" and "shoot the breeze," which should also be considered.*

gabby
adj Very talkative; garrulous and gossipy, as in "My taxi driver was the gabby sort"

all jaw, bigmouthed, flapjawed, full of wind, gassy, gimbaljawed, lippy, longwinded, motormouthed, satchelmouthed, talky, windy, yappy

gadget
n Any unspecified or unspecifiable usu small device or object; something one does not know the name of or does not wish to name

bitch, bugger, contraption, deedee, dingbat, dingus, doobob, doodad, doodle, doofunny, doohickey, doohinkus, doohinky, doojigger, doomajigger, doowhangam, doowhistle, doowillie, frobnitz, fucker, gidget, gigmaree, gilgadget, gilguy, gilhickey, gilhooley, gimmick, giz, gizmo, goofus, guy, hickey, hootenanny, hootmalalie, jigger, jimjick, kickshaw, little guy, mother, motherfucker, mucket, puppy, thingamajig, thingumabob, thingummy, thingy, whangdoodle, whatamahicky, whatchamacallit, whatsit, whoozis, widget, you-know-what

☞ *This is a partial list only. The terms may be multiplied enormously with variant spellings and with other spur-of-the-moment combinations of "do," "thing," and "what" with nonsense syllables. All told, these useful designators and euphemisms may potentially be the largest set of slang synonyms.*

gadgetry

n Ingenious or impressive devices, esp electronic or mechanical, as in "James Bond's gadgetry has saved his neck many times"

bells and whistles, gimmickry, gimmicks, Mickey Mouse

a gamble

n phr An uncertain venture; a matter of chance

chancy proposition, crap shoot, dicey proposition, horse race, iffy proposition, risky business, sporting proposition

gang bang

n phr An occasion when several males do the sex act serially with one woman

gang fuck, gang shag, train

gangster

n A member of a criminal gang; an organized-crime figure

button man, goombah, Mafioso, mobster, soldier

gay

1 *adj Homosexual, as in "Gay activists are pushing for antidiscrimination legislation"*

bent, fag, faggoty, faggy, fairy, fay, flaming, flitty, fruity, homo, kinky, lacy, light-footed, light on his feet, limp-wristed, Mary, nancy, Nelly, pansy, pink, queer, swish ☞ *"Gay" applies to both male and female homosexuals, but the other terms in this list are used nearly*

2 *n A male*
homosexual

exclusively of males. Female homosexuals are charac-
terized as "lez," "lezzie," "lesbo," "lizzy," or "dykey."
angel, camp, capon, daisy, dilly dude, drag queen, dyna,
fag, faggot, fairy, fay, fegelah, femme, flamer, flaming
asshole, flaming fruitbar, flit, flower, flute, fluter, foop,
fooper, freak, frit, fruit, fruitcake, girl, gump, home
boy, homo, jackie, jocker, limp-wrist, maricon, Mary,
mo, nancy, nancy boy, nelly, pansy, pato, pix, pogue,
[Brit] poof, [Brit] poofter, [Brit] poove, punk, queen,
queenie, queer, sissy, swish, three-letter man

☞ *These terms are all offensive.*

get a kick out of
v phr To enjoy
especially; delight in

dig, get a bang out of, get a charge out of, get off on, go
for, groove on

get by
v phr To do
acceptably well;
neither succeed nor
fail, but survive

cope, get along, get on, make out, manage, [Brit] muddle through, scrape along, scrape by, scruff, scruff along,
scuffle, scuffle along, skin through, squeak by, squeak
through

get down to brass
tacks
v phr To talk
seriously about
essential things

cut the shit, get down to cases, get down to the nitty
gritty, get to the bottom line, lay it on the line, level,
talk turkey

get even
v phr To take
revenge

even the score, get one's own back, get square, knot the
score, return the compliment, settle accounts, settle
the score, square accounts

get it in the neck
v phr To be severely punished or injured, as in "If my girl doesn't stop whining she's going to get it in the neck"

be shot down, be shot down in flames, be wiped out, get clobbered, get it, get one's lumps, get taken off at the knees, get the business

get it together
v phr To arrange one's life and affairs properly; become organized

bring this shit to a focus, get one's act together, get one's act together and take it on the road, get one's ducks in a row, get one's head together, get it all together, get one's shit together, get one's stuff together

get lucky
v phr To enjoy good luck

luck out, luck up

get me
question Do you understand me?

are we on the same wavelength, are you tuned in, catch, catch on, catch the drift, collar my jive, compree, comprenny, cool, coppish, dig, dig me, dontcha know, do you read me, get it, get the drift, get the message, get the picture, got it, got me, OK, read me, read my lips, right, savvy

get off someone's **back**
v phr To leave alone; stop annoying or nagging

back off, do not crowd someone, get off someone's case, get off someone's neck, get out of someone's face, let someone breathe

get on the ball

v phr To rally one's wits and energies; improve one's performance

get one's ass in gear, get one's finger out of one's ass, get one's head out of one's ass, get on the stick, get with it, pull up one's socks, spudge around, stir around, tie one's shoes

get on the bandwagon

v phr To join a popular trend, movement, etc

climb on the bandwagon, go along with the crowd, hop on the bandwagon, leap on the bandwagon

get the ax

v phr To be dismissed, discharged, etc

get the air, get the boot, get the bum's rush, get the hook, get the sack

get the lead out

v phr To hurry; get busy and play one's part

get a hump on, get a hustle on, get a move on, get one's ass, get one's ass in gear, get a wiggle on, get cracking, get cutting, get one's finger out of one's asshole, get going, get it on, get off one's ass, get off one's butt, get off one's dead ass, get off one's duff, get off the dime, get on one's horse, get on the stick, get the lead out of one's ass, hop to it, hump, hustle, hustle up, look alive, make it snappy, not stand around with one's finger up one's ass, pick 'em up and lay 'em down, pour it on, pour on the coal, quit fucking the dog, rustle one's bustle, shake a leg, shake it, shake it up, shake the lead out, show a leg, snap it up, snap to it, spudge around, step on it, stir one's stumps

ghetto box
n phr A large portable stereo radio and cassette player often carried and played loudly in public places

boogie box, box, coon box, ghetto blaster, thunderbox radio

gimmick
n Anything calculated to seize and rivet the attention, as in "We'll need a gimmick to sell it"

come-on, grabber, hook, pitch

gimpy
adj Having a limp or being lame

game, hoppy, limpy

gin mill
n phr A barroom; a saloon

boozer, fillmill, gargle factory, gin palace, gin parlor, groggery, grog-mill, guzzlery, guzzle shop, hoochery, waterhole, watering hole, watering place

give a miss
v phr To avoid; not choose, as in "I think I'll give that banquet a miss and just stay home"

give the go-by, pass up, skip, take a bye, take a rain check

give someone **a pain in the ass**
v phr To be distasteful, tedious, repellent, etc, as in "After the first few days that job gave me a pain in the ass"

frost someone's ass, get in someone's hair, give someone a pain, give someone a pain in the neck, give someone a swift pain in the ass, gripe someone's ass, gripe someone's balls, gripe someone's cookies, gripe someone's left nut, gripe someone's middle kidney, gripe someone's soul, miff, peeve, put someone's nose out of joint, rub one the wrong way

give someone **a ring**
v phr To call, esp on the telephone

give someone a blow, give someone a buzz, give someone a shout, [Brit] give someone a tinkle

give something **a shot**
v phr To have a try at; make an attempt

give something a crack, give something a go, give something a riffle, give something a rip, give something a ripple, give something a whack, have a crack at, have a go at, have a riffle at, have a rip at, have a ripple at, have a shot at, have a whack at, take a crack at, take a lick at, take a riffle at, take a rip at, take a ripple at, take a shot at, take a whack at

give someone **a slap on the wrist**
v phr To punish mildly

rap someone's knuckles

give five
v phr To greet with a handshake or a slapping of hands

give some skin, press the flesh, slap five, whip out

give someone his (or her) walking papers
v phr To dismiss or discharge; reject, as in "After the third time he cheated on her she gave him his walking papers"

give someone his (or her) running shoes, give someone his (or her) walking ticket, give someone the air

give the cold shoulder
v phr To snub; behave disdainfully

brush, brush off, chill, cold-shoulder, cut, cut dead, freeze, freeze out, give the beady eyeball, give the fish-eye, give the go-by, give the hairy eyeball, high-hat, put on the freeze, put on the frost, snoot, turn the cold shoulder, turn up one's nose, upstage

give someone the finger
v phr To make a contemptuous sign with the hand, middle finger extended

flip the bird, throw a bird

glad-hander
n A person who evinces a warmth and heartiness that is probably insincere; one who is designedly cordial

flesh-presser, handshaker, mitt-glommer, phony

glad rags
n phr One's best clothing

best bib and tucker, dress-ups, fancy rags, [Brit] full fig, Sunday best, Sunday-go-to-meeting clothes

glass arm
n phr A baseball pitcher's arm that is prone to injury and inflammation

crockery, putty arm

glass jaw
n phr A boxer's chin that cannot tolerate a hard punch

china chin

glitch
n A malfunction; a defect

bug, goof, hitch, kink, monkey-wrench in the works, screw-loose, slip-up, something screwy, wrinkle

glitzy
adj Blatantly scintillant; gaudy

day-glo, flashy, flossy, jazzy, loud, splashy, splurgy, zazz, zazzy

glob
n A mass of viscous matter

blob, gob

gloomy Gus
n phr A morose, melancholic person

crape-hanger, grinch, killjoy, party-poop, party-pooper, prophet of doom and gloom, turn-off, wet blanket

G-man
n An agent of the Federal Bureau of Investigation; a special agent

Feeb, Feebie, hard John

the go-ahead
n phr Permission or a signal to proceed; consent

the green light, the nod, the OK, permish, thumbs up

go back to square one
v phr To be forced to return to one's starting point; make a new beginning

be at jump street, be at square one, be at the git-go, go back and punt, go back to the old drawing board, scrub the slate clean, start from scratch, wipe the slate clean

go broke
v phr To become penniless; become insolvent

be cleaned out, be taken to the cleaners, be washed out, be washed up, be wiped out, go belly up, go bust, go to the cleaners, lose one's shirt, take a bath, tap out, wash out

go crazy
v phr To become insane; lose one's mind, as in "War is enough to make anyone go crazy"

blow one's cork, blow one's stack, blow one's top, crack up, flip, flip one's lid, flip out, flip one's wig, freak out, go ape, go apeshit, [Brit] go around the bend, go balmy, go bananas, go barmy, go bats, go batty, go bent, [Brit] go bonkers, go bonzo, go buggy, go bughouse, go bugs, go bugsy, go cockamamie, go cockeyed, go crackbrained, go cracked, [Brit] go crackers, go crackpot, go crackpotty, go crazy as a bedbug, go crazy as a coot, go crazy as a loon, go crazy as catshit, go cuckoo, go daffy, go dingdong, go dippy, go dopey, go dotty, go dumdum, go fruitcakey, go fruity, go funny, go ga-ga, go gonzo, go Gonzo City, go goofy, go half-baked, go half there, go haywire, go kooky, go loco, go loony, go loony-tune, go loopy, go lunchy, go mental, go meshugah, go nerts, go nertsy, go nuts, go nutso, go nutsy, go nutty, go nutty as a fruitcake, go off, go off one's chump, go off one's nut, go off one's rocker, go off the wall, go off one's trolley, go out of one's gourd, go out of one's skull, go out of one's tree, go potty, go psycho, go queer, go queer in the head, [Brit] go round the bend, go rumdum, go scatty, go schizo, go schizy, go screwball, go screwy, go squirrely, go tetched, go tetched in the head, go up the wall, go wacko, go wacky, go weird, go wild-ass, lose one's gourd, nut up, schiz out, slip one's trolley, snap, wig out

☞ *These terms are very often used loosely or figuratively.*

gofer
n A low-ranking subordinate

bench warmer, best boy, bottom man on the totem pole, doormat, gal Friday, go-for, gopher, grunt, guy Friday, hired help, lightweight, little shot, low-level Munchkin, low man on the totem pole, man Friday, peon, scrub, second fiddle, second-stringer, spear-carrier, stooge, third-stringer, utility infielder

go for
1 v phr To choose; prefer, as in "She always goes for the best wine"
2 SEE **DIG**

come down for, give the nod to, plump for, push, push for, vote for

go for it
*v phr To stake
everything on a
taxing try; take a
risk*

bet the farm, bet the house, bet the ranch, go for all the marbles, go for broke, go for the fences, go for the long ball, shoot the works, shoot one's wad

☞ *This term was widespread in the 1980s as an exhortation and was probably related to the contemporary obsession with sports and physical fitness.*

go into one's
dance
*v phr To begin a
prepared line of
pleading,
persuasion, selling,
seduction, etc, as in
"She's quiet most of
the time, but put
her with a client
and she'll go into
her dance"*

do one's number, go into one's act, go into one's dog and pony show, go into one's song and dance

go kerflooey
*v phr To cease to
function; break
down; collapse*

belly up, bust down, cash in, conk out, crap out, crash, fizzle, fizz out, get out of commission, get out of kilter, get out of whack, give out, give up the ghost, go belly up, go blooey, go down, go down the chute, go down the drain, go down the tubes, go flooey, go haywire, go kablooey, go kaput, go on the blink, go on the bum, go on the fritz, go up in smoke, go up the spout, gronk out, hit the skids, [Brit] pack up, peg out, poop out, pot out, tap out

gold mine
n phr A very profitable venture; a lucrative business

bonanza, gravy train, license to print money

goner
n A person or thing that is doomed beyond hope of saving

cooked goose, dead duck, dead meat, dead pigeon, dead rabbit, gone case, gone coon, gone gander, gone goose

goo
n Any viscous and unappealing fluid or mixture; anything slimy and nasty

glop, gook, goop, goozlum, guck, gumbo, gunk, jism, muck, mung, sludge, stickum

good guy
n phr A decent person; a reliable and admirable citizen, as in "It's hard to believe a good guy like him could be a spy"

ace, good egg, good head, good Joe, good sport, Mr Nice Guy, one-way guy, prince, regular fellow, regular guy, righteous egg, right gee, right guy, square dealer, square John, square shooter, supergopher
☞ *These terms, like "guy," are now used also of women.*

goody-goody
n A prim and ostentatiously virtuous person

bluenose, goody, goody two-shoes, holier-than-thou, Nice Nelly, old maid
☞ *This list is close to the one at "Bible-banger." Slang does not take virtue at the ideal evaluation.*

goof

1 *v To make a mistake; blunder, as in "The right fielder really goofed on that play"*

blot one's copybook, blow, blow it, bobble, boot, [Brit] drop a brick, drop one's bucket, drop the ball, [Brit] duff, flub, flub the dub, fluff, foozle, foul up, fuck up, get egg on one's face, goof up, louse up, make a blooper, make a boner, make a boo-boo, make a mess, muck up, pull a bloomer, pull a blooper, pull a bonehead play, pull a boner, pull a boo-boo, put one's foot in it, put one's foot in one's mouth, screw up, slip a cog, step on one's dick, trip up

2 SEE **FUCK UP**

go off half-cocked

v phr To make a premature response, esp an angry one

be quick-draw, be too quick on the draw, be too quick on the trigger, go off at the half-cock, shoot from the hip

goof off

1 *v phr To avoid work; shirk duty*

bunny-fuck, coast, conk off, dog it, dope off, drag-ass, drag one's ass, drag one's feet, drag it, dragtail, drag one's tail, fake off, fall down on the job, featherbed, float, flub, flub the dub, fluff off, fuck off, fuck the dog, goldbrick, goof around, hump the hound, jerk off, lay down on the job, lie on one's oars, lollygag, screw off, screw the pooch, sit on one's ass, sit on one's hands, skate, slack, sluff, [Brit] snurge, soldier, spin one's wheels, whip the dog

2 *v phr To pass time lazily and pleasantly; idle about, as in "I'm just going to goof off on this vacation"*

ass around, bat around, beat around, boogaloo, boogie, bum around, cat around, cruise around, cut didoes, cut up, dick, dick around, diddle, diddlybop, doodle, fart around, fiddle around, fiddlefart, fiddlefart around, fool around, fuck around, fuck off, fuck the dog, futz around, goof around, hack around, hang, hang around, hang out, horse, horse around, hump the hound, jack around, jerk off, kick, kick around, knock around, laze around,

[Brit] lollop around, lollygag, mellow out, mess around, Mickey Mouse around, monkey around, mooch around, [Brit] muck about, noodle, piddle around, play around, poot around, putz around, rail it, rat around, rat-fuck, schloomp, schloomp around, screw around, shuck, sit on one's ass, sit on one's butt, sit on one's duff, smoke and joke, stall around, suck around, veg, veg out

goof-off
n A person who regularly and chronically avoids work; a shirker

bunk lizard, coffee cooler, feather merchant, fluff-off, fuck-off, goldbrick, goldbricker, lard-ass, [Brit] lay-about, lazybones, piker, sack artist, screw-off, slacker

gook
1 *n An Asian or person of Asian extraction*
2 SEE **GOO**

dink, goo-goo, slant-eye, slope, slopie, zip
☞ *These offensive terms are applied most often to Vietnamese and other Southeast Asians.*

goon
n A rough, intimidating man, esp a paid ruffian; a thug

ape, bad baby, biff-guy, big tuna, bimbo, bozo, bruiser, cowboy, dropper, enforcer, gorill, gorilla, greaser, hard-boiled egg, hard case, heavy, heavy man, hood, hood-lum, hooligan, jaboney, knuckle-dragger, lobo, loogan, mugger, muscle, muscle man, muscler, persuader, plug-ugly, pretty boy, pug, rough customer, roughneck, shtarker, sidewinder, starker, strong-arm, strong-arm man, tough, tough baby, tough guy, tough mug, ugly customer, yegg

goon squad
n phr A group of ruffians, esp in the hire of a labor union, a corporation, etc

beef squad, strong-arm squad

goose
v To goad or otherwise stimulate to activity; energize

get someone off his (or her) dead ass, give a hotfoot, jazz up, juice up, perk up, poke, switch on, turn on
☞ *Other terms may be made by recalling that to "goose" is to cause someone to "get the lead out."*

goose bumps
n phr Gooseflesh

duck bumps

goosy
adj Sensitive; touchy, as in "He was inclined to be goosy about his business affairs"

miffy, prickly, quick on the draw, quick on the trigger, quick on the uptake, tetchy, thin-skinned

go over the hill
v phr To go absent without leave from a military unit

break barracks, go AWOL, hit the hump, take French leave

go over with a bang
v phr To succeed brilliantly; be enthusiastically approved

ace it, be a gas, be a gasser, be a hit, be a smash, be a smash hit, bring down the house, click, click big, come on like gangbusters, connect, go great guns, go like a house afire, go over, go over like a million bucks, go places, go to town, hit, [Brit] hit for six, hit it, hit pay dirt, hit the jackpot, kill them, knock someone's socks off, knock them dead, knock them out, lay them in the aisles, make it, make it big, make out like a bandit, pan out, put them away, put them in the aisles, put them on the floor, slaughter them, slay them, stop the show, strike oil, wow them

go public

v phr To reveal; be open about, as in "After a few weeks they thought they ought to go public with their report"

come out of the closet, take it to the street

go straight

v phr To renounce a life of crime and iniquity; reform, as in "Some people go straight even with little or no rehabilitation"

go legit, slipper, walk the straight and narrow, wipe one's nose

go through the mill

v phr To have practical experience of something; be thoroughly seasoned

earn one's ticket, pay one's dues, win one's wings

go to bat for

v phr To defend; take sides with

back up, go to the wall for, ride shotgun for, stand behind, stand up for, stick up for, stump for

go to hell

1 *v phr* To deteriorate; be on the road to ruin, as in *"The air quality in our town would go to hell if they built that shopping center here"*

come apart at the seams, come unglued, come unstuck, go downhill, go down the chute, go down the drain, go down the tubes, go to hell in a bucket, go to hell in a handbasket, go to perdition, go to pot, go to the dogs, go to wrack and ruin, go up the spout, hit the skids

2 SEE **FUCK YOU**

grab

v To acquire; gather

bag, catch, collar, cop, corral, dig up, drag down, get one's hands on, get hold of, get one's hooks into, glom on to, grab off, grub up, hook, knock down, land, latch on to, nab, nail, net, pull down, rake up, round up, scare up, scrape up, snag

grab-ass

n Sexual dalliance short of copulation; caressing, as in *"They played grab-ass for an hour before consummating their affair"*

bush patrol, canoodling, a feel, a feel-up, a grope, groping, hanky-panky, a love-up, lovey-dovey, slap and tickle

grabby

1 *adj* Captivating; very attractive, as in *"Get a load of that grabby hunk"*

catchy, hooky

2 *adj* Greedy; acquisitive; selfish

hoggish, hoggy, piggish, piggy

grand
n A thousand dollars

big one, G, gee, horse, K, ten yards, thou

grand slam
n phr A decisive and total victory

clean sweep, landslide, sweep, wipe-out

grandstand
v To play or perform in a brilliant and spectacular way, esp for the approval of an audience

grandstand it, hot dog, make a circus play, make a grandstand play, play to the gallery, profile, profile for the fans, showboat, show off, style

grandstander
n A person who habitually grandstands

glory-grabber, grandstand player, gunner, hot dog, showboat, showoff

gravy
n Money or other valuables beyond what one earns; a bonus

cake, easy money, easy pickings, found money, jelly, pie, velvet

grease monkey
n phr A mechanic, esp an automotive mechanic

greaseball, greasehound

grease someone's **palm**
v phr To bribe

cross someone's palm, oil someone's palm

greasy spoon
n phr A small,
cheap restaurant,
lunch room, or diner

beanery, bean wagon, chili joint, dog wagon, doughnut factory, doughnut foundry, doughnut house, doughnut joint, dump, eatery, grease joint, grease pit, grease trough, ham-and-eggery, ham joint, hashery, hash foundry, hashhouse, one-arm, one-arm joint, quick and dirty, quick and filthy, sloppy Joe's

great
adj Excellent;
wonderful

A-1, ace-high, aces, ah tuff, A-OK, awesome, bad, baddest, [Brit] bang on, bang-up, bangy, [Canadian] beauty, the berries, bio, bionic, bitchen, blip, blue-chip, boffo, [Australian] bonzer, boo, boss, brutal, bully, bumpin', champ, chewy, chill, chilly, class, classy, cock, cocky, cool, corking, crack, crackerjack, cracking, crazy, Cugat, dandy, darling, deadly, deadly boo, def, delish, devoon, dishy, divine, dope, double bitchen, down, dreamy, drooly, ducky, dynamite, elegant, endsville, evil, fab, fabby, faboo, fancy, fantabulous, far in, far out, fiendish, fiendish back, fierce, flash, fly, four-O, frabjous, frantic, fresh, froody, funky, gear, ginchy, gingerpeachy, gnarly, gone, gorgeous, the greatest, grooby, groovy, hando, hard, hash, heavenly, heavy, hellacious, high-class, high-rent, hipper-dipper, hot, hotsy-totsy, hounds, humdinging, hyper, ice, immense, intense, irie, jammy, jim-dandy, keen, key, kicky, killer, the kind, knockout, marvy, mean, mezz, mighty, the most, the mostest, nasty, neat, nifty, nitro, not too shabby, the nuts, on the beam, outasight, out of sight, out of this world, peacharooney, peachy, peachy-keen, plummy, potent, pretty radical, primo, rad, rattling, regular, righteous, ripping, ritzy, royal, scrumptious, serious, sexy, shag, sharp, skookum, slick, slurpy, smashing, smooth, snazzy, socko, solid, some kind of, something else, spanking, spiffy, stoking, stunning, super, superbo, super-duper, superfly, sweet, swell, swell-elegant, tawny, terrific, thrashing, thumping, the ticket, tickety-boo, tip-top, tits, toast, too much, top-drawer, top-hole, top-notch, tops, totally bitchen, tough, tubular, unreal, upscale, vicious, wailing, way out, weird, wicked, wig, wiggy, wild, [Brit] wizard, world-class, yummy, zero cool

☞ *The large number and rapid obsolescence of these terms reflects the use of slang as a sign of up-to-the-minute consciousness, of newness and glitter, of this day's "image."*

green around the gills

adj phr Sick; miserable; nauseated, as in "His cooking will make you feel green around the gills"

blah, blue around the gills, bum, crummy, off one's feed, out of sorts, pasty, peaked, peaky, punk, rocky, seedy, shaky, sick as a dog, sick as a pig, under the weather, wonky

greenhorn

n An inexperienced person; a newcomer; a neophyte

boot, buckwheater, cheechako, greeny, jaboney, Johnny-come-lately, [Brit] new boy, new kid on the block, rookie, rube, tenderfoot

grind

n A diligent student

bone, boner, dexter, dweeb, eager beaver, gradehound, greasy grind, grunt, gweebo, nerd, poler, sunshine girl, throat, tool, ween, weenie, wonk

groupie
1 *n A young woman who seeks to share the glamor of famous persons, esp rock-and-roll musicians, by offering help and sexual favors*
2 SEE **FAN**

bunny, star-fucker

grunt
1 *n An infantry soldier; a rifleman*
2 SEE the **DAMAGE**
3 SEE **GOFER**
4 SEE **GRIND**
5 SEE **SHIT**

blisterfoot, crunchie, dogface, dough, doughboy, doughfoot, line dog, line doggie, paddlefoot

gut course
n phr An easy college course

[Canadian] bird course, cinch, crib course, crip course, gut, lead-pipe course, Mickey Mouse course, pipe course, ride, setup, sluff course

guts
1 *n Courage; intrepidity*

balliness, balls, ballsiness, brass balls, [Latino] cojones, ginger, gravel, grit, intestinal fortitude, moxie, nerve, spizzerinctum, spunk, stuff

2 *n The insides of a person, machine, etc; the viscera*

innards, kishkes, tripes

gutsy
adj Courageous;
bold, as in "Picking
an ex-con to head
the department was
a gutsy move"

ballsy, braver than Dick Tracy, dead game, gritty, gutty, nervy, spunky, stand-up

guy
n A man; a male
person

apple, bean, bloke, boy, bozo, brother, bub, bucko, bud, bug, bugger, buster, cat, chap, character, chief, chum, clown, codger, cookie, cove, cuss, daddy, daddy-o, doc, dog, duck, dude, duffer, egg, fart, fella, feller, fucker, galoot, gazabo, gee, geezer, gent, gink, giz, gizmo, he-male, hombre, huckleberry, jamoke, jasper, Joe, [esp Brit] Johnny, joker, lad, man-jack, mister, monkey, mug, schmo, scout, shaver, son of a bee, son of a bitch, son of a gun, son of a so-and-so, sport, squirt, stiff, storch, stud, sucker, sumbitch, walyo

☞ *"Guy" is now often used for women, esp in the plural. This may or may not be a consequence of feminist consciousness.*

guzzle
v To drink liquor,
as in "He always
likes to guzzle on
payday"

bend the elbow, booze, chug-a-lug, crook the elbow, down a few, fight a bottle, gargle, hang a few on, have a dram, have a gargle, have a nip, hit the booze, hit the bottle, hit the sauce, juice, knock back, knock off, lap, lap up, liquor up, slug down, slurp, souse, splice the main brace, swig, swill, tank, tank up, tip the elbow, toss off, wet one's goozle, wet one's whistle

hack it
*v phr To succeed;
cope successfully*

breeze home, bring down the house, bring home the bacon, click, come out on top, come through, come up trumps, connect, cut it, cut the mustard, deliver the goods, fly, get home free, get off the ground, get places, hack, hit pay dirt, hit the mark, make a go of it, make it, make out like a bandit, make the cut, make the grade, make the riffle, play, pull it off, put it across, put it over, ring the bell, score, strike oil, turn the trick, win out

☞ *These terms are most often used in the negative.*

hairy
1 *adj Difficult;
arduous and
dangerous, as in
"Driving racing cars
is a hairy line of
work"*
2 SEE CREEPY

brutal, furry, heavy, hefty, mean, no cinch, no picnic, no snap, rough, rough as a cob, rugged, sticky, tough, tricky, wicked

half-assed
1 *adj Slipshod; careless, as in "He's a nice guy, but his work is always half-assed"*   half-baked, hit-or-miss, messy, skewgee, slam-bang, slapbang, slapdash, sloppy, sorry, sorry-ass
2 SEE **DUMB**
3 SEE **PIDDLY**

ham
v To overact; be self-dramatizing and overemotional, as in "Give her an audience and she starts to ham"   chew the ham, chew up the scenery, emote, ham it up

ham-handed
adj Awkward; undextrous   all thumbs, butterfingered, ham-fisted, klutzy, schleppy

hand it to someone
v phr To pay a compliment; praise someone for a success   hand someone a bouquet, hand someone a posy, pat someone on the back, take off one's hat to, throw bouquets at

hang on
v phr To accuse of; inculpate for, as in "How many charges can we hang on this guy?"   drop on, fasten on, finger for, paste on, pin on, point the finger at someone for, rap with

hang out with
v phr To associate with; consort with, as in "I don't like to hang out with drunkards"

be buddy-buddy with, be palsy-walsy with, buddy up with, buddy with, chum around with, chum with, gang up with, hang around with, hang with, have truck with, hook up with, join up with, line up with, pal up with, pal with, string with, team up with, throw in with, train with

hang tough
v phr To endure in a difficult plight; show pluck and persistence

grin and bear it, gut it out, hang in, hang in there, hang on, hold out, keep on trucking, macho it out, ride it out, stand the gaff, stick, stick in there, stick it out, take it, take it on the chin, tough it out

hard-on
n A penile erection

blue-veiner, bone, bone-on, boner, charge, horn, prong-on, stiff one

hash
n Hashish

Afghani, African black, bambalacha, black, black hash, black oil, black Russian, blond, blue cheese, candy, charas, cherry Leb, chocolate, chunk, citroli, dope smoke, green Moroccan, heavy hash, heesh, hog, honey oil, Indian oil, Indian rope, Leb, Lebanese, lightning hash, mud, Nepalese hash, Nepalese temple balls, Nepalese temple hash, oil, one, the one, Pakistani hash, powder, quarter moon, red Lebanese, red oil, sealing wax, sheesh, shishi, smash, sole, son of one, temple balls, temple bells, temple hash
☞ *The great number of slang terms for narcotics probably reflects both a need for coded reference to an illegal substance and a desire to be chic and up-to-date, in addition to the need to distinguish varieties.*

hash mark

*n phr A service
stripe, worn on the
sleeve to mark each
four-year period of
military service*

bean stripe, hash stripe, ignorant stripe

hassle

1 *n A disagreement;
a quarrel; a fight, as
in "I don't want any
hassle with you over
this"*

barney, beef, blowup, brush, donnybrook, duel, dust, dustup, fireworks, flare-up, fracas, fraction, go, hoedown, knock-down-drag-out, mix-up, one-on-one, pissing contest, pissing match, punch-out, rhubarb, row, ruckus, ruction, rumpus, run-in, scrap, set-to, shindy, [Brit] slanging match, spat, tangle, tiff

2 *v To quarrel;
actively disagree;
fight*

bicker, bump heads, duel, go at it, go round and round, go toe to toe, go to it, go to the mat, have a barney, have a pissing contest, have a pissing match, have a run-in, have a shindy, [Brit] have a slanging match, kick up a row, lock horns, make the fur fly, mix, mix it up, put on the gloves, row, ruckus, rumpus, scrap, set to, slug it out, spar, spat, tangle, tangle assholes, throw leather, thump, tiff, trade punches, wrangle

3 SEE **BUG**

hate someone's guts

*v phr To detest;
strongly dislike*

be down on, hate like poison, hate like sin, have a hardon for, have it in for, have no use for, not be seen dead with, not give a shit for, not give someone the time of day, not piss on someone's gums if his (or her) teeth were on fire, not piss up someone's ass if his (or her) guts were on fire, take a scunner at

have a ball
*v phr To enjoy
oneself thoroughly;
frolic; celebrate*

ball, boogie-woogie, cut loose, cut up, enjoy, get behind, get one's cookies, get down, get it on, get one's jollies, get one's kicks, get naked, get off, get one's rocks, go places and do things, go to town, groove, have lots of laughs, jam, jive and juke, kick out the jams, kick up one's heels, let oneself go, let loose, let off steam, live it up, make whoopee, paint the town red, party, raise a ruckus, raise hell, raise the roof, rat-fuck, whoop it up

have a field day
*v phr To be very
successful, esp at the
expense of an
opponent*

fatten up, lunch up

**have a hair up
one's ass**
*v phr To be very
irascible and touchy,
as in "I wouldn't
talk to him today,
he has a hair up his
ass"*

be feisty, have a bug up one's ass, have a bug up one's nose, have a chip on one's shoulder, have a hair up one's nose, have a short fuse

**have a hole in
one's head**
v phr To be stupid

be a quart low, be overdosed on dumb pills, blither, dither, drool, have a few buttons missing, have a few marbles missing, have a hole in one's wig, have a loose shingle, have a screw loose, have one's head up one's ass, have rocks in one's head, have shit for brains, have three bricks shy of a load, not find one's way to first base, not have a clue, not have all one's switches on, not have both oars in the water, not have brain one, not have brains enough to come in out of the rain, not have brains enough to walk and chew gum at the same time, not know one's ass from one's elbow, not know one's ass from third base, not know shit from Shinola, not play with a full deck

☞ *Hundreds of these expressions may be made by combining "be," "have," "not have," etc, with the terms for "dumb."*

☞ *Many of these terms share semantic territory with "not know shit from Shinola," which stresses ignorance rather than stupidity, and should also be considered.*

have a lech for
v phr To be especially desirous of; crave greatly

be antsy for, be crazy about, be ga-ga over, be high on, be hipped on, be nuts about, be stuck on, be sweet on, go for, go for in a big way, have a case on, have a crush on, have a hard-on for, have a mash on, have a thing for, have a weakness for, have a yen for, have eyes for, have hot nuts for, have hot pants for, have hot rocks for, have it bad for, have the hots for

☞ *This phrase is often used generally or figuratively.*

have a load on
v phr To be drunk

feel no pain, have a bag on, have an edge on

☞ *Hundreds of these terms may be made by combining "be" with the terms for "plastered."*

have balls
v phr To be courageous; be daring, as in "You gotta have balls to be in this line of work"

have brass balls, have cast-iron balls, have guts, have no nerves, have the nerve

have someone by the balls
v phr To have a decisive advantage over, as in "With evidence of his infidelity we really have him by the balls"

have by the curlies, have by the knickers, have by the nuts, have by the short hairs, have over a barrel, have the bulge on, have the drop on, have where the hair is short, hold the trump hand, hold the whip hand

have something cinched
v phr To be sure of a favorable outcome; be sure of success or victory, as in "After the second inning rally the Tigers had it cinched"

have a lock on, have hacked, have iced, have it made, have knocked, have made, have taped, have wired

have hot pants
v phr To be lustful; be sexually excited and desirous

cream one's jeans, have a hard-on, have a lech, have blue balls, have hot nuts, have hot rocks, have lead in one's pencil, have the hots, have the urge to merge, lech, lech after

have it both ways
v phr To hold and esp to profit from two contrary positions, as in "I'd like to support both candidates, but you can't have it both ways"

have your cake and eat it, work both sides of the street

have someone's
number
*v phr To know and
understand someone
thoroughly,
including deep
motives and likely
actions*

be onto someone, be wise to someone, have someone's measure, have someone pegged, have someone sized up, have someone taped, have someone's wavelength, know what makes someone tick, read someone, read someone like a book

have the rag on
v phr To menstruate

come around, fall off the roof, fly the red flag, have Baker flying, have the curse

one's **head off**
*adv phr At full tilt;
mightily, as in "He
had to holler his
head off before they
did anything"*

one's ass off, one's brains out, one's buns off

heavy
1 *adj Important;
consequential, as in
"They were into
heavy talk, no
trivia"*
2 SEE **BAD MAN**

big, heavyweight, hefty, high-powered, large

heeled
1 *adj Armed;
carrying a weapon*
2 SEE **LOADED**

carrying, carrying a rod, carrying the difference, packing heat, rodded, rodded up, [Brit] strapped

heist

1 *n* A robbery

bag job, boost, burn, caper, crib crime, crib job, five-finger discount, holdup, job, knockover, lift, pinch, rip-off, rustle, short heist, stickup, sting

2 *v* To steal; rob; burglarize, as in "They heisted nearly five million in cash"

bag, boost, burgle, burn, buzz, clip, crab, crack, crash, get busy, get paid, go south with, highjack, hoist, hold up, hook, hug, hustle, jackroll, jump, kick over, kipe, knock off, knock over, lift, loid, make, mooch, move, mug, nab, [Brit] nick, nip, pinch, pluck, put the grab on, rip off, roll, rumble, rustle, scarf, scoff, scoop, score, smooch, snaffle, snatch, snitch, stick up, swipe, take off, tip over, yoke

☞ *This list does not take account of the various types and modes of thievery.*

heist man

n phr A professional thief or holdup man; a robber, burglar, pickpocket, etc

booster, box man, cannon, cat bandit, cracksman, creeper, derrick, dip, dunnigan, file, fingersmith, five finger, five fingers, fork, gee whiz, goniff, gopher, grifter, gun, hijacker, holdup man, iceman, knucker, knucksman, lift, lifter, lush roller, lush worker, moll-buzzer, mugger, nabber, off artist, pennyweighter, pete-man, peter man, roller, rustler, safecracker, second-story man, stickup man, wire, yegg, yoker

☞ *This list includes thieves using various techniques, locales, etc. It is a curious fact that US slang lacks a widespread generalized term for "thief."*

hell around

v phr To lead a life of low pleasure, as in "I like to hell around with my pals till we can barely stand up"

bust loose, go on the loose, hell, knock around, let oneself go, tear around, tear-ass around, tom-cat around, whoop it up, whore around

hell breaks loose

sentence The situation deteriorates; trouble strikes

all hell breaks loose, it's every man for himself, it's Katie bar the door, the roof caves in, the roof falls in, the shit hits the fan, things come unstuck

a hell of a

adj phr Very remarkable, awful, admirable, distressing, etc, as in "We had a hell of a time when that pipe ruptured"

a bitch of a, a helluva, one bitch of a, one hell of a, some, some kind of a

he-man

1 *n An aggressively masculine man*

caveman, hairy-chest, hunk, macho, man's man, mensch

2 *adj Very masculine; blatantly virile*

hairy-chested, hunky, macho, two-fisted

3 SEE HUNK

hero

n A long sandwich of cheeses, sausage, etc, made from a loaf of bread cut lengthwise

grinder, hero sandwich, hoagie, poor boy, sub, submarine, submarine sandwich, torpedo

☞ *These terms are regionally distributed, hence not all are used in all parts of the US.*

hick

n A rural person; a rustic

apple-knocker, Arky, brush ape, chawbacon, Clem, clodhopper, clover-kicker, dark, gully-jumper, hayseed, hayseeder, Herkimer Jerkimer, hillbilly, honyock, honyocker, hoosier, jasper, jay, jaybird, jerk-off, John

Farmer, joskin, local yokel, nose-picker, Okie, plow jockey, pumpkin roller, redneck, Reuben, rube, shit-kicker, SK, sodbuster, stump-jumper, woodhick, yap, yokel

hideaway
n A hiding place; a place to escape attention or discovery

[Brit] bolt-hole, funk hole, hideout, hidey-hole, hole-up, scatter

hide out
v phr To conceal oneself; take cover

hole in, hole up, lay doggo, lay low, play possum, sit tight, tunnel

high
1 *adj Intoxicated with narcotics; drugged*

all lit up, amok, amuck, backed up, baked, basted, beaming, beaten, belted, bent, bent out of shape, blasted, blind, blitzed, blitzed out, blocked, blown out, bombed, bombed out, bonged out, boxed, buzzed, called, capped out, charged, charged up, coasting, coked, coked out, coked up, cooked up, crazy, delirious, destroyed, doped, doped up, dragged, drifty, fired, flattened, flipped, flipping, floating, flying, flying high, flying in the clouds, foxy, fractured, frazzled, fried, fried to the gills, frosted, frosty, frosty frozen, frozen, full, full blast, full of junk, fuzzy, gassed, geared, geared up, geed up, geezed, geezed up, getting a rolling buzz, getting a rush, glazed, gone, gonged, goofed, gorked, gorked out, gowed, gowed up, grifado, grooving, halvahed, heaped, hopped, hopped up, horsed, in, in a nod, in a session, in a zone, in flight, in orbit, in the air, in the pocket, in transit, jacked-up, jagged, jailhouse high, jolted, junked, junked up, keyed up, knocked out, leaping and stinking, loaded, locked, luded out, maxed, mohasky, muggled, muggled up, noddy, numbered out, on, on a bean trip, on a cloud, on a dope jag, on a joy ride, on cloud nine, on the gow, on the nod, on the stuff, ossified, out, out of it, overamped, overcharged, overdosed, packed up, passed out, polluted, poppied, potted, pottle-dripped, purring like a kitten, ripped, running amok, sent, set on one's ass, shot up, singing, sleighriding, smashed, snowed, snowed in, snowed up, spaced, spaced out, spacey, spiked, sprung, stoned, stoned to the eyes, straight, strung out, switched on, tall, tea'd up, there, torn up, totaled, tranqued, tripped out, tripping, trippy, turned on, twisted, up, wasted, way out, weirded out, whipped, wigged out, wiggy, wingy, wiped out, wired, wrecked, zipped, zoned, zoned out, zonked, zonked out, zonkers

2 *n The exhilarated or exalted feeling produced by a narcotic; a narcotic intoxication*
belt, blast, boot, buzz, charge, drag, flash, head, hit, jolt, kick, rush, splash, thrill, tingle, trip, zing

3 SEE **PLASTERED**

high-powered
adj Powerful; strong and effective, as in "She's a high-powered executive these days"
double-distilled, dynamite, hefty, high-geared, stemwinding, stronger than pig-shit, thumping

hike
1 *v To increase; raise, as in "They threaten to hike the rent next month"*
boost, crank up, heist, hike up, jack up, jump up, kite, pick up, step up, up

2 *n An increase; a raising or rising*
boost, jump, uptick

a hit
1 *n Anything*
sensational or
exciting, esp a
conspicuous success

barn-burner, blast, blockbuster, blood-curdler, boffo, bomb, bombshell, breath-taker, eye-popper, flabbergaster, gangbusters, gas, gasser, gut-thumper, heartstopper, jarrer, jolter, one for the book, phenom, riot, rip snorter, rouser, sensaysh, smash, smash-hit, snorter, sockdolager, sockeroo, something else, something to write home about, staggerer, standout, stunner, winner

2 SEE **a FIX**

hitchhike
v To get free rides
by standing beside a
road and signaling
drivers

hitch, hitch a lift, hitch a ride, thumb, thumb a lift, thumb a ride

hit it off
v phr To like one
another; get along
very well, as in "We
hit it off the first
time we met"

click, have great chemistry

hit man
n phr A gunman,
esp a professional
assassin

apache, blaster, blotter, bumpman, button man, croaker, driller, dropper, enforcer, gorilla, gun, gunman, gunpoke, gunsel, hatchet man, hired gun, hitter, iceman, plugger, ratboy, rod, rod boy, rodman, rubber, torpedo, trigger, trigger man

**hold someone's
feet to the fire**
*v phr To punish
severely and
publicly; make an
example of; crucify,
as in "The teacher
swore he'd hold my
feet to the fire if I
acted like that
again"*

let turn in the wind, nail to the cross, nail to the wall, stick it to

homer
v To hit a home run

hit a dinger, hit for the circuit, hit one out of there, make a circuit clout, park one, park it in the bleachers, power a homer

honest-to-God
1 *adj Genuine;
authentic; real*

aces, all wool and a yard wide, big as life, card-carrying, copper-bottomed, eighteen-carat, flat-ass, for real, for serious, for-sure, honest-to-goodness, honest-to-Pete, kosher, legit, McCoy, natural-born, no buts about it; no ifs, ands, or buts; no-shit, O G, on the level, on the up-and-up, really-truly, regular, simon-pure, solid, stone, straight, sure-enough, sure-thing, up-and-up

2 *adv phr Really;
truly*

I kid you not, I shit you not, no bull, no kidding, no shit, you better believe

honey
1 *n Beloved person;
sweetheart*

angel, angelface, babe, baby, baby-doll, babykins, bubbele, bubbie, buttercup, child, dearie, doll, doll-baby, dove, dreamboat, duckling, ducks, ducky, ducky-wucky, dumpling, heartthrob, hon, honey-bunch, honey-bunny, honey-child, honeypie, lamb, lambkins, lamby-pie, lollypop, love, lover, lovey, pet, poopsy,

poopsy-woopsy, precious, snooks, snooksy-wooksy, snookums, snooky, sugar, sugar-bun, sugar-pants, sweetheart, sweetie, sweetie-pants, sweetie-pie, sweet-kins, sweetness, sweet patootie, sweet potato, sweets, toots, tootsie, tootsie-pie, tootsy-wootsy

☞ *These terms are very often used as an endearment in address, as in "Yes, honey, I'll be home soon."*

2 SEE HUMDINGER

honk
1 *v To sound the horn of a car* beep, oogah, toot

2 SEE FEEL

hooked
adj Addicted to narcotics bamboozled, dipped, dirty, from Mount Shasta, gow-headed, having a monkey on one's back, hung out, hung up, in business, narkied, on, on the horse, on the mojo, on the monkey wagon, on the needle, on the pipe, on the stuff, pasted, poppy-headed, riding the poppy train, riding the witch's broom, shoveling the black stuff, strung, strung out, up against it

hooker
1 *n A prostitute* ass peddler, bat, B-girl, bim, bimbo, [Brit] bona roba, bum, butt peddler, call girl, cat, chippy, commercial beaver, dirtyleg, fille de joie, flatback, flesh peddler, floozy, ho, kelsey, lady of the evening, ler, notch girl, [Brit] Piccadilly commando, piece of trade, pro, pross, prossie, prosty, puta, putana, quiff, Sadie, Sadie Thompson, saleslady, sidewalk susie, skank, skeezer, tail peddler, working broad, working girl

☞ *Terms for a male prostitute do not abound, e.g., "call boy" and "male model," though many of the basically female terms can be used.*

2 SEE SNORT

hoopla

1 *n A clamorous commotion*

brouhaha, fireworks, flap, foofooraw, fuss, hoo-ha, how-de-do, racket, ruckus, rumpus, [Brit] shemozzle, shindy, to-do

2 SEE FLAK

horny

adj Sexually excited and desirous

antsy, goatish, hard, hard up, hot, hot as a three-dollar pistol, hot to trot, hunky, itching, itchy, rammy, randy, rooty, sexy, steamed, turned on

horse

n Heroin

ack-ack, antifreeze, Aunt Hazel, Aunt Noral, bad bundle, balot, big boy, big H, big Harry, black gold, black tar, blue sky, bonita, boy, bozo, brown, brown Rhine, brown rock, brown stuff, brown sugar, caballo, caca, China white, China white goods, Chinese, cobics, corgy, courage pills, crap, crown crap, deck, dog food, dogie, dopoe, downtown, dugee, dynamite, dyno, ferry dust, foolish powder, gammot, George smack, goldfinger, H, hairy, halvah, H and C, Harry, Hazel, H-cap, Henry, hero, him, hocus, hook, horse radish, hot and cold, jeegee, jive dojee, Jones, joy dust, joy flakes, joy powder, kenkoy, Lady H, matsakaw, mayo, McCoy, merchandise, Mexican mud, muscle, oil, old Steve, oroy, pack, piece, poison, powder, pulborn, pure, rat poison, red, red chicken, red rock, rock, salt, scag, scar, scat, schlechts, schlock, schmack, schmeck, schmeek, scott, shit, shriek, skid, slag, sleeper, smack, smeck, snow, sugar, syrup, tinik, TNT, Tootsie Roll, tragic magic, white nurse, white stuff, witch, witch Hazel

☞ *The great number of slang terms for narcotics probably reflects both a need for coded reference to an illegal substance and a desire to be chic and up-to-date, in addition to the need to distinguish varieties.*

horse around
v phr To joke and caper pleasurably; indulge in horseplay

carry on, cavort, cut capers, cut didoes, cut up, fart around, feel one's oats, fool around, frivol, kick up one's heels

the horselaugh
n phr A loud, nasty, and dismissive laugh at someone

the merry ha-ha

horse opera
n phr A cowboy movie; a western

bang-bang, giddyapper, horse opry, oateater, oater, oat opera, sagebrusher

horseplay
n Boisterous fun; uninhibited jollification

capers, didoes, high-jinks, monkeyshines, shenanigans

hot
1 *adj Very popular; very much courted and desired; very successful, as in "Clark Gable was a very hot movie star in his day"*

big, in, large, the rage, the thing

2 *adj Performing very well; enjoying a winning impetus*

in a bubble, in a zone, on a roll, on one's game

3 SEE **HORNY**

hot damn
interj An exclamation of delight, gratification, relish, etc

hot diggety, hot diggety damn, hot diggety dog, hot diggety doggety, hot dog, hot poo, hot shit, hot spit, hot ziggety, shit on wheels

hot pants
n phr Strong sexual desire; lust

blue balls, a hard-on, horniness, hot nuts, hot rocks, the hots, a lech, stonies

hot rod
n phr A car specially modified and fitted with a powerful or rebuilt engine so as to be much faster than one of the same stock design

A-bomb, bomb, bug, can, destroker, destroke rod, dragster, gow, gowed-up job, gow job, hauler, hopped-up job, hot iron, juiced-up jalopy, juiced-up job, rod, set of wheels, souped-up job, soup job, stepped-up job, street job, stroker, stroke rod

hot shot
n phr An especially gifted and effective person; an achiever

ball of fire, best thing since sliced bread, crowd-pleaser, fast burner, fireball, flash, go-getter, greatest thing since sliced bread, hot dog, hot dogger, hot number, hot rock, hot shit, hot stuff, hustler, no slouch, piss-cutter, pisser, pistol, shit on wheels, whiz, whiz kid, winner, wiz, world-beater

house-cleaning
n A reorganization of a business or government department, esp with dismissal of incompetent or dishonest employees

shake-up

a howl

n Something very funny; a hilarious show, occasion, etc

a boff, a boffo, a boffola, a hoot, a knee-slapper, a laff, a laff riot, a laugh, a laugh and a half, a laugher, a panic, a rib-tickler, a riot, a scream, a side-splitter, a stitch, a yuk, a yuk-yuk

how's tricks

sentence Hello; how are you?

hi ya, hi y'all, howdy, how goes it, how're you doing, how's every little thing, how's the world treating you, how's things, how's your hammer hanging, how they hanging, how you was, long time no see

hubby

n A husband

the lord and master, man, the man of the house, the mister, the old man, the worser half

humdinger

n Something remarkable, wonderful, superior, etc

ace, aceroo, aces, the article, barn-burner, bear, bear-cat, beaut, beauty, the best thing since sliced bread, a bitch, a bitch-kitty, blinger, the cat's balls, the cat's eyebrows, the cat's meow, the cat's nuts, the cat's pajamas, the cat's whiskers, champ, champion, the cheese, corker, crackerjack, daisy, dandy, darb, dill, dilly, dinger, doozy, the goods, a groove, honey, hooper-doo, hooperdooper, hot poo, hot shit, hot spit, hot stuff, hummer, jim-dandy, joe-darter, kick, killer, killer-diller, kill-out, knockout, lily, lollapalooza, lulu, the McCoy, the most, the nuts, oner, peach, peacherino, peacheroo, phenom, pip, pipperoo, pippin, piss-cutter, pisser, pistol, the real George, ringtailed snorter, ripsnorter, snorter, sockdolager, sockeroo, some punkins, something, something else, something to write home about, stemwinder, the stuff, stunner, sweetheart, tops, the tops, whiz, whizbang, winner, wow, wowser

hung
adj Having impressive male genitals

endowed, hung like a bull, hung like a horse, hung like a stallion, hung like a stud, well-endowed, well-hung

hungry
adj Very ambitious; threateningly self-improving, as in "The new employee's not just a hard worker, she's hungry"

bucking, [Brit] dead keen, eager, going for the jugular, lean and mean, on the make

hunk
1 *n An attractive man, esp one who is sexually attractive*

Adonis, beefcake, caveman, centerfold, collar ad, dreamboat, glamor puss, Greek god, he-man, hunk of beef, hunkorama, macho, pin-up boy, sex pot, smooth article, smoothie

2 SEE **HE-MAN**

hunky
1 *n A foreigner, esp an Eastern European laborer*

bohunk, ginzo

2 SEE **SEXY**

3 *adj Handsome; sexually attractive, as in "She was studying the hunky fellow at the next table"*

funky, laid out, Studley

4 SEE **HE-MAN**

hustle

1 *v To work as a prostitute*

2 SEE CON

3 SEE GET THE LEAD OUT

4 SEE HEIST

cruise, cruise for trade, go on track, hook, peddle ass, red-light, turn tricks

iffy
adj Uncertain; risky   [Brit] dicey, fifty-fifty, fluky, touch-and-go

I'll be damned
sentence and interj   I'll be, I'll be a dirty name, I'll be a dirty word, I'll be
May I be   a monkey's uncle, I'll be a son of a bitch, I'll be a son of
maltreated,   a gun, I'll be blowed, I'll be cow-kicked, I'll be danged,
confounded,   I'll be darned, I'll be ding-swizzled, I'll be dipped, I'll
accursed, etc; an   be dipped in shit, I'll be fucked, I'll be hanged, I'll be
exclamation of   hornswoggled, I'll be jiggered, I'll be jig-swiggered, I'll
surprise or   be switched
determination   ☞ *In every expression, "I'll be" may be replaced with
"I'm."*

in
adj Successful, as in   [Brit] home and dry, home free, in like Flynn, out of the
"After one more   woods
*all-out try he was
in"*

in a fog
adj phr In a   in a haze, in a muddle, in a zone, mooning, moony,
confused state;   nodding, noddy, spaced, spaced out, spacey
disoriented; dazed

the in group
n phr An exclusive group or clique of influential persons

insiders, old-boy network, old boys' system, those in the know, those in the loop

in hog heaven
adj phr In a position of ease and affluence; richly contented

fat, dumb, and happy; in clover, in fat city, in pig heaven, on top of the world, on velvet, pissing on ice

innards
n The viscera

guts, insides, kishkes, meatware, stuffings, tripes

in place
adv phr Available; effectuated or installed, as in "She has all her support systems in place"

aboard, on deck, on line, on tap

in stir
adv phr In prison

abroad, away, inside, out of circulation, out of town, up the river
☞ *This list may be greatly extended by making phraes with "in" or "in the" and terms under "the slammer."*

in the bag
adj phr Certain; as sure as if prearranged, as in "His election is in the bag"

all tied up, cinched, dead sure, iced, racked, taped, tied up, wired, wired up

in the driver's seat
adj phr In the position of authority and advantage; in control

in the catbird seat, sitting fat, sitting pretty

in the groove
adj phr Performing well and spontaneously; working seemingly without effort

getting down, getting off, grooving, in the pocket, in the zone, jamming, on the beam, winging

in the pipeline
adj phr Being prepared, processed, or worked on; imminent

in the hopper, in the works, on the fire

in there
adj phr Making a great effort; coping energetically, as in "The marketing department is always in there, finding new ways to sell our products"

in there pitching, on the spot, on top of it, right in there, right there

into
prep Currently interested in; practicing or absorbed in, as in "That year he was into Chinese cooking"

doing, hepped on, inta, wired into

it's a new ball game
sentence The situation has entirely altered; a new beginning must be made

all bets are off, back to the old drawing board, it's a whole 'nother thing, we're back at square one

it takes two to tango
sentence This cannot happen or have happened without more than one person or party, as in "She says that the divorce was all his fault, but it takes two to tango"

it's a two-way street, it's not a one-way street

izzatso
interj An exclamation of disbelief or defiance

applesauce, balls, baloney, bullshit, come off it, don't give me that shit, don't make me laugh, get out of here, the hell you say, hooey, in a pig's ass, like fun, no shit, says which, says who, says you, tell it to Sweeney, tell it to the Marines, who you kidding, you're full of hops, you're full of shit, you wouldn't shit me

J

Jack
n Mister; Sir; you there

Brother, Bub, Bud, Buddy, Buster, Butch, Chief, Dad, Daddy, Daddy-O, Doc, Fella, Guy, Hombre, Joe, Mac, Man, My Man, pal, Skipper, Sport
☞ *These are terms of address used by one man to another, either amiably or edged with hostility. They merge ordinary nicknames with terms for "man" and "fellow."*

jack off
v phr To masturbate

bang the bishop, beat one's dummy, beat one's log, beat one's meat, beat off, beat the hog, bring oneself off, choke the gopher, cuff one's meat, fist-fuck, flog one's meat, flong one's dong, fuck off, get oneself off, give oneself a hand job, jerk one's gherkin, jerk off, play with oneself, pound one's meat, pound one's peenie, pull oneself off, pull one's pud, rub off, screw off, stroke, [Brit] toss off, [Brit] wank, [Brit] wank off, whack off

jail bait
n A girl below the legal age of sexual consent

San Quentin pigeon, San Quentin quail

jalopy
n A car

ark, banger, beater, boat, boiler, bucket, bucket of bolts, buggy, bus, buzz-buggy, buzz-wagon, cage, chariot, clunk, clunker, cochecito, crate, four-wheeler, gas-guzzler, goat, grinder, heap, hoopy, iron, jitney, job, junker, junk-heap, lemon, lizzie, lunker, puddle jumper, ride, set of wheels, sheen, short, strugglebuggy, trans, transportation, tub, tuna wagon, vet, wheels, winter rat, wreck, zoom buggy

☞ *Many of these are used especially of old and ruinous cars, but they may be used appropriately of any car.*

Jane
n An average woman

Jane Doe, Jane Q Citizen, Jane Q Public, plain Jane

jazzed-up
adj Made faster, more exciting, fascinating, etc, as in "They promise a jazzed-up version of Uncle Remus"

gassed-up, goosed-up, hopped-up, jazzed, pepped-up, pumped-up, punched-up, revved-up, souped-up, zazzed-up

jazz up
v phr To make faster, more exciting, more stimulating, etc

gas up, goose, goose up, hop up, hype up, jack up, jazz, jim-jam, juice up, jump up, pep up, pump up, punch up, put balls on, put hair on, rev up, zazz up

jazzy
adj Exciting; stimulating

peppy, punchy, zappy, zazzy, zingy, zippy

Jeez

interj An exclamation of emphasis, surprise, disbelief, impatience, irritation, pain, etc

ay caramba, begorra, bless me, bless my soul, [Brit] blimey, boy, boy-howdy, brassafrax, brother, burbage, by cracky, by damn, by gad, by gee, by George, by golly, by jiminy, by jingo, by Jove, by thunder, chit, Chrisakes, Christ Almighty, Christ-on-a-crutch, [Brit] crikey, dammit, damn, damnation, dear me, doggone, for cat's sakes, for crying in the grog, for crying out loud, for goodness' sakes, for gosh sake, for heaven's sakes, for Pete's sake, for pity's sakes, for the love of Mike, for the love of Pete, gadzooks, gee, gee-whillikers, gee-whiz, George, glory hallelujah, God Almighty, goldamn, golly, golly gee, good gracious, goodness sakes alive, good night, [Brit] gorblimey, gosh all fishhooks, gosh almighty, goshdarn, gracious, gracious sakes alive, great leaping Jesus, great Scott, gunga, hail Columbia, heavens, heavens sakes, heavens to Betsy, hell, hell's bells, hey, hey-man, hijo, holy cats, holy cow, holy gee, holy hell, holy mackerel, holy Moses, holy shit, holy smokes, hoo-boy, hoo-ha, how about that, I declare, I swan, Jeepers, Jeepers Creepers, jeezy-peezy, Jesus, Jesus H. Christ, Judas priest, jumping Jehosaphat, jumping Jesus, law, leaping lizards, Lord have mercy, Lordy, man, man alive, my glory, my God, my gosh, my lands, ouch, poo, rats, sakes alive, shee, shee-it, sheesh, sheet, shit, shoot, suffering cats, ye gods, ye gods and little fishes, yikes, yipe, yipes

☞ *This interesting term represents both euphemism and blasphemy, and could be extended almost indefinitely.*

jerk

1 *n A tedious and ineffectual person, esp a man; a fool*

ass, bimbo, boob, bozo, chump, clown, cluck, corn dog, creep, dexter, dildo, dill, dingbat, dink, dipshit, dipstick, dolf, dork, drip, drizzle, drizzlepuss, drool, dud, dumdum, dummy, dweeb, eightball, fathead, fishball, foul ball, fuckhead, funk, fuzznuts, geek, geekoid, gink, goobatron, goober, goof, goon, grind, groover, grunch, grunge, gug, gumby, gump, gweebo, headache, Herkimer Jerkimer, hoakie, ho-dad, horse's ass, huckleberry, jackass, jack-off, jag, jag-off, Jerk McGee, jerk-off, joker, kink, kinko, klutz, lame, lop, lummox, lunk, lunkhead, meatball, Melvin, mince, mutt, nebbish, nerd, numbnuts, ook, outz, pain, pain in the ass, pain in the neck, peckerhead, pill, pinhead, plonk, pogue, poop, poor slob, poot, poot-butt, pud, punk, ringtail, sad apple, sap, saphead, scag, schlemiel, schlep, schlepper, schmo, schnook, schtoonk, shit-ass, shrimp, simp, skag, slob, snarf, squirt, stick, stiff, sucker, turkey, twerp, [Brit] twit, weenie, wimp, wonk, worm, yap, yo-yo, zhlub, zod

2 SEE DRAG

jerk town
n phr A small town

crossroads, East Jesus, filling station, jerkwater town, mudhole, noplaceville, one-horse town, one-stoplight town, podunk, tank town, whistle stop, wide place in the road

the jet set
n phr Wealthy, glamorous people

the beautiful people, the glitterati

a jiffy
n phr A very short time; an instant

as long as it takes to say Jack Robinson, the bat of a eye, a bit, a flash, half a mo, a hoop and a holler, a jif, a jiff, a jiffin, a jiffing, less than no time, a mo, no time, no time at all, a sec, a shake, a tick, a twink, a twinkling, two hoops and a holler, two shakes, two shakes of a lamb's tail, a wink

jiggers
interj An exclamation of alarm and warning, as in "Jiggers, here comes the boss"

cheese it, chickie

the jitters
n phr Fidgety nervousness; uneasy restlessness

the all-overs, butterflies, the dithers, the fantods, the fidgets, the heebie-jeebies, the jeebies, the jimjams, the jumps, the leaping heebies, the quivers, the screaming meemies, the shakes, shpilkes, the willies, the wimwams

jittery
adj Nervous; anxious

all of a doodah, all shook, all shook up, antsy, bouncing off the walls, clutched, clutchy, edgy, fretty, hitchy, hot and bothered, hyper, in a pucker, in a state, in a stew, in a sweat, in a swivet, in a tizzy, in the anxious seat, itchy, jumpy, nervous as a cat on a hot tin roof, nervous as a dog shitting razorblades, on edge, shook, shook up, uptight, wired, worried stiff, yantsy

jock
n An athlete

jockstrap, strap

Joe Blow
n phr Any man; the average man

every Tom Dick and Harry, ham-and-egger, Joe Schmo, Joe Six-Pack, Joe Storch, Joe Zilch, John, John Doe, Johnny, John Q Citizen, man on the street, one of the boys, one of the guys, ordinary guy, ordinary Joe, poor fish, poor John, Richard Roe, square John, Storch, zilch

Joe College

n phr A young man whose dress and manner betoken the nonacademic aspects of college life

Joe Yale, key, white shoe

joint

1 *n A marijuana cigarette*

ace, bam, bammy, belt, birdwood, bomb, bomber, boo reefer, booster stick, burnie, butt, canceled stick, cartucho, cattail, ceck, cigar, cocktail, dinky dow, doobie, double header, dream stick, dynamiter, fat jay, fatty, funny cigarette, gage butt, gasper, gold leaf special, gonga smudge, goober, good butt, goof butt, gooly butt, gow, gyve, hay butt, hot stick, J, jay, jay smoke, jive, jolt, J smoke, kick stick, killer, killer stick, leno, log, mezz, mezz roll, miggle, mighty mezz, ming, mooter, muggle, muggles, nail, nose burner, number, pin, pinner, reefer, riff, roach, root, skoofus, skrufus, spliff, splim, splint, stack, stencil, stick, stick of gage, stick of tea, tea, tea bag, tea-stick, thing, thirteen, thriller, thumb, torch, torpedo, tube, twist, vonce, weed, zol

☞ *The great number of slang terms for narcotics probably reflects both a need for coded reference to an illegal substance and a desire to be chic and up-to-date, in addition to the need to distinguish varieties.*

2 SEE **BAG**
3 SEE **COCK**
4 SEE **DIVE**
5 SEE the **SLAMMER**
6 SEE **WORKS**

jumped-up
adj Inflated, esp by artifice; made more imposing

jacked-up, puffed-up

junkie
1 *n A narcotics user or addict*

acidhead, ad, bangster, channel swimmer, coke freak, cokehead, cokey, cubehead, dip, dope fiend, dopehead, dopenik, doper, dopester, dreamer, druggie, drughead, feeblo, fiend, flier, freak, glassy-eye, goof, gowhead, gowster, grasshopper, hashhead, head, hog, hophead, hop merchant, hopster, hype shooter, jabber, junker, junk hawk, junk hog, junk hound, junk man, liner, mainliner, mainline shooter, meth freak, meth head, narco, needle fiend, needle jabber, needle nipper, needle pusher, needle rusher, pillhead, pill-popper, pinhead, pinjabber, pothead, puller, reefer, sleighrider, smack freak, smackhead, smecker, snowbird, space cadet, speedball, speedo, stoner, student, unkjay, vein shooter, weed eater, weedhead, zone, zoner

☞ *This list is not confined to any particular manner of injection or consumption, nor to any particular narcotic.*

2 SEE FAN

K

kaput
1 *adj Ruined;*
wrecked; inoperative

all washed up, ausgespielt, belly-up, blooey, buggered, burned out, clobbered, cooked, dead, dead in the water, dead meat, dished, done for, down and out, down for the count, down the chute, down the drain, down the pipe, down the tube, down the tubes, finished, floored, flummoxed, frazzled, fried, in the bag, in the dumper, in the tub, kayoed, laid out, one's name is mud, NG, nuked, on the rocks, on the skids, out of business, out of luck, out of the box, out on one's ass, out the window, pfft, played out, shit out of luck, shot, shot down in flames, snakebit, snake-bitten, S O L, south of the border, sunk, tapped out, toast, totaled, Tubesville, up the spout, washed up, wasted, whipped, wiped out

☞ *This list may be extended by using participial forms of terms under "go kerflooey."*

☞ *These terms share semantic territory with "out of luck," which should also be considered.*

2 SEE **FINISHED**

keep one's cool
*v phr To stay
unruffled; be calm,
as in "It's hard to
keep your cool when
you lose your job"*

go with the flow, keep a tight asshole, keep cool, keep one's hair on, keep one's pants on, keep one's shirt on, not bat an eye, not blink an eye, not blow a fuse, not blow a gasket, not get one's balls in an uproar, not get one's shit hot, not lose one's cool, not turn a hair

kibitzer
*n A person who
gives intrusive
advice; a meddler*

backseat driver, buttinsky, nark, Nosy Parker, Paul Pry, snoop, woppitzer, yenta

a kick
*n A delightful
sensation; a thrill, as
in "Seeing her again
was quite a kick"*

bang, belt, biff, blast, boot, buzz, charge, drive, flash, flip, groove, head, hit, jolt, large charge, lift, punch, rush, toot, up, upper, wallop, zing

kick ass
*v phr To punish;
assert authority;
discipline harshly*

attend to, bear down on, climb, climb one's frame, come down on, crack down on, fix, give hell, give it to, give merry hell, jump, jump all over, kick ass and take names, kick booty, let someone have it, light into, lower the boom, make it hot for, pitch into, put the wood to, read the riot act, settle someone's hash, skin alive, stack asses, strafe, throw the book at

kick back
*v phr To relax; rest
and restore oneself*

catch one's breath, ease up, knock off, lay back, lay chilly, lay up, mellow out, put one's feet up, take a break, take a breather, take a load off, take a load off one's feet, take five, take it easy, take ten, take time out, unkink, unlax, unwind, walk cool, wind down

kick in
v phr To give, pay, contribute

ante up, come across with, dish out, dish up, feed the kitty with, fork out, fork over, fork up, hand over, pony up, put out, shell out, slip, weigh in with

kicks
1 *n Pleasure; gratification*

bangs, cookies, [esp Brit] fun and games, happies, jollies, knocks, what turns you on

2 *n Shoes*

ends, kickers, leathers

kid
1 *n A child*

blister, boychick, brat, carpet rat, crumbcatcher, crumbcrusher, crumbgrinder, crumbsnatcher, curtain climber, drape ape, godfer, grommet, holy terror, house ape, imp, kiddo, kiddy, legbiter, little bugger, little devil, little dickens, little monkey, little pest, little pisher, little punk, little rascal, little shaver, mud lark, Munchkin, pisher, poot-butt, punk, punk kid, pup, puppy, rug ape, rug rat, slasher, snotnose, sprout, squirt, toddler, yard rat, young punk, young 'un

2 *v To joke; jest; banter*

crack funny, crack wise, jive, josh, make a funny, shuck, shuck and jive, wisecrack

3 *v To fool; deceive, as in "That can't be true; you're kidding me"*

give someone leg, goof on someone, have someone on, jack someone around, jerk someone around, jerk someone's chain, jerk someone off, pull someone's leg, put someone on, spoof, yank someone's chain

4 SEE SNOW

kid around
v phr To jest and banter; tease

boogaloo, boogie, fool around, jape, jive, josh, kid, lark, shuck, shuck and jive

kike

n A Jew

clipped dick, eagle-beak, Goldberg, Hebe, hooknose, Ike, Ikey, mockie, sheeny, Yid, zip top

☞ *These terms are deeply offensive.*

kinky

1 *adj Sexually deviant*

bent, far out, freaky, funky, funny, oddball, offbeat, off the wall, queer, rat fuck, strangioso, weird

2 SEE FLAKY

3 SEE GAY

kiss my ass

sentence I invite you to perform or submit to a humiliating act

bite my ass, bite this, cram it, fuck you, [Brit] get stuffed, go fuck yourself, ram it, screw you, shove it, [Brit] sod you, stick it, stick it in your ear, stick it up your ass, stick it where the sun doesn't shine, stuff it, up your ass, up yours, you know what you can do with it, you know where you can stick it

☞ *The distinction between "kiss my ass" and "fuck you" (also a main entry in this book) is not easy to draw. For a full repertory of powerful insults one should consider both.*

knock

1 *n A disparaging comment; an insult*

brickbat, bringdown, dig, ding, dirty crack, dirty dig, dump, dumping, nasty crack, pan, put-down, rank-out, rap, razz, rip, shot, slam, slap, slap in the face, sock, spitball, swipe

2 *v To criticize harshly, often unfairly; complain of; carp at*

bad-mouth, bring down, burn, dig at, dis, down, dump all over, dump on, jab, joan, lambaste, pan, pimp, poor-mouth, put down, put the shit on, rank out, rap, razz, rib, ride, rip, rip on, roast, run down, shoot on, slag, slag off, slam, slap, spitball, take a dig at, take a potshot at, take a swipe at, trash, zing

3 SEE BAD-MOUTH

knocked up
adj phr Pregnant

expecting, having a bun in the oven, in the family way, on the hill, preggers, preggy, prego, puffed, pumped, that way, wearing her apron high

knock off
1 *v phr* To stop, esp to stop working; desist, as in "I think I'll knock off early today"
2 SEE KICK BACK

bag it, belay, break off, call it a day, call it quits, can it, caulk off, check it in, come off, cut out, drop it, go to the showers, hang it up, lay down one's tools, lay off, [Brit] pack in, [esp Brit] pack it in, [esp Brit] pack up, secure, shut up shop, stow it, take a break, take five, take ten

knock out
v phr To make someone unconscious, esp with a blow

chill, coldcock, cork, cream, deck, drop, duke someone out, finish, flatten, kayo, knock cold, knock cuckoo, knock someone's lights out, knock stiff, knock the daylights out of, K O, lay out, lay out cold, lay out in lavender, put on the floor, put out like a light, stiffen

knock something out
v phr To make or produce, esp rather quickly, as in "I couldn't find time to knock the invitation out myself"

cobble up, knock something together, throw something together, whomp up

knock up
v phr To make pregnant

bump, fix up, get in trouble, put a bun in the oven

know one's **onions**
v phr To be
competent and
authoritative, esp in
one's work; have
impressive skill

have all the moves, have been around, have been through the mill, know all the answers, know all the moves, know all the tricks, know a thing or two, know backwards and forwards, know one's beans, know one's business, know from A to Z, know from the ground up, know one's stuff, know the ins and outs, know the ropes, know the score, know one's way around, know what it's all about, know what's what, know where it's at, not be born yesterday

kraut
n A German or
person of German
extraction

Boche, Dutchie, Dutchman, Fritz, Fritzie, Heinie, Hun, Jerry, krauthead, squarehead
☞ *These terms are considered offensive.*

kvetch
n A complainer, esp
a chronic
malcontent

beefer, bellyacher, bitcher, crab, crank, gripe, griper, grouch, grouchbag, groucher, grouse, grouser, grumbler, heat merchant, moaner, [Brit] moaning Minnie, picklepuss, sorehead, sourpan, sourpuss

L

ladies' man
n phr A man who pursues and otherwise devotes himself to women to an unusual degree

bad dude, bad-mother swinger, buck, cake-eater, Casanova, cat, chaser, Don Juan, drugstore cowboy, dude, God's gift to women, heartbreaker, hotshot, hound dog, lady-killer, Lothario, lounge lizard, lover-boy, make-out artist, masher, operator, playboy, poodle-faker, Romeo, sheik, skirt-chaser, smooth article, smoothie, smooth operator, sport, stud, studhammer, tomcat, wolf, woman-chaser

laid-back
adj Relaxed; unhurried

breezy, cas, chilly, cool, cooled out, easy, easy-going, mellow

latrine lawyer
n phr A soldier who is argumentative and authoritative among his peers with respect to his superiors, to rules and regulations, and to justice and expediency; a noisy meddler

clubhouse lawyer, forecastle lawyer, guardhouse lawyer, jailhouse lawyer, sea lawyer

☞ *While the entry term refers to soldiers, the modifiers in the list indicate similar types among other male groupings.*

a laugh
n phr Something very funny; a laughing matter

[Brit] a giggle, a hoot, a howl, a killer, a laugh and a half, a riot, a scream, a stitch

laundry list
n phr A bill of items to be obtained, requested, discussed, etc, as in "Once she has the microphone we'll have to listen to her whole laundry list of issues"

shopping list, want list, wish list

lay it on the line
v phr To speak candidly and straightforwardly; be plain

get down to brass tacks, go the hang-out road, lay it on the table, let one's hair down, let it all hang out, level, make no bones, pull no punches, put one's cards on the table, put it on the line, spill, spill one's guts, talk straight from the shoulder, talk turkey, tell it like it is

lay off
interj An exclamation of annoyance and warning

back off, butt out, get lost, get out of my hair, go fly a kite, go jump in the lake, go peddle your papers, go soak your head, keep your nose out of this, stick to your knitting, take a walk

lean on someone
v phr To put pressure on, esp with violence or the threat of it, as in "If he doesn't pay us today, we'll have to lean on him"

high-pressure, pressure, put the blocks to, put the heat on, put the squeeze on, twist someone's arm, work on

leatherneck
n A US Marine devil dog, gyrene, jarhead, seagoing bellhop

letdown
n A disap- [Brit] bringdown, comedown, [Brit] damp squib, dud,
pointment; a failure dull thud, false alarm, flash in the pan, frost, lemon,
of expectation misfire, nine days' wonder

let oneself go
v phr To behave in break out the jams, bust loose, cut loose, go hog wild,
an unrestrained kick out the jams, kick over the traces, let 'er rip, let
manner; be one's hair down, let it all hang out, let loose, loosen up,
uninhibited pull out all the stops

let it all hang out
v phr To speak get it off one's chest, get it out of one's system, go the
candidly; abandon hang-out road, let one's hair down, let it out, level, not
all concealment bottle it up, open up, spill one's guts, spill it, spit it out,
tell it like it is, unload

**a lick and a
promise**
n phr A hasty job; a once-over, a once-over lightly
*a cursory
performance, as in
"It's quitting time,
so all I can offer is a
lick and a promise"*

lickety-split
adv Very rapidly; at all out, balls to the wall, flat-out, full blast, full steam,
full speed hammer down, hell-bent, hell-bent for election, hell-
for-leather, in high gear, in overdrive, lickety-cut, like
a bat out of hell, like a blue streak, like a house afire, like
a scared rabbit, like a streak, like Billy Hell, like crazy,
like greased lightning, like hell, like mad, like sixty, like

thunder, on the double, to beat the band, to beat the devil, to beat the Dutch, wide open

lid
n A hat

bonnet, chapeau, Stetson

lightweight
n An inconsequential person; a trivial person

also-ran, busher, bush-leaguer, doormat, dud, eightball, featherweight, half-pint, limp-dick, little shot, loser, man with a paper ass, nebbish, no bargain, nobody, nobody to write home about, no great shakes, nonentity, nonstarter, no prize package, nothing to write home about, not much of a bargain, palooka, peanut, pip-squeak, pissant, poor fish, poor slob, punk, sad apple, sad sack, schlemazel, second-stringer, slob, small potatoes, small-timer, third-rater, tinhorn

☞ *These terms share semantic territory with "loser" and with "wimp," which should also be considered.*

like hell
1 *adv phr To an extreme degree; exceedingly, as in "This blister hurts like hell"*

one's ass off, one's brains out, hand over fist, one's head off, in a big way, in spades, in the worst way, like a house afire, like all creation, like all get-out, like anything, like Billy Hell, like blazes, like blue blazes, like blue hell, like everything, like it had gone out of style, like nobody's business, like sin, like sixty, like the deuce, like the devil, like the dickens, like there was no tomorrow, something awful, something fierce, to beat anything, to beat hell, to beat the band, to beat the deuce, to beat the devil, to beat the dickens, to beat the Dutch, to the max

2 *adv phr Never; not at all, as in "Like hell we did"*

fat chance, I'll be damned if, I'll be fucked if, in a pig's ass, in a pig's ear, in a pig's eye, like fun, like shit, my ass, my eye, nohow, no way, no way Jose, there's no way

limey
*n An English
person, esp a man*

beefeater, Brit, John Bull, lime-juicer
☞ *Strictly speaking, "Brit" applies to any native or
citizen in Great Britain, hence to the Welsh, Scots, Cor-
nish, Manx, etc, as well as the English. Both US and
British usage tends to be somewhat loose on this point.*

line
*n A try at
persuasion; a piece
of advocacy*

applesauce, fast line, jive, line of chatter, line of hooey,
pitch, routine, snow job, song, song and dance, spiel
☞ *These terms share semantic territory with "bullshit," which should also be considered.*

little bitty
*adj phr Very small;
tiny*

banty, bitsy, bitsy-witsy, bitty, bitty-witty, dinky,
eentsy-weentsy, half-pint, inky-dinky, itsy-bitsy, itsy-
witsy, itty-bitty, knee-high, little bitsy, peanut, peewee,
piddling, piddly, pint-size, pocket-size, poky, runty,
teentsy, teentsy-weentsy, teeny, teeny-weeny, two-by-
four, vestpocket, weenchy, weentsy

loaded
1 *adj Very rich;
affluent*

big rich, bloated, dirty, dirty with money, fat, filthy,
filthy rich, filthy with money, flush, heeled, holding, in
the bucks, in the chips, in the dough, in the money,
loose, lousy, lousy rich, made of money, nigger rich, on
the gravy boat, on the gravy train, oofy, rolling in it, six
feet up a bull's ass, stinking, stinking rich, well-heeled

2 SEE **HIGH**
3 SEE **PLASTERED**

loan shark
*n phr An
underworld usurer*

juice dealer, shy, shylock

long johns
n phr Long winter underwear

BVDs, John Ls, long-handle underwear, longies, long ones, woolies

long shot
n phr A person, horse, project, etc, that seems unlikely to win

dark horse, fooler, sleeper

loser
1 *n A person or thing that fails, esp habitually*

also-ran, boho, born loser, bust, clinker, dog, dud, dull tool, eightball, foul ball, lemon, never-was, nonstarter, pig-meat, poor slob, sad apple, sad sack, schlemiel, schmendrick, schmo, schnook, slob, total loss, turkey, wipe-out

2 SEE FLOP

lousy with
adj phr Abundant with, as in "The place was lousy with retired couples"

alive with, awash in, crawling with, loaded with, mangy with

lude
n A dose or capsule of methaqualone

Canadian quail, lemon, quack, quad, quas, soap, soaper, super soaper, wall banger

lush
n A heavy drinker; an inebriate

bar-fly, booze-fighter, booze-freak, boozehound, boozer, bottle-man, dipso, drunk, elbow bender, geek, ginhead, ginhound, guzzler, hooch-hound, juicehead, loadie, lusher, lushwell, oryide, rumbag, rumhound, rummy, rumpot, shikker, soak, sot, souse, sponge, stew, stewbum, wino

M
n Morphine

bang, barmecide, big M, birdie powder, birdie stuff, coby, cube, cube juice, em, glad stuff, goma, gonga dust, happy medicine, hard stuff, hell dust, hocus, joy dust, joy flakes, Marmon, Miss Emma, Miss Emma Jones, Miss Morph, moocah, morph, morphina, Mr Morpheus, number thirteen, piece, Red Cross, sister, sugar, sweet Jesus, sweet Morpheus, tab, uncle, white cross, white death, white goddess, white linen, white merchandise, white nurse, white powder, white silk, white stuff, white tape, wings, witch

mack
n A pimp

mackman, player, [chiefly Brit] ponce

make a killing
v phr To get a large, quick profit; win hugely

clean up, feather one's nest, hit the jackpot, make a bundle

make a scene

v phr To create a disturbance; exhibit noisy indignation; make a public outburst, as in "He made quite a scene when they told him he couldn't use his credit card"

carry on, cast a kitten, cut up, get into a swivet, get into a tizzy, have a conniption fit, have a cow, have a duckfit, have a fit, have a shit fit, have a tantrum, kick up a fuss, kick up a racket, kick up a row, kick up a stink, kick up a storm, make a how-de-do, make a stink, make a to-do, make fireworks, make waves, piss up a storm, raise a fuss, raise a hullaballoo, raise a ruckus, raise a stink, raise a storm, raise Cain, raise hell, raise sand, raise the devil, raise the roof, rattle cages, rock the boat, shit a brick, spit tacks, tear up the peapatch

☞ *These terms share semantic territory with "blow one's top," which should also be considered.*

the McCoy

n phr A person or thing of excellent quality; just what is wanted

the article, gem, the goods, mensch, real guy, the real McCoy, the right sort, the right stuff, sweetheart, the tops

☞ *Most of the terms at "humdinger" may be used in this sense. A person designated "the McCoy" is not precisely the same as a "good guy," because the former has more to do with sterling moral qualities than with simple geniality.*

meat wagon

n phr An ambulance

fruit wagon

Mick

n An Irishman or -woman or person of Irish extraction

bog-hopper, bog-trotter, harp, Mickey, mulligan, paddy
☞ *These terms are offensive.*

Mickey Finn
n phr A strong hypnotic or barbiturate dose, esp of chloral hydrate, put secretly into a drink

knockout drops, little Michael, little Mickey, mickey, peter

mish-mash
n A mixture; a miscellany, esp with ill-matching components

dog's breakfast, grab-bag, mess, odds and ends, rag-bag

mitt
n A hand

biscuit hook, bunch of fives, duke, fist, five, fiver, flapper, flipper, glom, glommer, hook, lunch hook, meat-hook, paw, some skin

mob scene
n phr A crowded occasion or place

fannybumper, Grand Central Station, sardine can

moneybags
n A wealthy person

bloated plute, Croesus, Daddy Warbucks, deep pockets, fat cat, jillionaire, lord of creation, Mister Money-bags, plute, [Brit] warm man

monicker
n A person's name

front name, handle, label, tag

monkey business
n phr Dubious behavior; dishonesty; deception

funny business, hank, hanky-pank, hanky-panky, hocus-pocus, hokey-poke, hokey-pokey, skullduggery

monster
adj Very large; huge

God-size, humongous, jumbo, king-size, moby, walloping, whacking, whambang, whopping

moocher
n A parasite; a habitual beggar and drone

beat, bum, bummer, cadger, deadbeat, deadhead, freeloader, moke, momzer, mooch, panhandler, schnorrer, scrounger, [Brit] spiv, sponge, sponger

moonlight
v To work at a job in addition to one's regular job

daylight, double, double in brass

the most
1 *n phr The superior person or thing; the best of all*

A number 1, A-1, the berries, burner, the cat's, the cat's balls, the cat's eyebrows, the cat's meow, the cat's nuts, the cat's pajamas, the cat's whiskers, the champ, the champion, the greatest, the mostest, oner, something else, too much, the tops

2 SEE **HUMDINGER**

mug shot
n phr A photograph of a person's face, esp the front and side views made for police records

art, mug

mule
1 *n An obstinate person*

bitter-ender, bulldog, bullethead, bullhead, diehard, donkey, hammerhead, hardhead, hardnose, hard nut to crack, pighead, stiffneck

2 SEE **PANTHER PISS**

mung
n Anything nasty; filth; ordure

crap, glop, grunch, grunge, muck, prut, scrunge, scunge, scuzz, scuzzo
☞ *These terms share semantic territory with "goo," which should also be considered.*

neck
v To kiss, embrace, and caress; dally amorously

boodle, box tonsils, canoe, canoodle, cuddle, do homework, fling woo, go on bush patrol, grab on, lollygag, love up, make out, park, perch, pet, pitch woo, play kissie, play kissie-kissie, play kissy-face, play kissy-facey, play kissy-poo, play lickey-face, play smacky lips, play snuggle-bunnies, play tonsil hockey, smash mouth, smooch, spoon, suck face, swap spit

nigger
n A black person

blackbird, blood, blue, blue-gum, blue-skin, boogie, boot, bro, brother, burrhead, chocolate drop, chungo bunny, clink, cluck, coon, darky, dinge, eightball, gee-chee, groid, hardhead, Hershey bar, hod, inky-dink, jar-head, jig, jigaboo, jit, jungle bunny, kinky-head, may-ate, nig, niggra, peola, schvartze, scuttle, shade, shad-mouth, shadow, skillet, smoke, spade, spook, zig, zigaboo
☞ *All these terms will give deep offense if used by nonblacks.*

night spot
n phr A nightclub

boite, club, lounge, nitery, room, trap

nit-pick
v To quibble over
trivia; cavil

chop logic, pick nits, split hairs
☞ *These terms share semantic territory with "blow up," which should also be considered.*

nix
v To veto; reject

bag, kill, negative, not buy, not sign off on, put the kibosh on, thumb down, turn down cold, turn thumbs down
☞ *These terms share semantic territory with "chuck," which should also be considered.*

no fooling
sentence I am
speaking seriously
and honestly

I kid you not, I'm not just whistling Dixie, I shit you not

nope
negation No; never

forget you, negative, nix, no deal, no dice, no go, no sale, no sirree, no soap, nothing doing, not on your life, not on your tintype, no way, no way Jose, uh uh

no shit
interj An
exclamation of
happy credulity, as
in "They bought my
story? No shit"

no jive, no kidding, you wouldn't shit me

not give a damn
v phr To be
indifferent to or
contemptuous of;
not care one whit

not give a dang, not give a darn, not give a dern, not give a flying fuck, not give a fuck, not give a hill of beans, not give a hoot, not give a rat's ass, not give a shit, not give diddly-damn, not give diddly-shit, not give spit, not give squat

☞ *This set may be enlarged enormously by substituting nearly any word for "shit" (that is, excrement) or "a shit," or any word for "zilch" (that is, nothing) in the formula.*

☞ *The terms share semantic territory with "one couldn't care less," which should also be considered. The distinction is one of impact, the terms above being much stronger than the others.*

not know shit from Shinola
v phr To be very ignorant; be hopelessly ill-informed; be stupid

know from nothing, not know one's ass from a hole in the ground, not know one's ass from first base, not know one's ass from one's elbow, not know beans, not know bubkes, not know diddly, not know diddly-damn, not know diddly-poo, not know diddly-poop, not know diddly-shit, not know diddly-squat, not know diddly-squirt, not know diddly-whoop, not know from nothing, not know shit, not know squat, not know zilch, not know zip, not know zippo

not worth a damn
adj phr Valueless; worthless

not worth a bucket of warm spit, not worth a plugged nickel, not worth a shit, not worth beans, not worth bubkes, not worth shit, not worth spit, not worth the powder to blow it to hell

☞ *The number of terms may be increased enormously by using nearly any word for "shit" (that is, excrement) or any word for "zilch" (that is, nothing) in the formula.*

nudnik
n An annoying person; a pest; a nuisance

nudge, pain, pain in the ass, pain in the neck, schlepper

nut

1 *n A crazy or very eccentric person; a lunatic*

bat, batty, bug, butterfly case, coot, crackbrain, crackpot, crazy, cuckoo, cupcake, daffydill, ding, ding-a-ling, dingbat, dip, flake, food for squirrels, freak, fruit, fruitcake, full-mooner, gonzo, goof, goofball, headcase, kook, loon, loonball, loony, loony-tune, loony-tunes, mental job, meshugana, nutball, nutbar, nutcake, nutcase, nutter, psycho, screwball, screw-loose, section eight, sickie, sicko, space cadet, space-out, squirrel, squirrel-food, wack, weirdie, weirdo, wombat

☞ *The semantic boundary between "eccentric person" and "insane person" is not easy to draw, so one should also see the entry for "oddball."*

2 SEE **BEAN**
3 SEE **FAN**

oddball

1 *n An eccentric person; a strange one*

bird, character, crank, creep, cueball, cupcake, dilly dude, ding-a-ling, dingbat, ding-dong, ferret, flake, foul ball, freak, fruit, fruitcake, geek, goober, goof, goofball, kook, nut, odd fish, odd stick, pod person, queer customer, queer duck, queer fish, [Brit] rum one, [Brit] rum customer, screwball, screw-loose, sickie, sicko, space cadet, space-out, spastic, spazz, spook, squirrel, twink, vert, wack, wacko, weirdie, weirdo, wombat, zod, zombie, zone, zoner

☞ *The semantic boundary between "eccentric person" and "insane person" is not easy to draw, so one should also see the entry for "nut."*

2 SEE **KINKY**

off one's feed

adj phr Not feeling or looking well; indisposed

not up to snuff, off color, peaked, peaky, poorish, punk, under the weather

OK

*affirmation Yes; I
agree; I accept that*

copacetic, definitely, hokey-dokey, ok, okay, oke, okey-doke, okey-dokey, okle-dokle, right, rightio, righto, right on, right you are, Roge, Roger, Roger-dodger, sure enough, sure nuff, sure thing, yeah, yeah man, yep, yes indeedy, yes sirree, yes sirree Bob, you bet, you betcha, yowzah, yup

☞ *These terms share semantic territory with "bet your ass," which should also be considered.*

the OK

*n phr Permission;
consent, as in "After
they thought it over
they gave me the
OK to start"*

the go, the go-ahead, the green light, the nod, the okay, thumbs up

old bag

*n phr An old
woman; a female
senior citizen*

hag, no spring chicken, old bat, old battle-ax, old broad, old dame, old doll, old girl, old hag, old heifer, old hen, old witch

old fart

*n phr An old man;
a male senior citizen*

alter kocker, codger, crock, dodo, duffer, fogy, fossil, futz, gaffer, geezer, gramps, old bird, old boy, old buzzard, old codger, old duffer, old fossil, old futz, old geezer, old poop, oldster, old-timer, pappy, pappy guy

old woman

*n phr One's wife;
one's helpmate*

ball-and-chain, bedmate, better half, frau, good wife, little woman, mat, missumis, old lady, squaw, trouble and strife, wifie

the once-over
n phr A look or glance of inspection; scrutiny

[Brit] dekko, the eye, gander, hinge, a load of, looksee, peek, peep, quick-over, slant, squint, [Brit] vetting

on hold
adv phr In postponement or abeyance

in a holding pattern, in cold storage, in mothballs, in the deep freeze, in the icebox, on ice, on the back burner, on the shelf

on someone's shit list
adv phr Ill-regarded by; hated and menaced by

in someone's bad books, on someone's get-lost list

on the ball
adj phr Skillful, alert, and effective; aware and effectual

on the stick, with it

on the blink
adj phr Not functioning; not operating; out of repair, as in "We can't process your order. Our computer's on the blink"

ausgespielt, blooey, buggered-up, bum, bust, busted, conked out, down, flooey, fritzed, fucked-up, haywire, jimmied-up, kerflooey, loused-up, off, on the bum, on the fritz, out of commission, out of kilter, out of whack, [Brit] packed-up, shot, snafu, snafued

on the cuff
*adv phr On credit,
as in "He bought a
couple of new suits
on the cuff"*

jawbone, on the arm, on the finger, on tick

on the double
*adv phr Quickly;
immediately, as in
"I want that thing
here and I want it
on the double"*

at the double, chop-chop, double-quick, hubba-hubba, immediately if not sooner, in a whoosh, in nothing flat, most rickety tick, PDQ, pronto, [Brit] quickstep, toot sweet

on the level
*adj phr Fair; even;
equable, as in "Are
you sure this deal is
on the level? Won't
somebody get
shafted?"*

[Australian] fair dinkum, level, on the legit, square

on the nose
*adj phr Precisely
right; exact, as in
"His stock-market
prediction was on
the nose"*

dead nut, on the bean, on the bull's-eye, on the button, on the dot, on the money, right on, slap on

on the QT
*adv phr Secretly;
quietly; not for
publication, as in
"I'll tell you this on
the QT"*

between you and me, between you and me and the bedpost, entre nous, hush-hush, off the record, strictly between us, under one's hat, under wraps

on the sauce
adj phr Drinking liquor, esp heavily

boozing, guzzling, on the bottle, on the juice, on the shikker

on someone's wavelength
adv phr In agreement; in harmony

grokking, hearing someone, on the same wavelength, tuned in

open one's yap
v phr To speak; say something, as in "When they asked her why, she didn't open her yap"

open one's face, open one's head, peep, pipe, pipe up, put one's oar in, put one's two cents in, put one's two cents' worth in, sing, sing out, warble

out
adj Unconscious

dead to the world, down for the count, out cold, out like a light, out of it

out of one's depth
adj phr In a situation where one cannot cope, esp because of inexperience or incapacity

in deep water, in over one's head, outclassed, out of one's league, over one's head

out of luck

adj phr Having little chance of success; in great difficulty, as in "If you want to pay by check, I'm afraid you're out of luck"

behind the eight ball, between a rock and a hard place, dead in the water, down on one's luck, hard put, hard up, in a bind, in a box, in a fix, in a hole, in a jam, in a mess, in a pickle, in a tight spot, in bad shape, in deep shit, in deep trouble, in deep water, in Dutch, in hot grease, in hot water, in the soup, on the hook, on the hot seat, on the ropes, on the spot, out of one's depth, shit out of luck, shot down in flames, S O L, sunk, up against it

☞ *These terms share semantic territory with "kaput," which should also be considered.*

pad
n One's room or dwelling

cave, coop, crash pad, crib, cubby, diggings, digs, hangout, hideout, hive, hutch, kip, layout, roost, setup, squat

paint the town red
v phr To carouse

bar-hop, bat, binge, booze, cut up, go on a bat, go on a bender, go on a binge, go on a tear, paint the town, [Brit] pubcrawl, raise hell, tear

pal
n A friend, esp a very close male friend

ace, asshole buddy, bosom buddy, buckwheat, bud, buddy, buddy-boy, buddy-buddy, buddyroo, buttfuck buddy, [Brit] butty, chum, [Australian] cobber, [Brit] cock, goombah, Holmes, homeboy, homey, landsman, main man, mellow, paesan, paisano, pally, palsy-walsy, pard, pardner, road dog, sidekick, walkboy

palsy-walsy
adj Very friendly

chummy, dovey, footsie, footsie-wootsie, huggy-huggy, kissy-huggy, like that, lovey-dovey, pally, thick, thick as thieves

panhandle
v To beg, esp by accosting people on the street

batter, ding, plingstem

panic
1 *v To become frightened; take alarm*

break out in assholes, flip, fudge one's undies, funk, get spooked, get the wind up, push the panic button, shit bullets, shit green, shit one's pants, suck air, sweat bullets

2 SEE **BREAK** someone **UP**

panther piss
n phr Inferior or bootleg liquor

bayou blue, bellywash, boilermaker's delight, bugjuice, busthead, cane corn, choke-dog, coffin varnish, corn juice, corn mule, dishwater, firewater, gage, goggle-eye, King Kong, Kong, lightning, moon, moonshine, moony, moose milk, mountain dew, mule, paint remover, panther, panther sweat, pig iron, pig sweat, popskull, prairie dew, redeye, rotgut, scrap iron, screech, sheep-dip, shellac, shine, shoe polish, snake poison, stump liquor, swipe, tangle-foot, tangle-leg, third rail, tiger sweat, varnish, varnish remover, white lightning, white mule, wild cat

paperhanger
n A person who passes counterfeit money

bill-poster, paper-layer, paper-pusher, pusher

park
v To put; place, as in "Where did you park the scissors?"

hide, stash

party hat
n phr The array of lights on the roof of a police car or emergency vehicle

cherry, gumball, Mickey Mouse ears

pass out
v phr To lose
consciousness

go out, go out like a light, go under, hear the birdies sing, hit the canvas, zonk, zonk out

pasteboard
1 *n A ticket of*
admission

board, ducat, duck, dukie, tab

2 *n A playing card*

board, book, broad, devil book, flat, rag

patsy
n A victim; a dupe

alvin, angel, boob, chicken, chump, clay pigeon, cousin, doormat, douchie, dumbjohn, easy make, easy mark, fall guy, fish, goat, goofus, gork, jay, [esp Brit] jiggins, [esp Brit] juggins, lamb, mark, monkey, mooch, [esp Brit] mug, pigeon, prune, pushover, schnook, setup, sitting duck, storch, sucker, tool, vic, yap, yold

pay dirt
n phr Profit

payoff, percentage, score, swag, take, velvet

pay one's dues
v phr To serve and
suffer such that one
earns what one gets,
as in "No one gets
very far in this line
of work without
paying his dues"

earn one's wings, go through the mill, have one's ticket punched

pay off
1 *v phr To be*
profitable
2 SEE **FIRE**

pan out

pearl-diver
n A person who   bubble dancer
washes dishes, esp
in a restaurant

peepers
n The eyes   baby blues, blinkers, daylights, glimmers, glims, lamps,
[Brit] mince pies, oglers, optics, peekers, peeps, pincers

peg
1 *v To identify;*   button down, finger, make, nail, nail down, pigeonhole,
classify   pin, pin down, put down for, spot as, tab
2 *v To throw*   chuck, chunk, let fly, shy, trun

pete
n A safe; a   box, can, crib, peet, pete-box, peter
strongbox

Philly
n Philadelphia   the big Pretzel, Phil, Quakertown, Sleepy Town

phony
1 *adj False;*   bogue, bogus, fake, hoked-up, hokey, hyped-up, phonus
counterfeit   balonus, phony as a three-dollar bill, plastic, plug,
plugged, pseudo, pumped-up, queer, stiff
2 *n Something false*   fake, falsy, fritzer, phonus balonus, phony baloney,
or counterfeit   puton
3 *n A person who*   actor, bluffer, boogerboo, fake, fakeroo, four-flusher,
affects some   fraud, glad-hander, handshaker, ho-dad, humbug,
identity, role,   pseud, quack
nature, etc; a poseur;
an impostor

pick-me-up
n A person or thing, esp a drink or snack, that invigorates; a stimulant

kick in the ass, pepper-upper, perker-upper, picker-upper, shot in the arm, shot in the ass

pick up the tab
v phr To pay; assume the expense, as in "I'll pick up the tab for the new park"

ante up, come across, cough over, cough up, dig down for, dish out, dish up, fork out, pay the freight, pick up the check, pop for, shell out for, spring for

piddly
adj Meager; trivial; paltry, as in "How could he expect her to accept such a piddly offer?"

bush, bush-league, chickenshit, diddly, five-and-dime, half-assed, half-pint, jeasly, jerkwater, measly, Mickey Mouse, narrow-gauge, peanut, peewee, penny ante, penny pool, pint-size, pippy-poo, pissant, pissy, pissy-ass, [esp Brit] poky, rinky-dink, runty, small-beer, small-bore, small-change, small-potato, small-time, softball, tinhorn, tinpot, two-bit, two-blink, two-by-four

piece
1 n A share; a portion; a financial interest, as in "He settled for a small salary and a piece of the gross"

piece of the racket, slice, slice of the melon, taste

2 SEE **ASS**
3 SEE **ROD**

pig

1 *n* *A glutton*   chow hound, gobbler, greedy-guts, hog, khazer, table finisher

2 SEE COP

3 SEE FLOOZY

pig out

v phr *To overeat; eat greedily, as in "When I get off this diet, I'm going to pig out on cake and ice cream"*   be a khazer, cram, dive in, eat like a horse, fork it in, gobble, hog it, hog it down, make a pig of oneself, pitch in, pork out, scarf out, shovel it in, stuff oneself

pimpmobile

n *Any very fancy and usu large car*   cuntmobile, hog, nerdmobile, rapemobile, rape wagon, sex wagon

pinko

n *A person of liberal or left-wing opinions*   commie, lefty, [Brit] lib-lab, parlor pink, pink, radiclib

pins

n *The legs, as in "Check out her pins"*   gams, hind legs, pegs, shanks, stems, sticks, stumps, trotters, underpinnings, wheels

piss

1 *v* *To urinate*   dangle one's hose, flash, leak, make a pit stop, pee, pee-pee, piddle, pump bilge, pump ship, take a leak, take a whizz, tinkle, wee-wee, whizz

2 *n* *Urine*   pee, pee-pee, wee-wee, whizz

3 SEE BEEF

a piss
n phr An act of urination

a leak, a pee, a piddle, a tinkle, a whizz

pissed off
adj phr Angry; indignant

bent out of shape, boiling, boiling mad, browned off, burned up, burning, chapped, cranky, dandered, drug, edged, fighting mad, fit to be tied, hacked, hacked off, het up, hopping mad, hot, hot and bothered, hot under the collar, huffy, in a huff, in a lather, in a lava, in a pucker, in a stew, in a sweat, in a swivet, in a tizzy, [Brit] in a wax, lathered, livid, mad, mad as a hornet, mad as a wet hen, miffed, miffy, on a tear, p'd, peed, peeved off, pissed, p o'd, pushed out of shape, raving mad, red-assed, red-necked, riled up, [Brit] shirty, sore, sore as a boil, steamed, steamed up, steaming, stuffy, t'd off, tearing mad, tee'd off, ticked, ticked off, torqued, [Brit] waxy

piss someone off
v phr To make someone angry; arouse keen indignation

burn someone's ass, burn someone's butt, burn someone off, burn someone up, frost, get a rise out of, get someone's back up, get someone's dander up, get someone's Irish up, hack someone, make someone hot under the collar, make someone mad, make someone sore, miff, pee someone off, piss, put someone's back up, [Brit] put someone's monkey up, put someone's nose out of joint, raise someone's dander, rile, steam, tee someone off, tick someone off

piss-off
n Anger; indignation, as in "He didn't conceal his piss-off at what they had done"

bile, burn, dander, Irish, mad, miff, pucker, R A, the redass, stew

piss-ugly
adj Very ugly;
repulsive

ugly as cat-shit

the pits
n phr The most
loathsome place or
situation
imaginable, as in
"She says her
university is the
pits"

the armpit, the asshole, Barf City

pizzazz
n Energy; vitality,
as in "If he had
more pizzazz he'd
be unbeatable"

bang, biff, bounce, drive, get-up-and-go, ginger, gism, hustle, jazz, kick, kick-ass, mohoska, moxie, oof, oomph, pep, pepper, piss and vinegar, poop, pow, punch, push, snap, spizzerinctum, spunk, starch, steam, zap, zing, zip, zippo, zizz, zowie

plastered
adj Drunk;
intoxicated with
alcohol

(very drunk) alkied, aped, bagged, basted, behind the cork, blind drunk, blitzed, blitzed out, bloated, blotto, blowed away, blue, boiled, bombed, boozed, boozed up, boozy, borahco, bottled, boxed, bunned, buzzed, buzzy, caged, canned, canned up, clobbered, cock-eyed, cooked, corked, corned, crashed, crocked, cronk, crumped out, dead drunk, dead to the world, decks awash, discouraged, drunk as a boiled owl, drunk as a coot, drunk as a fiddler's bitch, drunk as a lord, drunk as a skunk, edged, embalmed, faced, faint, far gone, feeling good, feeling no pain, flooey, flying high, fractured, fried, fried to the gills, fuzzled, gassed, ginned, ginned up, glassy-eyed, glazed, gone, gonged, grogged, had one too many, half-bagged, half-corned, half-crocked, half in the bag, half-lit, half-screwed, half seas over, half-shaved, half-shot, half-slewed, half-snaped, half-sprung, half-stewed, half under, happy, having a bun on, having a load on, having an edge on, having a skinful, having a snootful, having a snoot full, having one too many, high, high as a kite, hooched up, illuminated, impaired, in a bad way, in color, in one's cups, in the bag, juiced, juiced up, knocked out, laid out, lathered, liquored, liquored up, lit, lit up, lit up like a Christmas tree, loaded, looped, looping, lubricated, lushed, lushed up, mashed, muddled, obfuscated, oiled, on the shikker, organized, ossified, overtaken, petrified, pickled, pie-eyed, [Brit] pissed, plonked, plotzed, polluted, poo-pied, potted, reeling, ripe, ripped, riproaring drunk, roaring drunk, rocky, rummed up, saturated, sauced, schnockered, screwy, scronched, seeing pink elephants, shaved, shikker, shitfaced, shot, slewed, sloshed, slugged, smashed, snozzled, snuffy, soaked, soused, sozzled, spiffed, spifflicated, sprung, squiffed, squiffy, squiffy-eyed, stewed, stewed to the gills, stiff, stinking, stinking drunk, stinko, stitched, stoned, swacked, swacko, swizzled, swozzled, tangle-footed, tangle-legged, tanked, tanked up, tanky, three sheets to the wind, tight as a tick, tuned, under the influence, under the table, up to the ears, up to the eyeballs, up to the gills, waxed, wiped, wiped out, woozy, zonked, zonked out, zonkers

☞ *"To the ears," "to the gills," or "to the eyeballs" may be added to most of the adjectives as an intensifier; "half" may precede these adjectives as a moderating adverb.*

(slightly drunk) buzzy, happy, having a buzz, having a buzz on, having a slight edge, mellow, mildly impaired, pinked, pleasantly plastered, rosy, tiddly, tipsy, woozy

☞ *"Drunk" is one of the most prolific of slang concepts, probably because drunkenness has proffered the most persistent need of euphemism, both clever and defensive. Benjamin Franklin took note of this when he published a compilation of 225 terms for "drunk" (some fifteen of which are still current) as* The Drinker's Dictionary *in January 1737.*

platter
n A phonograph record

disc, plate

play ball
v phr To cooperate; collaborate; acquiesce, as in "They suggested bribery, but he wouldn't play ball"

go along, play, play along, play the game, stand still for

playboy
n A person devoted to partying and pleasure; a bon vivant

fun-seeker, gadabout, gay bird, gay dog, good time Charlie, man-about-town, sport

play dirty
v phr To use unethical, illegal, or injurious means; chicane

bend the rules, hit below the belt, play dirty pool, pull something funny, pull funny business, stack the cards, stretch the rules

play games
v phr To maneuver and manipulate cunningly; toy and gamble

angle, diddle around, fuck around, jockey, mess around

play hardball
v phr To be serious and determined to the point of callousness

go for the jugular, not play games, not play penny ante, play for keeps, play rough

play hooky
v phr To stay away from work and duty, esp from school

juke

play it safe
v phr To choose a cautious line of behavior; avoid much risk, as in "He played it safe and brought travelers' checks on vacation"

be on the safe side, cut one's losses, hedge one's bets, play safe

play second fiddle
v phr To be in an inferior position; lack power or will to lead

suck hind tit, take a back seat

play up to
v phr To ingratiate oneself with, esp by friendly flattery

buddy up to, butter up, make up to, play kissie with, run after, shine up to, suck up to

plug

1 *v To shoot or shoot at with a firearm* — blast, blaze away at, give a dose of lead poison to, let fly at, let loose at, let moonlight into, open up on, peg, perforate, plunk, pop at, pot, puncture, smoke, take a crack at, take a pop at, take a potshot at, zap

2 *v To progress or propel haltingly but doggedly, as in "I plugged at this book for many moons"* — hump and bump, plug along, plug away

3 *n A recommendation, as in "We would welcome plugs for this book"* — blurb, boost, build-up, plugola, puff, puff job, push

plug into

v phr To discover and exploit to one's advantage; tap — buy into, get aboard, get on board, tie into

poker face

n phr An expressionless face — deadpan, straight face

pooch

n A dog — bowwow, dorg, Fido, hound, man's best friend, mutt, pup, pup-dog, puppy, puppy-dog, purp, Rover

the poop

1 *n Information; data, as in "Give me the poop on our competition overseas"* — the dirt, the dope, [Brit] the gen, the goods, the info, the lowdown, the pif, the scoop, scuttlebutt, the skinny, the word

2 SEE **SHIT**

pooped
adj Very tired;
exhausted

all in, all shot, one's ass is dragging, ausgespielt, bagged, beat, beat out, beat to the ankles, beat to the ground, beat to the socks, blitzed, blitzed out, bone-tired, burned out, bushed, chewed, clanked, crapped out, dead, dead on one's feet, dog-tired, done, done in, done to a frazzle, dragged out, fagged, fagged out, feeped out, frazzled, fried, fucked out, had it, knocked out, on one's last legs, out on one's feet, paled, paled out, played out, plumb tuckered, poohed, poohed out, pooped out, punch-drunk, ready to drop, run ragged, shot, tapped out, one's tail is dragging, tuckered, tuckered out, worn to a frazzle

pop someone's
cherry
v phr To terminate
someone's virginity

cherrypop, cop someone's cherry

popeyed
adj Having
protruding eyes;
exophthalmic

bugeyed, goggle-eyed, googly-eyed, gotch-eyed

porn
n Pornography

porno, raunch, rough stuff

pot
n Marijuana;
cannabis sativa

Acapulco gold, Acapulco red, Angola black, ashes, Aunt Mary, baby, baby buds, bam, bambalacha, bammy, bang, bay, Bethesda gold, bhang, birdwood, black Columbus, black gold, black gungeon, black moat, black mold, black mole, black monte, black mota, blank, block mo, blue de hue, blue sage, blue-sky blond, bo bo, bo bo bush, boo, brand X, Breckenridge green, brifo, broccoli, buddha, buddha sticks, bull jive, bunk, bush, busy, butter flower, Cambodian trip weed, Cam red, Canadian black, canned goods, charge, chiba chiba, Chicago black, Chicago green, chira, churus, Colombian, Columbus black, conga, conga brown, Congo mataby, dagga, dew, ding, dirt grass, Dona Juanita, doobie, dope, dope smoke, dynamite, faggot, fennel, fu, funny stuff, gage, Gainesville green, gangster, ganja, garbage, gash, gates, gear, giggle smoke, gold, gold leaf, goof butt, grass, grass weed, greefa, green griff, greta, gunny, happy gas, happy grass, hay, hemp, herb, herbs, HOG, hooch, hot jay, ice bag, ice pack, incense, Indian, Indian hay, Indian hemp, Indian weed, jahooby, Jamaican, jay, Jersey green, jingo, jive, Johnson, joy smoke, J smoke, juane, juanita, juanita weed, ju ju, kaif, kanjac, keef, Kentucky blue, Kona gold, laughing grass, laughing tobacco, leaves, leper grass, Lipton's punk, loco weed, love weed, lozerose, lozies, M, mach, Mach Picchu, Maggie, Manhattan silver, Manhattan white, Mary, Mary and Johnny, Mary Ann, Mary Jane, Mary Warner, Mary Weaver, Mary Werner, Maui, Maui wowie, megg, mesca, Mex, Mexican, Mexican brown, Mexican green, Mexican red, the might mezz, MJ, M O, modams, mohasky, mojo, mooca, mootah, mooter, mootie, mu, mud, murder weed, musta, muta, New York white, noble weed, Oaxacan, one-toke weed, Panama gold, Panama red, patyo de gayina, pleiku pink, pod, powder, PR, Punta Rojas, ragweed, railroad weed, Rangoon, red, red gunyon, reefer, reefer weed, righteous bush, rocket, s, salt and pepper, Santa Maria gold, Santa Maria red, sativa, sausage, sess, shit, shuzit, sinsemilla, smoke, snop, stinkweed, straw, stuff, supremo, sweet lunch, sweet Mary, T, tea, Tennessee blue, Texas tea, Thai stick, Thai weed, Thunder weed, viper weed, wacky tobaccy, wacky weed, Wahegan, weed, wheat, wild weed, yerba, yesca, Zacatecas purple, zoom

☞ *The great number of slang terms for narcotics probably reflects both a need for coded reference to an illegal substance and a desire to be chic and up-to-date, in addition to the need to distinguish varieties.*

potbelly

n A protuberant stomach; a paunch

ballast, bay window, beer belly, bulge, corporation, fallen chest, German goiter, gut, jelly-belly, labonza, middle-age spread, Milwaukee goiter, Milwaukee tumor, pooched-out belly, porch, pot, potgut, pus-gut, pustle-gut, spare tire

pothead

n A user of marijuana, esp a heavy user

blower, blow top, bo-bo jockey, dopehead, doper, dopester, freak, Fu Manchu, goof, gouger, gowster, grass eater, grasshead, grasshopper, green, griefer, hay burner, hayhead, head, hophead, junkerman, lover, lusher, mugglehead, oiler, pot lush, puller, reefer, reefer hound, roach bender, tea blower, teahead, tea hound, teo, T-man, toker, twister, weed eater, weedhead, weed hound, weed twister

pow

1 *interj An imitation of a blow, collision, explosion, etc, used for sudden emphasis or to show sudden understanding, as in "And pow, there he was" or "Pow, the thing fell apart"*
2 SEE CLOUT

bam, bang, biff, bingo, blam, blap, blooey, bop, boppo, kerblooey, kerboom, kerplunk, kerthump, powie, smack, smacko, socko, whack, wham, whambang, whammo, zap, zowie

prissy
adj Overfastidious;
primly censorious

choosy, finicky, fusspotty, fussy, pernickety, persnickety, picky, prunish

private eye
n phr A private
detective

eye, op, peeper, tin star

pro
1 *n A serious*
performer or
practitioner; a
professional
2 SEE **HOOKER**

big boy, big girl, big lady, big man, suit
☞ *These terms mark the contrast between child and adult performance.*

proposition
v To invite or
request sexual favors

come on to, george, hit on, lay the make, make a move on, make a pass, mash, pass, pitch, put a move on, put the make on, put the moves on, throw a pass

prowl car
n phr A police
squad car

cherry top, cruiser, fuzz tub

psych someone up
v phr To arouse
someone
emotionally,
spiritually,
mentally, etc, to a
maximum effort;
raise to a state of
keen readiness and
capability

gear, gear someone up, pump someone up

pumped
adj In a state of excited preparedness and heightened keenness; keyed up

charged up, cranked up, geared, geared up, jazzed, leaning forward in the saddle, psyched, psyched up, pumped up, rarin' to go

punch-drunk
adj Dazed; exhibiting brain damage from repeated blows to the head

punchy, slap-happy, slug-nutty

punch line
n phr The last line or part of a joke, which makes it funny

gag line, kicker, payoff, punch, snapper, sock line, zinger

puss
n The face

beezer, clock, dial, gills, kisser, map, mask, mug, mush, pan, phiz

pussyfoot
v To be careful and hesitant; avoid direct and immediate action

beat around the bush, play it close to the chest, play it close to the vest, pussyfoot around, take it easy, take one step at a time, tap-dance, tiptoe, walk on eggs, walk on eggshells

pussy-whipped
adj Dominated by a woman, esp one's wife; hen-pecked

cunt-struck, whipped

a put-on
n phr A deception;
a trick

a con, a leg-pull, a number, a spoof

put on the ritz
v phr To make a
display of wealth
and luxury

dog it, give oneself airs, put on, put on airs, put on class, put on frills, put on swank, put on the dog, put on the high hat, ritz it, swank it

put the bite on
v phr To make a
request, esp for
money; importune

drop the lug on, hit, hit up, put the arm on, put the bee on, put the claw on, put the lug on, put the sleeve on, put the sting on, put the touch on, shake down, tap, touch, touch up

put-up job
n phr A pre-
arranged matter and
outcome; a contrived
affair, as in "It
wasn't a real
election, it was a
put-up job"

boat race, the fix, rigged fight, setup, tank job, wired job

put up or shut up
sentence Support
your statements,
boasts, opinions, etc,
with something
tangible

let's see the color of your money, put your money where your mouth is, talk is cheap

quickie

n A very quick sex act

bunny fuck, quick one, ram-bam thank you ma'am, wham-bam thank you ma'am

R

rabbi
n A patron and influential political friend, esp of a police officer

Chinaman

racket
n An occupation or concern, esp an illegal or somewhat shady one

dodge, game, graft, line, [Brit] line of country, number, scam

rack up
v phr To achieve; score or earn a total of, as in "The first year they racked up a 40% profit"

pile up, stack up

razzle-dazzle
n Adroit deception, as in "They were able to make their case without resort to razzle-dazzle"

dipsy-do, dipsy-doodle, double shuffle, fancy footwork, fast footwork, fast shuffle, flamdoodle, [Brit] gammon, hanky-pank, hanky-panky, hokey-pokey, hokum, jive, quick shuffle, razzmatazz, ring-a-ding, ring-a-ding-ding, smoke and mirrors

redneck

1 *n A bigoted and conventional person; a loutish ultraconservative*

Archie Bunker, hard-hat, neanderthal, no-neck

2 SEE **CRACKER**

rehash

v To review; discuss again; repeat

recap

rejigger

v To alter or readjust; tinker with, as in "I think we had better rejigger those cost estimates"

doctor, doctor up, fine-tune, fix up, rehaul, retool, revamp, trouble-shoot

ride the arm

v phr To collect a taxi fare without using the meter

arm it, highflag

rig

v To prearrange or tamper with a result or process, as in "It looked like a real rescue, but the whole thing was rigged"

cold deck, fake, fake up, fix, hold a boat race, put up, satchel, set up, stack, stack the cards, stack the deck, tank

roach clip
n phr A tweezerlike clip for holding a marijuana cigarette stub

airplane, crutch, Jefferson airplane, roach holder, roach pick

rocky
adj Dazed; weak and unsteady; confused, as in "I was a little rocky from lack of sleep"

dopey, foggy, fuddled, fuddleheaded, groggy, muzzy, out of it, out on one's feet, punchy, woozy

rod
1 *n A pistol*

artillery, belly gun, boomstick, bulldog, bulldozer, cannon, equalizer, fire stick, gat, hardware, heat, heater, hogleg, iron, jammies, John Roscoe, the noise, noise tool, oscar, pea shooter, persuader, piece, popper, roscoe, Saturday night special, shooting iron, sixgun, snubby, snug, zip gun

2 SEE COCK

rookie
n A newcomer; a novice; a tyro

boot, cruit, dumbjohn, fish, greenhorn, greeny, jellybean, John, Johnny-come-lately, [Brit] new boy, poggie, pogue, raw recruit, rook, snotnose, tenderfoot, wetnose, yardbird

rootin'-tootin'
adj Boisterous; rowdy; vigorous, as in "They had a rootin'-tootin' party going on"

harum-scarum, knock-down-drag-out, rambunctious, rampageous, riproaring, riproarious, rock 'em–sock 'em, rough-and-tumble, row-dow, rowdy-dow, rowdy-dowdy, slam-bang

rough up
v phr To hit and pummel; attack viciously

beat on, bushwhack, give the business, give the works, gorilla, haze, hit on, manhandle, massage, mess up, punish, stiff, stiff-arm, stomp, strong-arm, work over

roust
v Esp of police officers, to harass

chivvy, hassle, jack up, jam, lean on, take on, yank

rubber
n A condom

bag, Coney Island whitefish, fishskin, Frenchie, French letter, French safe, French tickler, Manhattan eel, pro, raincoat, rubber boots, safe, safety, scumbag, shower cap, skin

rubberneck
v To stare; gape

gander, gawk, gawp, goggle, goof at, rubber, take a gander

rug
n A toupee

divot, door mat, muff, sky rug

rumble
1 n A fight between street gangs

dance

2 n A police search or raid

bust-up, knockover, roust, tipover

3 SEE **HEIST**

run it up the flagpole
v phr To try out an idea, concept, etc, as in "Seems like a good idea, but let's run it up the flagpole first"

put one toe in first, run it up the flagpole and see if anybody salutes, test the water, try it on, try it on for size

rustle up

v phr To produce or provide, esp hastily, as in "With two minutes' warning I had to rustle up an alibi"

break out, knock out, promote, rassle up, rustle, scare up, scrape up, scrounge, scrounge up, whomp up

S

sack time
n phr Sleep

beauty sleep, beddy-bye, blanket drill, bunk fatigue, bunk habit, bye-bye, doss, kip, pad duty, rack duty, rack time, sack, sack drill, sack duty, shuteye, winks, Zs

sass
n Impudence; impertinent responses, as in "Just do what I say and don't give me any sass"

back-chat, back-talk, cheek, guff, lip, sauce

sawbones
n A physician or surgeon

bone-bender, bones, butcher, croaker, medic, medico, pill-bag, pill-peddler, pill-pusher, pill-roller

sawbuck
n A ten-dollar bill; ten dollars

dime-note, saw, tenner, ten-spot

scab

n A nonunion worker, esp one who attempts to break a strike

blackleg, boll weevil, fink, jackleg, rat, scissorbill

scads

n A large quantity or amount; many many

all kinds of, and then some, bags, barrels, bunches, a bundle, bundles, enough to choke a horse, a fistful, a flock, forty-'leven, gobs, hatfuls, a heap, heaps, a helluva lot, a jillion, jillions, lashings, loads, lots, a mess, more than you can shake a stick at, no end of, oceans, oodles, packs, piles, a power, a raft, rafts, seventy-leven, a shit-house full, a shit-load, a shitpot, a sight, a skillion, slathers, a slew, slews, a stack, stacks, umpteen, wads, a zillion, zillions

scalper

n A person who buys tickets to be sold at prices higher than is legally permitted

digger

scam

n A swindle; a confidence game; a fraud

bill of goods, bite, boiler room, bucket shop, bunco, bunco game, burn, the C, clip, clip game, con, the con, con game, con job, diddle, diddling, dipsy-do, dipsy-doodle, dodge, double cross, double shuffle, fast one, fast shuffle, fiddle, flam, flimflam, frigging, fucking, gig, grift, gyp, hanky-panky, hoke, hokey-pokey, hosing, hustle, hype, murphy, number, the old army game, racket, razzle-dazzle, razzmatazz, reaming, ripoff, rooking, runaround, sell, shakedown, shell game, skin game, skinning, slicker game, slickering, snow job, sting, sucker game, suckering, suck-in

☞ *Technically this list combines several types of fraud, but most of these terms can be used in the general sense.*

scarecrow
n An ugly person

bad broad, bag, bat, beast, beasty, board, buffarilla, clock stopper, cow, dog, doggy, double-bagger, douchebag, Elsie, faggot, fright, gargoyle, geech, hag, hatchetface, hatchet-puss, hog, horror, mess, no bargain, no prize package, picklepuss, scrag, scuzz, sight, skag, skank, skunk, snake, sourpuss, sweat hog, tusker, twobagger, vinegar-puss, witch

☞ *This list makes no distinction of gender, although some of the terms are specific to ugly women.*

scared shitless
adj phr Very frightened; terrified

fudging one's undies, goose-bumpy, goose-fleshy, in a funk, scared spitless, scared stiff, scared to death, shitting one's drawers, shitting one's pants, spooked, whiteknuckled

scare the shit out of
v phr To frighten very much

make someone's hair curl, put the fear of God into, scare shitless, scare spitless, scare stiff, scare the bejesus out of, scare the living shit out of, scare the pants off, scare the tar out of, scare witless, spook, throw a scare into

scarf
v To eat

chaw, chow, chow down, fall to, feed one's face, garbage down, get around, gorm, gorp, graze, grease down, grit, grub up, inhale, munch out, munch up, pitch in, polish off, put away, put it away, put on the feed bag, scarf up, scoff, snorf, stoke up, tuck away, tuck in

schlocky
adj Inferior; shoddy; cheap and gaudy

bargain-basement, cheapie, cheapo, cheapshit, cheesy, chintzy, crapoid, crappy, cruddy, crummy, dime-a-dozen, dimestore, five-and-dime, hanky-pank, junk, junky, low-rent, low-ride, Mickey Mouse, Model-T, NG, no-account, no-count, no-good, punk, south of the border, tacky, tatty, tinpot, trashy, two-bit

schmooz
n A conversation, esp a long and amiable one

blabfest, bull session, chatfest, chaw, chawfest, chin, chinfest, chin-wag, confab, gabfest, gam, gas, gum-beating, hash session, heart-to-heart, jaw, jawfest, jive session, palaver, pow-wow, rag-chew, rag-chewing, rap, rapping, rap session, RF session, set, talkfest, tongue-wag, visit

schnozz
n The nose

bazoo, beak, beezer, bill, boke, boko, bugle, honker, horn, muzzle, nozzle, proboscis, schnozzle, schnozzola, smeller, snoot, snout, snozzle, trumpet

score
1 v To buy or get narcotics

be put straight, cap, connect, cop, cop a buy, cop a fix, cop a match, deal, get through, hit, make a buy, make a meet, make the man, pick up, prime the pump

2 n Loot; booty

bacon, boodle, bundle, cop, goods, haul, hot stuff, pickin's, swag, take

screwed
adj Victimized; maltreated, as in "She really got screwed when she bought that car"

conned, diddled, frigged, fucked, fucked over, had; laid, relaid, and parlayed; screwed over, screwed, blued, and tattooed; shafted, shat on, shit on, suckered, taken, taken into camp, taken to the cleaners, yentzed
☞ *Other such terms may be made from the appropriate forms of the verbs "con" and "fuck."*

screw up
1 *v phr To spoil something, esp by bungling; confuse and ruin*

ass up, [Brit] balls up, ball up, bitch, bitch up, blow, blow high as a kite, blow it, bollix, bollix up, boot, bugger, bugger up, cook, crab, crock, crumb, crumb up, dish, dutch, finish, flummox, foul up, fritz, fuck up, goof up, gummix up, gum up, hash up, jigger, jimmy up, kibosh, louse up, make a hash of, make a mess of, make a muddle of, mess up, mommix, mommix up, muck up, muff, mung, mung up, pickle, play hell with, play merry hell with, plumber, put the kibosh on, queer, send to hell in a handbasket, shoot down, shoot down in flames, sink, snafu, snarl up, wipe out

☞ *The phrase "the works" or "the deal" may be added to nearly all these terms for fullness.*

2 SEE FUCK UP

scrub
v To cancel; eliminate; erase

abort, axe, bag, belay, blow, blow off, can, chuck, cut, deep-six, ditch, drop, kill, knock off, scrap, scratch, scrub, shit-can, spike, wash out, wooden-stake

scrunch
v To squeeze; consolidate, as in "We managed to scrunch all my stuff into one suitcase"

ooch, oonch, scooch, scrooch, scrooge, scrunch up

scut work
n phr Tedious work needing little thought or skill; drudgery

bullwork, dogwork, donkeywork, grunt labor, grunt work, scud, scut, shitwork

...hit
...n phr *A bowel*
...vement
...EE ASSHOLE

a crap, a dump, a poo, a poop, a squat

...list
...r *A usu fancied*
...f persons one
...not wish to
...iate with or
...or

drop-dead list

the shits
n phr *Diarrhea;*
loose bowels

the Aztec two-step, Basra belly, the craps, Delhi belly, the GIs, the GI shits, gyppy tummy, Hong Kong dog, Johnny Trots, Montezuma's revenge, the quickstep, the runs, the trots, turista

shooting gallery
n phr *A place*
where a narcotics
user can get a dose
or injection

launching pad, needle park

shoot the breeze
1 v phr *To chat*
amiably and
casually; converse

bat one's chops, bat one's gums, bat one's jaw, bat one's jowls, bat one's lip, bat the breeze, beat one's chops, beat one's gums, beat one's jaw, beat one's jowls, beat one's lip, bullshit, chew the fat, chew the rag, chin, chinjaw, chop one's teeth, confab, fan, flap one's chops, flap one's gums, flap one's jaw, flap one's jowls, flap one's lip, gab, gas, have a chinfest, have a gabfest, have a talkfest, hump one's chops, hump one's gums, hump one's jaw, hump one's jowls, hump one's lip, jaw, mouth off, [Brit] natter, palaver, patter, pop off, rap, run off at

213

the mouth, schmooz, shoot the bull, shoot the crap, shoot the fat, shoot the shit, sound off, wag the tongue, yack, yackety-yack

2 SEE BULLSHIT
3 SEE GAB

shoot up
v phr To take an injection or other dose of narcotic

back-track, back up, bang, boot, broach, bust the main-line, cave, cave-dig, ditch, douche, do up, down, drill, drop, flush, gate, geez, get off, get with it, give wings, go in the gutter, gutter, hit, hit the sewer, hit up, hop up, hype, jab, jab a vein, jack, jack off the spike, jack up, jerk off, jolt, kick the gong around, laugh and scratch, line, lip the dripper, main, mainline, pipe, pit, pop, raise a welt, register, send it home, sewer, shoot, shoot gravy, skin pop, spike up, splash, take off, tap, tie off, tie up

the shorts
n phr Lack of money; a shortage of funds

not a pot to piss in, financial embarrassment, not one dollar to rub against another, the tights

shorty
n A person of short stature

duckbutt, dusty butt, featherweight, half-pint, little drink of water, little squirt, midget, peanut, peewee, pip-squeak, runt, sawed-off runt, shrimp, squirt

show up
v phr To arrive; be present

blow in, bob up, breeze in, buzz in, check in, clock in, drag in, drop in, fall by, fall down, fall out, fall up, get in, hit town, make the scene, pop up, pull in, punch in, put in an appearance, ring in, roll in, show, sign in, time in, tool in, turn up, weigh in

shrink

n A psychiatrist, psychoanalyst, or other psychotherapist

bug doctor, couch doctor, guru, headpeeper, head-shrinker, nut doctor, shrinker

shut up

1 *v phr To be quiet; stop talking*

belt up, bottle it, button one's face, button one's lip, button up, caeto, clam up, cut the mouth, drink one's beer, dry up, dummy up, hang up, keep one's mouth shut, keep one's trap shut, not let out a peep, not say boo, pipe down, rest one's jaw, ring off, save one's breath, shush, shut one's bazoo, shut one's face, shut one's shit, shut one's trap, shut one's yap, sign off, stow it, stow the gab, zip one's lip, zip one's mouth

☞ *All these terms in the imperative, and the following interjections, may be used as stern or angry commands.*

2 *interj Be silent; hold your tongue*

at ease, bag your head, belay that, bottle it, can it, cork it, cut it out, cut the chat, cut the shit, knock it off, pack it up, save your breath, shet ep, shush your mouth, shut your ass, stow it

shyster

n A lawyer, esp an unscrupulous one

ambulance chaser, fixer, lip, mouthpiece, tongue

sissy

1 *n An effeminate male*

cream puff, cupcake, daisy, fancy-pants, flower, lily, Lord Fauntleroy, mama's boy, nance, nancy, pansy, pantywaist, Percy, Percy-boy, Percy-pants, sis, sissy-pants, softy, tootie fruity, weak sister

☞ *These terms share semantic territory with "wimp," which should also be considered.*

2 SEE GAY

sit tight

1 *v phr* *To wait patiently; be patient*

hang around, hang on, hold one's horses, hold it, hold the phone, keep one's hair on, keep one's pants on, keep one's shirt on, not hold one's breath, stay put

2 *v phr* *To retain one's position; refuse to shift, as in "The landlord offered me a thousand dollars to move, but I'm going to sit tight"*

die hard, hold out, stand one's ground, stand pat, stay put, stick to one's guns, take one's stand

the slammer

n phr *A jail or prison*

the academy, the bastille, the big, the big cage, the big house, the big joint, the big school, the bing, the boarding school, the brig, the bucket, the caboose, the cage, the calaboose, the calabozo, the can, the cannery, the clink, the clinker, the coalhole, the college, the collitch, the cooler, the coop, the fed pen, the hole, the hoosegow, the icebox, the joint, the jug, the lockup, the mill, the pen, the pogey, the pokey, the pound, the quad, the slam, the state pen, the stir, the tank

sleazebag

n *A disgusting person, esp a smelly,* · *filthy one; a moral and physical sloven*

chili-bowl, creep, crud, crumb, crumb-bun, dip, dirt-bag, dirtball, douchebag, filthbag, fishball, geek, mess, pus-bag, scum, scumbag, scumsucker, scurve, scut, scuzzbag, scuzzo, sleaze, sleazeball, slimebag, slime-ball, slimebucket, slob, sludgeball, weirdo, zhlub

☞ *Many of these terms are synonymous with those found under "asshole" and "jerk." The distinction is that while one despises a jerk and detests an asshole, one both despises and detests a sleazebag.*

sleep around
*v phr To be
sexually
promiscuous*

fool around, play around, play musical beds, swing

smack
1 *adv Exactly;
precisely, as in
"Smack on the hour
of three, she came"*
2 SEE **HORSE**

bam, [esp Brit] bang, bung, plonk, plump, plunk, slam-bang, slap, slap-bang, smack dab, spang, square

smart-ass
1 *n An impudent
and officious person;
a wiseacre*

armchair general, armchair strategist, bigmouth, ho-dad, know-it-all, smart aleck, smart guy, smartmouth, smarty, smartypants, wise apple, wise-ass, wise guy, wisenheimer

2 *adj Impudent;
disrespectfully
frivolous, as in
"That sort of
smart-ass remark is
going to get you in
trouble"*

cheeky, cute, flip, flip-lipped, sassy, smart, smart-alecky, smartmouth, wise, wise-ass

the smart money
*n phr The
predictions,
expectations, and
bets of those who
know best*

the educated money, the hip gee, the wise money

smarts
*n Intelligence;
competence*

brains, brain stuff, gray matter, know-how, moxie, savvy, something on the ball, the stuff, what it takes

smidgen
n A small amount cunt-hair, dab, dablet, lick, little bit, mite, skinch, skosh, smitch, tad, wee bit

a smoke
n An act of
smoking tobacco,
esp a cigarette, as in
"He said he was just
going out for a
smoke"

a burn, a butt, a cig, a coffin-nail, a drag, a fag, a gasper, a puff, a pull

smoke out
v phr To discover get a line on, sniff out, suss out, [Brit] winkle out

smoothie
1 *n A sophisticated* old smoothie, slicker, smooth article, smooth citizen,
and seductively smooth number, smooth operator, smooth potato
pleasant person
2 SEE LADIES' MAN

snafu
n A very confused [Brit] balls-up, Chinese fire call, Chinese fire drill, [Brit]
situation; chaos dog's dinner, fine how-de-do, flummox, foozle, foul-up, fuck-up, goat fuck, goat rope, goat screw, goof-up, hell of a mess, hurrah's nest, mell of a hess, mess, Mickey Mouse, mix-up, muss, pretty kettle of fish, rat's nest, sapfu, screw-up, shitstorm, stew, tuifu, unholy mess

snappy
1 *adj Stylish;* chic, classy, dressy, flossy, hip, mod, snazzy, trendy
modish, as in "She
had on a snappy
new skirt"
2 SEE ZINGY

sneakers
n *Rubber-soled sports shoes*

JC water-walkers, sneaks, tennies, tenny runners

snitch
n *A police informer or spy*

bat carrier, beefer, boogie, canary, cheese bun, cheese eater, copper, dime-dropper, dimer, faded boogie, finger, fink, geepo, nark, nightingale, nose, pigeon, rat, ratter, shamus, shiever, singer, snitcher, snitch jacket, squawk, squeaker, squeal, squealer, stool, stoolie, stool pigeon, tipster, weasel, whistle-blower, whistler, zuch

snooty
adj *Snobbish; haughty and disdainful; supercilious*

dicty, high and mighty, highfalutin', high-hat, high-hatty, hincty, hoity-toity, la-de-da, sniffy, snobby, snotty, standoffish, stuck-up, top-hat, uppish, uppity

snooze
v *To sleep; go to sleep; go to bed*

bag it, bag some Zs, cap out, catch Zs, caulk off, collar a nod, conk off, conk out, cop some Zs, cork off, crap out, crash, crawl into the hay, cut some Zs, cut Zs, dope off, doss, ear, fall out, flack out, flake out, flop, get some blanket drill, get some bunk fatigue, get some rack, get some sack time, get some shuteye, go beddie-bye, hit the great white biscuit, hit the hay, hit the pad, hit the sack, hit the trees, kip, pad down, pad out, pile up some Zs, pound one's ear, rack, rack out, roll in, sack out, saw logs, saw wood, stack some Zs, take a power nap, take forty winks, turn in, Z, Zee, [Brit] zizz

a snooze
n phr *A nap; a doze; sleep*

cat nap, forty winks, a kip, rack duty, rack time, sack drill, sack time, shuteye, some Zs, wink, [Brit] zizz, [Brit] zizzy

snort

1 *n A drink of liquor*

ball, bump, bumper, drag, dram, a finger, gargle, geezer, glug, guzzle, hook, hooker, jigger, jolt, kick, nip, peg, pull, shot, slug, slurp, snifter, spot, suck, swallow, swig, tot

2 *v To inhale cocaine*

blow, blow Charley, blow coke, get your nose cold, go on a sleigh ride, horn, kiss, scoop, see Steve, short, sniff, snowmobile, snozzle, toot, whiff

snow

v To deceive, esp with smooth persuasion; mislead

bamboozle, blow smoke, [Brit] bowl a googly, buffalo, deal from the bottom of the deck, diddle, dipsy-doodle, do a number, do a snow job, double shuffle, fake out, fast-shuffle, fast talk, flimflam, give a bum steer, give someone a line, give someone the business, have someone on, hornswoggle, humbug, hustle, hype, jerk someone's chain, jerk someone's string, kid, play for a sucker, pull a fast one, pull someone's chain, pull one's leg, pull someone's string, pull the wool over someone's eyes, put it over on, put someone on, put one over, rattle someone's chain, rope in, run a game, run a number, sell a bill of goods, slicker, snooker, snow-job, spoof, string along, sucker, take for a ride, take in, throw a curve, throw curves, use smoke and mirrors

☞ *These terms share semantic territory with those at "con," which should also be considered.*

snuff

v To kill; murder

blast, blot, blot out, blow away, blow out, bump, bump off, burn, burn down, bury, bushwhack, chill, clip, cut down, cut off, do in, drop, dry-gulch, dump, erase, finish off, fix, frag, get, give the business, give the heat, give the works, go out in the country with, grease, gun down, hit, ice, iron out, knock off, lay out, liquidate, off, polish off, push, push across, push off, put away, put on ice, rub, rub out, scrag, send to kingdom come, send west, set over, settle, settle someone's hash, snuff out, spoil, take care of, take for a ride, take off, take out, waste, wipe out, zap, zing

soap opera
n phr A radio or television daily dramatic series showing the painful, passionate, and riveting amours and disasters of more or less ordinary people

soap, soaper, sudser, suds scenario, washtub weeper

sock
1 *v To strike, esp with the fist; punch, as in "The dispute got serious when she socked him"*

bang, bash, belt, biff, blap, blast, boff, bonk, bop, brain, bust, clip, clock, clonk, clout, club, clunk, coldcock, conk, cork, crack, crown, ding, duke, dust, dust someone's jacket, fire on, give five to, give it to, give someone the works, go upside someone's face, go upside someone's head, hammer, hang a left on, hang a right on, haul off and land one, haul off on, hit on, hit upside someone's face, hit upside someone's head, hit someone where he (or she) lives, knock someone's block off, land a haymaker, land one, larrup, lather, lay one on, let someone have it, lower the boom, nail, paste, plant one on, poke, pop, pot, put the slug on, rock, rock and sock, slam, slug, smack, smear, soak, swat, tag, tan, thump, thwack, wallop, whack, wham, whang, whomp, whop ☞ *Many of these terms share semantic territory with "clobber," which should also be considered.*

2 *n A blow, esp with the fist; a punch*

bam, bang, bash, belt, biff, blap, bloop, blooper, bolo, bonk, bop, bust, clip, clout, crack, ding, haymaker, jab, klop in the chops, knock, knuckle sandwich, lam, the leather, lick, poke, pop, pow, roundhouse, shot, slam, smack, smash, swack, swat, swipe, thump, thwack, wallop, whack, wham, whop, zetz

3 SEE **KNOCK**

softie
n A person who is amiably compliant

easy mark, old softie, pushover, soft touch, squish
☞ *A "softie" is not a "dupe" or "patsy," but a kind person who wishes to please.*

soft-pedal
v To make less prominent; de-emphasize

belittle, play down, pull one's punches

soft soap
n phr Flattery; cajolement

applesauce, banana oil, blarney, bull, butter, eyewash, grease, grease job, oil, salve, soap, sweet talk

soft-soap
1 v To flatter; cajole, as in "We all started soft-soaping him about his speech"

blarney, build someone up, bull, bullshit someone, butter someone up, dish out the applesauce, dish out the baloney, fatmouth, feed someone a line, give someone a grease job, grease, honey up, lay it on thick, lay it on with a trowel, schmear, scratch someone's back, shoot someone a line, spread it on thick, sweeten someone up, sweet-talk

2 SEE **STROKE**

southpaw
n A left-handed person

cockeye, forkhander, lefty, portsider, sidewheeler, wrongarmer

so what
interj An
exclamation of
indifference, as in
"So you got a bonus
check, so what"

big deal, do tell, hoo-ha, so what else is new, what else is new, you wouldn't shit me

spare tire
n phr A usu fatty
surplus about the
waist

bulge, corporation, love handles, middle-age spread

specs
n Spectacles

cheaters, glims, goggles, windows

spell out
1 *v phr To explain;*
clarify, as in "I
didn't get it the first
time, so they spelled
it out for me"

break something down, brief, bring someone up to speed, clue, clue in, connect the dots, cue someone in, cut a take, cut it up, decode, draw a map, draw a picture, fill someone in, kick apart, lay out, poop someone up, put in plain English, [Brit] put someone in the picture, put in words of one syllable, run down, sort out, straighten someone out

2 *v phr To make*
precise; specify
clearly, as in "Next
we must spell out
the exact terms of
what you get"

button down, nail down

split
v To leave; depart

air out, amscray, ankle, ankle along, bag ass, bail, beat it, blast off, blaze, blow, blow away, boogie, book, book it, boot and saddle, bop off, breeze, breeze off, broom, bugger off, bug out, bunk, burn, burn rubber, butt out, buzz, buzz off, catch one's lid, chase oneself, chase along, check out, cheese it, clear out, clock out, cruise, cut, cut a, cut and run, cut ass, cut out, diddy now, dig out, drag ass, drag one's freight, drag it, duck out, dust, ease, ease on out, ease out, fade, fade away, fade out, flake off, fly the coop, fuck off, get going, get lost, get moving, get off the block, get off the dime, get on one's horse, get the hell out, git, go south, haul one's ashes, haul ass, haul it, head out, highball, hightail, hightail it, hike, hit out, hit the bricks, hit the road, hit the trail, hoof, hoof it, hook it, hop it, lam, light, light out, make like a banana split, make like a paper doll and cut out, make like a sheepherder, make like a tree and leave, make oneself scarce, make tracks, mosey, mosey along, nix out, patch out, peel out, [esp Brit] piss off, pop off, powder, pull one's freight, pull out, punch out, rabbit, rabbit-foot, ramble, rip off, [Brit] scarper, scoot, scram, screw, set sail, shag, shag ass, shemozzle, shove off, shuffle along, skate, skedaddle, skiddoo, skin out, skip, skip out, sky out, sky up, slide, slope, split the scene, take a douche, take a hike, take a powder, take a runout powder, take it on the lam, take off, take off like a bat out of hell, take off like a bigass bird, toddle along, toddle off, trot, truck, truck along, up stakes, vamoose, waltz off, warp out

☞ *Most of these, in the imperative, serve as more or less brusque commands.*

spoof

1 *v To lampoon, as in, "They loved to spoof his dancing style"*

send up

2 SEE **KID**

3 SEE **SNOW**

spook
1 *v To frighten;*
scare

bring scunnion, bring smoke, funk, give a turn, give the shakes, scare shitless, scare spitless, scare stiff, scare the hell out of, scare the life out of, scare the pants off of, scare the shit out of, scare to death, scare witless

2 SEE **NIGGER**

spotlight
v To single out
prominently;
emphasize

brightline, feature, give top billing to, headline, highlight, play up, shout up

square
1 *adj Conventional*
and conformistic in
behavior and
attitudes

Barbie-Doll, bogus, burbed-out, buttondown, buttoned down, clonish, drippy, drizzly, droid, four-square, fuddy-dud, fuddy-duddy, gray-flannel, groovy, hung-up, icky, Ken, kosher, L7, lame, plastic, ranky dank, squaresville, squeaky-clean, straight, straight-arrow, stuffy, swingin', uncool, unhep, unhipped, whitebread, white-bready, Wonder Bread

2 *n A conventional*
and conformistic
person

Babbitt, Barbie Doll, citizen, clone, clyde, cornball, cube, drip, drizzle, drizzlepuss, droid, Elk, flat hoop, flat tire, four-square, fuddy-dud, fuddy-duddy, jeff, Ken, nine-to-fiver, shim, Zelda, zoid

square deal
n phr Fair and
equal treatment;
honest dealing

even break, fair shake, good deal

squeal

v To be an informer, esp for the police; tattle, as in "He thought he'd gotten away with it, but his friend squealed"

beef, belch, blab, blow, blow the gaff, blow the whistle, canary, chirp, dime, drop a dime, drop the dime, eat cheese, finger someone, fink, go stool, holler, leak, mark, mouth on someone, nark, peach, put the claw on someone, put the finger on someone, rat, rat on, sell out, sing, sing out, snitch, spill one's guts, spill the beans, squawk, stool, talk, tell tales out of school, trick, weasel

squeezebox

n An accordion

groanbox, pushbox, stomach Steinway, windbox

stake someone to

v phr To give to someone, esp as a treat or gift, as in "Her dad staked her to a new car when she graduated"

blow someone to, come through with, deal out, dish out, dole out, hand out, slip someone, spot someone, stand someone

stall

v To delay; temporize; procrastinate

beat around the bush, buy time, drag one's feet, hem and haw, hold off, play for time, pussyfoot, stall around, stall for time, stooge around, tap-dance, waffle

standoff

n A balanced contest; a stalemate; a deadlock

dead heat, Mexican standoff, photo finish, six of one and half a dozen of the other, toss, toss-up, wash

stanza

n A period, an inning, a round, or some other division of a game or bout

canto, chapter, chukker, frame, heat, session, verse, waltz

stash
v To conceal; store or hoard, as in "I stashed my money in a safe place"

rathole, sock away, squirrel, squirrel away, stash away

stick it
1 *interj An exclamation of defiance at something offered or suggested, as in "He can take his apology and stick it"*
2 SEE **FUCK YOU**

cram it, put it in one's ear, ram it, shove it, stow it, stuff it

☞ *These expressions may be intensified by adding "up one's ass" or "in one's ear" or "where the sun doesn't shine."*

stick one's **neck out**
v phr To put oneself at risk; invite trouble, as in "If you tell them the truth you'll be sticking your neck out"

ask for it, chance it, go out on a limb, lead with one's chin, put one's ass on the line, stretch one's luck, take a flyer

stick out like a sore thumb
v phr To be very conspicuous; stand out starkly

be as plain as the nose on your face, be plain as a pikestaff, glare, hang out, have a high profile, hit one in the eye, shout, speak for itself, stare one in the face, stick out all over, stick out a mile

stick to one's
knitting
v phr To attend
strictly to one's own
affairs; not meddle

butt out, keep hands off, keep one's nose out, keep off the grass, leave it be, let sleeping dogs lie, let well enough alone, mind one's own business

sticky-fingered
adj Inclined to
steal; larcenous

light-fingered

stiff
n A corpse

crowbait, dead meat, fly-bait, goner, worm-food

stir-crazy
adj Insane,
stuporous,
hysterical, or
otherwise affected
mentally by
imprisonment

coop-happy, stir-bugs, stir-daffy, stir-simple

stone
1 *adv Utterly;*
totally
2 SEE
HONEST-TO-GOD

clean, dead, deadass, flat-ass, from A to Z; lock, stock, and barrel; plum, plumb, teetotally, wall-to-wall

straight
1 *adj Legitimate;*
honest and proper

by the book, clean, [Australian] dinkum, fair and square, kosher, legit, on the legit, on the level, on the square, on the up-and-up, square, straight-arrow, up-and-up, up front

2 *adj Honest and*
reliable; upright

frontal, legit, on the legit, on the level, on the square, on the up-and-up, out-front, straight-ahead, straight-

	arrow, straight from the shoulder, straight-shooting, straight-up, up-and-up, up-front
3 *n A person who does not use narcotics*	apple, brown shoes, do-righter, John, lame duck, square, square apple
4 *n A heterosexual man*	breeder, citizen, vanilla
5 *adj Heterosexual*	right-handed
6 SEE SQUARE	

the **straight dope**

| *n phr The truth; the unvarnished facts* | chapter and verse, [Brit] the gen, the gospel, the gospel truth, the honest-to-God truth, the lowdown, the pif, the scam, the skinny, the straight goods, the straight of it, the straight poop, the straight scoop, the straight skinny, straight talk, the veritable cack, warts and all, where it's at, the whole story |

stripper

| *n A strip-tease dancer* | ecdysiast, grinder, peeler |

stroke

1 *v To compliment; flatter and comfort, as in "Just stroke them a little, and they'll tend to agree with you"*	give warm fuzzies, massage someone's ego, soft-soap
2 *n Comforting and flattering praise; what one wants to hear*	ego massage, soft soap, sweet talk, warm fuzzies
3 SEE JACK OFF	

229

stuck-up
adj Haughty and conceited; snobbish

bigheaded, blown up, chesty, cocky, hatty, high-hat, high-hatty, hincty, hincty-ass, puffed up, stuck on oneself, swelled up, swellheaded, too big for one's britches, uppity

stud
1 *n A sexually promiscuous and prodigious man*

Casanova, chaser, cocksman, Don Juan, gash hound, heavycake, horndog, horny bastard, hot-nuts, hound dog, jelly-roll, lover-boy, make-out artist, masher, meathound, pistol Pete, rooster, skirt-chaser, stallion, studhammer, tom-cat, wolf, woman-chaser

2 SEE DUDE
3 SEE LADIES' MAN

suck
1 *v To be disgusting or extremely reprehensible; be of wretched quality, as in "This play really sucks"*

blow, rot, smell, stink, stink on ice, stink to high heaven, suck eggs, suck rope

2 SEE BLOW

sucker
1 *n Any specified object, esp one that is prodigious, troublesome, effective, etc, as in "He just couldn't get that sucker working"*

baby, bastard, bugger, cocksucker, fucker, momma, mother, motherfucker
☞ *It is odd to find only one overtly affectionate term in this cluster.*

2 SEE PATSY

sugar daddy
n phr A man who provides money, esp one who supports a mistress

daddy, John, old man, poppa, Santa Claus, sugar papa

Sunday punch
n phr A very hard blow

blockbuster, dynamite punch, haymaker, jolt, kayo, kayo shot, money punch, payoff punch, powerhouse punch

swabby
n A US Navy sailor

bluejacket, gob

swank
n Elegance; stylishness, as in "She took him to dinner at a place with lots of swank"

class, high tone, ritz, snazz, spiff

sweat
v To worry; fret

fuss, graum, lose sleep, stew

swell
1 *n An aristocrat; a rich and important person*
2 SEE GREAT

blue-blood, high-hat, nob, [Brit] toff, upper-cruster

swing
1 *v To be sexually promiscuous*
2 SEE FUCK

play musical beds, shack up, sleep around

swivet

n A fit of angry agitation, as in "He had a swivet when he realized they'd lost"

blowoff, blowup, catfit, conniption fit, duckfit, lather, pucker, snit, state, stew, tizzy, [Brit] wax, wingding

T

tab
n A promise to pay;   IOU, marker
written acknowl-
edgment of a debt

tail
1 *n A person who*   plaster, shadow, shagger
follows another for
surveillance
2 SEE ASS

take
n The proceeds of   gate, gross, handle, haul, loot, score
an event,
performance, period
of operation, etc, as
in "Our take this
quarter won't even
cover our costs"

take a beating
v phr To suffer a financial loss, esp to go bankrupt

be whitewashed, be wiped out, crack up, do an el foldo, drop a bundle, get it in the neck, go broke, go down for the count, go on the rocks, go to the cleaners, go to the wall, go under, take a bath, take it on the chin, tap out ☞ *These terms share semantic territory with "go ker-flooey," which should also be considered.*

take a crack at
v phr To make an attempt; have a try

get one's feet wet, give a fling, give a go, give a whirl, go at, have a crack, have a go, have a rip, have a ripple, have a shot, have a whack, make a stab, take a lick

take a dive
v phr To lose a prize-fight or other contest intentionally

dive, go in the tank, tank, throw

take care of numero uno
v phr To be primarily concerned with one's own profit, security, etc, as in "She doesn't worry about anyone else, she just takes care of numero uno"

feather one's nest, line one's nest, take care of number one

take someone down a peg
v phr To deflate or reduce, esp a pompous or vainglorious person

bring down, cut down to size, cut off at the knees, cut off someone's water, knock someone off his (or her) perch, prick someone's balloon, put a tuck in someone's tail, put someone's nose out of joint, put the skids to, send away with a flea in his (or her) ear, settle someone's hash, take down a notch, take the shine out of, take the starch out of, take the wind out of someone's sails, tell where to get off, tell where to head in, turn off someone's water

take it
v phr To accept and endure what one has deserved or pledged, as in "He can dish out abuse when it's called for but he sure can't take it"

bite the bullet, face the music, face up to it, grin and bear it, hang tough, hunker down, stand for it, stand the gaff, stand up and be counted, stay the course, stay the pace, stick it out, stick with it, take heat, take it on the chin, take it standing up, take one's lumps, take one's medicine, take the rap, tough it out

take on
v phr To challenge and oppose; accept combat with

buck, cross, go eyeball to eyeball with, go one on one with, go to bat against, go toe to toe with, go up against, stand up to, take a run at

talk someone into
v phr To persuade; actively influence

con, high-pressure, hook in, iggle, jaw, jawbone, pressure, sell, sell on, twist someone's arm

tan
1 *v To thrash; punish by spanking*

baste, burn someone's tail, dust someone's britches, dust someone's jacket, dust someone's pants, dust someone's trousers, fan someone's tail, give a dose of strap oil, lambaste, larrup, lather, paddle, paddlewhack, swinge, take it out of someone's hide, take the strop to, take to the woodshed, tan someone's hide, warm someone's seat, whale

2 SEE **SOCK**

tear-jerker
n A sentimental story, movie, song, etc

hard-luck story, sob story, sob stuff, tale of woe, weeper, weepie

tech
n A technician or engineer

techie, toolie

teenybopper
n A teenager or preteenager; an adolescent

bubble-gummer, the bubblegum set, grommet, teen, teener, the teen tribe, teenybop, teeny-rocker, tween-ager

that's the way the cookie crumbles
sentence Such is life; such are the mysterious ways of fate

c'est la vie, go figure, so what else is new, that's life, that's show biz, that's show business, that's the luck of the draw, that's the way the ball bounces, there you are, there you go, welcome to the club, what goes around comes around, win a few lose a few, you can't win them all

threads
n Clothing; dress

drapes, duds, fig, get-up, rags, rig-out, set of drapes, set of threads, togs, trappings, turnout, vines, weeds

ticker
n The heart

old ticker, pump, pumper

tickled
adj Pleased, as in "I was tickled that they had asked me"

happy as a clam, [Brit] happy as a sandboy, happy as can be, pleased as Punch, stoked, tickled pink, tickled silly, tickled to death, tickled to pieces

tightwad
n A parsimonious person; a miser

cheapskate, nickel-nurser, nickel-squeezer, penny-pincher, piker, pinchgut, pinchpenny, Scotsman, Scrooge

tin
n A police officer's badge

button, buzzer, potsy

tip
n A piece of information, as in "The cops got a tip about a drug deal"

hot tip, pointer, steer, tipoff

tits
1 *n A woman's breasts*

apples, bags, bazongas, bazooms, bazoonjies, big brown eyes, boobies, boobs, breastworks, cans, chi-chi, coconuts, globes, headlights, hooters, jugs, knockers, lungs, mangoes, maracas, melons, muffins, pair, snorbs, titties

2 SEE GREAT

toddle
v To walk, as in "After the party she toddled home"

amble, ankle, ankle along, bop, diddy-bop, ease, foot it, go by ankle express, hike, hit the sidewalk, hoof, hoof it, hoss it, leg it, march, mosey, mosey along, ooze, pad, percolate, pound the pavement, press the bricks, ride shank's mare, ride shank's pony, sashay, shag, shank it, shuffle, stump it, traipse, waltz

toke
1 *n A sucking or inhalation of a lighted cigarette, cigar, etc, esp a marijuana cigarette*

drag, puff, pull

2 SEE **BUTT**

Tommy gun
n phr A submachine gun

burp gun, chopper, typewriter

tootsies
n The feet

barkers, dogs, footsies, footsie-wootsies, hoofs, pedal extremities, puppies, pups, tootsie-wootsies, trotters

top-kick
n A first sergeant

first man, first shirt, first soldier, top, top sergeant

total
v To wreck; ruin, as in "She totaled the car not five minutes from home"

pile up, rack up, smack up, smash up, stack up, trash, waste, wipe out

tough
adj Severe and uncompromising; pugnacious and menacing, as in "Don't try any monkey business with them, they are very tough people"

butch, hard, hard as nails, hard-ass, hard-assed, hard-nose, hardnosed, hard-rock, kick-ass, raw, rough-ass, shit-kicking, stompass

tough shit
sentence That's bad luck; that's a shame   tough break, tough luck, tough nibs, tough noogies, tough rocks, tough tiddy, tough titty, TS

trendy
adj Following new trends in fashion, art, literature, etc; anxiously au courant   faddy, go-go, a go-go, hep, in, up-to-datey, with it

the tube
n Television; a television set   boob tube, eye, idiot box, one-eyed monster, [Brit] telly, video

umpty-umpth
adj Of a large and unspecified ordinal number, as in "I promised for the umpty-umpth time"

jillionth, umptieth, zillionth

Uncle Sam
n phr The US Government

Mister Whiskers, Uncle Sammy, Uncle Sugar, Uncle Whiskers

undies
n Underwear

drawers, skivvies, unmentionables

up front
1 *adv phr In advance; before any deductions or further payments, as in "She said she would want half her fee up front"*

in front, off the top

2 SEE **STRAIGHT**

the **upper crust**
n phr The social aristocracy; the elite

the best people, the blue-bloods, the class, the classes, the cream, the First Families, the four hundred, the high-hats, the nobs, the quality, the smart set, the swells

upstairs
adv In the brain or mind; mentally, as in "She was a little feeble upstairs"

brain-wise, in the noodle, in the upper story

up the creek
adj phr In trouble; beleaguered; in a dilemma

between a rock and a hard place, between the devil and the deep blue sea, in a corner, in a fix, in a hole, in a hot place, in a hot spot, in a jam, in a mess, in a mess of trouble, in a pickle, in a pinch, in a tight corner, in a tight hole, in a tough spot, in deep doo-doo, in deep shit, in deep trouble, in deep water, in Dutch, in over one's head, in the soup, jammed up, on the hot seat, on the spot, out of one's depth, out on a limb, painted into a corner, stymied, sucking canal water, under the gun, up against it, up shit creek, up shit creek without a paddle, up to one's ass in alligators, up to one's ass in rattlesnakes

up to one's **ass**
adj phr Overwhelmed; oversupplied; surfeited

asshole deep, awash in, knee deep, rolling in, snowed under, swimming in, up to one's ass in alligators, up to one's ass in rattlesnakes, up to one's eyeballs, up to one's eyebrows, up to here

up to here
adv phr In great quantity; to a surfeit, as in "I've taken insults up to here, and that's enough" and then some, coming out one's ears, till one can taste it, to spare, up the ass, up the kazoo, up to the eyeballs, up to the eyebrows

V

vanilla
adj Unadorned;   plain vanilla, your basic
simple; basic, as in
"It was a vanilla
treatment of a very
complex matter"

vibes
n What emanates   chemistry, karma, vibrations
from a person,
situation, etc,
inherently, and is
especially felt
between persons, as
in "She and I shared
vibes right from the
first"

W

walk

1 *v To break off negotiations, a relationship, etc, as in "The delegates said they'd walk if that rule went in"*

take a walk, walk out

2 *v phr To go on strike*

hit the bricks, stage a walkout, walk out

walk out on

v phr To abandon or relinquish, as in "They walked out on the project before it really had a chance"

break off, chuck, cut one's losses, drop, duck out on, give the kiss off, kiss off, leave flat, leave in the lurch, leave out in the cold, quit cold, run out on, skip out on, take a walk, throw over, throw overboard, toss up, waltz out on

warble

v To sing

belt out, canary, chirp, croon, groan, line out, pipe, wail, yodel

☞ *This list does not distinguish types or styles of singing.*

warm body
n phr A person regarded as merely such

anything that breathes, bench-warmer, chair-warmer, cipher, nebbish

way to go
interj An exclamation of delighted congratulation

attaboy, attagirl, aw right, congrats, go man go, good deal, good shit, hey, looking good, nice going, right on, take a bow, that'll do it, that's my boy, that's my girl

weasel
v To evade and equivocate; use deceptive language, as in "I asked him to help, but he just stood there weaseling"

duck, duck and weave, hem and haw, sidestep, tap dance, [Brit] waffle

weird
adj Abnormal in a sinister way; alarmingly strange

creepy, double-gaited, far out, fruity, funny, kinky, oddball, off the wall, psycho, queer, sick, sicko, sickroom, sicksicksick, spazzy, strangioso, wacko, wacky, way out, weird-ass, wigged out, wiggy, zerking

☞ *These terms share semantic territory with "flaky" and "crazy," which should also be considered.*

whammy
n The evil eye; a crippling curse

double whammy, hex, the Indian sign, jinx, triple whammy

what's-his-name
n An unspecified or unspecifiable person

what's-his-ass, what's-his-face, whoozis, whoozit

what's up
sentence What is happening; what is the question, problem, etc

buzza, hello Joe whaddaya know, sappnin, what cooks, what do you say, what gives, what goes, what say, what's been shaking, what's buzzin' cousin, what's cooking, what's doing, what's going down, what's happening, what's shaking, what's the deal, what's the dope, what's the good word, what's the scam, what's up doc, wuzzup, zup

wheeler-dealer
n A person busy with many affairs, esp officiously and conspiratorially

big macher, big shot, big-time operator, ganze macher, macher, operator, wire-puller

when the chips are down
adv phr When the time of decision or confrontation has come, as in "He always turns and runs when the chips are down"

in a pinch, in the clutch, in the crunch, in the squeeze, when it comes to the short strokes, when push comes to shove, when the balloon goes up, when the chips are on the table

where one is at
n phr One's viewpoint or attitudes; one's value system, as in "We must get the criminal justice system working, that's where I'm at"

where one's head is at, where one is coming from

white shoe
n phr A typical Ivy League student

Joe Yale, key, shoe, white buck

whitey
n A white person; a Caucasian

(all black unless otherwise labeled) [Latino] Anglo, blue-eyed devil, bright skin, buckra, Charley, Chuck, dap, devil, face, fay, [Chinese] ghost, gray, hack, hardhead, hay-eater, hincty, honky, jeff, kelt, keltch, maggot, the Man, marshmallow, Mr Charley, Mr Eddie, ofay, paddy, pale, paleface, patty, peck, peckerwood, pink, silk, vanilla, white meat, wood, yakoo

the whole shebang
n phr Everything; the totality

the boodle, the business, the devil and all, the kit and boodle, the kit and caboodle; lock, stock, and barrel; the megillah, the schmear, the shebang, the shooting match, the smear, the whole bag of tricks, the whole ball of wax, the whole business, the whole enchilada, the whole kit and caboodle, the whole megillah, the whole nine yards, the whole schmear, the whole shooting match, the whole show, the whole works, the works, you name it

whomp up
1 v phr To make, devise, or build, esp hastily; improvise, as in "I'm sure we can whomp up something for dinner"
2 SEE **COOK UP**

bash out, bat out, [Brit] cobble together, fake up, hammer out, rig up, whip out

whorehouse
n A brothel

call house, call joint, cathouse, crib, house of ill fame, house of ill repute, joy house, juke house, maison joie, massage parlor, notcherie, notch-house, rap club, rub parlor, sporting house

wimp
n An ineffectual person; a soft, silly person; a weakling

baby, big baby, bimbo, candy ass, Caspar Milquetoast, chicken, cookie-pusher, cream puff, cry baby, daisy, doormat, drip, drone, drool, dweeb, Ethel, feather-weight, flower, fraidy-cat, goody-goody, gutless wonder, ho-dad, jellyfish, jerk, lily, limp-dick, limp dishrag, lizzy, loser, mama's boy, milktoast, Milquetoast, neb, nebbish, nervous Nellie, nobody, nothing, ook, panty-waist, Percy, puppy, pushover, pussycat, putz, sad apple, sad sack, scaredy-cat, schlemiel, schmendrick, schmo, tootie fruity, turkey, weak sister, wuss, wussy
☞ *These terms share semantic territory with "light-weight" and "sissy," which should also be considered.*

wimpish
adj Weak and soft; effeminate; timorous, as in "The voters tend to despise wimpish responses"

candy-ass, candy-assed, chicken-hearted, chicken-liv-ered, drippy, gutless, lily-livered, milk-livered, mousy, pansified, paper-assed, rabbity, sissified, soft-ass, wimpo, wimpoid, wimpy

wing
n An arm

fin, flapper, flipper, fluke, soupbone

wingding
n A party or other usu noisy celebration

bash, [Brit] bean-feast, blast, blowoff, blowout, brawl, bust, clambake, [Brit] do, fest, festa, fiesta, fight, get-together, gig, hoedown, hoodang, hoo-ha, jamboree, jollification, kick-up, rally, [esp Brit] rave-up, ruckus, rumpus, shindig, shindy, struggle, whoopdedoo, wing, wingdinger

wing it
v phr To improvise; extemporize, as in "I didn't know all my lines, so I had to wing it some"

ad lib, cheek it, fake, fake it, play it by ear, shuck, vamp, vamp till ready, wing

win the porcelain hairnet
v phr To deserve a spectacularly useless reward; merit nothing but something absurd, as in "For that brilliant idea you win the porcelain hairnet"

win the barbwire garter, win the cast-iron overcoat, win the fur-lined bathtub, win the hand-painted door-mat, win the solid gold chamber pot

wise me up
sentence Tell me what you know

beam me aboard, beam me aboard Scotty, bring me up to speed, clue me in, [Brit] put me in the picture
☞ *Other such requests may be framed by using terms under "spell out."*

wise up
v phr To become shrewdly aware; apprehend reality

be beamed aboard, get next, get next to oneself, get smart, get the message, get the picture, get wise, get wise with oneself, get with it, pull your head out, pull your head out of your asshole, smarten up, tie one's shoes, use one's bean, use one's head, use one's noodle

with flying colors
adv phr In a bold and assured way; grandly, as in "She didn't just win, she won with flying colors"

high, wide, and handsome; in a walk, in spades, never looking back, with a bang, with bells on, with knobs on, without mussing a hair, with tits on

with it
adj phr Cognizant; in touch; stylish and au courant, as in "Whatever the now trend is, I'm not with it"

alive with the jive, cool, down with it, go-go, groovy, hep, hepped, hep to the jive, hip, hipped, in the groove, into it, jivey, light, mellow, mod, on the ball, on the beam, plugged in, really into it, right there, sharp, solid, state of the art, switched on, there, trendy, turned on, wise

the woods are full of something
sentence The thing indicated is in plentiful supply, as in "The woods are full of stand-up comics these days"

they are a dime a dozen, they are cut-rate, they are going for peanuts, they are thick on the ground, we have them and then some, we have them coming out our ears, we have them to burn, we have them to spare, we have them up the kazoo

wop
n An Italian or person of Italian extraction

dago, dino, Eytie, ginzo, greaseball, greaser, Guinea, spaghetti, walyo
☞ *These terms will give deep offense if used by persons outside the ethnic group.*

work
v To succeed; come to fruition

click, come off, fly, gel, get off the ground, get to first base, go over, make it, play, play in Peoria, swim, take fire, take off, work out

working stiff

n phr An ordinary working person

prole, stiff

work out

v phr To amend, repair, finish, etc, by careful effort, as in "It doesn't look promising, but we can work it out"

iron out, sort out

works

n The apparatus for injecting or otherwise using narcotics

artillery, bayonet, Bay State, biz, bong, boojie, cannon, collar, cook, cooker, cooking spoon, cotton, dinghiyen, dingus, dope gun, dripper, dropper, energy gun, engine, factory, fake, fakealoo, fit, G, gasket, gimmick, gimmicks, glass, glass gun, gun, hard nail, harpoon, head kit, hit spike, hop gun, horse and wagon, hype stick, ickey, jabber, Job's antidote, Johnson and Johnson, joint, kit, layout, light artillery, luer, machine, machinery, monkey drill, monkey pump, Mr Twenty-six, nail, needle, outfit, pin gun, point, prick, quill, rig, safety, satch cotton, set, sharp, spike, spike and dripper, spike and jolt, spoon, stabber, stem, tie, tools, Yale

☞ *This list does not take account of the various types and purposes of apparatus.*

☞ *The great number of slang terms for narcotics probably reflects both a need for coded reference to an illegal substance and a desire to be chic and up-to-date, in addition to the need to distinguish varieties.*

wow

v To delight extremely; impress powerfully and favorably, as in "She really wowed the opening-night audience"

bowl over, carve, choke someone up, crack them up, fracture, give a bang, give a boot, glaze someone over, go over, go over big, go over in a big way, go over like a million bucks, kill, knock someone cold, knock someone dead, knock someone for a loop, knock someone's lights out, knock someone out, knock someone's socks off, lay someone in the aisles, lay someone low, mow someone down, murder, put someone away, ring someone's bell, send, slaughter, slay, tickle the piss out of, tickle the shit out of, turn someone on

wrap up

v phr To complete; finish, as in "Let's wrap up this deal and go to lunch"

be through with, button up, call in one's chips, call it a day, call it quits, clean up, close out, close up, drop the curtain, fold up, mop up, pack in, pack up, polish off, put in the box, put the lid on, ring down the curtain, sew up, tie up, wind up, wrap

yap
1 *n The mouth* bazoo, chaps, chops, clam shells, clam trap, fish trap, flytrap, gills, gob, head, kisser, kissing trap, mug, mush, talk-trap, tater trap, trap

2 SEE **GAB**
3 SEE **JERK**

young squirt
n phr An adolescent poot-butt, punk, punk-kid, pup, snotnose, squirt, young
male; a youth punk

yours truly
pron phr I; me; little me, little old me; me, myself, and I; my lonesome,
myself, as in "Yours your Uncle Dudley
truly will take care
of that"

yuck
interj An exclamation of disgust and revulsion, as in "Yuck, did you see that he was eating pickles with ice cream?"

barf me out, ech, eeyuck, feh, gross me out, phew, ugh, yecch

yucky
adj Disgusting; loathsome

the armpits, Barf City, barfy, bletcherous, bogue, bum, cheesy, cocksucking, crapoid, crappy, crasty, creepy, creepy-crawly, cruddy, crummy, dirty, disgusto, fucking, fungus-faced, funky, gee, goat-smelling, godawful, greeby, grim, grody, gross, grotty, groudy, grungy, hairy, icky, messy, nasty, the pits, pukey, putrid, ratty, raunchy, rotchy, rotten, scroungy, scumsucking, scuzzy, shitty, sick, sicko, sicksicksick, skanky, sleaze-bag, sleazeball, sleaze-bucket, sleazo, sleazoid, sleazy, stinking, suck-off, tacky, vomitrocious, vomity, wormy, yecchy, Yucko City, zooey

Z

zero in
v phr To aim at or concentrate on a specific thing, person, etc; single out, as in "You have to zero in on the problem before you can start to solve it"

draw a bead, get down to cases, home in, narrow down on, pin down, pinpoint, spot, spotlight

zilch
1 *n Nothing; a minimal amount; an iota*

beans, Billy be damn, bubkes, a bucket of warm spit, [Brit] bugger-all, chopped liver, a damn, diddly, diddly-damn, diddly-poo, diddly-poop, diddly-shit, diddly-squat, diddly-squirt, diddly-whoop, dink, doodle-shit, doodly, doodly-shit, doodly-squat, dry spit on a hot day, a duck egg, a fart, a fig, a fuck, [Brit] fuck-all, a goose egg, a hill of beans, a hoot, a hooter, a hoot in hell, jack-shit, nada, nit, nix, one red cent, one thin dime, a plugged nickel, poo, poop, a rap, a rat's ass, a red cent, a row of pins, shit, a shit, shit-all, spit, squat, squirt, [Brit] sweet Fanny Adams, a thin dime, two hoots in hell, two whoops in hell, a whoop, zero, zip, zippo, zot, zotz

2 SEE ZIT

zingy
adj Full of energy and vigor

chipper, full of ginger, full of go, full of pep, full of piss and vinegar, gingery, gutsy, peppy, perky, punched-up, punchy, snappy, zappy, zippy

zit
n A minor skin lesion; a pimple; a blackhead

doohickey, goober, goophead, hickey, pip, zilch

zombie
n A mentally numb or dead person; a machinelike person

clone, plastic person, pod person

INDEX

Given a particular slang term or a concept in standard language, this index makes it possible to find the term's or the concept's slang synonyms in all their senses throughout the book.

In a typical index entry, the first line contains a slang word or phrase. Listed under it, in **boldface type,** are the main entries in the book where the word or phrase is cited as a synonym.

For example, the index entry for the slang word "ace" shows that "ace" appears in the book as a synonym for **angel dust, bingle, doll,** etc.

A second kind of index entry makes it possible to trace slang synonyms with only a concept in mind. These entries are headed by a nonslang term (for example, "agreement" and "body") and list the text entries where collections of synonyms express shades of this concept.

Finally, to make sure the index's coverage of the slang vocabulary is complete, all the main entry terms in the book appear in the index in their alphabetical positions. They may appear under an identical or near-identical head; **ace** is itself a main entry in the book, and this is signaled in the index entry by the appearance of the boldface **ace** with its three senses suggested. If there is no similar index head (as with **AC-DC**), the main entry term is given alone.

The index follows the same alphabetizing principles as the main text. In determining alphabetical position, the following were ignored: initial articles ("the," "a," and "an") and the nonspecific pronouns ("one," "one's," "oneself," "someone," "someone's," and "something"). For example, the index entry "throw someone a curve" immediately follows "throw a curve," and "one's head off" follows "headline."

A
  acid
  bennies
abandon
  walk out on
aboard
  in place
A-bomb
  hot rod
abort
  scrub
abroad
  in stir
absence
  play hooky
absorbed in
  into
absquatulate
  break out
abundant
  lousy with
the academy
  the slammer
Acapulco gold
  pot
accordion
  squeezebox
accuse
  hang on
AC-DC, "bisexual"
ace
  ace, "do well"
  ace, "expert"
  ace, "prison sentence"
  angel dust
  bingle
  doll
  good guy
  humdinger
  joint
  pal

ace-high
  great
ace in
  dig
ace in the hole
  case dough
ace it
  ace
  go over with a bang
aces
  great
  honest-to-God
  humdinger
achieve
  rack up
aching
  antsy
acid, "LSD"
acid funk
  bad trip
acidhead
  junkie
ack-ack
  horse
acquire
  grab
act, "imitation"
active person
  eager beaver
actor
  phony
act properly
  clean up one's act
addict
  junkie
addicted
  hooked
addlebrain
  ditz
  dope

addled
  ditsy
ad lib
  wing it
admire
  dig
Adonis
  hunk
adult movie
  blue movie
advance payment
  up front
affirmation
  OK
Afghani
  hash
aficionado
  fan
African black
  hash
Afro, "hair style"
Afro-Saxon
  fink
after-hours club
  blind pig
an age
  ages
agee
  cockeyed
aggravate
  bug
agony
  flak
agreement
  back out
  cut a deal
  on someone's wavelength
agricultural college
  cow college

A-hole
  asshole

aimies
  bennies

the air
  the axe

airbrain
  ditz
  dope

airbrained
  ditsy

airhead
  ditz
  dope

airheaded
  ditsy

air out
  split

airplane
  roach clip

alcohol
  beer bust
  binge
  blind pig
  booze
  brew
  gin mill
  guzzle
  have a load on
  lush
  on the sauce
  panther piss
  plastered
  the shakes
  snort

alert
  on the ball

alive with
  lousy with

alive with the jive
  with it

alkied
  plastered

alky
  booze

one's all
  best shot

all anyhow
  cockeyed
  fucked-up

all atwitter
  antsy

all bets are off
  it's a new ball game

alley cat
  floozy

all-fired
  damn

all hell breaks loose
  hell breaks loose

alligator
  dude

all in
  pooped

an all-nighter
  a bitch

all nohow
  cockeyed
  fucked-up

all of a doodah
  jittery

all one's got
  best shot

all out
  lickety-split
  flat-out

all-out try
  best shot

the all-overs
  the jitters

all shook up
  jittery

all shot
  pooped

all that jazz
  bullshit

all there
  cool

all the way
  flat-out

all thumbs
  ham-handed

all tied up
  in the bag

all washed up
  kaput

all wet
  full of shit

all wool and a yard wide
  honest-to-God

alma mammy
  collitch

aloof person
  cold fish

also-ran
  lightweight
  loser

alter kocker
  fogy
  old fart

alvin
  patsy

the amber brew
  brew

ambidextrous
  AC-DC

ambitious
  hungry

amble
  toddle

ambulance
  meat wagon

ambulance chaser
  shyster

amend
  work out

amen snorter
  Bible-banger

amoeba
  angel dust

amok
  high

amount
  little bitty
  scads
  shave
  smidgen

amp
  bennies

amphetamines
  bennies

amscray
  split

amuck
  high

amuse
  break someone up

amy
  bennies
  doll

Amy-John
  dyke

anchors
  binders

and then some
  up to here

angel
  angel, "patron"
  dish
  gay
  honey
  patsy

angelface
  dish
  honey

angel hair
  angel dust

anger
  blowup
  pissed off
  piss someone off
  piss-off

angle
  play games

Anglo
  whitey

Angola black
  pot

angry
  blow one's top

angry fit
  swivet

ankle
  split
  toddle

Annie Oakley, "free ticket"

annoy
  bug
  give someone a pain in the
    ass

annoyance
  nudnik

antagonize
  blow it with someone

the ante
  the damage

ante up
  cough up
  kick in
  pick up the tab

antifreeze
  horse

antigodlin
  cockeyed

antique
  fogy

antsy
  antsy, "excited"
  horny
  jittery

anus
  asshole

any person
  warm body

A-OK
  cool
  great

A-1
  great
  the most

apache
  hit man

ape
  crazy
  goon

aped
  plastered

apeshit
  crazy

apology
  excuse me all to hell

apparatus
  basket
  cock

apple
  cookie
  guy
  straight

apple butter
  bullshit

applehead
  dope

apple-knocker
  hick

apple-polish
  brown-nose

apples
  tits

applesauce
  bullshit
  izzatso
  line
  soft soap

approve
  buy

Arab
  camel-jammer

Archie Bunker
  redneck

aristocracy
  the upper crust

aristocrat
  swell

ark
  jalopy

Arky
  cracker
  hick

arm
  cop
  wing

armchair general
  bigmouth
  smart-ass

armed
  carry
  heeled

arm it
  ride the arm

the armpits
  the pits
  yucky

around the bend
  crazy

arrangement
  cut a deal

arrest
  bust
  fall

arrive
  show up

arse
  ass

arsy-varsy
  fucked-up

art
  mug shot

article
  cookie

the article
  humdinger
  the McCoy

artillery
  rod
  works

ashes
  pot

Asian
  gook

askew
  cockeyed

askewgee
  cockeyed

ask for it
  stick one's neck out

ass
  ass, "buttocks"
  ass, "sexual activity"
  ass, "the whole person"
  asshole
  jerk

ass around
  goof off

assassin
  hit man

ass backwards
  fucked-up

assfuck
  bugger

as shit, "very"

asshole, "anus"
asshole, "disliked person"

the asshole
  the pits

asshole buddy
  pal

asshole deep
  up to one's ass

one's ass is dragging
  pooped

ass-kisser
  brown-nose

associate
  hang out with

ass over tincups
  flat-out

ass peddler
  hooker

athlete
  jock

attaboy
  way to go

attack
  blast
  blind-side

attagirl
  way to go

attempt
  best shot
  a crack
  fish or cut bait
  a gamble
  give something a shot

take a crack at
  work
attend to
  fix someone
  kick ass
attic
  bean
attitude
  feisty
  have a hair up one's ass
  where one is at
attractive man
  hunk
  hunky
attractive woman
  dish
Aunt Hazel
  horse
auntie
  big O
Aunt Jane
  fink
Aunt Mary
  pot
Aunt Noral
  horse
Aunt Sally
  fink
Aurora Borealis
  angel dust
ausgespielt
  kaput
  on the blink
  pooped
authentic
  honest-to-God
authority
  in the driver's seat
available
  in place

average man
  Joe Blow
average woman
  Jane
avoid
  give a miss
avoid work
  goof off
avoirdupois
  blubber
awareness
  wise up
awash in
  lousy with
  up to one's ass
away
  in stir
awesome
  great
awful
  crummy
aw right
  way to go
axe
  chuck
  fire
  scrub
the axe, "dismissal"
ay caramba
  Jeez
the Aztec two-step
  the shits
azul
  cop
B
  bingle
b a
  bare-ass
Babbitt
  square

babbler
  blabbermouth
babe
  broad
  dish
  honey
baby
  broad
  cookie
  honey
  pot
  sucker
  wimp
baby blues
  peepers
baby doll
  broad
  honey
back, "support"
back-breaker, "hard job"
a back-breaker
  a bitch
back-chat
  sass
the back country
  the boondocks
back down
  back out
  fold
backed up
  high
backlog
  case dough
back off
  cool it
  get off someone's back
  lay off
back out
  back out, "renege"
  chicken out
  cop out

back porch
  ass
back-scratch
  brown-nose
back-scratcher
  brown-nose
back seat
  ass
backseat driver
  kibitzer
backside
  ass
back-slapper
  brown-nose
back-talk
  sass
back to the old drawing
    board
  it's a new ball game
back-track
  shoot up
back up
  back
  go to bat for
  shoot up
back way
  asshole
the backwoods
  the boondocks
bacon
  score
bad
  great
badass
  asshole
  bad man
  crummy
bad broad
  scarecrow
bad bundle
  horse

baddest
  great
baddie
  bad man
bad dude
  ladies' man
bad egg
  asshole
badge
  tin
bad hat
  bad man
bad head
  bad trip
bad hombre
  bad man
bad job
  asshole
bad lot
  asshole
bad luck
  tough shit
bad man, "villain"
bad medicine
  bad news
bad-mother swinger
  ladies' man
bad-mouth
  bad-mouth, "denigrate"
  knock
bad news, "trouble"
the bad news
  the damage
bad rap
  bum rap
bad scene
  bad news
  can of worms
a bad scene, "misfortune"

bad shit
  bad news
bad time
  cheat
bad trip
  a bad scene
  bad trip, "drug
      experience"
bag
  bag, "narcotics quantity"
  bag, "preference"
  bust
  chuck
  cut
  deck
  fire
  a fix
  floozy
  grab
  heist
  nix
  rubber
  scarecrow
  scrub
bag ass
  split
baggage
  floozy
bagged
  plastered
  pooped
bagger
  bingle
bag it
  knock off
  snooze
bag job
  heist
bag lady
  bum
bagman
  dealer

bag of wind
 bigmouth
 blabbermouth

bag of worms
 can of worms

bags
 tits

bag some Zs
 snooze

bag woman
 bum

bag your head
 shut up

bail
 split

baked
 high

bakehead
 dope

bald person
 baldie

bale of hay
 bag
 bundle
 deck

ball
 a fix
 fuck
 have a ball
 snort

a ball, "happy occasion"

ball-and-chain
 old woman

ballast
 potbelly

ball-buster
 back-breaker
 **ball-buster, "emasculating
  person"**

balled-up
 fucked-up

the ball game
 the bottom line

ballocks
 balls

ball of fire
 eager beaver
 hot shot

balloon
 bag
 deck
 fluff

balloonhead
 dope

balloon room
 dope den

balls
 balls, "testicles"
 bullshit
 guts
 izzatso

balls and bat
 basket

ballsiness
 guts

balls to the wall
 flat-out
 lickety-split

balls up
 screw up

balls-up
 boner
 snafu

ballsy
 gutsy

ball the jack
 barrel

ball up
 screw up

ball-wracker
 ball-buster

bally
 flack

ballyhoo
 flack

balmy
 crazy

baloney
 bullshit
 izzatso

balot
 horse

bam
 bennies
 joint
 pot
 pow
 smack
 sock

bambalacha
 hash
 pot

bambita
 bennies

bamboozle
 con
 snow

bamboozled
 hooked

bammy
 joint
 pot

bams
 bennies

banana
 cock

bananahead
 dope

banana oil
  bullshit
  soft soap
bananas
  crazy
bang
  blow grass
  clout
  dope
  a fix
  fuck
  a fuck
  a kick
  M
  pizzazz
  pot
  pow
  shoot up
  smack
  sock
bang-bang
  horse opera
banger
  banger, "engine cylinder"
  jalopy
bang on
  great
bangs
  kicks
bangster
  junkie
bang the bishop
  jack off
bang-up
  great
banjax
  clobber
bank bandit
  doll
bankroll
  angel
  bundle

bankruptcy
  take a beating
banty
  little bitty
bar
  bag
  deck
  gin mill
barb
  doll
barber
  blabbermouth
barbershop quartet
  Dutch rub
Barbie Doll
  square
barbiturate
  doll
bare-assed
  bare-ass
barf, "vomit"
Barf City
  the pits
  yucky
bar-fly
  lush
barfy
  yucky
bargain-basement
  schlocky
barge in
  butt in
bar-girl
  floozy
bar-hop
  paint the town red
barkers
  tootsies
barley broth
  brew

barmecide
  M
barmy
  crazy
barn-burner
  a hit
  humdinger
barney
  free-for-all
  hassle
barrel
  banger
barrel along
  barrel
barrel ass
  barrel
barrel house
  dive
barrelhouse bum
  bum
barrel of money
  bundle
base
  coke
baseball
  chapter
  homer
baseball hit
  bingle
bash
  a crack
  crummy
  sock
  wingding
bash out
  whomp up
basket
  basket, "male genitals"
  belly
basket case
  dope

Basra belly
 the shits

bassackwards
 fucked-up

bastard
 asshole
 back-breaker
 sucker

a bastard
 a bitch

baste
 tan

basted
 high
 plastered

the bastille
 the slammer

bat
 barrel
 binge
 hooker
 nut
 paint the town red
 scarecrow

bat around
 bat around, "discuss"
 goof off

bat carrier
 snitch

bat one's gums
 gab
 shoot the breeze

bathing beauty
 dish

the bat of a eye
 a jiffy

bat out
 whomp up

bats
 crazy

batter
 panhandle

battered
 beat-up

bat the breeze
 gab
 shoot the breeze

battle royal
 donnybrook
 free-for-all

batty
 crazy
 nut

bawl out
 chew out

bay
 pot

bayonet
 cock
 works

bayou blue
 panther piss

Bay State
 works

bay window
 potbelly

bazongas
 tits

bazoo
 schnozz
 yap

bazooms
 tits

bazoonjies
 tits

the beady eye
 the cold shoulder

beak
 schnozz

beaming
 high

beam me aboard
 wise me up

bean
 bean, "head"
 bean-eater
 bennies
 guy

bean-bandit
 bean-eater

bean counter, "clerk"

beaner
 bean-eater

beanery
 greasy spoon

bean-feast
 wingding

beanheaded
 dumb

beanpole, "tall person"

beans
 bennies
 bullshit
 dough
 zilch

beanstalk
 beanpole

bean stripe
 hash mark

bean wagon
 greasy spoon

bear
 humdinger

beard
 beaver

bearded clam
 cunt

bear down on
 chew out
 kick ass

bear hug
 clinch

beast
  acid
  scarecrow
beastly
  crummy
beasty
  scarecrow
beat
  beat, "surpass"
  broke
  con
  cool
  moocher
  pooped
beat all hollow
  beat
  clobber
beat around
  goof off
beat around the bush
  pussyfoot
  stall
beat one's chops
  gab
  shoot the breeze
beat one's dummy
  jack off
beaten
  high
beater
  jalopy
beat one's gums
  gab
  shoot the breeze
beat it
  break out
  split
beat off
  jack off
beat on
  rough up

beat out
  pooped
beat pad
  dope den
beat the bejesus out of
  clobber
beat the daylights out of
  clobber
beat the hell out of
  clobber
beat the hog
  jack off
beat the weeds
  blow grass
beat one's time
  beat
beat to the ground
  pooped
beat-up, "battered"
Beau Brummel
  dude
beaut
  dish
  humdinger
the beautiful people
  the jet set
beauty
  great
  humdinger
beauty queen
  dish
beauty sleep
  sack time
beaver
  beaver, "pubic hair"
  blue movie
  cunt
beddy
  dish
beddy-bye
  sack time

bedmate
  old woman
beef
  beef, "complain"
  beef, "complaint"
  blubber
  cock
  hassle
  squeal
the beef
  the damage
beefcake
  hunk
beefeater
  limey
beefer
  kvetch
  snitch
beef squad
  goon squad
beefwit
  dope
beef-witted
  dumb
a bee in one's bonnet,
    "obsession"
beep
  honk
beer
  brew
beer belly
  potbelly
beer party
  beer bust
beery
  corny
beetlebrain
  dope
beetleheaded
  dumb

beezer
  puss
  schnozz

beg
  bum
  panhandle

beggar's velvet
  dust bunny
  house moss

begin again
  go back to square one

beginning
  for openers
  from scratch

begorra
  Jeez

behavior
  flaky
  fly right
  play it safe

behind
  ass
  asshole

behind the cork
  plastered

behind the eight ball
  out of luck

beige
  dullsville

belay
  knock off
  scrub

belay that
  shut up

belch
  beef
  squeal

belfry
  bean

believe
  buy

belittle
  soft-pedal

bellow
  beef

bells and whistles
  gadgetry

belly, "stomach"

bellyache
  beef

bellyacher
  kvetch

belly-buster
  belly laugh
  belly-whopper

belly laugh, "laugh"

belly up
  croak
  go kerflooey
  kaput

belly-whopper
  belly laugh
  belly-whopper, "dive"

belongings
  basket
  cock

beloved person
  honey

below the belt
  dirty

belt
  high
  joint
  a kick
  sock

a belt
  a crack

belted
  high

belt out
  warble

belt over
  deck

belt up
  shut up

bench warmer
  gofer
  warm body

bender
  binge

bend over backwards
  bust one's ass

bend the elbow
  guzzle

bend the rules
  play dirty

bennies, "amphetamines"

bent
  crazy
  gay
  high
  kinky

bent out of shape
  high
  pissed off

benz
  bennies

bernice
  coke

berries
  dough

the berries
  big shot
  great
  the most

berry
  buck

be sick
  barf

best bet
  front runner

best bib and tucker
  glad rags

best boy
  gofer

best clothing
  glad rags

the best people
  the upper crust

best shot, "attempt"

best thing since sliced bread
  hot shot
  humdinger

bet
  bet one's ass

bet one's boots
  bet one's ass

bet dollars to doughnuts
  bet one's ass

Bethesda gold
  pot

bet on
  back

betrayal
  double cross

better half
  old woman

bet the farm
  bet one's ass
  go for it

bet the ranch
  bet one's ass
  go for it

between a rock and a hard
    place
  out of luck
  up the creek

between you and me
  on the QT

bet your ass, "definitely"

bevels
  crooked dice

BFD
  big deal

B-girl
  floozy
  hooker

bi
  AC-DC

Bibleback
  Christer

Bible-banger, "religionist"

the Bible Belt
  the boondocks

Bible-thumper
  Bible-banger

bicker
  hassle

biddy
  broad

biff
  clout
  a kick
  pizzazz
  pow
  sock

big
  big-league
  heavy
  hot

big as life
  honest-to-God

big boy
  big shot
  boss
  horse
  pro

big boys
  the brass

big bozo
  bruiser

big brass
  the brass

big breeze
  blabbermouth

big brown eyes
  tits

big bucks
  bundle

big bug
  big shot

big C
  coke

the big cage
  the slammer

big cheese
  big shot
  boss

big chief
  boss

big D
  acid

big deal
  **big deal, "important
    matter"**
  big shot
  so what

big enchilada
  big shot
  boss

biggie
  big deal
  big shot
  fatty

biggies
  the brass

big girl
  pro

big gun
  big shot

big guy
  big shot
  boss

big H
 horse
big Harry
 horse
bigheaded
 stuck-up
big hog
 bag
 deck
the big house
 the slammer
big John
 cop
the big joint
 the slammer
big lady
 pro
big-league, "important"
the big leagues, "top rank"
big M
 M
big macher
 big shot
 wheeler-dealer
big man
 big shot
 bruiser
 dealer
 pro
big money
 bundle
the big money
 the brass
bigmouth
 bigmouth, "pretentious
  talker"
 blabbermouth
 blow off
 smart-ass
bigmouthed
 gabby

big noise
 big shot
 blabbermouth
big O, "opium"
big one
 grand
bigoted person
 redneck
the big Pretzel
 Philly
big rich
 loaded
the bigs
 the big leagues
the big school
 the slammer
big shot
 big shot, "important
  person"
 boss
 wheeler-dealer
big stink
 beef
big stuff
 big shot
big-talk
 blow off
big-time
 big-league
the big time
 the big leagues
big-time operator
 eager beaver
 wheeler-dealer
big tuna
 bruiser
 goon
big wheel
 big shot

bike
 bike, "motorcycle"
 floozy
bile
 piss-off
bilge
 bullshit
 crap
 fuck up
bill
 schnozz
a bill, "hundred dollars"
Billie Hoke
 coke
billies
 dough
bill of goods
 scam
bill-poster
 paperhanger
billy
 billy club
Billy be damn
 zilch
bim
 broad
 hooker
bimbo
 broad
 floozy
 goon
 hooker
 jerk
 wimp
the bin
 booby hatch
bind, "predicament"
binders, "brakes"
bindle
 bag
 deck

bindle stiff
  bum

bing
  cooler
  a fix
  the slammer

binge
  binge, "spree"
  paint the town red

bingle
  bingle, "baseball hit"
  dope

bingo
  pow

bint
  broad

bionic
  great

bippy
  ass
  asshole

bird
  broad
  cookie
  dish
  oddball

the bird, "derisive noise"
the bird, "obscene
    gesture"

birdbrain
  dope

bird course
  gut course

birdie powder
  coke
  dope
  M

bisexual
  AC-DC

bit
  act

bag
bit, "prison sentence"

a bit
  a jiffy

bitch
  back-breaker
  a bad scene
  ball buster
  beef
  bitch, "disliked person"
  gadget
  screw up

a bitch
  a bitch, "effort"
  a bitch, "misfortune"
  humdinger

bitch box, "public address
    system"

bitchen
  great

bitcher
  kvetch

bitch-kitty
  back-breaker
  a bad scene
  humdinger

a bitch of a
  a hell of a

bitch up
  screw up

bitch-up
  boner

bite
  bite, "be credulous"
  bite, "share"
  blow
  con
  scam

the bite
  the damage

bite someone's head off
  chew out

bite one's lip
  blow grass

bite moose
  fuck you

biter
  con man

bite the bullet
  bite the bullet, "accept
      consequences"
  take it

bite the dust
  croak
  fold
  fuck up

bite this
  kiss my ass

bit of change
  dough

bit of fluff
  broad

bit of jam
  dish

bitsy
  little bitty

bitter-ender
  mule

biz
  bag
  deck
  works

blab
  gab
  squeal

blabberer
  blabbermouth

blabfest
  schmooz

black
blackball
hash
black beauty
bennies
doll
blackbird
nigger
black eye, "bruised eye"
black gold
horse
pot
black hash
hash
black hat
bad man
blackleg
scab
blacklist
blackball
Black Maria, "police van"
black moat
pot
black mold
pot
black mole
pot
black molly
doll
black monte
pot
black mota
pot
black oil
hash
black person
blood
nigger
black pill
big O

black Russian
hash
black snake
big O
black stuff
big O
black tabs
acid
black tar
horse
black whack
angel dust
blah
bullshit
down
dullsville
green around the gills
blah-blah
bullshit
chitchat
blahs
the blues
bullshit
blam
pow
blame
damn
blamed
damn
blank
clobber
pot
blank check, "license"
blanked
damn
blanket drill
sack time
blankety
damn

blankety-blank
blankety-blank,
"euphemism"
damn
blanks
dope
blap
pow
sock
blarney
bullshit
soft soap
blast
barrel
blast, "attack"
blow grass
clobber
a fix
flop
high
a hit
a kick
plug
snuff
sock
wingding
a blast
a ball
blasted
damn
high
blaster
hit man
blasting party
dope den
blast off
split
blat
chitchat
gab
blather
bullshit

blatter
 blabbermouth

blaze
 split

blaze away at
 plug

bleeding
 damn

bleeping
 blankety-blank
 damn

blessed
 damn

bless my soul
 Jeez

bletcherous
 yucky

bliggey
 blankety-blank

blimey
 Jeez

blimp
 fatty

blind
 high
 shill

blind drunk
 plastered

blind pig, "illegal saloon"

blind-side
 blind-side, "attack"
 con

blind tiger
 blind pig

Blind Tom, "sports official"

blinger
 humdinger

blinkers
 peepers

blinkety-blink
 damn

blinkie
 coke

blinking
 damn
 fucking

blip
 cool
 great

blister
 kid

blisterfoot
 grunt

blither
 have a hole in one's head

blithering idiot
 dope

blitz
 clobber
 cut

blitzed out
 high
 plastered
 pooped

bloated
 loaded
 plastered

bloated plute
 moneybags

blob
 glob

block
 bean

block box
 bag
 deck

blockbuster
 doll
 a hit
 Sunday punch

blocked
 high

blockhead
 dope

blockheaded
 dumb

block mo
 pot

bloke
 coke
 guy

blond
 hash

blood
 blood, "black person"
 nigger

blood brother
 blood

blood-curdler
 a hit

bloodhound
 dick

blood sister
 blood

bloody
 damn
 fucking

blooey
 kaput
 on the blink
 pow

bloomer
 boner

blooming
 damn
 fucking

blooper
 boner
 sock

blort
 coke

blot
  snuff
blot one's copybook
  blow it with someone
  goof
blot out
  snuff
blotter
  acid
  hit man
blotto
  plastered
blow
  blow, "expose secrets"
  blow, "perform
    cunnilingus"
  blow, "perform fellatio"
  blow, "spend
    extravagantly"
  blow grass
  blow off
  break out
  fluff
  fuck up
  goof
  screw up
  scrub
  snort
  split
  squeal
  suck
blow a fuse
  blow one's top
blow a stick
  blow grass
blow away
  clobber
  snuff
  split
blow coke
  snort
blow one's cool
  blow one's top

blow one's cork
  blow one's top
  crack up
  go crazy
blowed away
  plastered
blower
  bigmouth
  pothead
blow grass, "smoke
    marijuana"
blow grits
  barf
blowhard
  bigmouth
  blabbermouth
blow hard
  blow off
blow high as a kite
  screw up
blow in
  blow
  show up
blow it off
  cop out
blow it with someone,
    "antagonize"
blow job, "cunnilingus"
blow job, "fellatio"
blow one's mind
  crack up
blown out
  high
blown up
  stuck-up
blowoff
  blowup
  cinch
  swivet
  wingding

blow off
  blow off, "boast"
  bullshit
  come
  cop out
  scrub
blow off one's mouth
  blow off
  bullshit
blowout
  wingding
blow out
  snuff
blow out of the water
  clobber
blow one's own horn
  blow off
blow smoke
  blow grass
  blow off
  brown-nose
  snow
blow one's stack
  blow one's top
  crack up
  go crazy
blow the gaff
  squeal
blow the lid off
  blow
blow the whistle
  blow
  squeal
blow someone to
  stake someone to
blow top
  pothead
blow one's top
  blow grass
  blow one's top, "be angry"
  crack up

freak out
 go crazy

blow town
 break out

blowup
 blowup, "rage"
 crash
 hassle
 swivet

blow up
 blow one's top
 blow up, "exaggerate"
 fluff

blow up a storm
 beef

blow wide open
 blow

blubber, "fat"

blubberbrain
 dope

blubberbrained
 dumb

blubberhead
 dope

blubberheaded
 dumb

blubberpot
 fatty

blue
 cop
 dirty
 doll
 down
 nigger
 plastered

blue acid
 acid

blue angel
 bennies

blue around the gills
 green around the gills

blue balls
 hot pants

bluebird
 cop

blue blanket
 security blanket

blue-blood
 swell
 the upper crust

blueboy
 cop

blue cheer
 acid

blue cheese
 hash

blue-chip
 great

bluecoat
 cop

blue de hue
 pot

blue dot
 acid

blue-eyed devil
 whitey

blue flag
 acid

blue flick
 blue movie

blue funk
 the blues

blue-gum
 nigger

blue heaven
 acid

bluejacket
 swabby

blue liz
 Black Maria

blue man
 cop

blue meany
 asshole

blue mist
 acid

a blue moon
 ages

blue movie, "pornographic film"

bluenose
 Christer
 goody-goody

blue Owsley
 acid

the blues, "depression"

blue sage
 pot

blue-skin
 nigger

blue sky
 horse

blue-sky blond
 pot

blue splash
 acid

blue-veiner
 hard-on

bluff, "deceive"

bluffer
 phony

blunder
 boner
 fuck up
 goof

blunderheaded
 dumb

blurb
 plug
bo
 bum
board
 pasteboard
 scarecrow
boast
 blow off
boat
 Caddy
 jalopy
bobble
 boner
 goof
bobbler
 fuck-up
bobby
 cop
bo bo
 pot
bo-bo jockey
 pothead
bobtail, "military discharge"
bob up
 show up
Boche
 kraut
bod
 build
body
 ass
 asshole
 balls
 basket
 bean
 beaver
 belly
 black eye
 blubber
 build
 built

cauliflower ear
choppers
clit
cock
cum
cunt
falsies
fart
fatty
glass arm
glass jaw
goose bumps
hard-on
have the rag on
hung
innards
knocked up
mitt
peepers
pins
piss
a piss
poker face
potbelly
puss
schnozz
spare tire
stiff
ticker
tits
tootsies
wing
yap
zit
body-shake
 frisk
boff
 ass
 barf
 belly laugh
 fuck
 a fuck
 sock

a boff
 a howl
boffin
 ace
boffo
 ace
 belly laugh
 great
 a hit
 a howl
boffola
 belly laugh
 a howl
bog
 cop out
bogart
 bulldoze
bog-hopper
 Mick
bog house
 can
bog-trotter
 Mick
bogue
 phony
 yucky
bogus
 phony
 square
boho
 loser
boh-ring
 dullsville
bohunk
 dope
 hunky
boiled
 plastered
boiler
 jalopy

boiler room
 scam

boiling mad
 pissed off

boil in oil
 chew out

boisterous
 horse around
 horseplay
 rootin'-tootin'

boite
 night spot

boko
 schnozz

bold
 cheeky

bollix
 screw up

bollixed-up
 fucked-up

bollix up
 screw up

boll weevil
 scab

bolo
 sock

bolt-hole
 hideaway

bomb
 flop
 fuck up
 a hit
 hot rod
 joint

bombed
 high
 plastered

bomber
 joint

bombita
 bennies

bombshell
 a hit

bonanza
 gold mine

bona roba
 hooker

bone
 buck
 cock
 dough
 grind
 hard-on

bone-bender
 sawbones

bone-breaker
 back-breaker

bone factory
 bone factory, "hospital"
 boneyard

bonehead
 dope
 fuck-up

boneheaded
 dumb

bonehead play
 boner

bonehouse
 bone factory

bone-on
 hard-on

boner
 boner, "blunder"
 grind
 hard-on

bones
 sawbones

bone-tired
 pooped

bone up on
 brush up

boneyard, "cemetery"

bong
 works

bonged out
 high

bonita
 horse

bonk
 fuck
 sock

bonkers
 crazy

bonnet
 lid

bonus
 gravy

bonzer
 great

bonzo
 crazy

boo
 great
 pot

boob
 dope
 jerk
 patsy

boobies
 tits

boobish
 dumb

boo-boo
 boner

boobs
 tits

boob tube
 the tube

booby
  dope
booby hatch, "mental
    hospital"
boodle
  dough
  neck
  score
the boodle
  the whole shebang
boogaloo
  goof off
  kid around
boogerboo
  phony
boogie
  ass
  bugger
  fuck
  goof off
  kid around
  nigger
  snitch
  split
boogie box
  ghetto box
boogie-woogie
  have a ball
boojie
  works
book
  ace
  pasteboard
  split
the book, "performance
    record"
book it
  split
boom-boom
  ass
  fuck

boomstick
  rod
boondagger
  dyke
boondockers, "boots; shoes"
the boonies
  the boondocks
boo reefer
  joint
boost
  back
  heist
  hike
  plug
booster
  fan
  heist man
  shill
booster stick
  joint
boot
  boner
  chuck
  fire
  goof
  greenhorn
  high
  a kick
  nigger
  rookie
  screw up
  shoot up
the boot
  the axe
boot and saddle
  split
bootleg joint
  blind pig
bootlicker
  brown-nose
boot out
  bounce

boots
  boondockers
booty
  ass
  cunt
booze
  booze, "liquor"
  guzzle
  paint the town red
boozed up
  plastered
booze-freak
  lush
boozehound
  lush
booze joint
  dive
boozer
  dive
  gin mill
  lush
booze-up
  binge
boozing
  on the sauce
boozy
  plastered
bop
  ass
  fuck
  a fuck
  pow
  sock
  toddle
bop off
  split
boppo
  ace
  pow
borahco
  plastered

borax
  bullshit
  crap
boring
  dullsville
boring person
  drag
born loser
  loser
borrowed
  on the cuff
bosh
  bullshit
bosom buddy
  pal
boss
  big shot
  boss, "leader"
  boss, "manage"
  great
botheration
  flak
both hands, "prison
    sentence"
bottle
  bag
  deck
the bottle
  booze
bottle baby
  bum
bottled
  plastered
bottle it
  shut up
bottle-man
  lush
bottles
  bennies

bottleshop
  dive
bottom
  ass
  asshole
the bottom line, "decisive
    elements"
bottom man on the totem
    pole
  gofer
bounce
  bounce, "eject"
  fire
  pizzazz
bounce powder
  coke
bounce the goof balls
  blow grass
bouncing off the walls
  jittery
bouncy-bouncy
  ass
Bowery bum
  bum
bowl a googly
  snow
bowl over
  break someone up
  deck
  wow
bow out
  croak
bowwow
  pooch
box
  bind
  cunt
  ghetto box
  pete

boxed
  high
  plastered
box lunch
  fur pie
box man
  heist man
box of L
  bennies
box tonsils
  neck
boy
  guy
  horse
  Jeez
boychick
  kid
boy-howdy
  Jeez
bozette
  broad
bozo
  dope
  goon
  guy
  horse
  jerk
bracelets, "handcuffs"
braces
  bracelets
brack-brain
  dope
brack-brained
  ditsy
brag oneself up
  blow off
brain
  egghead
  sock
brainbox
  bean

brainery
  collitch
brainless
  dumb
brains
  smarts
one's brains out
  flat-out
  one's head off
  like hell
brainstorm
  brain wave
brain stuff
  smarts
brain tickler
  doll
brain ticklers
  bennies
brain wave, "idea"
brain-wise
  upstairs
brakes
  binders
brand X
  pot
brannigan
  binge
  donnybrook
  free-for-all
brashness
  chutzpa
brass
  chutzpa
  dough
the brass, "leaders"
brassafrax
  Jeez
brass balls
  guts
brassed off
  fed-up

brass hat
  big shot
brass hats
  the brass
brat
  kid
bravo
  bean-eater
brawl
  donnybrook
  free-for-all
  wingding
bread
  dough
bread basket
  belly
break a hamstring
  bust one's ass
break a stick
  blow grass
break barracks
  go over the hill
break chops
  bug
break something down
  spell out
break into jail
  fall
break one's neck
  bust one's ass
break off
  knock off
  walk
  walk out on
break out
  break out, "escape"
  rustle up
break out in assholes
  panic
break out the jams
  let oneself go

break up, "laugh"
break someone up, "amuse"
break wind
  fart
breasts
  tits
breastworks
  tits
breath-taker
  a hit
Breckenridge green
  pot
breeder
  straight
breed of cat
  cookie
breeze
  break out
  cinch
  gab
  split
breeze home
  hack it
breeze in
  show up
breeze off
  split
breezy
  laid-back
brew, "beer"
brew-out
  beer bust
brewskie
  brew
brew units
  big O
bribe
  grease someone's palm

brick
 bag
 deck
brickbat
 knock
brick gum
 big O
bricks
 crooked dice
brick-top, "red-head"
brief
 fill someone in
 spell out
briefed, "informed"
brifo
 pot
the brig
 the slammer
brightline
 spotlight
bright skin
 whitey
brillo
 beaver
bringdown
 knock
 letdown
bring down
 knock
 take someone down a peg
bring down the house
 go over with a bang
 hack it
bring home the bacon
 hack it
bring scunnion
 spook
bring up to speed
 fill someone in
 spell out

Brit
 limey
bro'
 blood
 nigger
broach
 shoot up
broad
 bitch
broad, "woman"
 dish
 floozy
 pasteboard
broccoli
 pot
brodie
 flop
broil
 free-for-all
broke, "penniless"
broken-down
 beat-up
broker
 dealer
bromide
 chestnut
Bronx cheer
 the bird
broom
 break out
 split
broomstick
 beanpole
brothel
 whorehouse
brother
 blood
 guy
 Jeez
 nigger

Brother
 Jack
brought up to speed
 briefed
brouhaha
 hoopla
brown
 asshole
 brown-nose
 bugger
 horse
brown dots
 acid
browned off
 fed-up
 pissed off
brown hash
 big O
brownhole
 bugger
brownie
 asshole
brownies
 bennies
brown-noser
 brown-nose
brown Rhine
 horse
brown rock
 horse
browns
 bennies
brown shoes
 straight
brown stuff
 big O
 horse
brown sugar
 horse
bruised eye
 black eye

bruiser
  bruiser, "big man"
  goon
brush
  cut
  give the cold shoulder
  hassle
the brush
  the boondocks
  the cold shoulder
brush ape
  hick
brush off
  cut
  give the cold shoulder
the brush-off
  the cold shoulder
brush up on
  brush up
brutal
  great
  hairy
brute
  back-breaker
  bruiser
  coke
BS
  bullshit
the B-side
  the flip side
B-29s
  bennies
bub
  guy
Bub
  Jack
bubbie
  honey
bubble-brain
  dope

bubble dancer
  pearl-diver
bubble-gummer
  teenybopper
bubblehead
  dope
bubkes
  zilch
buck
  buck, "defy"
  buck, "dollar"
  dude
  ladies' man
  take on
buckass private
  buck private
bucker
  brown-nose
buckeroo
  buck
bucket
  ass
  asshole
  banger
  barrel
  jalopy
the bucket
  the slammer
buckethead
  dope
bucket of bolts
  jalopy
a bucket of warm spit
  zilch
bucket shop
  scam
bucking
  hungry
buckle down
  bust one's ass

buck naked
  bare-ass
bucko
  guy
buck private, "soldier"
buckra
  whitey
bucks
  dough
buckshee
  free gratis
buck snort
  fart
buckwheat
  pal
buckwheater
  greenhorn
bud
  guy
  pal
Bud
  Jack
buddha
  pot
Buddhahead
  Chink
buddy
  pal
Buddy
  Jack
buddy-boy
  pal
buddy-buddy
  chummy
  pal
buddy up, "become
    friends"
buddy up to
  play up to

buddy up with
  hang out with

buff
  bare-ass
  fan

buffalo
  bulldoze
  snow

buffarilla
  scarecrow

bug
  bug, "annoy"
  bug, "racehorse"
  fan
  glitch
  guy
  hot rod
  nut

a bug
  a bee in one's bonnet

bug doctor
  shrink

bugeyed
  popeyed

bugged-up
  fucked-up

bugger
  asshole
  back-breaker
  bad man
  bugger, "sodomize"
  gadget
  guy
  screw up
  sucker

bugger-all
  zilch

buggered-up
  fucked-up
  kaput
  on the blink

bugger off
  split

bugger up
  screw up

buggy
  crazy
  jalopy

bughouse
  booby hatch
  crazy
  flophouse

bugjuice
  panther piss

bugle
  schnozz

bug out
  split

bugs
  crazy

build
  build, "physique"
  frame

buildup
  flack
  plug

build someone up
  soft-soap

built, "well developed"

bulb
  dope

bulge
  potbelly
  spare tire

bull
  bullshit
  cop
  dyke
  soft soap

bull artist
  bigmouth

bulldagger
  dyke

bulldink
  bullshit

bulldog
  mule
  rod

bulldoze
  bulldoze, "intimidate"
  clobber

bulldozer
  rod

bulldyke
  dyke

bullet bait
  buck private

bullethead
  mule

bullheaded, "obstinate"

bull in a china shop
  butterfingers

bull jive
  pot

bullrag
  bullshit

bull session
  schmooz

bullshine
  bullshit

bullshit
  blow off
  bullshit, "nonsense"
  bullshit, "speak nonsense"
  gab
  izzatso
  shoot the breeze

bullshit someone
  soft-soap

bullshit artist
  bigmouth

bullwork
 scut work

bully
 great

bullyrag
 bulldoze

bum
 ass
 asshole
 bum, "beg"
 bum, "vagrant"
 con
 crummy
 floozy
 green around the gills
 hooker
 moocher
 on the blink
 yucky

bum around
 goof off

bum bend
 bad trip

bumble bees
 bennies

bum deal
 bum rap
 the shaft

bum finger
 bum rap

bumfuck
 bugger

bumhole
 asshole

bummed out
 down

bummer
 asshole
 a bad scene
 bad trip
 bum
 moocher

bump
 fire
 knock up
 snort
 snuff

bumper
 snort

bump heads
 hassle

bumpin'
 great

bumpman
 hit man

bump off
 snuff

bum rap, "injustice"

the bum's rush
 the axe

bum trip
 a bad scene
 bad trip

bun-buster
 back-breaker

bunch
 bundle

bunch of fives
 mitt

bunco
 con
 con man
 scam

bunco artist
 con man
 shill

bundle
 broad
 bundle, "wealth"
 score

bung
 asshole
 smack

bunghole
 asshole
 bugger

bungler
 fuck-up

bunhead
 dope

bunk
 big O
 bullshit
 flack
 pot
 split

bunk habit
 sack time

bunk lizard
 goof-off

bunned
 plastered

bunny
 broad
 dish
 groupie

bunny fuck
 goof off
 quickie

bunny hug
 clinch

buns
 ass

burbed-out
 square

burese
 coke

burgle
 heist

burn
 barrel
 beat
 blow one's top
 bug
 con

fry
  heist
  knock
  piss-off
  scam
  snuff
  split
a burn
  a smoke
burn an Indian
  blow grass
burn artist
  con man
burn down
  snuff
burned out
  kaput
  pooped
burned up
  pissed off
burner
  con man
  the most
burnie
  joint
burnies
  coke
burning
  pissed off
burn out
  fold
burn rubber
  barrel
  split
burn the breeze
  barrel
burn the hay
  blow grass
burn the road
  barrel

burn up
  blow one's top
burn someone up
  piss someone off
burn up the highway
  barrel
burp gun
  Tommy gun
burrhead
  nigger
burst in
  butt in
bursting
  antsy
bury
  clobber
  snuff
bus
  jalopy
bush
  beaver
  bush, "mediocre"
  piddly
  pot
the bush
  the boondocks
bushed
  pooped
busher
  lightweight
bush-league
  bush
  crummy
  piddly
bush-leaguer
  lightweight
the bush leagues,
   "mediocrity"
bush patrol
  grab-ass

bushwah
  bullshit
bushwhack
  blind-side
  clobber
  rough up
  snuff
business
  basket
  cock
  shit
the business
  the whole shebang
businessman's lunch
  bennies
bust
  binge
  blow grass
  broke
bust, "arrest" (*v* and *n*)
  clobber
  crash
  flop
  flunk
  loser
  on the blink
  sock
  wingding
bust a gut
  break up
  bust one's ass
bust one's butt
  bust one's ass
bust down
  go kerflooey
busted
  broke
  on the blink
buster
  eager beaver
  guy

Buster
  Jack
busters
  crooked dice
busthead
  bum
  panther piss
bust hump
  bust one's ass
bust in
  butt in
busting
  antsy
bustler
  eager beaver
bust loose
  hell around
  let oneself go
bust out
  break out
bust-outs
  crooked dice
bust the mainline
  shoot up
bust-up
  rumble
busy
  pot
busy bee
  angel dust
busy person
  wheeler-dealer
butch
  dyke
  tough
Butch
  Jack
butcher
  clobber
  sawbones

butcher shop
  bone factory
but good
  flat-out
  for sure
butt
  ass
  asshole
  broad
  butt, "cigarette"
  butt, "cigarette stub"
  joint
a butt
  a smoke
buttbang
  bugger
butt-buster
  back-breaker
butt end
  ass
butter
  soft soap
butter-and-egg man
  angel
butterball
  fatty
buttercup
  honey
butterfingered
  ham-handed
butterfingers, "clumsy
    person"
butterflies
  the jitters
butter flower
  pot
butterfly case
  nut
butter no parsnips
  cut no ice

butter up
  play up to
butter someone up
  soft-soap
buttfuck
  bugger
buttfuck buddy
  pal
butthole
  asshole
butt in, "intrude"
buttinsky
  kibitzer
buttocks
  ass
button
  big O
  clit
  tin
button buster
  belly laugh
buttondown
  square
button down
  peg
  spell out
buttoned down
  square
button one's lip
  shut up
button man
  button man, "mobster"
  gangster
  hit man
button player
  button man
buttons
  chicken feed
button soldier
  button man

button up
  shut up
  wrap up
butt out
  lay off
  split
  stick to one's knitting
butt peddler
  hooker
butty
  pal
buy
  buy, "approve"
  buy, "believe"
  eat up
buy into
  buy
  plug into
buy it
  croak
buy narcotics
  score
buy the farm
  croak
buy time
  stall
buzz
  buzz, "telephone call"
  chitchat
  dirt
  gab
  heist
  high
  a kick
  split
buzza
  what's up
buzz-buggy
  jalopy
buzzed
  high
  plastered

buzzer
  tin
buzz in
  show up
buzz off
  split
buzz the brillo
  fuck
buzz-wagon
  jalopy
buzzy
  plastered
BVDs
  long johns
by ear, "instinctively"
bye-bye
  curtains
  sack time
by George
  Jeez
by guess and by God
  by ear
by the book
  straight
by the seat of one's pants
  by ear
C
  a bill
  coke
the C
  scam
caballo
  coke
  horse
cabbage
  dough
cabbagehead
  dope
cabbageheaded
  dumb

caboose
  ass
the caboose
  the slammer
caca
  horse
  shit
cack
  dish
cackle
  break up
cackle factory
  booby hatch
Cad
  Caddy
cadger
  moocher
Cadillac
  angel dust
  Caddy
  coke
caeto
  shut up
cage
  jalopy
the cage
  the slammer
caged
  plastered
cage rattler
  eager beaver
'cainer
  dealer
cake
  cinch
  cunt
  dish
  gravy
cake-eater
  dude
  ladies' man

cakes
  ass
cakewalk
  cinch
the calaboose
  the slammer
calendar art
  cheesecake
California sunshine
  acid
call down
  chew out
called
  high
call girl
  hooker
call house
  whorehouse
call it quits
  fold
  knock off
  wrap up
call joint
  whorehouse
call on the carpet
  chew out
call the shots
  boss
calm oneself
  cool it
Cambodian trip weed
  pot
camel-jammer, "Arab"
camp
  gay
can
  ass
  bag
  can, "toilet"
  chuck
  deck

fire
  hot rod
  pete
  scrub
the can
  the circular file
  the slammer
Canadian black
  pot
Canadian quail
  lude
canary
  broad
  snitch
  squeal
  warble
cancel
  chicken out
  scrub
canceled stick
  joint
candid speech
  let it all hang out
candy
  acid
  doll
  dope
  hash
candy ass
  wimp
candy-ass
  chicken
  wimpish
candy cee
  coke
candy man
  dealer
cane corn
  panther piss
can it
  knock off
  shut up

canned
  finished
  plastered
canned goods
  cherry
  pot
canned up
  plastered
the cannery
  the slammer
cannon
  heist man
  rod
  works
cannon fodder
  buck private
can of worms, "complex
    situation"
canoodle
  neck
canoodling
  grab-ass
cans
  tits
cantankerous
  feisty
canto
  chapter
  stanza
cap
  bag
  blow job
  deck
  score
caper
  binge
  caper, "robbery"
  heist
capers
  horseplay

capon
  gay
cap out
  snooze
capped out
  high
capper
  shill
car
  hot rod
  jalopy
  pimpmobile
card
  bag
  deck
card-carrying
  honest-to-God
card shark
  card sharp
careless
  half-assed
caress
  feel
caressing
  grab-ass
cargo
  bag
cargo cube
  deck
carload
  bundle
caronotics
  dope
carouse
  paint the town red
carpet rat
  kid
Carrie Nation
  coke
carrot-top
  brick-top

carry, "armed"
Carry
  coke
carry a lot of weight, "have
    influence"
carrying
  dirty
  heeled
carry on
  horse around
  make a scene
carry the difference
  carry
carry the mail
  barrel
cart, "transport"
carte blanche
  blank check
cartucho
  joint
cartwheel
  buck
cartwheels
  bennies
carve
  wow
carved in stone,
    "unchangeable"
cas
  laid-back
Casanova
  ladies' man
  stud
case dough, "emergency
    money"
case note
  buck
cash cow
  angel

cash in
  clean up
  go kerflooey
cash in one's chips
  croak
Caspar Milquetoast
  wimp
cast a kitten
  blow one's top
  make a scene
cat
  ass
  cunt
  dude
  guy
  hooker
  ladies' man
cat around
  cruise
  goof off
catawampus
  cockeyed
cat bandit
  heist man
catch
  catch, "hidden element"
  get me
  grab
catch one's breath
  kick back
catch cold
  catch redhanded
catch it
  catch hell
catch one's lid
  split
catch someone's lunch
  clobber
catch on
  dig
  get me

catch on the hop
  catch redhanded
catch the devil
  catch hell
catch the drift
  get me
catch-22, "contradiction"
catchy
  grabby
catch Zs
  snooze
catfit
  blowup
  swivet
cathouse
  flophouse
  whorehouse
cat nap
  a snooze
cats
  cookie
the cat's
  the most
cat's astrophe
  crash
the cat's meow
  humdinger
  the most
cattail
  joint
cauliflower ear, "damaged
    ear"
caulk off
  knock off
  snooze
caution
  pussyfoot
cave
  fold
  pad
  shoot up

cave in
  fold
  fuck up
caveman
  he-man
  hunk
cavort
  horse around
Cecil
  coke
ceck
  joint
cee
  coke
cemetery
  boneyard
cent
  buck
centerfold
  dish
  hunk
century
  a bill
certain
  cinched
  in the bag
certainly
  for sure
certainty
  cinch
c'est la vie
  that's the way the cookie
    crumbles
the chair, "electric chair"
chalk
  bennies
  coke
challenge
  take on

champ
  great
  humdinger
the champ
  the most
chance it
  stick one's neck out
chancy
  a gamble
change
  dough
channel swimmer
  junkie
chaotic
  fucked-up
chap
  guy
chapeau
  lid
chapped
  pissed off
chaps
  yap
chapter
  chapter, "game division;
    baseball inning"
  stanza
chapter and verse
  the straight dope
character
  cookie
  guy
  oddball
charas
  hash
charge
  hard-on
  high
  a pot

charged up
 high
 pumped

charge in
 butt in

charges
 the damage

chariot
 jalopy

Charley
 coke
 whitey

charmer
 dish

chart
 the book

chase along
 split

chase butterflies
 crack up

chaser
 ladies' man
 stud

chat
 shoot the breeze

chatfest
 schmooz

chatterbox
 blabbermouth

chaw
 scarf
 schmooz

chawbacon
 hick

chawfest
 schmooz

cheap
 chintzy
 crummy

cheapie
 schlocky

cheapskate
 tightwad

cheat, "philander"

cheaters
 specs

check
 check out

check in
 butt in
 show up

check it in
 knock off

check out
 check out, "examine"
 croak
 split

check the plumbing, "use a
   toilet"

check up on
 brush up

cheechako
 greenhorn

cheek
 chutzpa
 sass

cheek it
 bluff
 wing it

cheeks
 ass

cheeky
 cheeky, "rude"
 smart-ass

cheer for
 back

cheese
 barf
 bullshit
 coke

the cheese
 big shot
 humdinger

cheese bun
 snitch

cheesecake
 cheesecake, "seminude"
 cheesecake, "seminudity"
 dish

cheese eater
 snitch

cheesehead
 dope

cheese it
 break out
 jiggers
 split

cheesy
 crummy
 schlocky
 yucky

chemistry
 vibes

cherry
 cherry, "virgin"
 party hat

cherry Leb
 hash

cherry pie
 cinch

cherrypop
 pop someone's cherry

cherry top
 acid
 prowl car

chestnut, "trite story"

chesty
 stuck-up

chewallop
 belly-whopper

chew someone's ass out
  chew out
chewed
  pooped
chew out, "reprimand"
chew over
  bat around
chew the fat
  shoot the breeze
chew up the scenery
  ham
chewy
  great
chiba chiba
  pot
chic
  snappy
Chicago black
  pot
chi-chi
  tits
chick
  broad
  coke
  dish
chicken
  broad
  chicken, "coward"
  chicken, "cowardly"
  chicken out
  chickenshit
  patsy
  wimp
chicken feed, "little money"
chickenhead
  dope
chicken-hearted
  chicken
  wimpish
chicken out
  back out

chicken out, "withdraw
    from fear"
  cop out
chickenshit
  chickenshit, "petty spirit"
  piddly
chicory
  big O
chief
  acid
  guy
Chief
  Jack
chief cook and
    bottle-washer
  boss
child
  honey
  kid
chili-bowl
  sleazebag
chili-chomper
  bean-eater
chili joint
  greasy spoon
chill
  cool
  cut
  give the cold shoulder
  great
  knock out
  snuff
the chill
  the cold shoulder
chiller-diller
  chiller
chill out
  cool it
chilly
  great
  laid-back

chilly mo
  cold fish
chime in
  butt in
chin
  chitchat
  gab
  schmooz
  shoot the breeze
china
  choppers
china chin
  glass jaw
Chinaman
  rabbi
a Chinaman's chance
  a fat chance
China white
  horse
chin-chin
  chitchat
chinch pad
  flophouse
chinchy
  chintzy
Chinee
  Annie Oakley
  Chink
Chinese
  Chink
  horse
Chinese fire drill
  snafu
Chinese molasses
  big O
chinfest
  schmooz
chinjaw
  shoot the breeze
chink
  cunt

Chink, "Chinese person"
chin music
  chitchat
  gab
chinning
  gab
Chino
  Chink
chintzy
  chintzy, "stingy"
  schlocky
chin-wag
  schmooz
chipper
  full of piss and vinegar
  zingy
chippy
  broad
  cheat
  floozy
  hooker
chips
  dough
chiquita
  dish
chira
  pot
chirp
  squeal
  warble
chisel
  bum
  con
chisel down
  shave
chiseler
  con man
chisel in
  butt in
chit
  Jeez

chitchat, "conversation"
chitter-chatter
  chitchat
chivvy
  bug
  roust
chloral hydrate
  Mickey Finn
chocha
  cunt
chocolate
  big O
  hash
chocolate drop
  nigger
chogie
  barrel
choke
  choke up
choke-dog
  panther piss
choke the gopher
  jack off
choke up
  choke up, "panic"
  freeze up
choke someone up
  wow
Cholly
  coke
chooch
  cunt
choose
  go for
choosy
  prissy
the chop
  the axe
chop-chop
  on the double

chop logic
  nit-pick
chopped liver
  zilch
chopper
  Tommy gun
choppers, "teeth"
chops
  yap
chop one's teeth
  shoot the breeze
chow
  chow, "food"
  scarf
chowderhead
  dope
chow down
  scarf
chow hound
  pig
Christ Almighty
  Jeez
Christer
  Bible-banger
  Christer, "pious person"
Christinas
  bennies
Christmas roll
  doll
Christmas tree
  doll
Christmas trees
  bennies
chubbette
  fatty
chuck
  barf
  bounce
  chuck, "throw away"
  peg

scrub
  walk out on
Chuck
  whitey
the chuck
  the axe
chucke
  bean-eater
chuck it
  fold
chucklehead
  dope
chuckleheaded
  dumb
chuck you, Farley
  fuck you
chuey
  bean-eater
chug-a-lug
  guzzle
chukker
  chapter
  stanza
chum
  guy
  pal
chum around with
  hang out with
chummy
  chummy, "friendly"
  palsy-walsy
chump
  bean
  dope
  jerk
  patsy
chum up
  buddy up
chum with
  hang out with

chungo bunny
  nigger
chunk
  ass
  hash
  peg
churus
  pot
chutzpa, "brashness"
cigar
  joint
cigarette
  butt
  a smoke
cigarette stub
  butt
cigarrode
  angel dust
ciggy
  butt
cinch
  cinch, "certainty"
  cinch, "easy task"
  clinch
  gut course
cinched
  cinched, "certain"
  in the bag
cinchers
  binders
cinder bull
  cop
cipher
  warm body
the circular file,
    "wastebasket"
citizen
  cookie
  square
  straight

citroli
  hash
city slicker
  dude
CJ
  angel dust
c-jam
  coke
clam
  boner
  cunt
clambake
  wingding
clamp down, "enforce"
clamps
  bracelets
clams
  dough
clam shells
  yap
clam trap
  yap
clam up
  shut up
clank
  freeze up
clanked
  pooped
clanker
  buck
the clanks
  the shakes
clank up
  freeze up
clapped-out
  beat-up
claptrap
  bullshit
class
  great

swank
  the upper crust

classy
  classy, "prestigious"
  great
  snappy

claw
  bust

clay eater
  cracker

clay pigeon
  cinch
  patsy

clean
  broke
  clean, "innocent"
  clean, "narcotics-free"
  stone
  straight

clean as a whistle
  clean

clean someone's clock
  clobber

cleaned out
  broke

clean sweep
  grand slam

clean up
  clean up, "profit"
  make a killing
  wrap up

clean up one's act, "act
    properly"

clean up the floor with
  clobber

clear
  clean

clear light
  acid

clear out
  break out
  split

clear to hell
  flat-out

Clem
  hick

clerk
  bean counter

click
  buddy up
  go over with a bang
  hack it
  hit it off
  work

click big
  go over with a bang

cliffhanger, "suspense"

climb
  chew out
  kick ass

climb down
  come down a peg

climb one's frame
  kick ass

climb on the bandwagon
  get on the bandwagon

climb the wall
  blow one's top

clinch, "conclude"
clinch, "embrace"

the clincher
  the bottom line

clink
  nigger

the clink
  the slammer

clinker
  boner
  catch

flop
loser

the clinker
  the slammer

clip
  barrel
  bust
  con
  heist
  scam
  snuff
  sock

a clip, "each one"

clip artist
  con man

clip game
  scam

clipped dick
  kike

clique
  the in group

clitoris
  clit

clobber
  beat
  clobber, "defeat"

clobbered
  kaput
  plastered

clock
  puss
  sock

clock in
  show up

clock out
  split

clock stopper
  scarecrow

clod
  dope

clodhopper
  hick

clodhoppers
  boondockers

clodpated
  dumb

clone
  double
  square
  zombie

clonk
  sock

close
  chintzy

close out
  wrap up

close shave
  cliffhanger

close up
  wrap up

clothes horse
  dude

clothes pole
  beanpole

clothing
  boondockers
  doll up
  glad rags
  kicks
  lid
  long johns
  sneakers
  threads
  undies

clottish
  dumb

cloud nine
  fat city

clout
  clout, "power"
  sock

clover-kicker
  hick

clown
  cookie
  guy
  jerk

club
  cock
  dope den
  night spot
  sock

clubhouse lawyer
  latrine lawyer

cluck
  cookie
  dope
  jerk
  nigger

cluckhead
  dope

clue
  fill someone in
  spell out

clued in
  briefed

clue me in
  wise me up

clumsy
  ham-handed

clumsy person
  butterfingers

clunk
  dope
  jalopy
  sock

clunker
  butterfingers
  flop
  jalopy

clunkhead
  dope

clunky
  dumb

clutch
  bind
  clinch

clutched
  jittery

clutch up
  choke up

clutchy
  jittery

clyde
  square

C-note
  a bill

the coalhole
  the slammer

coast
  goof off

coasting
  high

coast-to-coasts
  bennies

cobber
  pal

cobble up
  knock something out
  whomp up

cobics
  horse

coby
  M

coca
  coke

cocaine
  coke

cochecito
  jalopy

cock
  cock, "penis"

great
pal
cockamamie
crazy
cockeye
southpaw
cockeyed
cockeyed, "askew"
crazy
fucked-up
plastered
cockiness
chutzpa
cocksman
stud
cocksucker
asshole
cocksucker, "fellator"
sucker
cocksucking
yucky
cocktail
joint
cock-teaser, "sexual arouser"
cocky
cheeky
great
stuck-up
coconut
bean
coke
coconuts
tits
codger
guy
old fart
coffee
acid
coffee and cakes
chicken feed

coffee cooler
goof-off
coffin-nail
butt
a smoke
cognizant
with it
coin
dough
coin money
clean up
coin of the realm
dough
cojones
balls
guts
coke, "cocaine"
coked
high
coked up
high
cokehead
dope
junkie
cola
coke
cold
cinched
cold as hell
dead to rights
cold cash
dough
coldcock
clobber
knock out
sock
cold deck
rig
cold decker
con man

cold fish, "aloof person"
cold haul
con
cold in hand
broke
cold pack
cinch
cold-shoulder
cut
give the cold shoulder
the cold shoulder, "snub"
collar
bust
grab
works
collar ad
hunk
collar a nod
snooze
collar the jive
dig
get me
college
collitch
the college
the slammer
college man
Joe College
college student
white shoe
collitch, "college"
the collitch
the slammer
colly
dig
Colombian
pot
Columbo
angel dust

Columbus black
  pot
come
  come, "experience
    orgasm"
  cum
come a cropper
  fuck up
come across
  pick up the tab
come across with
  cough up
  kick in
come again, "repeat"
come apart at the seams
  go to hell
come around
  have the rag on
come barging in
  butt in
comedown
  letdown
come down
  come off
come down a peg, "be
    humiliated"
come down hard on
  chew out
come down on
  chew out
  fix someone
  kick ass
come-freak
  cocksucker
come off
  come
  come off, "happen"
  knock off
  work
come off it
  izzatso

come off one's perch
  come down a peg
come on
  come on strong
come-on
  gimmick
  shill
come on like gangbusters
  come on strong
  go over with a bang
come-on man
  shill
come on strong, "succeed
    brilliantly"
come on to
  proposition
come out of the closet
  come out
  go public
come out on top
  beat
  hack it
come-queen
  cocksucker
come through
  hack it
come through with
  cough up
  stake someone to
come unstuck
  come unglued
  go to hell
come up trumps
  hack it
coming out one's ears
  up to here
commercial beaver
  hooker
commie
  pinko

commit suicide
  cut one's own throat
commode
  can
commotion
  hoopla
communications
  give someone a ring
comp
  Annie Oakley
  freebie
competence
  know one's onions
complain
  beef
complainer
  kvetch
complaint
  beef
complete
  wrap up
complex situation
  can of worms
compliant person
  softie
compliment
  hand it to someone
comprehend
  dig
  get me
  have someone's number
compute
  figure
con
  bullshit
  con, "convict"
  con, "swindle"
  a put-on
  scam
  talk someone into
con artist
  con man

conceal
  stash

conceited
  stuck-up

conclude
  clinch

condom
  rubber

conehead
  egghead

Coney Island whitefish
  rubber

confab
  schmooz
  shoot the breeze

confidence
  bet one's ass

conflict
  hassle

conformist
  square

confused
  in a fog

confusion
  snafu

conga
  pot

con game
  scam

Congo mataby
  pot

congratulation
  way to go

con job
  scam

conk
  bean
  clobber
  sock

conk-buster
  egghead

conked out
  on the blink

conk off
  croak
  goof off
  snooze

conk out
  croak
  fold
  go kerflooey
  snooze

con man, "swindler"

connect
  go over with a bang
  hack it
  score

connection
  dealer

connector
  dealer

connect the dots
  spell out

conned
  screwed

conniption fit
  blowup
  swivet

consarned
  damn

conservative person
  fogy

conspicuous
  stick out like a sore thumb

constructed
  built

contented
  in hog heaven

contentious person
  latrine lawyer

contradiction
  catch-22

contraption
  gadget

contribute
  kick in

convenience
  can

conversation
  chitchat
  schmooz

convict
  con

convulse
  break someone up

cooch
  cunt

cook
  come off
  fry
  screw up
  works

cooked
  kaput
  plastered

cooked goose
  goner

cooked up
  high

cooker
  works

cook someone's goose
  clobber

cookie
  coke

cookie, "any person"
  guy

cookie mud
  big O

cookie-pusher
  wimp

cookies
  kicks

cooking
  cool

cooking spoon
  works

cook up, "devise"

cool
  cool, "disengaged"
  cool, "good"
  get me
  great
  laid-back
  with it

cooler, "jail"

the cooler
  the slammer

cool it, "calm oneself"

cool million
  bundle

cool out
  cool it

coon
  nigger

coon box
  ghetto box

a coon's age
  ages

coop
  pad

the coop
  the slammer

cooperate
  play ball

cooperation
  it takes two to tango

coop-happy
  stir-crazy

coot
  dope
  nut

cooz
  ass

broad
  floozy

cop
  bust

cop, "police officer"
  grab
  score

copacetic
  cool
  OK

cop a feel
  feel

cop a gander at
  check out

cop an attitude
  beef

cop someone's cherry
  pop someone's cherry

cope
  get by

copeck
  buck

copilot
  bennies

coping
  in there

cop it
  croak

cop man
  dealer

cop out
  back out
  cop out, "evade"

copper
  cop
  snitch

coppish
  get me

the cops, "police"

cop some Zs
  snooze

copulation
  fuck
  a fuck
  gang bang

corgy
  horse

Corine
  coke

cork
  knock out
  sock

corked
  plastered

corker
  humdinger

corking
  great

cork it
  shut up

cork off
  snooze

corn, "old-fashioned music"
corn, "sentimentality"

cornball
  corny
  square

corn dog
  jerk

corned
  plastered

corn-fed
  corny

cornhole
  asshole
  bugger

corn juice
  panther piss

corny, "sentimental"

corny joke
  chestnut

corporation
  potbelly
  spare tire
corpse
  stiff
corral
  grab
cost
  set someone back
cotics
  dope
cotton
  works
cotton-pickin
  crummy
  damn
couch doctor
  shrink
cough over
  cough up
  pick up the tab
one couldn't care less, "be
  indifferent"
counterfeit
  paperhanger
a country mile, "distance"
county mounty
  cop
couple of fives back to back
  both hands
courage
  guts
  gutsy
  have balls
courage pill
  doll
  horse
cousin
  patsy
couze
  cunt

cove
  guy
cover girl
  dish
cow
  broad
  scarecrow
coward
  chicken
cowboy
  cowboy, "criminal"
  dealer
  goon
cowboy movie
  horse opera
cow college, "agricultural
  college"
cowflap
  bullshit
cow tech
  cow college
cozmos
  angel dust
crab
  back out
  beef
  heist
  kvetch
  screw up
crabby
  feisty
crack
  ass
  broad
  coke
  crack, "joke"
  crack up
  cunt
  dish
  great
  heist
  sock

a crack
  a clip
  a crack, "attempt"
crack a deal
  cut a deal
crackbrain
  nut
crackbrained
  crazy
crack down on
  blast
  chew out
  fix someone
  kick ass
cracked
  crazy
  flaky
cracker
  acid
  cracker, "Southerner"
cracker factory
  booby hatch
crackerjack
  great
  humdinger
crackers
  crazy
crack funny
  kid
crack hand
  ace
cracking
  great
crack one's jaw
  blow off
crackpot
  crazy
  nut
cracksman
  heist man

crack the whip
  boss
crack up
  break up
  crack up, "collapse
    emotionally"
  go crazy
  take a beating
  wow
crack-up
  crash
crack wise
  kid
cram
  brush up
  pig out
cram it
  fuck you
  kiss my ass
  stick it
crammed
  fed-up
crank
  bennies
  kvetch
  oddball
cranked up
  pumped
crank up
  hike
cranky
  flaky
  pissed off
crap
  bullshit
  crap, "inferior things"
  flack
  horse
  mung
  shit
a crap
  a shit

crap can
  can
crape-hanger
  gloomy Gus
crapoid
  schlocky
  yucky
crapola
  bullshit
crap out
  flop
  fold
  fuck up
  go kerflooey
  snooze
crapped out
  pooped
crapper
  bigmouth
  can
crappy
  crummy
  schlocky
  yucky
the craps
  the shits
crap shoot
  a gamble
crash
  crash, "disaster"
  crash, "fail disastrously"
  fuck up
  go kerflooey
  heist
  snooze
crashed
  plastered
crashing bore
  drag
crash pad
  dope den
  pad

crasty
  yucky
crate
  jalopy
crave
  have a lech for
crawdad
  back out
crawl
  chew out
  fuck
crawling with
  lousy with
crazy
  crazy, "insane"
  great
  high
  nut
crazy about
  have a lech for
crazy house
  booby hatch
cream
  ace
  big O
  clobber
  con
  cum
  knock out
the cream
  the upper crust
cream one's jeans
  have hot pants
cream puff
  sissy
  wimp
creamstick
  cock
cream up
  ace

credulity
  bite

creep
  jerk
  oddball
  sleazebag

creeper
  heist man

the creeps
  the shakes

creepy
  creepy, "terrifying"
  weird
  yucky

cretinoid
  dope
  dumb

crib
  dive
  flophouse
  pad
  pete
  whorehouse

crib course
  gut course

crib crime
  heist

crikey
  Jeez

crime
  ace
  bit
  both hands
  button man
  caper
  con
  con man
  cooler
  cowboy
  crooked dice
  fall
  gangster
  grease someone's palm

heist
heist man
hit man
in stir
jail bait
loan shark
paperhanger
pete
racket
rig
scalper
scam
score
the slammer
snuff
sticky-fingered

criminal
  cowboy
  gangster

crimp
  card sharp

crink
  bennies

crip course
  gut course

cris
  bennies

Crisco
  fatty

cristal
  angel dust

criticism
  flak

criticize harshly
  knock

critter
  cookie

croak, "death"
croak, "die"

croaker
  hit man
  sawbones

croaker joint
  bone factory

crock
  bullshit
  clobber
  old fart
  screw up

crocked
  plastered

crockery
  choppers
  glass arm

crock of shit
  bullshit

Croesus
  moneybags

cronk
  plastered

crook
  con man

crooked
  dirty

crooked dice, "altered dice"

crook the elbow
  guzzle

croon
  warble

cross
  double cross
  take on

cross someone's palm
  grease someone's palm

crossroads
  bennies
  jerk town

cross-tops
  bennies

cross-up
  boner
  double cross

crowbait
  stiff
crowd
  crowd, "press"
  mob scene
crowd someone's act
  butt in
crowd-pleaser
  hot shot
crown
  bean
  sock
crown crap
  horse
crud
  bullshit
  sleazebag
cruddy
  crummy
  schlocky
  yucky
cruft
  crap
cruise
  cruise, "search for sexual
    opportunities"
  hustle
  split
cruise around
  goof off
cruiser
  prowl car
cruit
  rookie
crumb
  asshole
  screw up
  sleazebag
crumbcrusher
  kid

crumb house
  flophouse
crumbs
  chicken feed
crumbun
  crummy
crumb up
  screw up
crummy
  crummy, "inferior"
  dirty
  green around the gills
  schlocky
  yucky
crumped out
  plastered
crumpet
  bean
  dish
crunch
  bind
crunchie
  grunt
crush out
  break out
crust
  chutzpa
crusty
  feisty
crutch
  roach clip
cry
  blubber
cry baby
  wimp
crying
  fucking
crystal
  angel dust
  bennies

C-spot
  a bill
cubby
  pad
cube
  acid
  bag
  M
  square
cubehead
  junkie
cube juice
  M
cuckoo
  crazy
  nut
cuddle
  neck
cuddle-bunny
  dish
cueball
  baldie
  oddball
cue in
  spell out
cuff one's meat
  jack off
cuffo
  free gratis
cuffs
  bracelets
Cugat
  great
cum, "semen"
cunnilingus
  blow
  blow job
  cunt-lapper
  fur pie
cunt
  ass

bitch
broad
cunt, "vulva"

cuntface
asshole

cunt-hair
smidgen

cunthead
asshole

cunt-lapper, "performer of
cunnilingus"

cunt meat
broad

cuntmobile
pimpmobile

cunt-struck
pussy-whipped

cupcake
dish
nut
oddball
sissy

cupcakes
acid
ass

cup of tea
bag

curse
whammy

cursed
damn

curtain climber
kid

curtains, "death"

curvaceous
built

curve
con

cush
dough

cushion
a fix

cushy
classy

cuss
cookie
guy

cussed
damn
feisty

cuss out
chew out

customer
cookie

cut
barrel
bite
cut, "fail to attend"
cut, "snub"
divvy
give the cold shoulder
scrub
shave
split

cut a deal, "agree"

cut a fart
fart

cut and run
split

cut someone a new asshole
chew out

cut a take
spell out

cut capers
horse around

cut dead
cut
give the cold shoulder

cut didoes
goof off
horse around

cut down
snuff

cut down to size
take someone down a peg

cute
smart-ass

cutie
broad
dish

cutie-pie
dish

cut in
butt in

cut it
hack it

cut it out
shut up

cut it up
spell out

cut loose
have a ball
let oneself go

cut one's losses
play it safe
walk out on

cut no ice, "be ineffective"

cut off
snuff

cut off at the knees
take someone down a peg

cut out
knock off
split

cut one's own throat,
"disable oneself"

cut-rate
bush

cut some Zs
snooze

cut the chat
  shut up

cut the cheese
  fart

cut the crap
  clean up one's act

cut the mouth
  shut up

cut the mustard
  hack it

cut the shit
  get down to brass tacks
  shut up

cut up
  divvy
  goof off
  have a ball
  horse around
  make a scene
  paint the town red

cut Zs
  snooze

cyclones
  angel dust

D
  acid
  dick
  dirt

dab
  smidgen

dab hand
  ace

Dad
  Jack

dadblamed
  damn

daddy
  guy
  sugar daddy

Daddy
  Jack

daddy longlegs
  beanpole

daddy-o
  guy

Daddy-O
  Jack

Daddy Warbucks
  moneybags

dadgasted
  damn

daffy
  crazy
  ditsy

dagga
  pot

dagnabbed
  damn

dago
  wop

daisy
  gay
  humdinger
  sissy
  wimp

the damage, "charges"

damaged ear
  cauliflower ear

dame
  broad

dammit
  Jeez

damn
  damn, "cursed"
  fucking
  Jeez

a damn
  zilch

one's damndest
  best shot

damp squib
  flop
  letdown

dance
  rumble

dander
  piss-off

dandered
  pissed off

dandy
  great
  humdinger

dang
  cock
  damn
  sexy

danged
  damn

dangle one's hose
  piss

dap
  whitey

dapper man
  dude

darb
  humdinger

darbies
  bracelets

dark
  hick

dark horse
  long shot

darky
  nigger

darling
  great

darn
  damn

date bait
  dish

day-glo
  glitzy
daylight
  moonlight
daylights
  peepers
dazed
  punch-drunk
  rocky
dazzler
  dish
DD
  bobtail
dead
  dullsville
  finished
  kaput
  pooped
  stone
deadass
  drag
  stone
deadbeat
  moocher
dead broke
  broke
dead cinch
  cinch
dead cut
  the cold shoulder
dead drunk
  plastered
dead duck
  goner
deadfanny
  drag
dead from the neck up
  dumb
dead game
  gutsy

deadhead
  dope
  moocher
dead heat
  standoff
dead in the water
  kaput
  out of luck
dead keen
  hungry
deadlock
  standoff
deadly
  great
dead meat
  goner
  kaput
  stiff
deadneck
  drag
dead nut
  on the nose
dead one
  drag
dead on one's feet
  pooped
deadpan
  poker face
dead pigeon
  goner
dead ringer
  double
dead sure
  for sure
  in the bag
dead-sure thing
  cinch
deadsville
  dullsville
dead to rights,
    "inescapably"

dead to the world
  out
  plastered
dead wrong
  full of shit
deal
  cut a deal
  score
dealer, "narcotics seller"
deal from the bottom of the
    deck
  snow
deal out
  stake someone to
dearie
  broad
  honey
dear me
  Jeez
death
  croak
  curtains
debut
  come out
deceive
  bluff
  kid
  snow
decent person
  doll
  good guy
deception
  monkey business
  a put-on
  razzle-dazzle
deck
  bag
  deck, "knock down"
  deck, "narcotics quantity"
  horse
  knock out

deck out
 doll up
decode
 spell out
decrease
 shave
deeda
 acid
deedee
 gadget
dee-jay
 disc jockey
deek
 dick
de-emphasis
 soft-pedal
deep pockets
 bundle
 moneybags
deep shit
 bad news
deep-six
 chuck
 scrub
deep sixed
 finished
deep trouble
 bad news
def
 great
defeat
 clobber
defecation
 shit
 a shit
defend
 go to bat for
defiance
 izzatso
 stick it

definitely
 bet your ass
 OK
deflate
 take someone down a peg
defy
 buck
deke
 con
dekko
 the once-over
delay
 stall
Delhi belly
 the shits
delight
 hot damn
 wow
delirious
 high
delirium tremens
 the shakes
delish
 great
deliver the goods
 hack it
delysid
 acid
demi-rep
 floozy
demon rum
 booze
denigrate
 bad-mouth
dense
 dumb
depart
 go over the hill
 split
depressed
 down

depression
 the blues
derisive noise
 the bird
dern
 damn
 fucking
derrick
 heist man
derriere
 ass
desk jockey, "office worker"
despatchers
 crooked dice
destroker
 hot rod
destroke rod
 hot rod
destroyed
 high
detective
 dick
 private eye
deteriorate
 come unglued
 go to hell
deterioration
 hell breaks loose
Detroit pink
 angel dust
deuce
 bag
 damn
 deck
deuce bag
 bag
 deck
developed
 built
deviant sex
 kinky

device
  gadget
  gadgetry
  gimmick
devil
  whitey
the devil and all
  the whole shebang
devil book
  pasteboard
devil dog
  leatherneck
devil dust
  angel dust
devise
  cook up
  whomp up
devoon
  great
devotee
  fan
dew
  pot
dexies
  bennies
dexter
  grind
  jerk
dial
  puss
diamonds
  balls
diarrhea
  the shits
dib
  dough
dibble
  cock
dice
  crooked dice

dicey
  a gamble
  iffy
dick
  asshole
  bugger
  cock
  cop
  dick, "detective"
  fuck
  goof off
dick around with
  fool around with
dick-brained
  crazy
dickhead
  asshole
dick-lick
  blow
dick-licker
  cocksucker
dick with
  fool around with
dicky
  cock
dicty
  classy
  snooty
diddle
  con
  fingerfuck
  fuck
  goof off
  scam
  snow
diddle around
  play games
diddle around with
  fool around with
diddle away
  blow

diddled
  screwed
diddle-damn
  damn
diddlehead
  ditz
diddler
  con man
diddle with
  fool around with
diddling
  ass
  scam
diddly
  piddly
  zilch
diddlybop
  goof off
diddy-bop
  toddle
diddy now
  split
didoes
  horseplay
die
  croak
  fry
diehard
  fogy
  mule
die hard
  sit tight
die laughing
  break up
diesel-dyke
  dyke
difficult
  hairy
dig
  check out
  dig, "admire"

dig, "comprehend"
get a kick out of
get me
knock

dig down for
cough up
pick up the tab

digger
scalper

diggings
pad

dig me
get me

dig out
split

digs
pad

dig up
cough up
grab

dildo
jerk

dildock
card sharp

dilly
humdinger

dilly dude
gay
oddball

dim
dumb

dim bulb
dope

dime
squeal

dime-a-dozen
bush
schlocky

dime bag
bag
deck

dime-dropper
snitch

dime-note
sawbuck

dime of buzz
angel dust

dimer
snitch

dimestore
schlocky

dimwit
dope

dim-witted
dumb

dinch
butt

dinero
dough

ding
knock
nut
panhandle
pot
sock

ding-a-ling
nut
oddball

dingbat
dope
gadget
jerk
nut
oddball

dingbusted
damn

ding-dong
cock
crazy
donnybrook
dope
oddball

dinge
nigger

dinged
damn

dinger
bingle
humdinger

dinghiyen
works

dingswizzled
damn

dingus
gadget
works

dingy
broke
dumb

dink
cock
gook
jerk
zilch

dinkum
straight

dinky
crummy
little bitty

dinky dow
joint

dino
wop

dip
asshole
dope
heist man
junkie
nut
sleazebag

dipped
hooked

dipper
angel dust

dippy
  crazy
  ditsy
dipshit
  asshole
  crummy
  dope
  jerk
dipso
  lush
dipstick
  asshole
  jerk
dipsy
  ditsy
dipsy-doodle
  con
  con man
  double cross
  razzle-dazzle
  scam
  snow
dip one's wick
  fuck
direct speech
  lay it on the line
dirt
  dirt, "gossip"
  the poop
dirtbag
  asshole
  sleazebag
dirt chute
  asshole
dirt grass
  pot
dirt road
  asshole
dirty
  dirty, "dishonest"
  dirty, "obscene"

dirty, "possessing
  narcotics"
  hooked
  loaded
  yucky
dirty bum
  asshole
dirty crack
  knock
dirtyleg
  floozy
  hooker
dirty movie
  blue movie
dirty pool
  dirty
  dirty tricks
dirty rat
  asshole
dirty tricks, "dishonest
  practices"
dirty with money
  loaded
dirty work
  dirty tricks
dis
  knock
disabled persons
  fruit salad
disappointment
  letdown
disaster
  a bad scene
  crash
disc
  platter
disc jockey, "radio
  performer"
discombobulate
  bug

discouraged
  plastered
discover
  smoke out
discuss
  bat around
disengaged
  cool
disgusting
  suck
  yucky
disgusting person
  sleazebag
dish
  bag
  broad
  cookie
  dish, "attractive woman"
  screw up
dished
  kaput
dish of tea
  bag
dishonest
  dirty
  put-up job
  rig
dish out
  blow
  cough up
  kick in
  pick up the tab
  stake someone to
dishwasher
  pearl-diver
dishwater
  panther piss
dishy
  great
disliked person
  asshole
  bitch

311

jerk
nudnik
on someone's shit list
scarecrow
shit list
sleazebag
dismiss
fire
dismissal
the axe
get the ax
give someone his (or her)
walking papers
disparage
knock
disreputable place
dive
distance
a country mile
disturbance
make a scene
ditch
chuck
scrub
shoot up
dither
have a hole in one's head
the dithers
the jitters
ditsy, "scatterbrained"
dittybop
dope
ditz, "scatterbrain"
dive
belly-whopper
dive, "disreputable place"
take a dive
dive in
pig out
divide
divvy

divine
great
divot
rug
divvy
bite
divvy up
divvy
dizzy
ditsy
dumb
DJ
disc jockey
do
blow grass
do, "use narcotics"
shit
wingding
D O A
angel dust
do a deal
cut a deal
do a number on
clobber
con
doc
guy
Doc
Jack
dock rat
bum
doctor up
doctor
rejigger
Doctor White
coke
do one's damndest
bust one's ass
dodge
racket
scam

dodo
dope
fogy
old fart
does a bear shit in the
woods, "flippant
answer"
dog
bug
dish
flop
guy
loser
pooch
scarecrow
dog-ass
crummy
Dogberry
cop
dog-eared
beat-up
dogface
grunt
dogfight
free-for-all
dog food
horse
doggery
dive
doggo
crummy
doggone
damn
Jeez
doggy
crummy
scarecrow
dogie
horse
dog it
bum

goof off
put on the ritz

dog out
doll up

dogs
tootsies

a dog's age
ages

dog's breakfast
mish-mash

dog's dinner
snafu

dogshit
bullshit
crap

dog-tired
pooped

dog up
doll up

dog wagon
greasy spoon

dogwork
scut work

do in
clobber
snuff

doing
into

do it
fuck

doker
shill

doldrums
the blues

dole out
stake someone to

dolf
jerk

doll
broad
dish

doll, "barbiturate"
doll, "decent person"
honey

dollar
buck

dollars
a bill

doll-baby
honey

dollface
dish

dollop
broad

doll out
doll up

doll up, "dress one's best"

dolly
broad
dish
doll

dome
bean

domes
acid

dominoes
bennies

Dona Juanita
pot

donc
pooped

done for
finished
kaput

done in
pooped

dong
cock

donicker
can

Don Juan
ladies' man
stud

donkey
mule

donkey's years
ages

donkeywork
scut work

donnybrook
donnybrook, "brawl"
free-for-all
hassle

do one's number
go into one's dance

doobie
joint
pot

doodad
gadget

doodle
cock
con
crap
cunt
gadget
goof off

doodly
zilch

doodly-squat
zilch

doo-doo
shit

doo-doo head
dope

doofunny
gadget

doohickey
gadget
zit

doomajigger
 gadget

doormat
 gofer
 lightweight
 patsy
 rug
 wimp

door pops
 crooked dice

do over
 con

doowhistle
 gadget

doozy
 humdinger

dopatorium
 dope den

dope
 the book
 butt
 dope, "narcotic"
 dope, "stupid person"
 great
 the poop
 pot

dope booster
 dealer

dope den, "marijuana
  venue"

doped up
 high

dope fiend
 junkie

dope gun
 works

dopehead
 junkie
 pothead

dope off
 goof off
 snooze

dope peddler
 dealer

doper
 junkie
 pothead

dope sheet
 the book

dope smoke
 hash
 pot

dopester
 junkie
 pothead

dope stick
 butt

dopey
 crazy
 ditsy
 dumb
 rocky

dopium
 big O

dopoe
 horse

do-re-mi
 dough

dorg
 pooch

do-righter
 straight

dork
 cock
 jerk

dorky
 dumb

dose
 dish

doss
 sack time
 snooze

doss house
 flophouse

dot
 acid

do tell
 so what

do the Dutch, "commit
  suicide"

dotty
 crazy

double
 double, "duplicate"
 moonlight

double-bagger
 scarecrow

double-barrel
 big-league

double bitchen
 great

double-clutcher
 asshole

double-clutching
 damn

doublecross
 con
 scam

double cross, "betrayal"

double-crosser
 con man

double deal
 double cross

double-distilled
 high-powered

double-dome
 egghead

double Dutch
 double-talk

double finn
 both hands

double-gaited
  AC-DC
  weird

double header
  joint

double in brass
  moonlight

double-O
  check out

double-quick
  on the double

double shuffle
  double cross
  razzle-dazzle
  scam
  snow

double-talk, "unintelligible
  language"

double-trouble
  bad news

double whammy
  whammy

double X
  double cross

doubloons
  dough

douche
  shoot up

douchebag
  scarecrow
  sleazebag

douchie
  patsy

dough, "money"

doughboy
  buck private
  grunt

dough-head
  dope

doughnut factory
  greasy spoon

doughpop
  clobber

do up
  blow grass
  clobber
  do
  a fix
  fix up
  shoot up

dove
  honey

dovey
  palsy-walsy

down
  buy
  cool
  deck
  depressed
  down, "depressed"
  great
  knock
  on the blink
  shoot up

down and out
  broke
  kaput

downer
  a bad scene
  bad trip
  doll

down for the count
  broke
  kaput
  out

down in the dumps
  down

down on one's luck
  out of luck

down the drain
  kaput

downtown
  horse

down trip
  a bad scene
  bad trip

drag
  bad trip
  blow grass
  butt
  cart
  clout
  drag, "boring person"
  high
  a smoke
  snort
  toke

drag one's ass
  goof off

drag down
  grab

drag one's feet
  goof off
  stall

dragged
  high

dragged out
  pooped

draggy
  dullsville

drag in
  show up

drag it
  goof off
  split

drag queen
  gay

dragster
  hot rod

dragsville
  dullsville

dragtail
  goof off

dram
 snort
drama
 soap opera
dramshop
 dive
drape ape
 kid
drapes
 threads
dratted
 damn
draw a bead
 zero in
draw a lot of water
 carry a lot of weight
draw a picture
 spell out
drawers
 undies
dream beads
 big O
dreamboat
 dish
 honey
 hunk
dreambox
 bean
dreamer
 junkie
dream girl
 dish
dream stick
 joint
dreamy
 great
dreck
 crap
 shit
dress down
 chew out

dress up
 doll up
dress-ups
 glad rags
dressy
 snappy
drifter
 bum
drifty
 high
drill
 shoot up
driller
 hit man
drink
 guzzle
 snort
drink one's beer
 shut up
drink Texas tea
 blow grass
drink to
 buy
drip
 drag
 jerk
 square
 wimp
dripper
 works
drippy
 corny
 square
 wimpish
drive
 a kick
 pizzazz
drivers
 bennies
drive the big bus
 barf

drive very fast
 floor it
droid
 square
drone
 wimp
drool
 corn
 have a hole in one's head
 jerk
 wimp
drooly
 great
drop
 blow
 deck
 fall
 fire
 knock out
 scrub
 shave
 shoot up
 snuff
 walk out on
drop a brick
 goof
drop a bundle
 take a beating
drop a dime
 squeal
drop a joint
 blow grass
drop one's bucket
 goof
drop case
 dope
drop dead
 fuck you
drop-dead list
 shit list
drop in
 show up

drop it
  knock off

drop kick
  dope

drop one's load
  come
  shit

drop on
  hang on

dropper
  cowboy
  goon
  hit man
  works

drop shot
  dope

drop the ball
  fuck up
  goof

drop the curtain
  wrap up

drop the dime
  squeal

drop the lug on
  bum
  put the bite on

drub
  clobber

druggie
  junkie

drugstore cowboy
  dude
  ladies' man

drum-beater
  flack

drunk
  have a load on
  lush
  on the sauce
  plastered

drunkard
  lush

dry booze
  dope

dry-gulch
  clobber
  snuff

dry up
  fluff
  shut up

the DTs
  the shakes

dub
  duffer
  fuck-up

ducat
  buck
  pasteboard

ducats
  dough

duck
  cookie
  guy
  pasteboard
  weasel

duck bumps
  goose bumps

duckbutt
  shorty

a duck egg
  zilch

duckfit
  blowup
  swivet

duckling
  honey

duck out
  break out
  split

duck out on
  walk out on

ducks
  honey

duck soup
  cinch
  easy as pie

duck-squeezer,
  "environmentalist"

ducky
  cool
  great
  honey

duct
  coke

dud
  crummy
  flop
  jerk
  letdown
  lightweight
  loser

dude
  dude, "dapper man"
  guy
  ladies' man

dude up
  doll up

duds
  threads

duff
  ass
  goof

duffer
  butterfingers
  duffer, "poor performer"
  guy
  old fart

dufus
  dope
  dumb

dugee
  horse

duke
  mitt
  sock

duke someone out
  knock out

dukes-up
  feisty

dukie
  pasteboard

dull
  dullsville

dull thud
  letdown

dull tool
  drag
  loser

dumb, "stupid"

dumbard
  dope

dumbbell
  dope
  dumb

dumb Dora
  ditz
  dope

dumbjohn
  patsy
  rookie

dumbo
  boner
  dope

dumdum
  crazy
  dope
  dumb
  jerk

dummy
  cock
  dope
  jerk

dummy dust
  angel dust

dummy up
  shut up

dump
  barf
  chuck
  clobber
  dive
  dump, "repulsive place"
  greasy spoon
  knock
  snuff

a dump
  a shit

dump all over
  knock

dump a load
  shit

dumpish
  down

dumpling
  honey

dump on
  bad-mouth
  knock

dumps
  the blues

dunderheaded
  dumb

dunnigan
  heist man

duplicate
  double

dust
  angel dust
  barrel
  break out
  coke
  dust bunny
  hassle

  sock
  split

dust bunnies
  house moss

dust bunny, "dust"

duster
  ass

dust kitty
  dust bunny

dust off
  clobber

dustup
  hassle

dusty butt
  shorty

dutch
  screw up

Dutchman
  kraut

Dutch rub, "torment"

dweeb
  grind
  jerk
  wimp

dwelling
  pad

dyke, "lesbian"

dyna
  gay

dynamite
  coke
  great
  high-powered
  horse
  pot

dynamite punch
  Sunday punch

dynamiter
  joint

dynamite stocks
  bennies

dyno
  horse
eager
  hungry
eager beaver
  eager beaver, "active
    person"
  grind
eagle-beak
  kike
eagle day, "pay day"
eagle-eye
  dick
eagle freak
  duck-squeezer
ear
  cauliflower ear
  snooze
earbanger
  brown-nose
ear-bender
  blabbermouth
earn one's wings
  go through the mill
  pay one's dues
earth
  angel dust
ease out
  split
ease up
  kick back
easing powder
  dope
Eastern European
  hunky
East Jesus
  jerk town
East Jesus State
  cow college

easy
  easy as pie
  laid-back
easy course
  gut course
easy digging
  cinch
easy-going
  laid-back
easy lay
  floozy
easy mark
  patsy
  softie
easy meat
  cinch
easy money
  gravy
easy task
  cinch
eat
  blow
  eat up
  scarf
eat cheese
  squeal
eat crow
  come down a peg
eat dirt, "be humiliated"
eater
  cocksucker
eatery
  greasy spoon
eat for breakfast
  clobber
eat high off the hog
  eat high on the hog
eat humble pie
  come down a peg
eatin' stuff
  dish

eat it
  blow
  eat dirt
  fuck you
eat like a horse
  pig out
eat out
  chew out
eats
  chow
  a feed
eat shit
  come down a peg
  eat dirt
eat up
  bite
  buy
  dig
  eat up, "accept readily"
  flip
eccentric
  flaky
eccentric person
  oddball
ecdysiast
  stripper
ech
  yuck
ecofreak
  duck-squeezer
edged
  pissed off
  plastered
edgy
  jittery
Edsel
  flop
the educated money
  the smart money
education
  flunk

eentsy-weentsy
little bitty

eeyuck
yuck

eff
fuck

effective person
hot shot

effing
damn

effort
a bitch
bust one's ass
flat-out
flop
in there

egg
cookie
egghead
guy

eggsucker
brown-nose

ego massage
stroke

egotist
grandstander

eightball
jerk
lightweight
loser
nigger

eighteen-carat
honest-to-God

eighty-six
chuck

eject
bounce

elbow
bag
cop
deck

elbow bender
lush

elbow in
butt in

electric chair
the chair

electric Kool Aid
acid

elegant
great

elephant
angel dust
fatty

elevation
big O

el foldo
flop

Elk
square

Elsie
scarecrow

em
M

emanations
vibes

embalmed
plastered

embrace
clinch
neck

emergency money
case dough

emote
ham

emphasize
spotlight

the end of the line
curtains

endowed
hung

ends
kicks

endsville
great

endure
hang tough
take it

energetic
full of piss and vinegar
zingy

energy
pizzazz

energy gun
works

enforce
clamp down

enforcer
goon
hit man

engine
works

engine cylinder
banger

English person
limey

enjoy
have a ball

entre nous
on the QT

environmentalist
duck-squeezer

equalizer
rod

equipment
basket

erase
snuff

erection
hard-on

escape
break out

Ethel
  wimp

euchre
  con

euphemism
  blankety-blank

evade
  cop out

evasion
  weasel

even break
  square deal

event
  a ball

even the score
  get even

everything
  the whole shebang

every Tom Dick and Harry
  Joe Blow

every which way
  cockeyed
  fucked-up

evil
  great

exact
  on the nose

exactly
  smack

exaggerate
  blow up

examine
  check out

exceedingly
  like hell

excellence
  the McCoy

excellent
  great

excess baggage,
    "unnecessary person"

excessive talker
  blabbermouth

excited
  antsy
  pumped

excited sexually
  horny

exciting
  jazzed-up
  jazz up
  jazzy

exclamation
  I'll be damned
  Jeez
  jiggers
  no shit
  pow
  so what
  stick it
  way to go
  yuck

excrement
  shit

excuse me all to hell,
    "apology"

execs
  the brass

exhaust pipe
  asshole

exit
  croak

expecting
  knocked up

experience
  go through the mill
  pay one's dues

expert
  ace

expire
  fold

explain
  spell out

exploit
  plug into

expose secrets
  blow

extremely
  fucking

eye
  check out
  dick
  private eye
  the tube

the eye
  the once-over

eyeball
  check out

eyeful
  dish

eyeglasses
  specs

eye-opener
  bennies

eye-popper
  a hit

eyes
  peepers
  popeyed

eyewash
  bullshit
  flack
  soft soap

Eytie
  wop

fab
  great

fabby
  great

face
  chutzpa
  cookie

poker face
  puss
  whitey
face card
  big shot
faced
  plastered
face the music
  bite the bullet
  take it
factory
  works
faddy
  trendy
fade
  fink
  split
fade away
  split
fag
  butt
  gay
  a smoke
fagged out
  pooped
faggot
  gay
  pot
  scarecrow
fail
  crash
  flop
  fold
failure
  flop
  loser
fair
  on the level
fair and square
  straight

fair dinkum
  on the level
fair shake
  square deal
fair-to-middling
  bush
fairy
  gay
fairy lady
  dyke
fairy powder
  dope
fake
  phony
  rig
  wing it
  works
fakealoo
  works
fake it
  bluff
  wing it
fake off
  goof off
fake out
  a bad scene
  con
  snow
fakeroo
  phony
fake up
  rig
  whomp up
fall, "be arrested"
fall about
  break up
fall apart
  blow one's top
fall down
  show up

fall down on the job
  flop
  goof off
fall flat
  flop
  fuck up
fall for
  bite
  buy
  eat up
fall guy
  patsy
fall off the roof
  have the rag on
fall on one's face
  flop
fall out
  break up
  fall
  show up
  snooze
fall to
  scarf
false
  phony
false alarm
  letdown
falsies, "false breasts"
the family jewels
  balls
fan
  fan, "devotee"
  frisk
  gab
  shoot the breeze
fancy
  great
fancy Dan
  classy
  dude

fancy footwork
 razzle-dazzle

fancypants
 dude
 sissy

fancy rags
 glad rags

fancy-schmancy
 classy

fancy up
 doll up

fangs
 choppers

fanny
 ass
 cunt

fannybumper
 mob scene

fantabulous
 great

the fantods
 the jitters

far gone
 plastered

far in
 great

farm
 croak

farmer
 dope

far out
 cool
 great
 kinky
 weird

far piece
 a country mile

fart
 cookie
 fart, "flatulate"
 guy

fart around
 goof off
 horse around

fashion plate
 dude

fast burner
 hot shot

fast chick
 floozy

fasten on
 hang on

fast footwork
 razzle-dazzle

fast one
 scam

fast shuffle
 double cross
 razzle-dazzle
 scam
 snow

fast-talk
 bullshit
 con
 snow

fat
 blubber
 fatty
 loaded

fat-ass
 fatty

fatbrain
 dope

fatbrained
 dumb

fat cat
 moneybags

fat chance
 like hell

a fat chance, "no chance"

fat city, "ideal situation"

fat, dumb, and happy
 in hog heaven

fate
 that's the way the cookie
  crumbles

fathead
 dope
 jerk

fatheaded
 dumb

fat jay
 joint

fatmouth
 bullshit
 gab
 soft-soap

fatso
 fatty

fatten up
 have a field day

fatty, "fat person"

favorite
 front runner

fay
 gay
 whitey

fear
 freeze up

featherbed
 goof off

feather-brained
 dumb

feather merchant
 goof-off

feather one's nest
 make a killing
 take care of numero uno

featherweight
 lightweight
 shorty
 wimp

feature
  spotlight
Federal agent
  G-man
fed-up, "satiated"
feeb
  dope
Feeb
  G-man
feeblo
  dope
  junkie
feed
  chow
  dope
  dough
a feed, "meal"
feed and grain man
  dealer
feed bag
  bag
  deck
feed one's face
  scarf
feed the fish
  barf
feed the kitty
  kick in
feel, "caress"
a feel
  grab-ass
feel no pain
  have a load on
  plastered
feel one's oats
  full of piss and vinegar
  horse around
feel up
  feel
  grab-ass

feeped out
  pooped
feet
  tootsies
fegelah
  gay
feh
  yuck
feisty
  bullheaded
  feisty, "irascible"
  full of piss and vinegar
fella
  guy
Fella
  Jack
fellatio
  blow
  blow job
femme
  broad
  dyke
  gay
fennel
  pot
ferret
  oddball
ferry dust
  horse
fest
  wingding
fetcher
  dish
fiddle
  con
  doctor
  scam
fiddle around
  goof off
fiddle around with
  fool around with

fiddle-faddle
  bullshit
fiddlefart
  goof off
fiddler
  con man
Fiddler's Green
  fat city
fiddle with
  doctor
  fool around with
the fidgets
  the jitters
Fido
  pooch
fiend
  fan
  junkie
fiendish
  great
fierce
  great
fiesta
  wingding
fifty-fifty
  iffy
fig
  threads
a fig
  zilch
fight
  buck
  donnybrook
  rumble
  wingding
fighting
  deck
  free-for-all
  knock out
fighting mad
  pissed off

fig up
  doll up
figure, "make sense"
file
  fuck
  heist man
file 13
  the circular file
fille de joie
  hooker
filled in
  briefed
fill someone in
  fill someone in, "inform"
  spell out
filling station
  jerk town
fillmill
  gin mill
filly
  broad
filth
  mung
filthbag
  sleazebag
filthy
  dirty
  loaded
filthy lucre
  dough
filthy rich
  loaded
filthy with, "having much"
fin
  fin, "five dollars"
  wing
financial embarrassment
  the shorts
fine hammer
  dish

fine how-de-do
  snafu
fine kettle of fish
  bind
the finest
  the cops
fine-tune
  rejigger
finger
  bag
  cop
  deck
  fingerfuck
  peg
  snitch
finger someone
  squeal
a finger
  snort
the finger
  the bird
fingerfuck, "insert a finger
  into the vulva"
fingersmith
  heist man
finicky
  prissy
finiff
  fin
finish
  clobber
  fix someone
  knock out
  screw up
finished
  finished, "ruined"
  kaput
finish off
  clobber
  snuff

fink
  asshole
  fink, "traitor"
  scab
  snitch
  squeal
fink out
  back out
fire, "dismiss"
firearm
  heeled
  plug
  rod
  Tommy gun
fireball
  eager beaver
  hot shot
fired
  high
fire-eating
  feisty
fire on
  sock
fire-plug
  big O
fire stick
  rod
firetrap
  dive
  dump
fire up
  blow grass
firewater
  booze
  panther piss
fireworks
  flak
  hassle
  hoopla
the First Families
  the upper crust

first man
  top-kick
first off
  for openers
fish
  buck
  cookie
  floozy
  patsy
  rookie
fishball
  jerk
  sleazebag
the fish-eye
  the cold shoulder
fish or cut bait, "take
    action"
fishskin
  rubber
fish trap
  yap
fist
  mitt
fist-fuck
  jack off
fit
  works
fit to be tied
  pissed off
five
  mitt
five-and-dime
  piddly
  schlocky
five-by-five
  fatty
five dollars
  fin
five finger
  heist man

five fingers
  heist man
fiver
  fin
  mitt
fives
  bennies
five-spot
  fin
fix
  bind
  clobber
  kick ass
  rig
  snuff
a fix, "narcotics dose"
a fix, "situation"
the fix
  put-up job
fix someone, "punish"
fixer
  dealer
  shyster
fix someone's hash
  clobber
  fix someone
fix up
  fix up, "put in order"
  knock up
  rejigger
fizz
  dumb
  flop
fizzle
  flop
  fuck up
  go kerflooey
flab
  blubber
flabbergaster
  a hit

flack
  flack, "publicist"
  flack, "publicity"
  flak
flack out
  snooze
flag
  bust
flag it
  flunk
flak
  flack
  flak, "criticism"
  flak, "trouble"
flake
  angel dust
  bust
  coke
  dope
  flaky
  nut
  oddball
flake off
  bug
  split
flake out
  snooze
flaky, "eccentric"
flam
  scam
flamdoodle
  bullshit
  razzle-dazzle
flamer
  eager beaver
  gay
flaming
  gay
flap
  flak
  hoopla

flapdoodle
 bullshit
 corn
flapjaw
 blabbermouth
 gab
flapper
 mitt
 wing
flare-up
 blowup
 hassle
flash
 ace
 acid
 bag
 barf
 great
 high
 hot shot
 a kick
 piss
a flash
 a jiffy
flash one's hash
 barf
flash in the pan
 letdown
flash on
 dig
flash-sport
 dude
flashy
 glitzy
flat
 broke
 pasteboard
flat-ass
 broke
 honest-to-God
 stone

flatback
 hooker
flat blues
 acid
flat broke
 broke
flatfoot
 cop
 dick
flathead
 cop
 dope
flatheaded
 dumb
flat hoop
 square
flat on one's ass
 broke
flat-out
 flat-out, "unrestrainedly"
 lickety-split
flats
 acid
 crooked dice
flatten
 clobber
 deck
 knock out
flattened
 high
flatter
 stroke
flattery
 soft-soap
flat tire
 drag
 square
flatulate
 fart
fleabag
 flophouse

a flea in one's nose
 a bee in one's bonnet
flea powder
 dope
fleatrap
 flophouse
fleece
 con
fleecer
 con man
flesh
 cheesecake
flesh flick
 blue movie
flesh peddler
 hooker
flesh-presser
 glad-hander
flic
 cop
flick it in
 cop out
flier
 junkie
flimflam
 con
 scam
 snow
flimflam man
 con man
a fling
 a crack
fling woo
 neck
flip
 bad trip
 blow one's top
 cheeky
 crack up
 flip, "respond excitedly"
 freak out

go crazy
a kick
panic
smart-ass
flip one's lid
blow one's top
crack up
go crazy
flip out
bad trip
blow one's top
flip
freak out
go crazy
flipped
high
flipper
mitt
wing
the flip side, "opposite side"
flip the bird
give someone the finger
flit
gay
flivver
flop
float
goof off
floater
bum
floating
high
flong one's dong
jack off
flooey
on the blink
plastered
floor
barrel
deck

floored
kaput
floor it
barrel
floor it, "drive very fast"
floozy
floozy, "promiscuous
woman"
hooker
flop
flop, "fail"
flop, "failure"
fuck up
snooze
flop joint
flophouse
Florida snow
coke
flossy
classy
glitzy
snappy
flower
gay
sissy
wimp
flub
boner
butterfingers
dope
fluff
goof
goof off
fluff
broad
fluff, "forget lines"
goof
fluffhead
ditz
fluffheaded
ditsy

fluff off
goof off
fluke
wing
flukum
flop
fluky
iffy
flummadiddle
bullshit
flummox
boner
flop
screw up
snafu
flummoxed
fucked-up
kaput
flunk, "fail in school"
flush
cut
flunk
loaded
shoot up
flusher
can
flush it
flunk
flute
cock
gay
fly
barrel
great
hack it
work
fly-bait
stiff
fly bull
cop

flying high
  high
  plastered

fly low
  barrel

fly off the handle
  blow one's top

fly right, "behave properly"

fly the coop
  break out
  split

fly the red flag
  have the rag on

flytrap
  yap

fog
  barrel

foggy
  rocky

fogy
  fogy, "conservative
    person"
  fogy, "old person"
  old fart

foil
  bag
  deck

fold
  cop out
  flop
  fold, "fail"
  fuck up
  wrap up

folding green
  dough

folding money
  dough

follower
  groupie

fonky
  cool

food
  chow
  a feed
  pig out

food for squirrels
  crazy
  nut

foo-foo dust
  coke

foofooraw
  donnybrook
  hoopla

fool around
  goof off
  horse around
  kid around
  sleep around

fool around with, "tamper
  with"

fool away
  blow

fooler
  long shot

fool-headed
  dumb

foolish powder
  coke
  horse

fool with
  fool around with

foon
  big O

foop
  gay

fooper
  gay

football
  bennies

foot it
  toddle

footsie
  palsy-walsy

footsies
  tootsies

footsie-wootsie
  palsy-walsy

foozle
  boner
  fogy
  fuck up
  goof
  snafu

foozler
  butterfingers
  fuck-up

for a fact
  for sure

for all one's worth
  flat-out

for certain
  for sure

for crying out loud
  Jeez

forecastle lawyer
  latrine lawyer

foreigner
  hunky

forever and amen
  for keeps

for free
  free gratis

for fun
  for kicks

forget it, "pardon"

forget lines
  fluff

for good
  for keeps

for goodness' sakes
  Jeez

329

for heaven's sakes
  Jeez

fork
  fuck
  heist man

for keeps, "permanently"

forkhander
  southpaw

for kicks, "for pleasure"

forking
  damn

fork it in
  pig out

fork out
  blow
  cough up
  kick in
  pick up the tab

form
  the book

for nothing
  free gratis

for openers, "as a
    beginning"

for Pete's sake
  Jeez

for pity's sakes
  Jeez

for real
  for sure
  honest-to-God

for starters
  for openers

for sure, "certainly"

for-sure
  honest-to-God

for the birds
  crummy

for the hell of it
  for kicks

for the love of Mike
  Jeez

forty ways to Sunday
  flat-out

forty winks
  a snooze

forwards
  bennies

fossil
  fogy
  old fart

foul
  dirty

foul ball
  jerk
  loser
  oddball

fouled-up
  fucked-up

foulup
  boner

foul up
  fuck up
  goof
  screw up
  snafu

found money
  gravy

four-flusher
  con man
  phony

the four hundred
  the upper crust

four-letter man
  asshole
  dope

four-O
  great

four-square
  square

four-star
  big-league

four-way hit
  acid

four-wheeler
  jalopy

fox
  con
  dish
  floozy

foxy
  high
  sexy

frabjous
  great

fracas
  free-for-all
  hassle

fracture
  break someone up
  wow

fractured
  high
  plastered

frag
  snuff

fraidy-cat
  chicken
  wimp

frail
  broad

frail job
  dish

frame
  bum rap
  frame, "incriminate
    falsely"
  stanza

frame-up
  bum rap

frantic
 great

frapping
 damn

frau
 broad
 old woman

fraud
 phony

frazzled
 high
 kaput
 pooped

freak
 fan
 flip
 freak out
 gay
 junkie
 nut
 oddball
 pothead

freaking
 damn

freak out
 bad trip
 crack up
 flip
 freak out, "experience a
   bad narcotics reaction"
 go crazy

freaky
 kinky

freebase
 coke

freebie
 Annie Oakley
 freebie, "something free of
   charge"
 free gratis

free-for-all, "brawl"

freeload
 bum

freeloader
 moocher

free lunch
 freebie

free ticket
 Annie Oakley
 blank check

freeze out
 cut
 give the cold shoulder

freeze up, "panic"

French
 blow
 fur pie

Frenchie
 rubber

French job
 blow job

French kiss, "kiss"

French letter
 rubber

French person
 Frog

French safe
 rubber

fresh
 cheeky
 chutzpa
 cool
 great

fresh up
 brush up

fretty
 jittery

fribble away
 blow

fried
 fucked-up
 high

kaput
 plastered
 pooped

friend
 pal

friendly
 chummy
 palsy-walsy

friendship
 buddy up

frig
 ass
 con
 fingerfuck
 fuck
 a fuck

frigged
 screwed

frigging
 ass
 damn
 fucking
 scam

fright
 scarecrow

frighten
 scare the shit out of
 spook

frightened
 panic
 scared shitless

frisk, "search"

frisking powder
 coke

frit
 gay

fritter away
 blow

fritz
 screw up

Fritz
  kraut

fritzed
  on the blink

fritzer
  phony

frivol away
  blow
  horse around

'fro
  Afro

frobnitz
  gadget

frog-eater
  Frog

frogging
  damn

Froggy
  Frog

frogskin
  buck
  dough

frolic
  caper

from A to Z
  stone

from hunger
  crummy

from scratch, "from the
  beginning"

from the ground up
  flat-out
  from scratch

front
  shill

frontal
  straight

front name
  monicker

front office
  the brass

frontpage
  big-league

front runner, "probable
  winner"

froody
  great

frost
  flop
  letdown
  piss someone off

the frost
  the cold shoulder

frost someone's ass
  give someone a pain in the
  ass

frosted
  high

frosty
  high

froth
  brew

fruitcake
  gay
  nut
  oddball

fruitcakey
  crazy

fruit salad, "disabled
  person"

fruit wagon
  meat wagon

fruity
  crazy
  gay
  weird

fry
  crash

fry, "die in the electric
  chair"

fu
  pot

fubar
  fucked-up

fuck
  ass
  asshole
  con
  fuck, "copulate"
  fuck, "copulation"
  fuck, "maltreat"
  zilch

a fuck, "copulation"

fuck around
  fool around with
  goof off
  play games

fuck book, "pornographic
  book"

fucked
  screwed

fucked out
  pooped

fucked-up
  fucked-up, "chaotic"
  on the blink

fucker
  asshole
  gadget
  guy
  sucker

fuck film
  blue movie

fuckhead
  asshole
  jerk

fucking
  ass
  damn

fucking, "conspicuous and
  complete"

fucking, "extremely"
  scam
  yucky

a fucking
 the shaft
fucking ay
 bet your ass
fucking well told
 bet your ass
fuck off
 goof off
 jack off
 split
fuck over
 fuck
fuck up
 fuck
 fuck up, "blunder"
 goof
 screw up
fuck-up
 boner
 fuck-up, "bungler"
 snafu
fuck with
 doctor
 fool around with
fuck you
 fuck you, "expression of
  strong defiance"
 kiss my ass
fuck you and the horse you
  rode in on
 fuck you
fud
 fogy
fuddled
 rocky
fuddy-duddy
 fogy
 square
fudge
 cook up
 doctor

fudging one's undies
 panic
 scared shitless
fuel
 angel dust
full
 high
fullams
 crooked dice
full blast
 flat-out
 high
 lickety-split
full court press
 best shot
full fig
 glad rags
full moon
 bag
 deck
full-mooner
 nut
full of baloney
 full of shit
full of beans
 full of piss and vinegar
 full of shit
full steam
 lickety-split
full up
 fed-up
Fu Manchu
 pothead
fumble-fist
 butterfingers
 fuck-up
fumtu
 fucked-up
fun
 big O

horse around
horseplay
fun and games
 kicks
funk
 the blues
 chicken out
 freeze up
 jerk
 panic
 spook
funk hole
 hideaway
funk out
 back out
 chicken out
funky
 cool
 great
 hunky
 kinky
 yucky
funny
 crazy
 flaky
 howl
 kinky
 weird
funny business
 dirty tricks
 monkey business
funny cigarette
 joint
funny farm
 booby hatch
funny stuff
 pot
fun-seeker
 playboy
furburger
 cunt

dish
  fur pie

furry
  creepy
  hairy

fuss
  hoopla
  sweat

fussy
  prissy

futy
  cunt
  fuck

futz
  con
  fuck
  a fuck
  old fart

futz around
  goof off

futz around with
  fool around with

futzed-up
  fucked-up

the fuzz
  the cops

fuzzled
  plastered

fuzznuts
  jerk

fuzz tub
  prowl car

fuzzy
  cinch
  cop
  high

fuzzy one
  doll

G
  grand
  works

gab
  chitchat

gab, "speak"
gab, "speech"
  shoot the breeze

gabber
  blabbermouth

gabble
  chitchat
  gab

gabby, "talkative"

gabfest
  schmooz

gadabout
  playboy

gadget, "device"

gadgetry, "device"

gadzooks
  Jeez

gaffer
  old fart

gag
  crack

ga-ga
  crazy
  ditsy

gage
  panther piss
  pot

gage butt
  joint

gag line
  punch line

Gainesville green
  pot

gal
  broad

gal Friday
  gofer

gall
  chutzpa

galley-west
  cockeyed
  fucked-up

galoot
  guy

gam
  schmooz

a gamble, "chance"

game
  gimpy
  racket

gammon
  razzle-dazzle

gammot
  horse

gams
  pins

gamy
  dirty

gander
  check out
  the once-over
  rubberneck

gang
  bag
  deck

gang bang, "copulation"

gangbusters
  a hit

ganger
  dope

gangster, "criminal"

ganja
  pot

ganze macher
  wheeler-dealer

garbage
  bullshit

crap
dope
pot

garbage down
  scarf

garden variety
  bush

gargle
  guzzle
  snort

gargle factory
  dive
  gin mill

gargoyle
  scarecrow

gas
  bullshit
  chitchat
  flop
  gab
  a hit
  schmooz
  shoot the breeze

a gas
  a ball

gasbag
  bigmouth
  blabbermouth

Gas City
  a ball

gas-guzzler
  jalopy

gash
  ass
  bullshit
  cunt
  floozy
  pot

gash hound
  stud

gasket
  works

gasman
  bigmouth
  flack

gasper
  butt
  joint
  a smoke

gassed
  high
  plastered

gassed-up
  jazzed-up

gasser
  flop
  a hit

gassy
  gabby

gas up
  jazz up

gat
  rod

gate
  shoot up
  take

the gate
  the axe

gatemouth
  bigmouth
  blabbermouth

gates
  pot

gaudy
  glitzy

gawk
  rubberneck

gay, "homosexual"
gay, "homosexual male"

gay bird
  playboy

gay-cat
  dude

gay deceivers
  falsies

gay dog
  playboy

gazabo
  guy

gazer
  cop
  dick

gazoo
  ass
  asshole

GB
  doll

gear
  great
  pot
  psych someone up

gearbox
  dope

geared
  high
  pumped

geared up
  high
  pumped

gearhead
  dope

gear someone up
  psych someone up

gee
  dough
  grand
  guy
  Jeez
  yucky

geech
  scarecrow

geechee
  nigger

gee-dee
  damn

geed up
  high

geek
  jerk
  lush
  oddball
  sleazebag

geepo
  snitch

geets
  dough

gee whiz
  heist man
  Jeez

geez
  dope
  shoot up

geezed
  high

geezer
  dope
  fogy
  guy
  old fart
  snort

gel
  work

gelatin
  acid

gelt
  dough

gem
  the McCoy

the gen
  the poop
  the straight dope

gendarme
  cop

genitals
  hung

gent
  cookie
  guy

George
  Jeez

George smack
  horse

German goiter
  potbelly

German person
  kraut

get
  bug
  dig
  snuff

get a bang out of
  dig
  flip
  get a kick out of

get one's act together
  clean up one's act
  get it together

get one's back up
  blow one's top

get a kick out of
  dig

get a line on
  smoke out

get a little on the side
  cheat

get a load of
  check out

get along
  get by
  hit it off

get a move on
  get the lead out

get a rise out of
  piss someone off

get a wiggle on
  get the lead out

get someone's back up
  piss someone off

get behind
  back
  have a ball

get by, "perform
    minimally"

get cold feet
  chicken out

get cracking
  get the lead out

get down
  blow grass
  have a ball

get down on
  bug

get down to cases
  get down to brass tacks
  lay it on the line
  zero in

get even, "avenge"

get one's feet wet
  take a crack at

get someone's goat
  bug

get going
  get the lead out
  split

get one's hands on
  grab

get hold of
  grab

get one's hooks into
  grab

get in one's hair
  bug
  give someone a pain in the
    ass

get into the act
 butt in

get in trouble
 knock up

get one's Irish up
 blow one's top

get it
 catch hell
 get it in the neck
 get me

get it all together
 get it together

get it in the neck
 get it in the neck, "be
  injured"
 take a beating

get it off
 come

get it off one's chest
 let it all hang out

get it off with
 fuck

get it on
 blow grass
 get the lead out
 have a ball

get it out of one's system
 let it all hang out

get it straight
 dig

get it together
 clean up one's act
 get it together, "organize
  life"

get one's jollies
 have a ball

get laid
 fuck

get lost
 fuck you

lay off
 split

get lucky, "enjoy luck"

get mad
 blow one's top

get me, "comprehend"

get moving
 split

get naked
 have a ball

get next to
 brown-nose

get off
 blow grass
 have a ball
 shoot up

get off someone's case
 get off someone's back

get off one's high horse
 come down a peg

get off on
 dig
 get a kick out of

get off the dime
 get the lead out
 split

get off the ground
 hack it
 work

get off with
 fuck

get on
 blow grass
 get by

get on board
 plug into

get on someone's case
 bug
 crowd

get on someone's list
 blow it with someone

get on someone's nerves
 bug

get on the ball
 clean up one's act
 get on the ball, "improve"

get on the bandwagon, "join
  a popular trend"

get on the stick
 get on the ball
 get the lead out

get out of here
 izzatso

get out of my hair
 lay off

get one's own back
 get even

get smart
 wise up

get some rack
 snooze

get sore
 blow one's top

get straight
 clean up one's act

get the air
 get the ax

get the business
 get it in the neck

get the drift
 dig
 get me

get the hang of
 dig

get the hell out
 split

get the idea
 dig

get the lead out of one's ass
 get the lead out

get the picture
 dig

get me
 wise up

get the sack
 get the ax

get through
 score

get to
 bug

get to first base
 work

get-together
 wingding

get to the bottom line
 get down to brass tacks

get tough with
 bulldoze

get under one's skin
 bug

get up
 brush up
 doll up
 threads

get-up-and-go
 pizzazz

get wise
 dig
 wise up

get with it
 clean up one's act
 dig
 get on the ball
 shoot up
 wise up

ghetto blaster
 ghetto box

ghost
 acid
 whitey

ghost turd
 dust bunny

ghow
 big O

GI
 buck private

gibble-gabble
 blabbermouth
 chitchat
 gab

giddy
 ditsy

giddyapper
 horse opera

giddybrain
 ditz

gidget
 gadget

gig
 asshole
 cunt
 scam
 wingding

a giggle
 a laugh

giggle smoke
 pot

giggy
 asshole
 cunt

gigmaree
 gadget

GI Joe
 buck private

gilhooley
 gadget

gills
 puss
 yap

gimbaljawed
 gabby

gimmick
 bag
 gadget
 gimmick, "device"
 works

gimmicks
 gadgetry
 works

gimpy, "limping"

gin
 coke
 donnybrook
 free-for-all

ginch
 ass
 broad
 cunt

ginchy
 great
 sexy

ginger
 guts
 pizzazz

gingerpeachy
 great

gingery
 zingy

ginhead
 lush

gink
 cookie
 guy
 jerk

gin mill
 dive
 gin mill, "bar"

ginned up
 plastered

ginzo
 hunky
 wop

girl
  coke
  gay
  jail bait
girlie
  broad
  cheesecake
the GIs
  the shits
gism
  cum
  pizzazz
git
  split
give
  stake someone to
give someone a bad time
  bug
give a go
  take a crack at
give a good talking to
  chew out
give a look at
  check out
give a miss, "avoid"
give someone a pain in the
    ass, "annoy"
give a piece of one's mind
  chew out
give someone a ring,
    "telephone"
give something a shot, "try"
give someone a slap on the
    wrist, "punish mildly"
give a turn
  spook
giveaway
  freebie
give away
  blow

give a whirl
  take a crack at
give five, "shake hands"
give five to
  sock
give good head
  blow
give hail Columbia
  chew out
give head
  blow
give hell
  chew out
  kick ass
give someone his (or her)
    walking papers,
    "dismiss"
give in
  fold
give it to
  kick ass
  sock
give it to someone in the
    neck
  fix someone
give merry hell
  chew out
  kick ass
give out
  croak
  fold
  fuck
  go kerflooey
give some skin
  give five
give the axe
  fire
give the bum's rush
  bounce
  fire

give the business
  chew out
  clobber
  rough up
  snuff
give someone the business
  con
  fix someone
  snow
give the cold shoulder,
    "snub"
give the devil
  chew out
give the door
  fire
give the finger
  fuck
give someone the finger,
    "insult"
give the gate
  fire
give the go-by
  cut
  give a miss
  give the cold shoulder
give the nod to
  go for
give the once-over
  check out
give the shakes
  spook
give the works
  chew out
  clobber
  rough up
  snuff
give up the ghost
  croak
  go kerflooey
give what-for
  chew out

gizmo
  gadget
  guy

glad
  coke

glad-hander
  glad-hander, "insincere
    greeter"
  phony

glad rags, "best clothing"

glad stuff
  big O
  M

glamor girl
  dish

glamorous people
  the jet set

glamor puss
  dish
  hunk

glare
  stick out like a sore thumb

glass
  bennies
  works

glass arm, "vulnerable arm"

glass jaw, "vulnerable chin"

glazed
  high
  plastered

glim
  check out

glimmers
  peepers

glitch, "malfunction"

the glitterati
  the jet set

glitzy, "gaudy"

glob, "viscous mass"

globes
  tits

glom
  check out
  mitt

glommer
  mitt

glom on to
  grab

gloomy Gus,
    "melancholiac"

glop
  corn
  goo
  mung

gloppy
  corny

glory-grabber
  grandstander

glory hallelujah
  Jeez

gluey
  corny

glug
  snort

glutton
  pig

G-man, "Federal agent"

gnarly
  crummy
  great

gnatbrain
  dope

gnome
  bean counter

go
  come off
  hassle

a go
  a clip
  a crack

the go
  the OK

goad
  goose

the go-ahead
  the go-ahead, "permission"
  the OK

go all the way
  bust one's ass
  fuck

go along
  play ball

go along with
  buy
  get on the bandwagon

go ape
  blow one's top
  crack up
  go crazy

go ape over
  flip
  go crazy

go at
  chew out
  take a crack at

goat fuck
  snafu

goatish
  horny

go at it
  fuck
  hassle

gob
  glob
  swabby
  yap

go back to square one,
    "begin again"

go bananas
  crack up
  go crazy

go bananas over
flip

gobble
blow
pig out

gobble down
bite

gobbledygook
double-talk

gobbler
cocksucker
pig

gobble up
eat up
flip

go beddie-bye
snooze

go belly up
crash
croak
flop
fuck up
go broke
go kerflooey

go bonkers
go crazy

go broke
go broke, "become insolvent"
take a beating

gobs
bundle

go bust
go broke

the go-by
the cold shoulder

go crazy, "become insane"

godawful
crummy
damn
fucking
yucky

goddamn
damn

godfather
boss

godfer
kid

go down
come off
crash
go kerflooey

go down for the count
flop
take a beating

go downhill
go to hell

go down in flames
crash

go down on
blow

go down the drain
fuck up
go kerflooey
go to hell

God's gift to women
ladies' man

go easy
cool it

gofer, "subordinate"

go figure
that's the way the cookie crumbles

go fly a kite
fuck you
lay off

go for
bite
buy
dig
flip
get a kick out of

go for, "choose"
have a lech for

go-for
gofer

go for broke
bust one's ass
go for it

go for in a big way
have a lech for

go for it
bust one's ass
go for it, "risk all"

go fuck yourself
fuck you
kiss my ass

go-getter
eager beaver
hot shot

goggle
rubberneck

goggle-eye
panther piss

goggle-eyed
popeyed

goggles
specs

go-go
full of piss and vinegar
trendy
with it

a go-go
trendy

go great guns
ace
go over with a bang

go haywire
go crazy
go kerflooey

go hog wild
let oneself go

go home in a box
  croak

goies
  bennies

go into one's dance,
    "persuade"

go jump in the lake
  lay off

go kerflooey, "stop
    functioning"

gold
  coke
  dough
  pot

goldamn
  damn
  Jeez

Goldberg
  kike

gold braid
  the brass

goldbrick
  goof off

goldbricker
  goof-off

golden girl
  coke

goldern
  damn

goldfinger
  horse

gold leaf
  pot

gold leaf special
  joint

gold mine, "profit"

go like a bat out of hell
  barrel

golly
  Jeez

go-long
  Black Maria

goma
  big O
  M

go man go
  way to go

goms
  cop

gone
  cool
  great
  high
  plastered

goner
  goner, "doomed one"
  stiff

goney
  dope

gonga dust
  M

gonga smudge
  joint

gonged
  high
  plastered

goniff
  heist man

gonzo
  crazy
  nut

goo
  corn
  cum
  goo, "viscous fluid"

goober
  jerk
  joint
  oddball
  zit

good
  cool

good deal
  square deal
  way to go

good egg
  good guy

good gracious
  Jeez

good head
  blow job
  good guy

good Joe
  good guy

good-looker
  dish

good old boy
  cracker

goods
  dope
  score

the goods
  clout
  humdinger
  the McCoy
  the poop

good sport
  good guy

good time Charlie
  playboy

good-time man
  dealer

good way
  a country mile

good wife
  old woman

goody
  Christer
  goody-goody
  wimp

goody two-shoes
  goody-goody

goof
  blow grass
  boner
  dope
  fuck-up
  glitch
  goof, "blunder"
  jerk
  junkie
  nut
  oddball
  pothead

goof around
  goof off

goofball
  doll
  dope
  a fix
  nut
  oddball

goof butt
  joint
  pot

goofed
  high

goofer
  doll
  dope
  fuck-up

go off half-cocked, "act
    prematurely"

go off one's rocker
  crack up
  go crazy

go off the deep end
  blow one's top
  crack up

goof off, "avoid work"
goof off, "idle pleasure"
goof-off, "shirker"

goof-up
  boner
  butterfingers
  fuck-up
  goof
  screw up
  snafu

goofus
  dope
  flaky
  fuck-up
  gadget
  patsy

goofy
  crazy
  ditsy
  dope
  dumb
  flaky

goofy dust
  coke

goog
  black eye

googly-eyed
  popeyed

goo-goo
  crazy
  ditsy
  gook

gook
  crap
  goo
  gook, "Asian"

gooly butt
  joint

goombah
  gangster
  pal

goon
  angel dust
  goon, "ruffian"
  jerk

goon dust
  angel dust

go one on one with
  take on

gooney
  dope

goon squad, "ruffians"

goop
  dope
  goo

goopgobbler
  cocksucker

goophead
  zit

goopy
  corny

goose
  goose, "goad"
  jazz up

goose bumps, "gooseflesh"

goose-bumpy
  scared shitless

goosed-up
  jazzed-up

a goose egg
  zilch

gooseflesh
  goose bumps

goose it
  floor it

goose up
  jazz up

goosy, "touchy"

go out
  pass out

go out like a light
  pass out

go out of one's skull
  blow one's top

crack up
go crazy

go out of one's way
bust one's ass

go out on a limb
stick one's neck out

go over
bat around
go over with a bang
work
wow

go over big
wow

go overboard for
flip

go over in a big way
wow

go over like a lead balloon
flop

go over the hill, "depart"

go over the wall
break out

go over with a bang, "succeed"

goozlum
goo

go peddle your papers
lay off

go pfft
flop

gopher
gofer
heist man

go places
go over with a bang

go places and do things
have a ball

go public, "reveal"

gorblimey
Jeez

gorgeous
great

gorilla
bulldoze
clobber
cowboy
goon
hit man
rough up

gork
patsy

gorked
high

gorm
scarf

gormless
dumb

go round and round
hassle

go round the bend
go crazy

gorp
scarf

goshawful
damn
fucking

goshdarn
damn
Jeez

go soak your head
fuck you
lay off

go south
crash
flop
heist
split

the gospel
the straight dope

gossip
dirt

go straight
fly right
go straight, "reform"

gotcha
bust

gotch-eyed
popeyed

go the extra mile
bust one's ass

go the limit
bust one's ass
fuck

go the whole hog
bust one's ass

go through the mill
go through the mill, "acquire practical experience"
pay one's dues

got it
get me

go to bat for
back
go to bat for, "defend"

go toe to toe
hassle
take on

go to hell
come unglued
fuck you
go to hell, "deteriorate"

go to it
fuck
hassle

go to pieces
come unglued
crack up

go to pot
come unglued
go to hell

go to the dogs
  come unglued
  go to hell

go to the mat
  back
  hassle

go to the powder room
  check the plumbing

go to the wall
  bust one's ass
  take a beating

go to town
  barrel
  fuck
  go over with a bang
  have a ball

go to wrack and ruin
  go to hell

gouge
  con

gouger
  con man
  pothead

go under
  fuck up
  pass out
  take a beating

go up against
  buck
  take on

go up in someone's face
  chew out

go up in one's line
  fluff

go up in smoke
  go kerflooey

go up the spout
  fuck up
  go kerflooey
  go to hell

gourd
  bean

governor
  boss

gow
  big O
  cheesecake
  hot rod
  joint

gow crust
  big O

gowed
  high

gowed-up job
  hot rod

gowhead
  junkie

go with the flow
  keep one's cool

gow job
  hot rod

gowster
  junkie
  pothead

goynk
  big O

grab
  bust
  grab, "acquire"

grab-ass, "caressing"

grab-bag
  mish-mash

grabber
  gimmick

grabby, "attractive"

grabby, "greedy"

grab on
  neck

grad
  cool

gradehound
  grind

grads
  bennies

graft
  racket

gram
  bag
  deck

gramps
  old fart

grand, "thousand
    dollars"

Grand Central Station
  mob scene

grandly
  with flying colors

grand slam, "victory"

grandstander, "egotist"

grandstand it
  grandstand

grandstand player
  grandstander

grape parfait
  acid

grasp the nettle
  bite the bullet

grass
  pot

grassback
  floozy

grasshead
  pothead

graum
  sweat

gravel
  bug
  guts

gravy
  cinch

dough
  gravy, "bonus"
gravy train
  gold mine
gray
  whitey
gray-flannel
  square
gray matter
  smarts
graze
  scarf
grease
  big O
  clout
  snuff
  soft soap
  soft-soap
greaseball
  bean-eater
  grease monkey
  wop
grease down
  scarf
grease-gut
  bean-eater
greasehound
  grease monkey
grease job
  soft soap
grease monkey, "mechanic"
grease someone's palm,
    "bribe"
greaser
  bean-eater
  goon
  wop
greasy spoon, "restaurant"
the greatest
  great
  the most

greatest thing since sliced
    bread
  hot shot
the great one
  big shot
great Scott
  Jeez
greeby
  yucky
greedy
  grabby
greedy-guts
  pig
greefa
  pot
Greek
  bugger
  double-talk
Greek god
  hunk
green
  angel dust
  dough
  pothead
green around the gills,
    "nauseated"
green ashes
  big O
greenbacks
  dough
green dragon
  acid
  bennies
  doll
green folding
  dough
green griff
  pot
greenhorn
  greenhorn, "neophyte"
  rookie

greenie
  duck-squeezer
greenies
  bennies
the green light
  the go-ahead
  the OK
green Moroccan
  hash
green mud
  big O
green powder
  big O
green stuff
  dough
green swirls
  acid
green tea
  angel dust
green wedge
  acid
greeny
  greenhorn
  rookie
greta
  pot
grette
  butt
grief
  flak
griefer
  pothead
grifado
  high
grift
  scam
grifter
  bum
  con man
  heist man

grim
  yucky
grin and bear it
  hang tough
  take it
grinch
  gloomy Gus
grind
  back-breaker
  grind, "diligent student"
  jerk
grinder
  hero
  jalopy
  stripper
grinders
  choppers
gripe
  beef
  bug
  kvetch
griper
  kvetch
gilt
  butt
  guts
  scarf
grits
  chow
gritty
  gutsy
groan
  warble
groanbox
  squeezebox
groceries
  chow
grody
  yucky

grog
  booze
  dope
grogged
  plastered
groggery
  gin mill
groggy
  rocky
grog merchant
  dealer
groid
  nigger
grok
  dig
grokking
  on someone's
    wavelength
grommet
  kid
  teenybopper
gronk out
  go kerflooey
grooby
  great
groove
  bag
  dig
  have a ball
  a kick
a groove
  a ball
  humdinger
groove on
  dig
  get a kick out of
groover
  jerk
grooving
  high
  in the groove

groovy
  cool
  great
  square
  with it
grope
  feel
  grab-ass
gross
  crummy
  take
  yucky
grouch
  beef
  kvetch
groucher
  kvetch
grouchy
  feisty
groudy
  yucky
ground rations
  ass
groupie
  fan
  groupie, "follower"
grouse
  beef
  kvetch
grouser
  kvetch
growl
  beef
growler
  bitch box
grub
  chow
  a feed
grub-staker
  angel

grub up
  grab
  scarf

grumbler
  kvetch

grumps
  the blues

grunch
  jerk
  mung

grunge
  fuck
  jerk
  mung

grungy
  crummy
  yucky

grunt
  gofer
  grind
  grunt, "infantry soldier"
  shit

the grunt
  the damage

grunt work
  scut work

guardhouse lawyer
  latrine lawyer

guck
  goo

guesser
  Blind Tom

guff
  bullshit
  chitchat
  gab
  sass

gug
  jerk

guilty
  catch redhanded

Guinea
  wop

gully-jumper
  hick

gully-low
  dirty

gulp down
  bite

gum
  big O
  gab

gumball
  party hat

gum-beater
  blabbermouth

gum-beating
  bullshit
  schmooz

gumbo
  goo

gumby
  jerk

gumfoot
  cop

gummed-up
  fucked-up

gummix up
  screw up

gummy
  corny

gump
  dope
  gay
  jerk

gumshoe
  cop
  dick

gum up
  fuck up
  screw up

gun
  heist man
  hit man
  works

gun down
  snuff

gunga
  dumb
  Jeez

gung ho
  antsy
  full of piss and vinegar

gunk
  goo

gunman
  hit man

gunner
  grandstander

gunny
  pot

gunpoke
  hit man

gunsel
  hit man

guru
  shrink

gushy
  corny

gussy up
  doll up

gut
  belly
  gut course
  potbelly

gut-buster
  back-breaker
  belly laugh
  belly-whopper

gut course, "easy course"

gutless
  chicken
  wimpish
gutless wonder
  wimp
guts
  chutzpa
  guts, "courage"
  guts, "viscera"
  innards
gutsy
  gutsy, "courageous"
  zingy
gutter
  shoot up
gut-thumper
  a hit
gutty
  cheeky
  gutsy
guy
  cookie
  gadget
  guy, "male person"
Guy
  Jack
guzzle
  binge
  guzzle, "drink"
  snort
guzzler
  lush
guzzle shop
  gin mill
guzzling
  on the sauce
gweebo
  grind
  jerk
gyp
  con

con man
  scam
gyp artist
  con man
gyppy tummy
  the shits
gyrene
  leatherneck
gyve
  joint
H
  horse
hack
  hack it
  whitey
a hack
  a crack
hack around
  goof off
hacked
  pissed off
hacker
  butterfingers
  duffer
hack it, "succeed"
had
  screwed
had it
  finished
  pooped
hag
  old bag
  scarecrow
hail Columbia
  Jeez
hair pie
  blow job
  cunt
  fur pie
hairsplitter
  cock

hairy
  creepy
  hairy, "difficult"
  horse
  yucky
hairy-chested
  he-man
the hairy eyeball
  the cold shoulder
half
  bag
  deck
half a mo
  a jiffy
half-assed
  crummy
  dumb
  half-assed, "careless"
  piddly
half-baked
  crazy
  crummy
  dumb
  half-assed
half bundle
  bag
  deck
half-cracked
  flaky
half in the bag
  plastered
half load
  bag
  deck
half-pint
  lightweight
  little bitty
  piddly
  shorty
halvah
  horse

halvahed
  high
ham, "overact"
ham-and-egger
  Joe Blow
ham-and-eggery
  greasy spoon
ham-fisted
  ham-handed
ham it up
  ham
hammer
  broad
  cock
  dish
  sock
hammer down
  flat-out
  lickety-split
hammerhead
  mule
hammer out
  whomp up
hand
  mitt
H and C
  coke
  horse
handcuffs
  bracelets
hand someone his (or her)
    head
  clobber
hand it to someone,
    "compliment"
handkerchief-head
  fink
handle
  feel
  monicker
  take

handle the reins
  boss
hando
  great
hand out
  stake someone to
hand over
  kick in
hand over fist
  like hell
handshake
  give five
handshaker
  glad-hander
  phony
hang
  goof off
hang around
  goof off
  sit tight
hang around with
  hang out with
hang in
  hang tough
hang it easy
  cool it
hang it up
  knock off
hang loose
  cool it
hang on
  hang on, "accuse"
  hang tough
  sit tight
hang one on
  clobber
hangout
  pad
hang out
  goof off
  stick out like a sore thumb

hang out with, "associate
    with"
hang together
  figure
hang tough
  hang tough, "endure"
  take it
hang up
  shut up
hanky-panky
  grab-ass
  monkey business
  razzle-dazzle
  scam
happen
  come off
happies
  kicks
happy dust
  dope
happy
  plastered
  tickled
harass
  roust
hard
  great
  horny
  tough
hard-assed
  tough
hardball
  big-league
  the big leagues
hard-boiled egg
  bad man
  goon
hard case
  goon
hard cash
  dough

hard coin
  bundle

hard-hat
  redneck

hardhead
  mule
  nigger
  whitey

hardheaded
  bullheaded

hard job
  back-breaker

hard John
  G-man

hard-legs
  dude

hard-luck story
  tear-jerker

hardnose
  mule
  tough

hardnosed
  bullheaded
  feisty
  tough

hard nut to crack
  mule

hard-on, "erection"

a hard-on
  hot pants

hard put
  out of luck

hard row to hoe
  back-breaker

hard stuff
  booze
  M

hard up
  horny
  out of luck

hardware
  rod

har-har
  break up

harness bull
  cop

harp
  Mick

harpoon
  works

Harry
  horse

harum-scarum
  rootin'-tootin'

hash
  bat around
  dope
  great
  hash, "hashish"

hashery
  greasy spoon

hashhead
  junkie

hashhouse
  greasy spoon

hashish
  hash

hash mark, "service stripe"

hash over
  bat around

hash session
  schmooz

hash stripe
  hash mark

hash up
  screw up

hassle
  bug
  hassle, "conflict"
  roust

hasty job
  a lick and a promise

hat
  lid

hatchet-face
  scarecrow

a hatchet job
  the axe

hatchet man
  hit man

hate
  hate someone's guts

hatrack
  beanpole

hatty
  stuck-up

haul
  score
  take

haul ass
  barrel
  split

hauler
  hot rod

haul in
  bust

haul it
  split

haul over the coals
  chew out

haul the mail
  barrel

have
  con

have someone
  fuck

have a bag on
  have a load on

have a ball, "enjoy"

have a bellyful
fed-up

have a bird
blow one's top

have a bug up one's ass
have a hair up one's ass

have a case on
have a lech for

have a catfit
blow one's top

have a chip on one's
shoulder
have a hair up one's ass

have a conniption fit
blow one's top
make a scene

have a crack at
give something a shot
take a crack at

have a crush on
have a lech for

have a few marbles missing
have a hole in one's head

have a field day, "succeed"

have a fit
blow one's top
make a scene

have a gander at
check out

have a go at
give something a shot
take a crack at

have a hair up one's ass,
"be touchy"

have a hard-on for
hate someone's guts
have a lech for
have hot pants

have a hole in one's head,
"be stupid"

have a lech for, "crave"

have a load on, "be drunk"

have a lock on
have something cinched

have a looksee
check out

have an attitude
beef

have a party
fuck

have a screw loose
have a hole in one's head

have a shit fit
blow one's top
make a scene

have a short fuse
have a hair up one's ass

have a shot at
give something a shot
take a crack at

have a tantrum
make a scene

have a thing for
have a lech for

have balls, "be courageous"

have bang to rights
catch redhanded

have someone by the balls,
"have a decisive
advantage"

have by the short hairs
have someone by the balls

have clout
carry a lot of weight

have cold
catch redhanded

have dead to rights
catch redhanded

have egg in one's beer
eat high on the hog

have eyes for
have a lech for

have for breakfast
clobber

have guts
have balls

have hacked
have something cinched

have one's head up one's
ass
have a hole in one's head

have hot pants, "lust for"

have it all over
beat

have it bad for
have a lech for

have it both ways, "have
with certainty"

have it down pat
dig

have it good
eat high on the hog

have it in for
hate someone's guts

have it made
eat high on the hog
have something cinched

have it pegged
dig

have kittens
blow one's top

have knocked
have something cinched

have someone's lunch
clobber

have made
have something cinched

have no use for
hate someone's guts

have someone on
   kid
   snow
have over a barrel
   have someone by the balls
have someone pegged
   have someone's number
have rocks in one's head
   have a hole in one's head
have taped
   have something cinched
have someone taped
   have someone's number
have the curse
   have the rag on
have the drop on
   have someone by the balls
have the hots
   have a lech for
   have hot pants
have the last word
   boss
have the nerve
   have balls
have the rag on,
   "menstruate"
have one's ticket punched
   pay one's dues
have wired
   have something cinched
have your cake and eat it
   have it both ways
Hawaiian sunshine
   acid
hawkshaw
   dick
hay
   chicken feed
   pot

hay butt
   joint
hay-eater
   whitey
hayhead
   pothead
haymaker
   sock
   Sunday punch
hayseed
   hick
haywire
   cockeyed
   crazy
   flaky
   full of shit
   on the blink
haze
   acid
   rough up
Hazel
   horse
H-cap
   horse
head
   bean
   blow job
   can
   cookie
   dish
   fur pie
   high
   junkie
   a kick
   pothead
   yap
headache
   bad news
   drag
   jerk
headcase
   nut

head cheese
   boss
head job
   blow job
head kit
   works
headlights
   tits
headline
   spotlight
one's head off
   flat-out
   one's head off, "mightily"
   like hell
head out
   split
head over heels
   flat-out
headpiece
   bean
headshrinker
   shrink
head up
   boss
heap
   jalopy
heaped
   high
heart
   ticker
heartbreaker
   ladies' man
hear the birdies sing
   pass out
hearts
   bennies
hearts and flowers
   corn
heart-stopper
   a hit

heartthrob
  honey

heart-to-heart
  schmooz

heat
  flak
  rod
  stanza

the heat
  the cops

heater
  rod

heat merchant
  kvetch

heave
  barf

the heave-ho
  the axe

heaven and hell
  angel dust

heaven dust
  coke

heavenly
  great

heavens to Betsy
  Jeez

heavy
  bad man
  big-league
  big shot
  bruiser
  cool
  goon
  great
  hairy
  heavy, "important"

heavy breathing
  ass

heavycake
  stud

heavy coin
  bundle

heavy hash
  hash

heavy man
  goon

heavy money
  bundle

heavy sledding
  back-breaker

heavyweight
  ace
  big-league
  big shot
  bruiser
  fatty
  heavy

Hebe
  kike

hedge one's bets
  play it safe

the heebie-jeebies
  the jitters
  the shakes

heel
  asshole
  shill

heeled
  heeled, "armed"
  loaded

heeler
  asshole

heesh
  dope
  hash

hefty
  big-league
  hairy
  heavy
  high-powered

heifer
  broad

heinie
  ass
  asshole

Heinie
  kraut

heist
  heist, "robbery"
  heist, "steal"
  hike

heist man, "thief"

hell
  barrel
  a bitch
  hell around
  Jeez

hellacious
  great

hell around, "pursue
  pleasure"

hell-bender
  binge

hell-bent
  lickety-split

hell breaks loose, "things
  deteriorate"

hell dust
  M

heller
  eager beaver

hellhole
  dive
  dump

a hell of a, "remarkable"

hell of a mess
  bind
  snafu

hell of a note
  bind
  a bitch

hell on wheels
 a bitch

hell's bells
 Jeez

hell to pay
 bind

a helluva
 a hell of a

the hell you say
 izzatso

helter-skelter
 fucked-up

he-man
 he-man, "aggressively
  masculine"
 he-man, "masculine male"
 hunk

hem and haw
 stall
 weasel

hemorrhage
 blowup

hemp
 pot

hen
 broad

hen-pecked
 pussy-whipped

Henry
 horse

hep
 cool
 trendy
 with it

hepcat
 dude

hepped
 with it

hepped on
 into

hepped up
 antsy

her
 coke

herbs
 pot

Herkimer Jerkimer
 hick
 jerk

herms
 angel dust

hero
 hero, "sandwich"
 horse

heroin
 horse

hero sandwich
 hero

Hershey bar
 nigger

heterosexual
 straight

het up
 antsy
 pissed off

hex
 whammy

hey
 Jeez
 way to go

hick, "rural person"

hickdom
 the boondocks

hickey
 gadget
 zit

hickory
 billy club

hicksville
 corny
 dullsville

hidden element
 catch

hide
 broad
 hide out
 park

hideaway, "hiding place"

hideout
 hideaway
 pad

hide out, "hide"

higgledy-piggledy
 fucked-up

high
 high, "intoxicated"
 high, "intoxication"
 plastered

high and mighty
 snooty

highball
 barrel
 split

highbrow
 egghead

high-class
 classy
 great

higher-up
 big shot

highfalutin
 classy
 snooty

highflag
 ride the arm

high-geared
 high-powered

high-grade
 classy

high-hat
 classy
 cut

give the cold shoulder
  snooty
  stuck-up
  swell
  the upper crust
highjack
  heist
high-jinks
  horseplay
highlight
  spotlight
high muckety-muck
  big shot
highpockets
  beanpole
high-power
  big-league
high-powered
  heavy
  high-powered, "powerful"
high-pressure
  lean on someone
  talk someone into
high-rent
  classy
  great
hightail it
  barrel
  break out
  split
high-toned
  classy
high-up
  big shot
high, wide, and handsome
  with flying colors
hijacker
  heist man
hijo
  Jeez

hike
hike, "increase" (v and n)
  split
  toddle
hilarity
  a howl
hillbilly
  cracker
  hick
a hill of beans
  zilch
him
  horse
himself
  big shot
  boss
hincty
  snooty
  stuck-up
  whitey
hind end
  ass
hind legs
  pins
hindside
  ass
hinge
  the once-over
hip
  cool
  snappy
  with it
the hip gee
  the smart money
hipped
  with it
hipper-dipper
  great
hippo
  fatty

hips
  curtains
hired gun
  hit man
hired help
  gofer
his highness
  boss
his nibs
  big shot
  boss
hit
  blow grass
  a crack
  a fix
  go over with a bang
  high
  a kick
  put the bite on
  score
  shoot up
  snuff
a hit, "success"
hit below the belt
  play dirty
hitch
  bit
  catch
  glitch
  hitchhike
hitch a ride
  hitchhike
hitchy
  antsy
  jittery
hitfest
  donnybrook
hit for six
  go over with a bang
hit it
  ace
  go over with a bang

hit it big
 clean up
hit it off
 buddy up
 hit it off, "get along"
hit man, "assassin"
hit on
 proposition
 rough up
 sock
hit-or-miss
 half-assed
hit out
 split
hit pay dirt
 go over with a bang
 hack it
hits
 crooked dice
hit spike
 works
hitter
 hit man
hit the bottle
 guzzle
hit the bricks
 split
 walk
hit the canvas
 pass out
hit the ceiling
 blow one's top
hit the hay
 blow grass
 snooze
hit the jackpot
 come on strong
 go over with a bang
 make a killing
hit the mark
 hack it

hit the road
 split
hit the sack
 snooze
hit the sauce
 guzzle
hit the sidewalk
 toddle
hit the skids
 go kerflooey
 go to hell
hit the trail
 split
hitting on all six
 cool
hit town
 show up
hit up
 bum
 put the bite on
 shoot up
hit someone where he (or
  she) lives
 clobber
 sock
hizzoner
 Blind Tom
ho
 hooker
hoagie
 hero
hoakie
 jerk
hobble
 bind
hobo
 bum
hock
 bug
hockey
 bullshit

cum
 shit
hocus
 coke
 horse
 M
hocus-pocus
 monkey business
hod
 nigger
ho-dad
 bigmouth
 jerk
 phony
 smart-ass
 wimp
ho-daddy
 bigmouth
hoedown
 donnybrook
 hassle
 wingding
hog
 angel dust
 bike
 cock
 hash
 junkie
 pig
 pimpmobile
 pot
 scarecrow
the hog
 angel dust
hoggish
 grabby
hoggy
 grabby
hog heaven
 fat city
hog it
 pig out

hogleg
  rod
hogwash
  bullshit
ho-hum
  dullsville
hoist
  heist
hoity-toity
  classy
  snooty
hoka toka
  blow grass
hoke
  bullshit
  flack
  scam
hoked-up
  phony
hoke up
  cook up
hokey
  phony
hokey-pokey
  bullshit
  flack
  monkey business
  razzle-dazzle
  scam
hokum
  bullshit
  flack
  razzle-dazzle
hokus
  dope
holder
  dealer
hold someone's feet to the
    fire, "punish"
hold one's horses
  cool it
  sit tight

holding
  dirty
  loaded
hold it
  cool it
  sit tight
hold off
  stall
hold out
  hang tough
  sit tight
hold the phone
  sit tight
hold the whip hand
  have someone by the balls
hold together
  figure
hold up
  figure
  heist
holdup man
  heist man
hold water
  figure
hole
  ass
  asshole
  banger
  bind
  cooler
  cunt
  dive
  dump
the hole
  the slammer
hole up
  hide out
hole-up
  hideaway
holier-than-thou
  Christer
  goody-goody

holler
  beef
  squeal
holler quits
  fold
holly-golly
  bullshit
  flak
Holmes
  pal
holy cats
  Jeez
holy cow
  Jeez
Holy Joe
  Bible-banger
  Christer
holy mackerel
  Jeez
holy Moses
  Jeez
holy smokes
  Jeez
holy terror
  eager beaver
  kid
hombre
  guy
Hombre
  Jack
home and dry
  in
homeboy
  gay
  pal
home free
  in
home in
  zero in
home run
  homer

homo
 gay
homosexual
 gay
homosexuality
 come out
hon
 honey
honcho
 big shot
 boss
 the brass
hondo
 fan
honest
 straight
honest-to-God, "authentic"
honest-to-God, "truly"
the honest-to-God truth
 the straight dope
honest-to-goodness
 honest-to-God
honey
 broad
 dish
 doll
 honey, "beloved person"
 humdinger
honey oil
 hash
honeypie
 honey
honeypot
 cunt
honey up
 brown-nose
 soft-soap
Hong Kong dog
 the shits
honk
 barrel

feel
honk, "sound the horn"
honked up
 antsy
honker
 schnozz
honky
 whitey
honky-tonk
 dive
honyocker
 hick
hooch
 ass
 booze
 pot
hooched up
 plastered
hoochery
 gin mill
hooch-hound
 lush
hood
 cowboy
 goon
hoodang
 wingding
hoodlum
 cowboy
 goon
hooey
 bullshit
 izzatso
hoof it
 split
 toddle
hoofs
 tootsies
hoo-ha
 donnybrook
 hoopla

Jeez
 so what
 wingding
hoohaw
 big shot
hook
 con
 gimmick
 grab
 heist
 horse
 hustle
 mitt
 snort
the hook
 the axe
hooked, "addicted"
hooker
 hooker, "prostitute"
 snort
hook in
 talk someone into
hook it
 split
hooknose
 kike
hook up with
 hang out with
hooky
 grabby
hooley
 binge
hooligan
 goon
a hoop and a holler
 a jiffy
hooperdooper
 humdinger
hoopla
 flack

flak
hoopla, "commotion"

hoopy
jalopy

the hoosegow
the slammer

hoosier
hick

a hoot
a howl
a laugh
zilch

hootchie-cootchie
ass

a hoot in hell
zilch

hootmalalie
gadget

hoover
blow

hop
big O
bullshit

hopfest
beer bust

hop gun
works

hophead
junkie
pothead

hop it
split

hop on the bandwagon
get on the bandwagon

hopped up
antsy
full of piss and vinegar
high
jazzed-up

hopped-up job
hot rod

hopping mad
pissed off

hoppy
gimpy

hopster
junkie

hop to it
get the lead out

hop up
jazz up
shoot up

horizontal bop
a fuck

horked
antsy

horn
cock
hard-on
schnozz
snort

hornblowing
flack

horndog
stud

horn in
butt in

horniness
hot pants

hornswoggle
con
snow

horny, "excited sexually"

horny bastard
stud

horror
scarecrow

horror film
chiller

the horrors
the shakes

horse
fuck
goof off
grand
horse, "heroin"

horse and wagon
works

horse around
goof off
horse around, "be boisterous"

horsed
high

horsefeathers
bullshit

horseheads
bennies

horselaugh
belly laugh

the horselaugh, "laugh"

horse opry
horse opera

horseplay, "fun"

horse race
a gamble

horse radish
horse

horses
crooked dice

horse's ass
asshole
jerk

horseshit
bullshit
chickenshit

hose
cock
con
fuck

hose job
blow job

hoser
  con man

hosing
  scam
  the shaft

hospital
  bone factory

hoss it
  toddle

hot
  antsy
  dirty
  great
  horny
  hot, "performing well"
  hot, "popular"
  pissed off

a hot
  a feed

hot air
  bullshit
  chitchat
  flack

hot-air artist
  bigmouth
  blabbermouth

hot and bothered
  jittery
  pissed off

hot and cold
  coke
  horse

hot as a three-dollar pistol
  horny

hotbox
  cunt

hot diggety
  hot damn

hot dish
  dish

hot dog
  grandstand
  grandstander
  hot damn
  hot shot

hot dogger
  hot shot

hot-eyed
  antsy

hot favorite
  front runner

hotfoot
  barrel

hot grease
  bad news

hot horse
  front runner

hot iron
  hot rod

hot jay
  pot

hot notion
  brain wave

hot number
  dish
  hot shot

hot pants, "sexual desire"

hot patootie
  dish

hot poo
  hot damn
  humdinger

hot rock
  hot shot

hot rocks
  hot pants

hot rod, "car"

the hots
  hot pants

hot seat
  the chair

hot shit
  hot damn
  hot shot
  humdinger

hotshot
  ace
  big shot
  dude
  eager beaver
  ladies' man

hot shot, "effective person"

hot sketch
  dish

hot spit
  hot damn
  humdinger

hot spot
  bind

hot squat
  the chair

hot stick
  joint

hot stuff
  ace
  dope
  hot shot
  humdinger
  score

hotsy-totsy
  cool
  great

hot tip
  tip

hot to trot
  antsy
  horny

hot under the collar
  pissed off

hot water
  bad news
  bind
hot ziggety
  hot damn
hound
  asshole
  bug
  pooch
hound dog
  ladies' man
  stud
house ape
  kid
house-cleaning,
      "reorganization"
house dick
  dick
house moss
  dust bunny
house nigger
  fink
house of ill repute
  whorehouse
how about that
  Jeez
how-de-do
  bind
  a fix
  flak
  hoopla
how goes it
  how's tricks
howl
  beef
a howl
  a howl, "hilarity"
  a laugh
howler
  boner

how's that?
  come again
how's things
  how's tricks
hubba-hubba
  on the double
hubby, "husband"
huckleberry
  guy
  jerk
huffy
  feisty
  pissed off
hug
  clinch
  heist
hugger-mugger
  fucked-up
huggy-huggy
  palsy-walsy
hulk
  bruiser
hully-gully
  bullshit
human dynamo
  eager beaver
humbug
  phony
  snow
humdinger, "remarkable
      person or thing"
hummer
  dope
  humdinger
hummer hustler
  eager beaver
humongous
  monster
hump
  ass
  barrel

cart
  fuck
  a fuck
  get the lead out
hump one's chops
  shoot the breeze
humpery
  ass
hump the hound
  goof off
hump the sage
  blow grass
humpy
  sexy
Hun
  kraut
hung, "having impressive
      male genitals"
hung like a bull
  hung
hungry, "ambitious"
hung up
  hooked
  square
hunk
  ass
  bag
  deck
  he-man
  hunk, "attractive man"
hunker down
  take it
hunk of change
  dough
hunky
  built
  cool
  he-man
  horny
  hunky, "attractive"
  hunky, "foreigner"
  sexy

hunky-dory
  cool
hurrah's nest
  bad news
  snafu
hurry
  get the lead out
hurtburger
  flop
hurting
  antsy
husband
  hubby
hush-hush
  on the QT
hustle
  con
  get the lead out
  heist
  hustle, "prostitute oneself"
  pizzazz
  scam
  snow
hustler
  con man
  hot shot
hustle up
  get the lead out
hutch
  pad
hyena
  asshole
hype
  con
  dealer
  a fix
  flack
  scam
  shoot up
  snow
hype artist
  flack

hyped-up
  antsy
  phony
hyper
  antsy
  flack
  great
  jittery
hype stick
  works
hype up
  cook up
  jazz up
ice
  clinch
  clobber
  coke
  cool
  cut
  great
  snuff
the ice
  the cold shoulder
ice bag
  pot
iceberg
  cold fish
icebox
  cooler
  the slammer
ice cream
  dope
ice cream man
  dealer
iced
  in the bag
ice maiden
  cold fish
iceman
  heist man
  hit man

ice out
  cut
ice pack
  pot
icky
  corny
  square
  yucky
idea
  brain wave
ideal situation
  fat city
identify
  peg
idiot box
  the tube
iffy, "uncertain"
iffy proposition
  a gamble
iggle
  talk someone into
ignorance
  not know shit from Shinola
ignorant stripe
  hash mark
Ike
  kike
I kid you not
  honest-to-God
  no fooling
ill
  off one's feed
I'll be
  I'll be damned
I'll be damned if
  like hell
I'll drink to that
  bet your ass
illegal saloon
  blind pig

ill-regarded
  on someone's shit list

I'll tell the world
  bet your ass

illuminated
  plastered

I'm all right Jack
  fuck you

imitation
  act

immediately
  on the double

immense
  great

I'm not just whistling Dixie
  no fooling

imp
  kid

impaired
  plastered

impassive
  poker face

important
  big deal
  big-league
  heavy

important money
  bundle

important person
  big shot

importune
  put the bite on

improve
  get on the ball

improvise
  wing it

impudence
  sass
  smart-ass

impudent person
  smart-ass

in
  high
  hot
  in, "successful"
  trendy

in a bad way
  plastered

in a big way
  like hell

in a bind
  out of luck

in a box
  out of luck

in a bubble
  hot

in a corner
  up the creek

in a dither
  antsy

in a flutter
  antsy

in a fog, "confused"

in a funk
  down
  scared shitless

in a haze
  in a fog

in a holding pattern
  on hold

in a hole
  out of luck
  up the creek

in a huff
  pissed off

in a jam
  out of luck
  up the creek

in a lather
  antsy
  pissed off

in a mess
  out of luck
  up the creek

in a muddle
  in a fog

in-and-out
  ass

in a pickle
  out of luck
  up the creek

in a pig's ass
  izzatso
  like hell

in a pinch
  up the creek
  when the chips are down

in a pucker
  jittery
  pissed off

in a session
  high

in a state
  antsy
  jittery

in a stew
  jittery
  pissed off

in a sweat
  antsy
  jittery
  pissed off

in a tight spot
  out of luck

in a tizzy
  antsy
  jittery
  pissed off

in a tough spot
  up the creek

in a walk
  with flying colors

in a zone
  high
  hot
  in a fog
in bad shape
  out of luck
in-betweens
  bennies
in one's birthday suit
  bare-ass
in business
  hooked
incapacity
  out of one's depth
in cement
  carved in stone
incense
  pot
incentive
  coke
in clover
  in hog heaven
in cold storage
  on hold
increase
  hike
in one's cups
  plastered
in deep trouble
  out of luck
  up the creek
Indian hemp
  pot
Indian rope
  hash
the Indian sign
  whammy
indifference
  one couldn't care less
  not give a damn
  so what

in Dutch
  out of luck
  up the creek
ineffective
  cut no ice
inescapably
  dead to rights
infantry soldier
  grunt
in fat city
  in hog heaven
inferior
  crummy
  schlocky
inferior liquor
  panther piss
inferior position
  play second fiddle
inferior things
  crap
inflated
  jumped-up
influence
  carry a lot of weight
info
  the poop
inform
  fill someone in
information
  the poop
  tip
  wise me up
informed
  briefed
informer
  snitch
in front
  up front
in good shape
  cool

ingratiation
  play up to
in great shape
  cool
the in group, "clique"
inhalation
  snort
  toke
inhale
  scarf
in high gear
  lickety-split
in hog heaven, "contented"
in hot water
  out of luck
injury
  get it in the neck
injustice
  bum rap
in kilter
  cool
inky-dink
  nigger
inky-dinky
  little bitty
in like Flynn
  in
in mothballs
  on hold
innards
  chutzpa
  guts
  innards, "viscera"
inning
  chapter
innocent
  clean
in nothing flat
  on the double

in orbit
 high
in-out
 ass
in overdrive
 lickety-split
in over one's head
 out of one's depth
 up the creek
in pig heaven
 in hog heaven
in place, "available"
inquiry
 what's up
insane
 crazy
 go crazy
insane person
 nut
inside
 in stir
insiders
 the in group
insides
 innards
insincere greeting
 glad-hander
insolvent
 go broke
in spades
 flat-out
 like hell
 with flying colors
inspection
 the once-over
instant Zen
 acid
instinctively
 by ear
in stir, "imprisoned"

insult
 fink
 give someone the finger
 kiss my ass
 knock
 the bird
intelligence
 smarts
intense
 great
intestinal fortitude
 guts
in the altogether
 bare-ass
in the bag
 cinched
 in the bag, "certain"
 kaput
 plastered
in the buff
 bare-ass
in the catbird seat
 in the driver's seat
in the chips
 loaded
in the clear
 clean
in the clutch
 when the chips are down
in the crunch
 when the chips are down
in the deep freeze
 on hold
in the doldrums
 down
in the dough
 loaded
in the driver's seat, "having
  authority"
in the dumper
 kaput

in the dumps
 down
in the family way
 knocked up
in the groove
 in the groove, "performing
  well"
 with it
in the hopper
 in the pipeline
in the icebox
 on hold
in the money
 loaded
in the pipeline, "imminent"
in the pocket
 high
 in the groove
in the raw
 bare-ass
in there pitching
 in there
in the soup
 out of luck
 up the creek
in the works
 in the pipeline
in the worst way
 like hell
intimidate
 bulldoze
intimidation
 lean on someone
into, "absorbed in"
into it
 with it
in town
 cool
in transit

in trouble
  up the creek

intrude
  butt in

IOU
  tab

irascible
  feisty

irie
  great

Irish person
  Mick

iron
  bike
  jalopy
  rod

iron man
  buck

iron out
  snuff
  work out

irritate
  bug

irritation
  Jeez

ishkabibble
  one couldn't care less

iso
  cooler

Italian person
  wop

itchy
  antsy
  horny
  jittery

item
  cookie

it's a new ball game, "the situation has changed"

it's nothing
  forget it

itsy-bitsy
  little bitty

it takes two to tango, "this matter entails cooperation"

ivories
  choppers

ivory-dome
  dope
  egghead

izzatso, "expression of disbelief"

J
  joint

jab
  bust
  a fix
  knock
  shoot up
  sock

jabber
  gab
  junkie
  works

jabberer
  blabbermouth

jabberjack
  bullshit

jaboney
  goon
  greenhorn

jack
  dough
  shoot up

Jack, "Mister"

jack around
  fool around with
  goof off

jack someone around
  kid

jackass
  dope
  jerk

jacked-up
  high
  jumped-up

jackie
  gay

jackleg
  con man
  scab

jack off, "masturbate"

jack-off
  jerk

jack off the spike
  shoot up

jackroll
  heist

jack up
  chew out
  clobber
  hike
  jazz up
  roust
  shoot up

jag
  binge
  jerk

jagged
  high

jag-off
  jerk

jahooby
  pot

jail
  cooler
  the slammer

jail bait, "young girl"

jailbird
  con

jailhouse lawyer
  latrine lawyer
jake
  cop
jakes
  can
jalopy, "car"
jam
  bennies
  bind
  coke
  cunt
  fuck
  have a ball
  roust
Jamaican
  pot
jamboree
  wingding
jam Cecil
  bennies
jammed up
  up the creek
jammies
  rod
jamming
  in the groove
jammy
  great
jamoke
  guy
jane
  broad
  can
Jane Doe
  Jane
jang
  cock
jape
  kid around

jarhead
  dope
  leatherneck
  nigger
jarrer
  a hit
jasper
  cookie
  guy
  hick
jaw
  chitchat
  gab
  schmooz
  shoot the breeze
  talk someone into
jawbone
  on the cuff
  talk someone into
jawfest
  schmooz
jay
  hick
  joint
  patsy
  pot
jaybird
  hick
jay smoke
  joint
jazz
  ass
  bullshit
  clout
  dirt
  fuck
  a fuck
  jazz up
  pizzazz
jazz-bo
  dude

jazzed
  jazzed-up
  pumped
jazz up
  goose
  jazz up, "make more
    exciting"
jazzy
  glitzy
  jazzy, "exciting"
JC water-walkers
  sneakers
jeasly
  piddly
the jeebies
  the jitters
jeegee
  horse
Jeepers Creepers
  Jeez
jeff
  square
  whitey
Jefferson airplane
  roach clip
jelly
  cinch
  cunt
  gravy
jellybean
  bennies
  dope
  rookie
jelly-belly
  fatty
  potbelly
jellyfish
  chicken
  wimp
jelly-roll
  ass

cunt
stud

jenny
broad

jerk
asshole
drag
jerk, "tedious person"
wimp

jerk someone around
bug
kid

jerk someone's chain
bug
con
kid
snow

jerk off
goof off
jack off
shoot up

jerk someone off
kid

jerk-off
hick
jerk

jerk town, "small town"

jerkwater
piddly

jerkwater town
jerk town

Jerry
kraut

Jersey green
pot

Jesus H. Christ
Jeez

jet fuel
angel dust

the jet set, "glamorous
people"

Jew canoe
Caddy

jewelry
basket

Jewish person
kike

jibber-jabber
double-talk
gab

a jif
a jiffy

jig
nigger

jigaboo
nigger

jigger
cock
gadget
screw up
snort

jiggers, "exclamation of
warning"

jiggerypokery
bullshit
dirty tricks

jiggins
dope
patsy

jiggle
cheesecake

jig-jig
ass

jillionaire
moneybags

jillionth
umpty-umpth

jim-dandy
great
humdinger

jim-jam
jazz up

the jimjams
the jitters
the shakes

jimjick
gadget

jimmied-up
on the blink

jimmy in
butt in

jimmy up
screw up

jingle
buzz

jingleberries
balls

jinglebrains
ditz

jingo
pot

jinx
whammy

jism
clout
cum
goo

jit
nigger

jitney
jalopy

the jitters, "nervousness"

jittery, "nervous"

jive
bullshit
chitchat
flack
joint
kid
kid around
line
pot
razzle-dazzle

jive and juke
  have a ball

jive-ass
  bullshit

jive dojee
  horse

jive session
  schmooz

jivey
  with it

jizz
  cum

joan
  knock

job
  blow job
  broad
  caper
  cookie
  heist
  jalopy

jobber
  dealer

jobbie
  cookie

Job's antidote
  works

jock
  cock
  disc jockey
  jock, "athlete"

jocker
  gay

jockey
  play games

jockstrap
  jock

Joe
  buck private
  guy

Jack
  Joe Blow

Joe College, "college man"

Joe Millerism
  chestnut

Joe Yale
  Joe College
  white shoe

john
  can

John
  cock
  Joe Blow
  rookie
  straight
  sugar daddy

John Barleycorn
  booze

John Bull
  limey

John Doe
  Joe Blow

John Dogface
  buck private

John Farmer
  hick

John Law
  cop

John Ls
  long johns

johnny
  can

Johnny
  cock
  guy
  Joe Blow

Johnny-come-lately
  greenhorn
  rookie

Johnny Trots
  the shits

John Q Citizen
  Joe Blow

John Roscoe
  rod

johnson
  cock
  pot

Johnson and Johnson
  works

joint
  bag
  butt
  cock
  dive
  dump
  joint, "marijuana
    cigarette"
  the slammer
  works

join up with
  hang out with

joke
  crack
  kid
  kid around

joker
  catch
  cookie
  guy
  jerk

jollies
  kicks

jollification
  wingding

jolly beans
  bennies

jolt
  bit
  clobber
  clout
  high
  joint

a kick
shoot up
snort
Sunday punch
jolted
high
jolter
a hit
joltheaded
dumb
jones
cock
horse
josh
kid
kid around
joskin
hick
joy dust
coke
horse
M
joy house
whorehouse
joyjuice
booze
joy knob
cock
joy pellet
bennies
doll
joy pop
a fix
joy powder
coke
horse
joy prick
a fix
joy smoke
pot

joy stick
cock
J smoke
joint
pot
juane
pot
Judas priest
Jeez
jug
bag
deck
the slammer
juggins
dope
patsy
juggle
doctor
juggler
dealer
juggle with
doctor
jughead
dope
jugheaded
dumb
jugs
tits
juice
angel dust
booze
clout
cum
guzzle
juiced
plastered
juice dealer
loan shark
juiced-up job
hot rod

juicehead
lush
juice-joint
dive
juice up
goose
jazz up
juicy
dirty
juicy morsel
dirt
ju ju
pot
juke
play hooky
juke house
whorehouse
jumbo
bruiser
fatty
monster
jump
fry
fuck
heist
hike
kick ass
jump all over
chew out
fix someone
kick ass
jump someone's bones
fuck
jump down someone's
throat
chew out
jumped-up, "inflated"
jumping Jehosaphat
Jeez
jump on
chew out

371

the jumps
 the jitters
 the shakes
jump salty
 blow one's top
jump up
 hike
 jazz up
jumpy
 jittery
jungle bunny
 nigger
junk
 chuck
 crap
 crummy
 schlocky
junked up
 high
junker
 dealer
 jalopy
 junkie
junk-heap
 jalopy
junkie
 fan
 junkie, "addict"
junk peddler
 dealer
junky
 crummy
 schlocky
just for the hell of it
 for kicks
K
 angel dust
 grand
kafooster
 bullshit

kaif
 pot
kale
 dough
kanjac
 pot
Kaps
 angel dust
kaput
 finished
 kaput, "ruined"
karma
 vibes
kayo
 clobber
 knock out
 Sunday punch
kayoed
 kaput
kayo shot
 Sunday punch
kazoo
 ass
 asshole
 can
K-blast
 angel dust
kee
 bag
 deck
keef
 pot
keek
 a fix
keel over
 fuck up
keen
 antsy
 great
keep cool
 keep one's cool

keeper of mistress
 sugar daddy
keep hands off
 stick to one's knitting
keep one's mouth shut
 shut up
keep one's nose clean
 fly right
keep on trucking
 hang tough
keep posted
 fill someone in
keep one's shirt on
 cool it
 keep one's cool
 sit tight
keep one's trap shut
 shut up
keep your nose out of this
 lay off
keg
 bag
 deck
kegger
 beer bust
keg party
 beer bust
keister
 ass
 asshole
kelsey
 hooker
kelt
 whitey
keltch
 whitey
Ken
 square
kenkoy
 horse

Kentucky blue
  pot
kerboom
  pow
kerflooey
  on the blink
kerflummoxed
  fucked-up
a kettle of fish
  a fix
key
  bag
  great
  Joe College
  white shoe
keyed up
  antsy
  high
khazer
  pig
khazeray
  crap
ki
  bag
kibitz
  butt in
kibitzer, "meddler"
kibosh
  screw up
kick
  bag
  beef
  bobtail
  clout
  fire
  goof off
  high
  humdinger
  pizzazz
  snort
a kick, "pleasure"

kick apart
  spell out
kick around
  bat around
  goof off
kick ass, "punish"
kick-ass
  clout
  pizzazz
  tough
kick back, "relax"
kicked out
  finished
kicker
  catch
  punch line
kick in
  cough up
  croak
  kick in, "contribute"
kick in the ass
  pick-me-up
kick off
  croak
kick out
  bounce
kick out the jams
  have a ball
  let oneself go
kick over
  heist
kick over the traces
  let oneself go
kicks, "pleasure"
kicks, "shoes"
kickshaw
  gadget
kick stick
  joint
kick the bucket
  croak

kick the gong around
  shoot up
kick the shit out of
  clobber
kick the tires
  check out
kick-up
  donnybrook
  wingding
kick up a fuss
  beef
  make a scene
kick up a storm
  beef
  make a scene
kick up one's heels
  have a ball
  horse around
kicky
  great
kid
  kid, "child"
  kid, "deceive"
  kid, "joke"
  kid around
  snow
kid oneself
  buy
kiddo
  kid
kid stuff
  cinch
kike, "Jewish person"
kill
  break someone up
  go over with a bang
  nix
  scrub
  snuff
  wow
killer
  back-breaker

great
  humdinger
  joint
a killer
  a bitch
  a laugh
killer-diller
  humdinger
killer stick
  joint
killerweed
  angel dust
killjoy
  gloomy Gus
killout
  humdinger
kingfish
  boss
King Kong
  doll
  panther piss
kingpin
  boss
king-size
  monster
king's ransom
  bundle
kink
  glitch
  jerk
kinky
  flaky
  gay
  kinky, "sexually deviant"
  weird
kip
  pad
  sack time
  snooze
kipe
  heist

kishkes
  belly
  guts
  innards
kiss
  French kiss
  neck
  snort
kiss ass
  brown-nose
kisser
  puss
  yap
kiss goodbye
  chuck
kiss my ass
  fuck you
  kiss my ass, "expression of
    defiance"
kiss off
  the axe
  cut
  fire
  walk out on
kissy-huggy
  palsy-walsy
kit
  works
the kit and caboodle
  the whole shebang
kitchen
  belly
kite
  bag
  deck
  hike
kitten
  dust bunny
Kitty
  Caddy
klooch
  broad

klutz
  butterfingers
  dope
  jerk
klutzy
  dumb
  ham-handed
knee-bender
  Bible-banger
knee deep
  up to one's ass
knee-high
  little bitty
knee-slapper
  belly laugh
  a howl
knife in the arm
  a fix
knob
  bean
  cock
knob job
  blow job
knock
  bad-mouth
  bust
  knock, "criticize
    harshly"
  knock, "disparage"
  sock
the knock
  the damage
knock around
  bat around
  goof off
  hell around
knock back
  guzzle
knock someone back
  set someone back

knock someone's block off
  clobber
  sock
knock cold
  knock out
knock dead
  break someone up
knock down
  deck
  grab
  shave
knock-down-drag-out
  donnybrook
  flat-out
  free-for-all
  hassle
  rootin'-tootin'
knocked
  cinched
knocked out
  high
  plastered
  pooped
knocked up, "pregnant"
knockers
  tits
knock for a loop
  clobber
knock someone for a loop
  wow
knock someone into the
    middle of next week
  clobber
knock it off
  shut up
knock someone's lights out
  clobber
  knock out
  wow
knock off
  clobber
  fuck

guzzle
  heist
  kick back
  knock off, "cease work"
  scrub
  snuff
knock someone off his (or
    her) perch
  take someone down a peg
knockout
  dish
  great
  humdinger
knock out
  clobber
  knock out, "make
    unconscious"
  rustle up
knock oneself out
  bust one's ass
knock someone out
  wow
knockout drops
  Mickey Finn
knockover
  heist
  rumble
knocks
  kicks
knock someone's socks off
  go over with a bang
  wow
knock stiff
  knock out
knock the daylights out
    of
  clobber
  knock out
knock them dead
  go over with a bang
  wow

knock something together
  knock something out
knock up, "impregnate"
knothead
  dope
knot the score
  get even
know a thing or two
  know one's onions
know from nothing
  not know shit from Shinola
know-how
  smarts
know-it-all
  smart-ass
know one's onions, "be
    competent"
know what makes someone
    tick
  have someone's number
knucker
  heist man
knuckle
  bean
knuckle down
  bust one's ass
knuckle-dragger
  goon
knucklehead
  dope
knuckleheaded
  dumb
knuckle sandwich
  sock
knuckle under
  fold
knucksman
  heist man
K O
  knock out

Kona gold
  pot
kook
  nut
  oddball
kooky
  crazy
  ditsy
Kools
  angel dust
kopecks
  dough
kosher
  honest-to-God
  square
  straight
kraut, "German person"
kvetch
  beef
  kvetch, "complainer"
ky
  bag
L
  acid
label
  monicker
labonza
  belly
  potbelly
lack-brained
  dumb
lack of money
  the shorts
lackwitted
  dumb
lacy
  gay
lad
  guy
la-de-da
  classy

dude
  snooty
ladies' man,
    "womanizer"
lady
  broad
the Lady
  coke
Lady H
  horse
lady-killer
  dude
  ladies' man
lady of the evening
  hooker
Lady Snow
  coke
Lady White
  coke
  dope
a laff
  a howl
a laff riot
  a howl
lag
  bit
lagger
  con
laid-back, "relaxed"
laid out
  hunky
  kaput
  plastered
laid, relaid, and
    parlayed
  screwed
lajara
  cop
lam
  break out

sock
  split
lamb
  honey
  patsy
lambaste
  blast
  clobber
  knock
  tan
lamby-pie
  honey
lame
  dumb
  jerk
  square
lamebrain
  dope
lamebrained
  dumb
lame duck
  straight
lampoon
  spoof
lamps
  peepers
land
  catch redhanded
  grab
land on
  chew out
land one
  sock
landslide
  grand slam
landsman
  pal
lap up
  bite
  buy
  guzzle

lard-ass
 fatty
 goof-off
lardhead
 dope
large
 big-league
 heavy
 hot
 monster
large charge
 a kick
large number
 umpty-umpth
large order
 back-breaker
large quantity
 scads
lark
 kid around
larrup
 sock
 tan
lassie
 broad
last roundup
 curtains
latch on
 dig
latch on to
 grab
the latest
 dirt
lather
 blowup
 clobber
 sock
 swivel
 tan
lathered
 pissed off
 plastered

Latino
 bean-eater
latrine
 can
latrine lawyer, "contentious
 person"
L A turnabouts
 bennies
laugh
 belly laugh
 break up
 the horselaugh
 a howl
 a laugh
laugh and scratch
 shoot up
laughing academy
 booby hatch
laughing grass
 pot
laughing soup
 booze
launching pad
 shooting gallery
laundry list,
 "agenda"
lav
 can
the law
 cop
lawyer
 shyster
lay
 ass
 fuck
 a fuck
layabout
 goof-off
lay a fart
 fart

lay an egg
 flop
 fuck up
lay back
 kick back
lay doggo
 hide out
lay down
 cough up
lay down on the job
 goof off
lay down the law
 chew out
lay down one's tools
 knock off
lay flat
 deck
lay in the aisles
 break someone up
lay into
 blast
 chew out
lay it on
 bullshit
lay it on the line
 get down to brass tacks
 lay it on the line, "speak
 directly"
lay it on thick
 blow off
 soft-soap
lay it on with a trowel
 bullshit
 soft-soap
lay low
 break someone up
 hide out
lay off
 knock off
 lay off, "exclamation of
 warning"

lay on
 fill someone in
lay one
 fart
lay one on
 sock
layout
 dive
 pad
 works
lay out
 blow
 clobber
 deck
 knock out
 snuff
 spell out
lay oneself out
 bust one's ass
lay out cold
 knock out
lay out in lavender
 deck
 knock out
lay pipe
 fuck
lay the make
 proposition
lay them in the aisles
 go over with a
  bang
 wow
lay tube
 fuck
lay up
 kick back
laze around
 goof off
lazybones
 goof-off

LBJ
 acid
lead balloon
 flop
leader
 boss
leaders
 the brass
lead-pipe cinch
 cinch
lead-pipe course
 gut course
lead with one's chin
 stick one's neck out
the leaf
 coke
leak
 piss
 squeal
lean and mean
 hungry
lean green
 dough
leaning forward in the
  saddle
 pumped
lean on
 bulldoze
 crowd
 roust
lean on someone,
 "intimidate"
leapers
 bennies
leaping and stinking
 high
the leaping heebies
 the jitters
leaping lizards
 Jeez

leap on the bandwagon
 get on the bandwagon
the leather
 sock
leather dew
 dope
leatherneck, "Marine"
leathers
 kicks
leave in the lurch
 walk out on
leave it be
 stick to one's knitting
leave out in the cold
 walk out on
leaves
 pot
Leb
 hash
Lebanese
 hash
a lech
 hot pants
lech after
 have hot pants
lefty
 pinko
 southpaw
leg
 broad
leg art
 cheesecake
legbiter
 kid
legit
 honest-to-God
 straight
leg it
 toddle

legitimate
  straight
a leg-pull
  a put-on
legs
  pins
lemkee
  big O
lemon
  crap
  dope
  flop
  jalopy
  letdown
  loser
  lude
lemonade
  dope
leno
  joint
leper grass
  pot
ler
  hooker
lesbian
  dyke
less than no time
  a jiffy
let a fart
  fart
let someone breathe
  get off someone's back
letdown, "disappointment"
let 'er rip
  let oneself go
let fly
  peg
let fly at
  blast
  plug

let oneself go, "be
  uninhibited"
let one's hair down
  lay it on the line
  let oneself go
  let it all hang out
let have it
  blast
  chew out
let someone have it
  clobber
  fix someone
  kick ass
  sock
let her rip
  barrel
let in on
  fill someone in
let it all hang out
  blow
  lay it on the line
  let oneself go
  let it all hang out, "speak
    candidly"
let loose
  have a ball
  let oneself go
let loose at
  blast
  plug
let's have it again
  come again
let sleeping dogs lie
  stick to one's knitting
let's see the color of your
  money
  put up or shut up
lettuce
  dough

let someone turn in the
  wind
  hold someone's feet to the
    fire
let well enough alone
  stick to one's knitting
let wind
  fart
level
  get down to brass tacks
  lay it on the line
  let it all hang out
  on the level
lez
  dyke
liberal
  pinko
license to print money
  gold mine
lick
  beat
  blow
  clobber
  a crack
  smidgen
  sock
a lick and a promise, "hasty
  job"
lick ass
  brown-nose
lickety-split
  flat-out
  lickety-split, "rapidly"
lick to a frazzle
  clobber
lid
  bag
  deck
  lid, "hat"
lid poppers
  bennies

lie on one's oars
  goof off
lift
  heist
  heist man
  a kick
lifter
  heist man
light
  doll
  split
  with it
light artillery
  works
light-fingered
  sticky-fingered
light-footed
  gay
light into
  blast
  chew out
  kick ass
lightning
  bennies
  panther piss
lightning hash
  hash
lightning smoke
  big O
light on his feet
  gay
light out
  split
lights
  party hat
lights out
  curtains
light up
  blow grass
light upstairs
  dumb

lightweight
  gofer
  lightweight, "trivial
    person"
like
  back
  hit it off
like a bat out of hell
  lickety-split
like all get-out
  like hell
like falling off a log
  easy as pie
like fun
  izzatso
  like hell
like hell, "exceedingly"
like hell, "never"
like shit through a tin horn
  flat-out
like shooting fish in a
    barrel
  easy as pie
like sixty
  lickety-split
  like hell
like stealing candy from a
    baby
  easy as pie
lily
  humdinger
  sissy
  wimp
lily-livered
  chicken
  wimpish
lily white
  clean
lime-juicer
  limey

limp-dick
  lightweight
  wimp
limp dishrag
  wimp
limping
  gimpy
limp-wrist
  gay
line
  a fix
  line, "try at persuasion"
  racket
  shoot up
line dog
  grunt
line one's nest
  take care of numero uno
line of chatter
  line
line of country
  bag
  racket
line of hooey
  line
line out
  warble
line one's pockets
  clean up
liner
  junkie
line shot
  a fix
line up with
  hang out with
lip
  gab
  sass
  shyster
lip mover
  dope

lip proppers
  bennies

lippy
  cheeky
  gabby

lipstick on a dipstick
  blow job

lip the dripper
  shoot up

Lipton's punk
  pot

liquidate
  clobber
  snuff

liquor
  booze

liquored up
  plastered

list
  laundry list

lit
  plastered

little bit
  little bitty
  smidgen

little boy in the boat
  clit

little devil
  kid

little drink of water
  shorty

little guy
  gadget

little Mickey
  Mickey Finn

little money
  chicken feed

little old me
  yours truly

little pisher
  kid

little shaver
  kid

little shot
  gofer
  lightweight

little squirt
  shorty

little woman
  old woman

lit up
  plastered

lit up like a Christmas tree
  plastered

live high on the hog
  eat high on the hog

live it up
  have a ball

live wire
  eager beaver

livid
  pissed off

living doll
  doll

living picture
  double

lizzie
  jalopy

lizzy
  wimp

load
  bag
  deck

loaded
  high
  loaded, "wealthy"
  plastered

loaded with
  filthy with
  lousy with

loadie
  lush

a load of
  the once-over

load of dirt
  dirt

load of wind
  blabbermouth

loan shark, "usurer"

loaves
  ass

lobo
  cowboy
  goon

lobster
  butterfingers

local yokel
  hick

lock
  cinch

locked
  high

lock horns
  hassle

lock, stock, and
    barrel
  stone
  the whole shebang

the lockup
  the slammer

loco
  crazy

loco weed
  pot

locus
  dope

log
  joint

loid
  heist

lollapalooza
  humdinger

lollygag
  goof off
  neck
lollypop
  honey
long
  bag
  deck
long chalk
  a country mile
long drink of water
  beanpole
long green
  dough
longhair
  egghead
long-handle underwear
  long johns
long shot, "unlikely winner"
long time
  ages
long time no see
  how's tricks
longwinded
  gabby
loo
  can
loogan
  dope
  goon
look
  check out
  the once-over
look-alike
  double
look alive
  get the lead out
looker
  dish

look-in
  bite
looking good
  way to go
looksee
  the once-over
loony
  crazy
  nut
loony bin
  booby hatch
loony-tune
  crazy
  nut
looped
  plastered
loopy
  crazy
  ditsy
  flaky
loose
  cool
  loaded
loosen up
  let oneself go
looseygoosey
  cool
loot
  dough
  score
  take
lop
  jerk
lopper-jawed
  cockeyed
the lord and
    master
  hubby
Lord Fauntleroy
  sissy

lords of creation
  the brass
  moneybags
Lordy
  Jeez
lose consciousness
  pass out
lose one's cool
  blow one's top
lose one's gourd
  go crazy
lose intentionally
  take a dive
lose-lose situation
  catch-22
lose one's marbles
  crack up
lose out
  fuck up
loser
  con
  flop
  lightweight
  loser, "failure"
  wimp
lose one's shirt
  go broke
lose sleep
  sweat
lose one's wig
  blow one's top
Lothario
  ladies' man
loud
  glitzy
loudmouth
  bigmouth
  blabbermouth
  blow off
loud-talk
  blow off

lounge
  night spot
lounge lizard
  ladies' man
louse
  asshole
loused-up
  on the blink
louse up
  goof
  screw up
lousy
  crummy
  loaded
lousy deal
  bum rap
  the shaft
lousy rich
  loaded
lousy with, "abundant in"
love
  honey
love handles
  spare tire
love juice
  cum
lovely
  dish
lovely magic
  angel dust
love-muscle
  cock
lover
  honey
  pothead
lover-boy
  ladies' man
  stud
Love Saves
  acid

love up
  grab-ass
  neck
love weed
  pot
lovey
  honey
lovey-dovey
  grab-ass
  palsy-walsy
low
  bad trip
low-down
  crummy
  down
the lowdown
  dirt
  the poop
  the straight dope
lower the boom
  fix someone
  kick ass
  sock
low-fullams
  crooked dice
low-level Munchkin
  gofer
low-life
  bum
low man on the totem pole
  gofer
low-rent
  bush
  crummy
  floozy
  schlocky
lozies
  pot
LSD
  acid

L7
  square
lubber
  butterfingers
lubricated
  plastered
luck out
  get lucky
lucre
  dough
Lucy in the sky with
    diamonds
  acid
lude, "methaqualone"
luded out
  high
luer
  works
lug
  cart
lulu
  dish
  humdinger
lummox
  butterfingers
  dope
  jerk
lump
  dope
lumpish
  dumb
lump it
  eat dirt
lunch box
  dope
lunch hook
  mitt
lunch up
  have a field day

lunchy
  crazy
  dumb
lung
  banger
lungs
  tits
lunker
  jalopy
lunkhead
  dope
  jerk
lunkheaded
  dumb
luscious
  sexy
lush, "drunkard"
lushed up
  plastered
lusher
  lush
  pothead
lush roller
  heist man
luxo
  classy
M
  M, "morphine"
  pot
Mac
  Jack
mach
  pot
macher
  big shot
  wheeler-dealer
machinery
  works
macho
  he-man
  hunk

macho it out
  hang tough
Mach Picchu
  pot
mack, "procurer"
mackman
  mack
mad
  pissed off
  piss-off
made of money
  loaded
mad money
  case dough
Mafioso
  gangster
Maggie
  pot
maggot
  butt
  whitey
magic dust
  angel dust
magoo
  big shot
mahogany juice
  big O
mahoska
  dope
maiden
  bug
mainline
  a fix
  shoot up
mainliner
  junkie
main man
  pal
main squeeze
  boss

maison joie
  whorehouse
major-league
  big-league
the major leagues
  the big leagues
make
  check out
  dig
  fuck
  heist
  peg
  shit
a make
  ass
make a big stink
  blow up
make a break for it
  break out
make a bundle
  clean up
  make a killing
make a buy
  score
make a circuit clout
  homer
make a circus play
  grandstand
make a deal
  cut a deal
make a federal case
  blow up
make a full-court press
  bust one's ass
make a funny
  kid
make a fuss
  beef
make a go of it
  hack it

make a grandstand play
grandstand
make a hash of
screw up
make a how-de-do
make a scene
make a killing
clean up
make a killing, "profit"
make a meet
score
make a mess
goof
screw up
make a mint
clean up
make a move on
proposition
make an ascension
fluff
make a pass
proposition
make a patsy of
con
make a pig of oneself
pig out
make a pinch
bust
make a pit stop
piss
make a scene, "cause a disturbance"
make a stab
take a crack at
make a stink
beef
make a scene
make big money
clean up
make book
bet one's ass

make someone's hair curl
scare the shit out of
make hash of
clobber
make it
fuck
go over with a bang
hack it
work
make it big
go over with a bang
make it hot for
chew out
fix someone
kick ass
make it snappy
get the lead out
make mincemeat of
clobber
make no bones
lay it on the line
make no never-mind
cut no ice
make official
clinch
make out
get by
neck
make-out artist
ladies' man
stud
make out like a bandit
come on strong
go over with a bang
hack it
make out with
fuck
make someone say
uncle
clobber

make oneself scarce
break out
split
make sense
figure
make short work of
clobber
makes no never mind
forget it
make someone sore
piss someone off
make the cut
hack it
make the fur fly
hassle
make the grade
hack it
make the man
score
make the riffle
hack it
make the scene
show up
make tracks
barrel
split
make up to
play up to
make waves
make a scene
make whoopee
have a ball
malarkey
bullshit
male
he-man
male genitals
basket
male person
guy

malfunction
  glitch
maltreat
  fuck
maltreated
  screwed
mama
  broad
mama's boy
  sissy
  wimp
mamber
  blood
man
  dyke
  hubby
  Jeez
  sugar daddy
Man
  Jack
the Man
  boss
  cop
  the cops
  whitey
man-about-town
  playboy
manage
  boss
  get by
man alive
  Jeez
man Friday
  gofer
mangoes
  tits
mangy
  crummy
mangy with
  lousy with

manhandle
  bulldoze
  rough up
Manhattan eel
  rubber
Manhattan white
  pot
man-hole
  cunt
man in the boat
  clit
man in the front office
  boss
manipulate
  play games
man-jack
  guy
man mountain
  bruiser
the man of the house
  hubby
man on the street
  Joe Blow
man's best friend
  pooch
man's man
  he-man
man upstairs
  boss
man with a paper ass
  lightweight
map
  puss
maracas
  tits
marble city
  boneyard
marble-dome
  dope

marble orchard
  boneyard
march
  toddle
mare
  broad
maricon
  gay
marijuana
  pot
marijuana cigarette
  joint
marijuana stub-holder
  roach clip
marijuana user
  pothead
marijuana venue
  dope den
Marine
  leatherneck
mark
  patsy
  squeal
marker
  tab
marmalade
  bullshit
Marmon
  M
marshmallow
  whitey
marvy
  great
Mary
  dyke
  gay
  pot
Mary Jane
  pot
Mary Owsley
  acid

masculine
  he-man

mash
  proposition

mashed
  plastered

masher
  ladies' man
  stud

mask
  puss

massacre
  clobber

massage
  clobber
  rough up

massage someone's ego
  stroke

massage parlor
  whorehouse

mastermind
  boss

masturbate
  jack off

mat
  broad
  old woman

match
  bag
  deck

matsakaw
  horse

Maui
  pot

maul
  clobber

mavin
  ace

maxed
  high

max out
  ace

mayate
  nigger

mayo
  coke
  horse

mazuma
  dough

the McCoy
  honest-to-God
  horse
  humdinger
  the McCoy, "excellence"

meal
  a feed

meal ticket
  angel

mean
  feisty
  great
  hairy

mean bean
  ace

mean green
  angel dust
  dough

meanie
  bad man

measly
  crummy
  piddly

meat
  ass
  bag
  basket
  cock
  cunt

the meat and potatoes
  the bottom line

meat-axe
  clobber

meatball
  dope
  jerk

meathead
  dope

meatheaded
  dumb

meathook
  mitt

meathound
  stud

meat wagon, "ambulance"

meatware
  innards

mechanic
  card sharp
  grease monkey

meddler
  kibitzer

medic
  sawbones

mediocre
  bush

mediocrity
  the bush leagues

med mojo
  coke

megabucks
  bundle

megg
  pot

the megillah
  the whole shebang

melancholy
  down
  gloomy Gus

melee
  free-for-all

mell of a hess
  bind
  snafu

mellow
 cool
 laid-back
 pal
 plastered
 with it
mellow out
 goof off
 kick back
melonhead
 dope
melons
 tits
meltdown
 crash
melted out
 broke
Melvin
 jerk
member
 cock
memory hole
 the circular file
me, myself, and I
 yours truly
mensch
 he-man
 the McCoy
menstruate
 have the rag on
mental
 crazy
mental hospital
 booby hatch
mental job
 nut
mentally
 upstairs
mentally numb person
 zombie

merchandise
 dope
 horse
the merry ha-ha
 the horselaugh
mesca
 pot
Mescin
 bean-eater
meshugah
 crazy
meshugana
 nut
mess
 bind
 can of worms
 mish-mash
 scarecrow
 sleazebag
 snafu
mess around
 goof off
 play games
mess around with
 fool around with
messed-up
 fucked-up
mess someone over
 fuck
mess up
 clobber
 rough up
 screw up
mess with
 doctor
 fool around with
messy
 fucked-up
 half-assed
 yucky
methaqualone
 lude

meth head
 junkie
Mex
 pot
Mexican standoff
 standoff
mezonny
 dough
mezz
 great
 joint
MF
 asshole
Mick, "Irish person"
mickey
 Mickey Finn
Mickey
 Mick
Mickey Finn, "chloral
 hydrate"
Mickey Mouse
 chickenshit
 corn
 crap
 crummy
 dope
 gadgetry
 piddly
 schlocky
 snafu
Mickey Mouse around
 goof off
Mickey Mouse course
 gut course
Mickey Mouse ears
 party hat
microdots
 acid
microgram
 bag

middle
 belly

middle-age spread
 potbelly
 spare tire

middle leg
 cock

the middle of nowhere
 the boondocks

midget
 shorty

midnight oil
 big O

miff
 bug
 give someone a pain in the
  ass
 piss someone off
 piss-off

miffed
 pissed off

miggle
 joint

mightily
 one's head off

mighty
 fucking
 great

mighty Joe Young
 doll

mighty mezz
 joint
 pot

mighty Quinn
 acid

mildly impaired
 plastered

military
 bobtail
 buck private
 go over the hill

grunt
 hash mark
 latrine lawyer
 leatherneck
 swabby
 top-kick

military discharge
 bobtail

milk
 con

milk-livered
 chicken
 wimpish

milk the cash cow
 clean up

milktoast
 wimp

milk wagon
 Black Maria

the mill
 the slammer

milligram
 bag

Milquetoast
 chicken
 wimp

Milwaukee goiter
 potbelly

mince
 jerk

mince pies
 peepers

mind detergent
 acid

mind-fucker
 bad news
 a bad scene

mind one's own business
 stick to one's knitting

ming
 joint

mink
 dish

the minor leagues
 the bush leagues

mint
 bundle

mintweed
 angel dust

miscue
 boner

miser
 tightwad

misfire
 letdown

misfortune
 a bad scene
 a bitch

mish-mash
 can of worms
 mish-mash, "mixture"

miss
 broad

Miss Emma
 M

misses
 crooked dice

missie
 broad

missing some marbles
 dumb

missionary
 dealer

missis
 broad

Miss Morph
 M

miss the boat
 blow it with someone
 fuck up

missumis
 old woman

389

mist
  angel dust

mistaken
  full of shit

mister
  guy

Mister
  Jack

the mister
  hubby

Mister Bad Guy
  bad man

Mister Big
  boss

Mister Moneybags
  moneybags

Mister Tom
  fink

Mister Whiskers
  Uncle Sam

mite
  mitt, "hand"
  smidgen

mitt-glommer
  glad-hander

mitts
  bracelets

mix it up
  hassle

mixture
  mish-mash

mix-up
  free-for-all
  hassle
  snafu

MJ
  pot

mo
  gay

M O
  pot

a mo
  a jiffy

moan
  beef

moaner
  kvetch

mob scene, "crowd"

mobster
  button man
  gangster

moby
  monster

mockie
  kike

mocus
  fucked-up

mod
  snappy
  with it

modams
  pot

Model-T
  schlocky

modoc
  dope

mohasky
  high
  pot

mohoska
  clout
  pizzazz

mojo
  dope
  pot

moke
  moocher

molasses
  big O

moll
  broad

moll-buzzer
  heist man

momma
  broad
  sucker

mommix
  screw up

mommixed-up
  fucked-up

momzer
  asshole
  moocher

mon
  dough

Monday morning
    quarterback
  bigmouth

money
  angel
  a bill
  blow
  broke
  buck
  bundle
  case dough
  chicken feed
  cough up
  the damage
  dough
  fin
  freebie
  free gratis
  go broke
  grand
  gravy
  grease someone's palm
  kick in
  loaded
  make a killing
  moneybags
  paperhanger
  pick up the tab
  sawbuck
  set someone back

the shorts
  tab
  take
  tightwad

moneybags, "wealthy
    person"

money punch
  Sunday punch

monicker, "name"

monkey
  guy
  patsy

monkey around
  fool around with
  goof off

monkey business
  dirty tricks
  monkey business,
    "deception"

monkey cocaine
  coke

monkeydoodle
  bullshit

monkey drill
  works

monkey dust
  angel dust

monkeyshines
  horseplay

monkey talk
  double-talk

monkey with
  fool around with

monkey-wrench in the
    works
  glitch

monster, "large"

Montezuma's revenge
  the shits

a month of Sundays
  ages

moo
  dough

moocah
  M
  pot

mooch
  bum
  dope
  heist
  moocher
  patsy

mooch around
  goof off

moocher
  bum
  moocher, "parasite"

moolah
  dough

moon
  bag
  deck
  panther piss

mooning

moonlight, "work at a
    second job"

moonshine
  bullshit
  flack
  panther piss

moose
  bruiser

moose milk
  panther piss

mooter
  joint
  pot

mope
  dope

mopey
  down

mop up
  wrap up

mop up the floor with
  clobber

mopus
  dough

morphine
  M

morsel
  dish

mortal lock
  cinch

mosey along
  split
  toddle

mosquito
  coke

mossback
  fogy

the most
  great
  humdinger
  the most, "superior one"

the mostest
  great
  the most

mother
  asshole
  damn
  dealer
  gadget
  sucker

motherfucker
  asshole
  gadget
  sucker

motherfucking
  damn

motorcycle
  bike

motor-mouth
  blabbermouth
motor-mouthed
  gabby
mouldy
  crummy
mountain dew
  panther piss
mouse
  black eye
  broad
  feel
mousy
  chicken
  wimpish
mouth
  yap
mouthbreather
  dope
mouth off
  blow off
  bullshit
  gab
  shoot the breeze
mouth on someone
  squeal
mouthpiece
  shyster
move
  heist
move someone back
  set someone back
movies
  horse opera
mow down
  break someone up
  clobber
  wow
moxie
  chutzpa
  clout

guts
pizzazz
smarts
mox nix aus
  one couldn't care
    less
  forget it
Mr Charley
  whitey
Mr Morpheus
  M
Mr Nice Guy
  doll
  good guy
Mr Twenty-six
  works
mu
  pot
mucho dinero
  bundle
muck
  big shot
  goo
  mung
muck about
  fool around with
  goof off
mucked-up
  fucked-up
mucker
  asshole
mucket
  gadget
muckety-mucks
  the brass
muck up
  goof
  screw up
muck-up
  boner

muck with
  fool around with
mucky-muck
  big shot
mud
  hash
  pot
muddled
  plastered
muddlehead
  ditz
muddle-headed
  dumb
muddle through
  get by
mudhole
  jerk town
mud lark
  kid
muff
  beaver
  boner
  cunt
  fuck up
  rug
  screw up
muff-diver
  cunt-lapper
muffer
  butterfingers
  duffer
muffins
  tits
mug
  guy
  heist
  mug shot
  patsy
  puss
  yap

mugger
  goon
  heist man
muggle
  joint
muggled
  high
mugglehead
  pothead
muggles
  joint
mug shot, "photograph"
muhfuh
  asshole
mule
  mule, "obstinate person"
  panther piss
mulish
  bullheaded
mullethead
  dope
mulletheaded
  dumb
mulligan
  Mick
mulligrubs
  the blues
mumbo-jumbo
  bullshit
  double-talk
Munchkin
  kid
munch out
  scarf
mung
  goo
  mung, "filth"
  screw up
munsh
  big O

murder
  bad news
  clobber
  wow
murder weed
  pot
murphy
  con
  scam
muscle
  clout
  a fix
  goon
  horse
musclehead
  dope
muscle in
  butt in
muscle man
  goon
mush
  bullshit
  corn
  puss
  yap
mush-head
  dope
mushheaded
  dumb
mushy
  corny
muss
  snafu
mussed-up
  fucked-up
musta
  pot
mutt
  dope
  jerk
  pooch

muttonhead
  dope
muttonheaded
  dumb
muzzle
  schnozz
muzzler
  cop
muzzy
  rocky
my ass
  like hell
my eye
  like hell
my God
  Jeez
my lonesome
  yours truly
My Man
  Jack
nab
  bust
  cop
  grab
  heist
nabber
  heist man
nabob
  big shot
nada
  zilch
nail
  bust
  catch redhanded
  dig
  fuck
  grab
  joint
  peg
  sock
  works

nail down
 clinch
 peg
 spell out

nailed down
 cinched

nail it
 barrel
 floor it

nail someone to the wall
 hold someone's feet to the
  fire

naked
 bare-ass

name
 monicker

the name of the game
 the bottom line

one's name is mud
 kaput

nancy
 gay
 sissy

narc
 cop
 dick

narco
 cop
 junkie

narcotic injection
 shoot up

narcotics
 acid
 angel dust
 bad trip
 bag
 bennies
 big O
 blow grass
 coke
 dealer
 deck

dirty
do
doll
dope
dope den
a fix
freak out
hash
high
hooked
horse
joint
junkie
lude
M
pot
pothead
roach clip
score
shooting gallery
shoot up
snort
toke
works

narcotics apparatus
 works

narcotics dose
 a fix

narcotics experience
 freak out

narcotics-free
 clean
 straight

narcotics intoxication
 high

narcotics possession
 dirty

narcotics quantity
 bag
 deck

narcotics seller
 dealer

narcotics use
 do

narcotics venue
 shooting gallery

nark
 kibitzer
 shill
 snitch
 squeal

narkied
 hooked

narrow down on
 zero in

narrow-gauge
 bush
 piddly

narrow squeak
 cliffhanger

nasty
 great
 yucky

nasty bits
 basket

nasty crack
 knock

natch
 bet your ass

natter
 chitchat
 gab
 shoot the breeze

natural
 cinch

natural-born
 honest-to-God

naughty
 dirty

nauseated
 green around the gills

Navy
 butt

neanderthal
  redneck

near thing
  cliffhanger

neat
  cool
  great

neaten up
  fix up

neb
  wimp

nebbie
  doll

nebbish
  jerk
  lightweight
  warm body
  wimp

the necessary
  dough

neck, "kiss"

needle
  bug
  works

needle candy
  dope

needle park
  shooting gallery

negative
  nix
  nope

nelly
  gay

nemmie
  doll

neophyte
  greenhorn
  rookie

Nepalese hash
  hash

nerd
  grind
  jerk

nerdmobile
  pimpmobile

nerts
  crazy

nerve
  chutzpa
  guts

nervous
  cool
  jittery

nervous Nellie
  wimp

nervousness
  the jitters

nervy
  cheeky
  gutsy

nest egg
  case dough

net
  grab

never looking back
  with flying colors

never-was
  loser

new kid on the block
  greenhorn

new magic
  angel dust

new situation
  it's a new ball game

New York white
  pot

NG
  kaput
  schlocky

nice girl
  floozy

nice going
  way to go

nice hunk of change
  bundle

Nice Nelly
  Christer
  goody-goody

nick
  bust
  heist

nickel bag
  bag
  deck

nickels and dimes
  chicken feed

nickel-squeezer
  tightwad

nifty
  great

nifty number
  dish

nigger, "black person"

nigger rich
  loaded

nightclub
  night spot

nightingale
  snitch

night spot, "nightclub"

nightstick
  billy club

nimby
  doll

nincompoop
  dope

nine days' wonder
  letdown

nine-to-fiver
  square

ninny
  ditz
  dope

nip
  heist
  snort

nippers
  bracelets

nit
  zilch

nitery
  night spot

nit-pick, "quibble"

nitro
  great

the nitty-gritty
  the bottom line

nitwit
  dope

nitwitted
  dumb

nix
  nix, "reject"
  nope
  zilch

nix out
  split

no-account
  crummy
  schlocky

nob
  swell

no bargain
  lightweight
  scarecrow

no big deal
  forget it

noble weed
  pot

nobody
  lightweight
  wimp

nobody home
  crazy

nobody to write home
    about
  lightweight

the nobs
  the upper crust

no bull
  honest-to-God

no buts about it
  for sure
  honest-to-God

no chance
  a fat chance

no cinch
  hairy

nocks
  dope

no-count
  schlocky

the nod
  the go-ahead
  the OK

noddy
  dope
  high
  in a fog

no dice
  nope

no end
  as shit

no fooling, "expression of
    honesty"

noggin
  bean

no go
  nope

no-good
  crummy
  schlocky

no great shakes
  lightweight

nohow
  like hell

no ifs, ands, or buts
  for sure
  honest-to-God

noise
  gab

noise tool
  rod

no jive
  no shit

no kidding
  honest-to-God
  no shit

no-neck
  redneck

nonentity
  lightweight

nonfunctioning
  on the blink

nonsense
  bullshit

nonstarter
  lightweight
  loser

nonunion worker
  scab

noodle
  bean
  dope
  goof off

noodlehead
  dope

noogie
  Dutch rub

nooky
  ass
  cunt
nope, "negation"
no picnic
  a bitch
  hairy
noplaceville
  jerk town
no prize package
  lightweight
  scarecrow
no problem
  forget it
no sale
  nope
nose
  coke
  schnozz
  snitch
the nosebag
  chow
nose burner
  joint
nose candy
  coke
  dope
nose in
  butt in
nose-picker
  hick
nose powder
  coke
nosh
  cheat
no shit
  honest-to-God
  izzatso
no shit, "expression of
  credulity"

no sirree
  nope
no slouch
  ace
  hot shot
no snap
  hairy
no soap
  nope
no spring chicken
  old bag
no sweat
  easy as pie
  forget it
Nosy Parker
  kibitzer
not all there
  crazy
  dumb
not a pot to piss in
  the shorts
not a prayer
  a fat chance
not bat an eye
  keep one's cool
not be born yesterday
  know one's onions
not be seen dead with
  hate someone's guts
not blink an eye
  keep one's cool
not blow a gasket
  cool it
  keep one's cool
not bottle it up
  let it all hang out
not buy
  nix
notch
  ass
  cunt

notcherie
  whorehouse
notch girl
  hooker
not cricket
  dirty
not cut the mustard
  fuck up
no tea party
  a bitch
not get one's balls in an
    uproar
  cool it
  keep one's cool
not get to first base
  fuck up
not give a shit
  not give a damn
not give someone the time
    of day
  hate someone's guts
not hack it
  fuck up
not have a clue
  have a hole in one's head
not have brains enough to
    come in out of the rain
  have a hole in one's head
nothing
  wimp
  zilch
nothing doing
  nope
nothing to write home
    about
  lightweight
not hold one's breath
  sit tight
no time at all
  a jiffy

not know one's ass from
   one's elbow
  have a hole in one's head
  not know shit from Shinola

not let out a peep
  shut up

not lose one's cool
  keep one's cool

not make a diff of
  bitterence
  cut no ice

not make the grade
  fuck up

not meddle
  stick to one's knitting

not much of a bargain
  lightweight

not on your life
  nope

not play games
  play hardball

not play with a full deck
  have a hole in one's head

not right bright
  dumb

not say boo
  shut up

not sign off on
  nix

not tightly wrapped
  crazy

not too shabby
  great

not turn a hair
  keep one's cool

not up to snuff
  off one's feed

not worth a plugged nickel
  not worth a damn

no two ways about it
  for sure

nougat
  dope

no way
  like hell
  nope

no-win situation
  catch-22

nozzle
  schnozz

nudge
  bug
  nudnik

nuggets
  bennies
  dough

nuke
  clobber

nuked
  kaput

numb
  dumb

number
  act
  cookie
  joint
  a put-on
  racket
  scam

number cruncher
  bean counter

numbered out
  high

number one
  boss

numbers
  the book

number thirteen
  M

number three
  coke

number two
  shit

numbnuts
  jerk

numbskull
  dope

numbskulled
  dumb

numero uno
  boss

nut
  bean
  fan

nut, "insane person"
  oddball

nutcase
  nut

nut college
  booby hatch

nut-cruncher
  ball-buster

nut doctor
  shrink

nut house
  booby hatch

nuts
  balls
  crazy

the nuts
  great
  humdinger

nutty
  crazy
  flaky

nut up
  go crazy

nympho
  floozy

O
  bag
  big O
  deck

Oakley
  Annie Oakley

oater
  horse opera

Oaxacan
  pot

obfuscated
  plastered

obscene
  dirty

obsession
  a bee in one's bonnet

obstinate
  bullheaded

obstinate person
  mule

occupation
  grease monkey
  racket
  sawbones
  shrink
  shyster

oddball
  kinky
  oddball, "eccentric
    person"
  weird

odd man out
  excess baggage

odds and ends
  mish-mash

odds-on favorite
  front runner

odds splitter
  crooked dice

odd stick
  oddball

of a sort
  bush

ofay
  whitey

off
  crazy
  fuck
  on the blink
  snuff

off artist
  heist man

offbeat
  kinky

off one's bird
  crazy

off-color
  dirty

off one's feed
  green around the gills
  off one's feed, "ill"

off one's head
  crazy

office worker
  desk jockey

off the cob
  corny

off the habit
  clean

off the record
  on the QT

off the top
  up front

off the wall
  crazy
  kinky
  weird

off-tone
  dirty

of sorts
  bush

O G
  honest-to-God

oglers
  peepers

Ohio bag
  bag
  deck

oil
  bullshit
  hash
  horse
  soft soap

oil bags
  ass

oiled
  plastered

oiler
  bean-eater
  pothead

oil someone's palm
  grease someone's palm

oink
  cop

OK
  buy
  cool
  get me
  OK, "affirmation"

the OK
  the go-ahead
  the OK, "permission"

okey-dokey
  cool
  OK

Okie
  cracker
  hick

the old army game
  scam

old bat
  old bag

old-boy network
  the in group
old fart, "old man"
old-fashioned music
  corn
old geezer
  old fart
the old heave-ho
  the axe
oldie
  chestnut
old lady
  old woman
old Madge
  coke
old maid
  goody-goody
old man
  boss
  old fart
  sugar daddy
the old man
  hubby
Old Man Trouble
  bad news
old person
  fogy
old Siwash
  cow college
old slave
  coke
Old Smoky
  the chair
old smoothie
  smoothie
old softie
  softie
Old Sparky
  the chair

oldster
  fogy
  old fart
old Steve
  horse
old ticker
  ticker
old-timer
  fogy
  old fart
old woman
  old bag
  old woman, "wife"
on
  high
  hooked
on a roll
  hot
on a tear
  pissed off
once-over
  check out
the once-over, "inspection"
a once-over lightly
  a lick and a promise
on cloud nine
  high
on deck
  in place
the one
  hash
on one's ear
  broke
one-arm joint
  greasy spoon
one bitch of a
  a hell of a
one could care less
  one couldn't care less

on edge
  jittery
one-eyed monster
  the tube
one for the book
  a hit
one hell of a
  a hell of a
one-horse
  bush
one-horse town
  jerk town
one hundred dollars
  a bill
one-liner
  crack
one of the boys
  Joe Blow
one-on-one
  hassle
oner
  humdinger
  the most
one red cent
  zilch
oneself
  yours truly
one-spot
  ace
  buck
one-stoplight town
  jerk town
the one that wrote the book
  ace
one thin dime
  zilch
one-toke weed
  pot
one too many
  excess baggage

one-way guy
  doll
  good guy
one-way hit
  acid
on one's game
  hot
on someone's get-lost list
  on someone's shit list
on hold, "postponed"
on ice
  cinched
  on hold
onion
  bean
on one's last legs
  pooped
on line
  in place
on tap
  in place
on the arm
  free gratis
  on the cuff
on the back burner
  on hold
on the ball
  on the ball, "alert"
  with it
on the beam
  great
  in the groove
  with it
on the bean
  on the nose
on the blink,
    "nonfunctioning"
on the bottle
  on the sauce

on the bum
  on the blink
on the button
  on the nose
on the cob
  corny
on the cuff
  free gratis
  on the cuff, "borrowed"
on the dot
  on the nose
on the double
  lickety-split
  on the double,
    "immediately"
on the finger
  on the cuff
on the fire
  in the pipeline
on the fritz
  on the blink
on the gow
  high
on the gravy train
  loaded
on the hill
  knocked up
on the hog
  broke
on the hook
  out of luck
on the horse
  hooked
on the hot seat
  out of luck
  up the creek
on the house
  free gratis
on the juice
  on the sauce

on the legit
  on the level
  straight
on the level
  fly right
  honest-to-God
  on the level, "fair"
  straight
on the make
  hungry
on the mojo
  hooked
on the money
  on the nose
on the monkey wagon
  hooked
on the needle
  hooked
on the nod
  high
on the nose, "exact"
on the pipe
  hooked
on the QT, "secretly"
on the rims
  broke
on the rocks
  broke
  kaput
on the ropes
  out of luck
on the same wavelength
  on someone's wavelength
on the sauce, "drinking
    liquor"
on the shelf
  on hold
on the shikker
  on the sauce
  plastered

on the skids
  kaput

on the spot
  in there
  out of luck
  up the creek

on the square
  straight

on the stick
  on the ball

on the stuff
  high
  hooked

on the up-and-up
  fly right
  honest-to-God
  straight

on tick
  on the cuff

onto
  have someone's number

on top of it
  in there

on top of the world
  in hog heaven

on one's uppers
  broke

ooch
  scrunch

oof
  clout
  pizzazz

oofless
  broke
  dullsville

oofus
  dope
  dough

oofy
  loaded

oogah
  honk

ook
  jerk
  wimp

ookus
  dough

oomph
  clout
  pizzazz

oomph girl
  dish

oonch
  scrunch

oops
  barf

ooze
  toddle

op
  dick
  private eye

Op
  big O

open-and-shut
  cinched

open one's face
  open one's yap

open up
  let it all hang out

open up on
  plug

open one's yap, "speak"

operator
  eager beaver
  ladies' man
  wheeler-dealer

opium
  big O

opportunity
  a fat chance

opposite side
  the flip side

optics
  peepers

orange crush
  cop

orange cryst
  angel dust

orange cubes
  acid

orange peaches
  bennies

ordinary guy
  Joe Blow

Oreo
  fink

organized
  plastered

organized life
  get it together

orgasm
  come

ork
  barf

ornery
  feisty

oroy
  horse

oryide
  lush

oscar
  rod

ossifer
  cop

ossified
  dumb
  high
  plastered

ostentatious car
  pimpmobile

ostracize
  blackball
the other side of the coin
  the flip side
ouch
  Jeez
ounce man
  dealer
our betters
  the brass
out
  cool
  high
  out, "unconscious"
outasight
  great
the outback
  the boondocks
outclassed
  out of one's depth
out cold
  out
outer
  acid
outfit
  works
out-front
  straight
out in left field
  fucked-up
out in the cold
  finished
out like a light
  out
out of business
  kaput
out of circulation
  in stir
out of commission
  on the blink

out of one's depth
  out of one's depth,
  "incapable"
  out of luck
  up the creek
out of one's gourd
  crazy
out of it
  finished
  high
  out
  rocky
out of one's league
  out of one's depth
out of luck
  kaput
  out of luck, "unfortunate"
out of sight
  great
out of one's skull
  crazy
out of sorts
  green around the gills
out of the box
  kaput
out of the woods
  in
out of this world
  great
out of town
  in stir
out of whack
  on the blink
out on a limb
  up the creek
out on one's ass
  finished
  kaput
out on one's ear
  finished

out on one's feet
  pooped
  rocky
outpoint
  beat
out the window
  kaput
out to lunch
  crazy
outz
  jerk
oven
  cooler
overact
  ham
overdosed
  high
overeat
  pig out
over one's head
  out of one's depth
overtaken
  plastered
Owsley
  acid
O Z
  bag
  deck
pachuco
  bean-eater
pack
  carry
  cart
  horse
package
  bundle
  dish
packed up
  high
  on the blink

packet
bundle

pack fudge
bugger

pack heat
carry

pack in
knock off
wrap up

packing heat
heeled

pack it in
knock off

pack it up
shut up

pack some mud
bugger

pack the mail
barrel

pack up
go kerflooey
knock off
wrap up

pad
pad, "dwelling"
toddle

paddle
tan

paddlefoot
grunt

paddlewhack
tan

pad down
frisk
snooze

pad duty
sack time

paddy
cop
Mick
whitey

paddy wagon
Black Maria

pad out
snooze

paesan
pal

pain
jerk
nudnik

painful rubbing
Dutch rub

pain in the ass
bad news
a bad scene
drag
jerk
nudnik

painted into a corner
up the creek

paint remover
panther piss

paint the town red
have a ball
paint the town red,
**   "carouse"**

pair
tits

paisano
pal

Pakistani hash
hash

pal
Jack
pal, "friend"

palaver
gab
schmooz
shoot the breeze

paled
pooped

paleface
whitey

palm oil
dough

palooka
lightweight

palsy-walsy
chummy
pal
palsy-walsy, "friendly"

pal together
buddy up

pal up with
hang out with

pan
bad-mouth
knock
puss

Panama gold
pot

pancake turner
disc jockey

panhandle, "beg"

panhandler
moocher

panic
break someone up
panic, "become
**   frightened"**

a panic
a howl

panjandrum
big shot

pan juice
big O

pan out
go over with a bang
pay off

pansified
wimpish

pansy
 gay
 sissy

panther sweat
 panther piss

pantry
 belly

pantywaist
 sissy
 wimp

paper
 Annie Oakley
 bag
 deck

paper-assed
 wimpish

paper-pusher
 paperhanger

paper tiger
 bigmouth

paperweight
 desk jockey

pappy
 old fart

paradise
 coke

parallel parking
 a fuck

paralyzing tension
 choke up

parasite
 moocher

pardner
 pal

pardon
 forget it

pardon me for living
 excuse me all to hell

park
 neck
 park, "place"

park it in the bleachers
 homer

parlor pink
 pinko

part cheeks
 bugger

part that goes over the
   fence last
 ass

party
 ass
 cookie
 fuck
 a fuck
 have a ball
 wingding

party hat, "lights"

party-pooper
 gloomy Gus

pass
 proposition

passed out
 high

passers
 crooked dice

pass out
 croak
 pass out, "lose
   consciousness"

pass up
 give a miss

paste
 clobber
 sock

pasteboard, "playing card"

pasteboard, "ticket of
   admission"

pasteboard shark
 card sharp

pasted
 hooked

paste on
 hang on

pasty
 green around the gills

patch out
 split

pate
 bean

pato
 gay

pat oneself on the back
 blow off

pat someone on the back
 hand it to someone

patootie
 ass
 dish

patron
 angel
 rabbi

patsy, "victim"

patter
 gab
 shoot the breeze

patty
 whitey

patyo de gayina
 pot

Paul Pry
 kibitzer

paunch
 potbelly

paw
 feel
 mitt

pay
 cough up

pay a bill
 pick up the tab

pay day
 eagle day

pay one's dues
  go through the mill
  pay one's dues, "acquire
    practical experience"

payoff
  pay dirt
  punch line

pay off
  fire
  pay off, "yield profit"

the payoff
  the bottom line
  curtains

payoff punch
  Sunday punch

pay the freight
  pick up the tab

pay the piper
  bite the bullet

PCP
  angel dust

p'd
  pissed off

PDQ
  on the double

peabrain
  dope

peabrained
  dumb

peace
  acid
  angel dust

peach
  dish
  humdinger
  squeal

peachy
  great

peahead
  dope

peaheaded
  dumb

peaked
  green around the gills
  off one's feed

peanut
  doll
  lightweight
  little bitty
  piddly
  shorty

peanut-brained
  dumb

peanuts
  chicken feed

pearl-diver, "dishwasher"

pearlies
  choppers

pea shooter
  rod

peck
  cracker
  whitey

pecker
  cock

peckerhead
  asshole
  jerk

peckerwood
  cracker
  whitey

peddle ass
  hustle

peddler
  dealer

pee
  piss

a pee
  a piss

peed
  pissed off

peek
  the once-over

peekers
  peepers

peeler
  cop
  stripper

peel out
  split

peenie
  cock

pee someone off
  piss someone off

peep
  the once-over
  open one's yap

pee one's pants
  break up

pee-pee
  piss

peeper
  private eye

peepers
  peepers, "eyes"
  shades

peeps
  peepers

peet
  pete

peeve
  bug
  give someone a pain in the
    ass

peeved off
  pissed off

peewee
  little bitty
  piddly
  shorty

peg
  peg, "identify"

peg, "throw"
  plug
  snort

peg out
  croak
  fuck up
  go kerflooey

pegs
  pins

pekoe
  big O

the pen
  the slammer

pencil pusher
  desk jockey

penis
  cock

penniless
  broke

penny ante
  piddly

penny-pincher
  tightwad

penny pool
  piddly

pennyweighter
  heist man

pen-pusher
  desk jockey

pen yen
  big O

peola
  nigger

peon
  gofer

people upstairs
  the brass

pep
  pizzazz

pep-em-ups
  bennies

pepped-up
  jazzed-up

pepper
  pizzazz

pepper-belly
  bean-eater

pepper-upper
  pick-me-up

pep pills
  bennies

peppy
  full of piss and vinegar
  jazzy
  zingy

pep up
  jazz up

percentage
  bite
  pay dirt

perch
  neck

percolate
  toddle

Percy
  sissy
  wimp

a per-each
  a clip

perforate
  plug

perform
  fuck

performance record
  the book

performing well
  hot
  in the groove

perform minimally
  get by

perform spectacularly
  grandstand

perico
  coke

perishing
  antsy

perker-upper
  pick-me-up

perk up
  goose

perky
  zingy

permanently
  for keeps

permission
  the go-ahead
  the OK

perplex
  can of worms

persnickety
  prissy

person
  ace
  ass
  asshole
  bad man
  baldie
  ball-buster
  bean counter
  bean-eater
  beanpole
  bigmouth
  big shot
  bitch
  blood
  boss
  the brass
  brick-top
  broad
  brown-nose
  bruiser
  bum
  butterfingers

button man
camel-jammer
Chink
cold fish
con
con man
cookie
cracker
cunt-lapper
desk jockey
disc jockey
dish
ditz
doll
dope
drag
duck-squeezer
dude
duffer
dyke
eager beaver
egghead
excess baggage
fan
fink
flack
floozy
fogy
Frog
front runner
gangster
gay
glad-hander
gloomy Gus
G-man
gofer
goner
good guy
goody-goody
goof-off
gook
goon
greenhorn
grind
groupie
grunt

guy
heist man
he-man
hick
hit man
honey
hooker
hot shot
hubby
humdinger
hunk
hunky
Jack
jail bait
Jane
jerk
Joe Blow
Joe College
kibitzer
kid
kike
kraut
kvetch
ladies' man
latrine lawyer
leatherneck
lightweight
limey
loan shark
loser
Mick
monicker
mule
nigger
nudnik
nut
oddball
old bag
old fart
old woman
pal
patsy
phony
pig
pinko
playboy

pothead
private eye
pro
redneck
scab
scalper
scarecrow
shill
shorty
shrink
shyster
sissy
sleazebag
smar

persons
  the in group
  the jet set

persuade
  talk someone into

persuader
  goon
  rod

persuasion
  go into one's dance
  line

pesky
  damn

peso
  buck

pesos
  dough

pet
  broad
  feel
  honey
  neck

pete-box
  pete

pete-man
  heist man

peter
  cock

Mickey Finn
pete
peter-eater
  cocksucker
Peter Funk
  shill
peter man
  heist man
peter out
  fold
  fuck up
Peter Pan
  angel dust
petrified
  plastered
petty spirit
  chickenshit
pfft
  flop
  kaput
phenom
  a hit
  humdinger
phew
  yuck
Philadelphia
  Philly
philander
  cheat
Philly, "Philadelphia"
phiz
  puss
phonies
  crooked dice
phonograph record
  platter
phony
  glad-hander
  phony, "false"
  phony, "false one"

phony baloney
  bullshit
  phony
phony rap
  bum rap
photo finish
  standoff
photograph
  mug shot
phutz
  con
  fuck
  a fuck
phutzing
  ass
physician
  sawbones
physique
  build
Piccadilly commando
  hooker
piccolo player
  cocksucker
pick 'em up and lay 'em
    down
  get the lead out
picker-upper
  pick-me-up
pickin's
  score
pickle
  bind
  screw up
pickled
  plastered
picklepuss
  kvetch
  scarecrow
pick-me-up, "stimulant"

pick nits
  nit-pick
pick on
  bug
pickup
  bust
pick up
  blow grass
  bust
  check out
  hike
  score
pick up on
  dig
pick up the check
  pick up the tab
picky
  prissy
a picnic
  a ball
  cinch
piddle
  piss
a piddle
  a piss
piddle around
  goof off
piddle away
  blow
piddling
  bush
  little bitty
piddly
  little bitty
  piddly, "trivial"
pie
  cinch
  gravy
piece
  ass
  bit

bite
broad
coke
deck
floozy
a fuck
horse
M
piece, "share"
rod

piece of ass
ass
floozy
a fuck

piece of butt
ass

piece of cake
cinch

piece of cash
bundle

piece of change
dough

piece of cheese
cookie

piece of crap
crap

piece of jack
dough

piece of shit
asshole
bullshit
crap

piece of tail
ass
floozy
a fuck

piece of the racket
piece

piece of trade
hooker

piece pillow
bag

piece up
divvy

pie-eyed
plastered

pie-faced
dumb

piety
Christer

pie wagon
Black Maria

the pif
the poop
the straight dope

piffle
bullshit

pig
cop
floozy
pig, "glutton"

pigeon
patsy
shill
snitch

pigeonhole
peg

pigfucker
asshole

piggish
grabby

piggy
grabby

pighead
mule

pigheaded
bullheaded

pig heaven
fat city

pig iron
panther piss

pig killer
angel dust

pig-meat
loser

pig out, "overeat"

pigs
crooked dice

pig sweat
panther piss

piker
goof-off
tightwad

piki
big O

pile into
blast
chew out

pile it up
bullshit

pile of shit
bullshit

piles
bundle

pile up
rack up
total

pile up some Zs
snooze

pill
doll
drag
jerk

pillhead
junkie

pillow
deck

pill-peddler
sawbones

pill pillow
big O

pill-popper
 junkie

pill-pusher
 sawbones

pimp
 knock

pimp dust
 coke

pimple
 bean
 zit

pimpmobile, "ostentatious
 car"

pimp stick
 butt

pin
 check out
 joint
 peg

pincers
 peepers

pinch
 bind
 bust
 heist

pinch a loaf
 shit

pinchpenny
 tightwad

pin down
 peg
 zero in

pin someone's ears back
 chew out

pinga
 cock

ping in the wing
 a fix

pin gun
 works

pinhead
 dope
 jerk
 junkie

pinheaded
 dumb

pinjabber
 junkie

pink
 gay
 pinko
 whitey

pinked
 plastered

pinko, "liberal"

pink Owsley
 acid

pink-slip
 fire

the pink slip
 the axe

pink swirl
 acid

pinner
 joint

pin on
 hang on

pinpoint
 zero in

pins, "legs"

pin shot
 a fix

pinto bean
 bean-eater

pint-size
 little bitty
 piddly

pinup
 cheesecake

pin-up
 dish
 hunk

pious person
 Christer

pip
 humdinger
 zit

the pip
 the blues

pipe
 check out
 cinch
 open one's yap
 shoot up
 warble

pipe course
 gut course

pipe down
 shut up

pipe up
 open one's yap

pipperoo
 humdinger

pippy-poo
 piddly

pip-squeak
 lightweight
 shorty

pisher
 kid

piss
 beef
 crummy
 piss, "urinate"
 piss, "urine"
 piss someone off

a piss, "urination"

piss and vinegar
 pizzazz

pissant
  asshole
  lightweight
  piddly

piss away
  blow

piss-cutter
  ace
  eager beaver
  hot shot
  humdinger

pissed
  pissed off
  plastered

pisser
  ace
  back-breaker
  eager beaver
  hot shot
  humdinger

pisshead
  asshole

pissing contest
  hassle

pissing on ice
  in hog heaven

piss off
  split

piss someone off, "anger
    someone"

piss-off, "anger"

piss one's pants
  break up

piss on ice
  eat high on the hog

piss on you
  fuck you

piss or get off the pot
  fish or cut bait

piss-poor
  broke
  crummy

piss-ugly, "ugly"

piss up a storm
  beef
  make a scene

pissy
  crummy
  piddly

pissy-ass
  bush
  piddly

pistol
  ace
  eager beaver
  hot shot
  humdinger

pistol Pete
  stud

pit
  cunt
  shoot up

pitch
  bugger
  flack
  gimmick
  line
  proposition

pitch in
  pig out
  scarf

pitch into
  blast
  chew out
  kick ass

pitch woo
  neck

the pits
  the pits, "wretched place"
  yucky

pix
  gay

pixies
  bennies

pixilated
  crazy
  flaky

pizzazz
  clout
  pizzazz, "energy"

place
  dive
  park

places
  the boondocks
  night spot

plack shit
  big O

plain Jane
  Jane

plain vanilla
  vanilla

plank
  fuck

plank down
  cough up

plant
  shill

plant one on
  sock

plaster
  buck
  tail

plastered, "drunk"

plaster saint
  Christer

plastic
  phony
  square

plastic person
  zombie

plate
dude
platter

play
hack it
play ball
work

play along
play ball

play around
cheat
goof off
sleep around
play ball,
"cooperate"

play bouncy-bouncy
fuck

playboy
ladies' man
playboy, "pleasure-
seeker"

play dirty pool
play dirty

play down
soft-pedal

played out
kaput
pooped

player
mack

play footsie
buddy up

play for a sucker
con
snow

play for keeps
play hardball

play for time
stall

play games, "manipulate"

play grab-ass
feel

play hardball, "be serious"

play hell with
screw up

play hide-the-weenie
fuck

play hooky, "be absent"

playing card
pasteboard

play in Peoria
work

play it by ear
wing it

play it close to the chest
pussyfoot

play it cool
cool it

play it safe, "avoid risk"

play kissie-kissie
neck

play kissie with
play up to

play lickey-face
neck

play merry hell with
screw up

play musical beds
sleep around
swing

play possum
hide out

play rough
play hardball

play safe
play it safe

play second fiddle, "occupy
an inferior position"

play slap and tickle
feel

play smacky lips
neck

play stinky-pink
fingerfuck

play the dozens on
con

play the game
play ball

play the skin flute
blow

play tonsil hockey
neck

play to the gallery
grandstand

play up
spotlight

play up to
brown-nose
play up to, "ingratiate"

play with oneself
jack off

pleased as Punch
tickled

pleaser
floozy

pleasure
for kicks
get a kick out of
have a ball
hell around
a kick
kicks

pleasure-seeker
playboy

pleiku pink
pot

plingstem
panhandle

plonk
jerk
smack

plonked
 plastered
plow
 fuck
plow into
 blast
 chew out
plow jockey
 hick
pluck
 con
 fuck
 heist
plug
 phony
 plug, "progress steadily"
 plug, "recommendation"
 plug, "shoot"
plug along
 plug
plug for
 back
plugged
 phony
plugged in
 with it
a plugged nickel
 zilch
plugger
 hit man
plugging
 flack
plug into, "exploit"
plugola
 plug
plug-ugly
 cowboy
 goon
plum
 fucking
 stone

plumb
 fucking
 stone
plumber
 screw up
plumb tuckered
 pooped
plummy
 great
plump
 smack
plump for
 go for
plumpie
 fatty
plunk
 buck
 plug
 smack
plunk down
 cough up
plush
 classy
plute
 moneybags
pocket one's pride
 eat dirt
pocket-size
 little bitty
pod
 pot
p o'd
 pissed off
pod person
 dope
 oddball
 zombie
podunk
 jerk town
the pogey
 the slammer

poggie
 rookie
pogo pogo
 coke
pogue
 gay
 jerk
 rookie
point
 works
pointed head
 dope
 egghead
pointer
 tip
point the finger at someone
 for
 hang on
pointy-headed
 dumb
poison
 bad news
 coke
 horse
poke
 blow grass
 dough
 fuck
 a fuck
 goose
 sock
poke one's nose into
 butt in
poker
 cock
poker face, "impassive face"
the pokey
 the slammer
poky
 little bitty
 piddly

pole
  cock

poler
  grind

police
  billy club
  Black Maria
  bracelets
  bust
  cop
  the cops
  dick
  frisk
  mug shot
  party hat
  prowl car
  rabbi
  roust
  rumble
  snitch
  tin

police badge
  tin

police car
  prowl car

police officer
  cop

police up
  fix up

police van
  Black Maria

polish apples
  brown-nose

polish off
  clobber
  scarf
  snuff
  wrap up

polish up
  brush up

polluted
  high
  plastered

pom-pom
  ass

ponce
  mack

pong
  Chink

pony up
  cough up
  kick in

poo
  Jeez
  shit
  zilch

pooch, "dog"

pooched-out belly
  potbelly

poodle-faker
  ladies' man

poof
  gay

pooh-bah
  big shot
  boss

poontang
  ass
  cunt

poo out
  fold

poop
  ass
  clout
  dope
  jerk
  pizzazz
  shit
  zilch

a poop
  a shit

the poop, "information"

poop chute
  asshole

pooped out
  pooped

pooped up
  briefed

poophole
  asshole

poopied
  plastered

poo-poo
  asshole
  shit

poop out
  fold
  fuck up
  go kerflooey

poop someone up
  spell out

poopsy
  honey

poopsy-woopsy
  honey

poop up
  fill someone in

poor boy
  hero

poor fish
  Joe Blow
  lightweight

poorish
  off one's feed

the poor man's
  bush

poor-mouth
  bad-mouth
  knock

poor performer
  duffer

poor slob
  jerk
  lightweight
  loser

poot
  crap
  jerk
  shit
poot around
  goof off
poot-butt
  jerk
  kid
  young squirt
poove
  gay
pop
  ass
  a fix
  fuck
  shoot up
  sock
a pop
  a clip
pop at
  plug
pop someone's cherry, "end
    someone's virginity"
pop one's cookies
  come
pop one's cork
  blow one's top
popeyed
  cockeyed
  popeyed, "having
    protruding eyes"
pop for
  pick up the tab
popo
  ass
popoff
  bigmouth
pop off
  blow off
  bullshit
  croak

gab
  shoot the breeze
  split
pop off at the mouth
  blow off
poppa
  sugar daddy
popper
  rod
poppet
  dish
poppied
  high
poppy
  big O
poppycock
  bullshit
poppy-headed
  hooked
poppy rain
  big O
poppy train
  big O
popskull
  panther piss
popular
  hot
popular trend
  get on the bandwagon
pop up
  show up
porch
  potbelly
pork
  cock
  fuck
pork out
  pig out
porky
  fatty

porno
  porn
pornographic book
  fuck book
pornographic film
  blue movie
pornography
  fuck book
  porn
porthole
  asshole
portsider
  southpaw
posh
  classy
post
  fill someone in
postponed
  on hold
pot
  can
  dope
  dope den
  plug
  pot, "marijuana"
  potbelly
  sock
potato
  bean
  buck
potatoes
  dough
potatohead
  dope
potato patch
  fruit salad
potbelly, "paunch"
potchkie around with
  fool around with
potent
  great

potgut
  potbelly
pothead
  junkie
  pothead, "marijuana user"
pothouse
  dive
pot lush
  pothead
pot out
  blow grass
  go kerflooey
potsy
  tin
potted
  high
  plastered
pottle-dripped
  high
potty
  can
  crazy
  ditsy
pound
  fuck
the pound
  the slammer
poundcake
  dish
pound one's ear
  snooze
pound one's meat
  jack off
pound the pavement
  toddle
pour down the drain
  blow
pour it on
  barrel
  come on strong
  get the lead out

pour on the coal
  barrel
  get the lead out
pow
  clout
  pizzazz
  pow, "sound of a blow"
  sock
powder
  break out
  clobber
  coke
  hash
  horse
  pot
  split
powdered joy
  dope
power
  the brass
  clout
power a homer
  homer
powerful
  high-powered
power hit
  blow grass
powerhouse
  ace
  eager beaver
powerhouse punch
  Sunday punch
powers that be
  the brass
powie
  pow
pow-wow
  schmooz
pox
  big O

PR
  flack
  pot
practical experience
  go through the mill
practice
  brush up
prairie dew
  panther piss
praise
  stroke
prank
  doll up
prat
  ass
prat-prowl
  frisk
prattle
  gab
pray to the porcelain god
  barf
precious
  honey
precise statement
  spell out
predicament
  bind
preference
  bag
preggers
  knocked up
pregnant
  knocked up
  knock up
prematurily
  go off half-cocked
preparation
  in the pipeline
prepped
  briefed

press
 crowd

press the bricks
 toddle

press the flesh
 give five

pressure
 crowd
 lean on someone
 talk someone into

prestigious
 classy

pretentious talker
 bigmouth

pretty boy
 goon

pretty ear
 cauliflower ear

pretty kettle of fish
 snafu

pretty penny
 bundle

pretty pickle
 bind

pretty radical
 great

pretty scary
 cool

prick
 asshole
 cock
 works

prick someone's balloon
 take someone down a peg

prickly
 goosy

prick-teaser
 cock-teaser

prim
 prissy

primed
 briefed

prime the pump
 score

primo
 great

primp
 doll up

prince
 doll
 good guy

prink
 doll up

prison
 in stir
 stir-crazy

prison sentence
 ace
 bit
 both hands

prissy, "prim"

prittle-prattle
 chitchat

private eye
 dick
 private eye, "detective"

privates
 basket

Private Slipinshits
 buck private

pro
 hooker
 pro, "professional"
 rubber

probable winner
 front runner

proboscis
 schnozz

procurer
 mack

prod
 a fix

produce
 knock something out
 rustle up

professional
 pro

profile
 grandstand

profit
 clean up
 gold mine
 make a killing
 pay dirt

prog
 chow

progress steadily
 plug

prole
 working stiff

promiscuity
 swing

promiscuous woman
 floozy

promise to pay
 tab

promo
 flack

promote
 rustle up

prong
 cock
 fuck

prong-on
 hard-on

pronto
 on the double

prop
 a fix

proper behavior
 fly right

prophet of doom and gloom
  gloomy Gus

proposition, "invite to sex"

props
  falsies

prosper
  eat high on the hog

pross
  hooker

prostitute
  hooker
  hustle

prostitution
  hooker
  whorehouse

prosty
  hooker

protruding eyes
  popeyed

the provinces
  the boondocks

prowl
  frisk

prowl car, "police car"

prune
  patsy

prunish
  prissy

prut
  mung

pseudo
  phony

psyched
  antsy
  pumped

psychiatrist
  shrink

psycho
  crazy
  nut
  weird

psych someone up, "arouse"

PT
  cock-teaser

pub
  flack

pubcrawl
  paint the town red

pubes
  beaver

public address system
  bitch box

publicity
  flack

publicity person
  flack

pucker
  flak
  piss-off
  swivet

pucker-assed
  chicken

pud
  cock
  jerk

puddinghead
  dope

puddingheaded
  dumb

puddle jumper
  jalopy

pudgy-wudgy
  fatty

puff
  big O
  flack
  plug
  a smoke
  toke

puffed
  knocked up

puffed up
  jumped-up
  stuck-up

puffery
  flack

puff job
  plug

puffy
  angel dust

pug
  goon

puke
  barf

pukey
  yucky

pulborn
  horse

pull
  blow grass
  clout
  a smoke
  snort
  toke

pull a boner
  goof

pull a fast one
  con
  snow

pull an el foldo
  flop
  fold

pull someone's chain
  con
  snow

pull down
  grab

puller
  junkie
  pothead

pull one's freight
  split
pull funny business
  play dirty
pull in
  bust
  show up
pull in one's horns
  come down a peg
  cool it
pull it off
  hack it
pull one's leg
  snow
pull someone's leg
  kid
pull no punches
  lay it on the line
pull oneself off
  jack off
pull out
  split
pull out all the stops
  let oneself go
pull one's pud
  jack off
pull one's punches
  cool it
  soft-pedal
pull something funny
  play dirty
pull someone's string
  con
  snow
pull the wool over
    someone's eyes
  con
  snow
pull up one's socks
  clean up one's act

fly right
get on the ball
pull your head out
  wise up
pulverize
  clobber
pummel
  rough up
pump
  fuck
  ticker
pump bilge
  piss
pumped
  knocked up
  pumped, "excited"
pumped up
  jazzed up
  phony
  pumped
pumper
  ticker
pumpkin
  bean
pumpkinhead
  dope
pumpkinheaded
  dumb
pumpkin roller
  hick
pump ship
  piss
pump up
  blow up
  jazz up
pump someone up
  psych someone up
punch
  clout
  a kick
  pizzazz

punch line
  sock
  Sunday punch
punchboard
  floozy
punch-drunk
  pooped
  punch-drunk, "dazed"
punched-up
  jazzed-up
  zingy
punch in
  show up
punch line, "funny
    statement"
punch out
  split
punch-out
  hassle
punch someone out
  clobber
punch up
  jazz up
punchy
  jazzy
  punch-drunk
  rocky
  zingy
puncture
  plug
pundit
  ace
punish
  fix someone
  hold someone's feet to the
    fire
  kick ass
  rough up
punish mildly
  give someone a slap on the
    wrist

punk
  asshole
  bugger
  crummy
  gay
  green around the gills
  jerk
  kid
  lightweight
  off one's feed
  schlocky
  young squirt
punk kid
  kid
  young squirt
punk out
  cop out
Punta Rojas
  pot
pup
  kid
  pooch
  young squirt
puppies
  tootsies
puppy
  gadget
  kid
  pooch
  wimp
pure
  horse
pure love
  acid
purp
  pooch
purple haze
  acid
purple heart
  bennies
  doll

purring like a kitten
  high
pus-bag
  sleazebag
pus-gut
  fatty
  potbelly
push
  bug
  clout
  crowd
  dealer
  floozy
  go for
  pizzazz
  plug
  snuff
pushbox
  squeezebox
push someone's button
  bug
pushed out of shape
  pissed off
pusher
  dealer
  paperhanger
push for
  go for
push off
  snuff
pushover
  cinch
  floozy
  patsy
  softie
  wimp
push-push
  ass
push the panic
    button
  panic

push up daisies
  croak
puss, "face"
pussy
  ass
  broad
  cunt
pussycat
  broad
  doll
  wimp
pussyfoot
  pussyfoot, "be careful"
  stall
pussy-whipped,
    "hen-pecked"
pustle-gut
  fatty
  potbelly
put
  fuck
puta
  floozy
  hooker
put a bun in the oven
  knock up
put a move on
  proposition
putana
  hooker
put one's ass on the line
  stick one's neck out
put a tuck in someone's tail
  take someone down a peg
put away
  clinch
  clobber
  scarf
  snuff
put someone away
  wow

put someone back
  set someone back

put one's back into it
  bust one's ass

put balls on
  jazz up

put one's cards on the table
  lay it on the line

put down
  knock

put down for
  peg

put one's feet up
  kick back

put one's foot in one's
    mouth
  goof

put hair on
  jazz up

put in an appearance
  show up

put in order
  fix up

put in plain English
  spell out

put in stitches
  break someone up

put in the bag
  clinch

put in the box
  wrap up

put in the can
  clinch

put in the picture
  briefed
  fill someone in

put someone in the picture
  spell out

put in the shade
  beat

put in words of one syllable
  spell out

put it across
  hack it

put it away
  scarf

put it in one's ear
  stick it

put it in your ear
  fuck you

put it on the line
  lay it on the line

put it over
  hack it

put it over on
  snow

put it to someone
  fuck

put it to the wood
  barrel

put me in the picture
  wise me up

put one's money on
  back

put someone's nose out of
    joint
  give someone a pain in the
    ass
  piss someone off
  take someone down a
    peg

puton
  phony

a put-on, "deception"

put someone on
  kid
  snow

put on airs
  put on the ritz

put on one's best bib and
    tucker
  doll up

put one over
  snow

put one toe in first
  run it up the flagpole

put on frills
  put on the ritz

put on ice
  clinch
  snuff

put on one's Sunday clothes
  doll up

put on swank
  put on the ritz

put on the crap list
  blackball

put on the ditch list
  blackball

put on the dog
  doll up
  put on the ritz

put on the feed bag
  scarf

put on the floor
  knock out

put on the frost
  cut
  give the cold shoulder

put on the gloves
  hassle

put on the high hat
  cut
  put on the ritz

put on the rack
  chew out

put on the ritz, "display
    wealth"

put on the shit list
  blackball

put out
 fuck
 kick in
put out like a light
 knock out
putrid
 crummy
 yucky
put the arm on
 bum
 bust
 put the bite on
put the blocks to
 clobber
 fuck
 lean on someone
put the chill on
 cut
put the claw on
 bust
 put the bite on
 squeal
put the collar on
 bust
put the eye on
 check out
put the fear of God into
 chew out
 scare the shit out of
put the finger on someone
 squeal
put the freeze on
 cut
 give the cold shoulder
put the gakk on
 chew out
put the grab on
 heist
put the hammer down
 barrel
 floor it

put the heat on
 crowd
 lean on someone
put the kibosh on
 nix
 screw up
put the lid on
 wrap up
put the lug on
 bum
 put the bite on
put the make on
 proposition
put them in the aisles
 go over with a bang
put the moves on
 proposition
put the pedal to the metal
 barrel
 floor it
put the screws to
 crowd
put the shit on
 knock
put the skids to
 bounce
 chuck
 clobber
 take someone down a peg
put the sleeve on
 bust
 put the bite on
put the slug on
 sock
put the squeeze on
 crowd
 lean on someone
put the touch on
 bum
 put the bite on

put the wood to
 kick ass
put through the wringer
 chew out
put together
 cook up
put one's two cent's worth
 in
 butt in
 open one's yap
putty arm
 glass arm
putty-head
 dope
put up
 rig
put up a squawk
 beef
put-up job, "dishonest
 prearrangement"
put someone wise
 fill someone in
put your money where your
 mouth is
 put up or shut up
putz
 asshole
 cock
 wimp
putz around
 goof off
putz around with
 fool around with
quack
 lude
 phony
quad
 lude
the quad
 the slammer

quail
 broad
 dish

Quakertown
 Philly

the quality
 the upper crust

quarrel
 hassle

quarter bag
 bag
 deck

quarter moon
 hash

quarter ounce
 bag

quas
 lude

queen
 gay

queer
 crazy
 flaky
 gay
 kinky
 phony
 screw up
 weird

queer duck
 oddball

queer in the head
 crazy

queer it with someone
 blow it with someone

quibble
 nit-pick

quick and dirty
 greasy spoon

quick one
 quickie

quick on the trigger
 goosy

quick-over
 the once-over

quick push
 floozy

quick sex
 quickie

quick shuffle
 razzle-dazzle

quickstep
 on the double

the quickstep
 the shits

quiff
 floozy
 hooker

quill
 works

quim
 ass
 cunt

quit cold
 walk out on

quit fucking the dog
 get the lead out

the quivers
 the jitters

R A
 piss-off

rabbi, "patron"

rabbit
 split

rabbit's foot
 security blanket

rabbity
 chicken
 wimpish

racehorse
 bug
 coke

racked
 cinched
 in the bag

racket
 flak
 hoopla
 racket, "occupation"
 scam

rack out
 chew out
 snooze

rack time
 sack time
 a snooze

rack up
 rack up, "achieve"
 total

racy
 dirty

rad
 great

radiclib
 pinko

radio
 ghetto box

radio performer
 disc jockey

rafts
 bundle

rag
 pasteboard

rag and a bone and a hank
 of hair
 broad

rag-bag
 mish-mash

rag-chewing
 gab
 schmooz

rage
 blowup

the rage
  hot
Raggedy Ann
  acid
raggedy-pants
  crummy
raghead
  camel-jammer
rag out
  doll up
rags
  threads
ragweed
  pot
raid
  rumble
rail it
  goof off
railroad
  bulldoze
railroad weed
  pot
raincoat
  rubber
raise a ruckus
  beef
  have a ball
  make a scene
raise a welt
  shoot up
raise Cain
  beef
  make a scene
raise someone's dander
  piss someone off
raise hell
  have a ball
  make a scene
  paint the town red
raise hell with
  chew out

raise the dickens with
  chew out
raise the roof
  beef
  have a ball
  make a scene
rake it in
  clean up
rake-off
  bite
rake over the coals
  chew out
rake up
  grab
rake up one side and down
      the other
  chew out
rally
  wingding
ralph up
  barf
ram-bam thank you ma'am
  quickie
ramble
  split
ramble-scramble
  fucked-up
rambunctious
  full of piss and vinegar
  rootin'-tootin'
ram it
  fuck you
  kiss my ass
  stick it
rammy
  horny
rampageous
  rootin'-tootin'
ramrod
  cock

ramshackle
  beat-up
randan
  binge
randy
  horny
rane
  coke
ranged
  antsy
Rangoon
  pot
rank
  the big leagues
  bug
  crummy
rank-out
  knock
ranky dank
  square
rap
  bad-mouth
  gab
  knock
  schmooz
  shoot the breeze
a rap
  zilch
rap club
  whorehouse
rapemobile
  pimpmobile
rap someone's knuckles
  give someone a slap on the
      wrist
rapping
  gab
  schmooz
rap session
  schmooz

425

rap with
  hang on
rare back
  bust one's ass
rarin' to go
  antsy
  full of piss and vinegar
  pumped
raspberry
  the bird
rassle up
  rustle up
rat
  asshole
  bad man
  scab
  snitch
  squeal
rat around
  goof off
rat-ass
  crummy
ratboy
  hit man
ratchet-mouth
  blabbermouth
rat-fink
  asshole
rat-fuck
  asshole
  cool
  goof off
  have a ball
  kinky
rathole
  dive
  dump
  stash
rat on
  squeal

rat out
  back out
  cop out
rat poison
  horse
rats
  Jeez
a rat's ass
  zilch
rat's nest
  snafu
ratter
  snitch
rattle
  gab
rattlebrain
  ditz
rattlebrained
  ditsy
rattle someone's cage
  bug
rattle cages
  make a scene
rattle someone's chain
  con
  snow
rattletongue
  blabbermouth
rattling
  great
ratty
  beat-up
  crummy
  yucky
raunch
  fuck
  porn
raunchy
  crummy
  dirty
  yucky

rave about
  flip
rave-up
  wingding
raving beauty
  dish
raving mad
  pissed off
raw
  dirty
  tough
raw deal
  bum rap
a raw deal
  the shaft
raw recruit
  rookie
razoo
  the bird
razor
  divvy
razz
  knock
the razz
  the bird
razzle-dazzle, "deception"
razzmatazz
  corn
  razzle-dazzle
  scam
reach back
  bust one's ass
read
  dig
read someone
  have someone's
    number
readiness
  in the pipeline

readjust
  rejigger

read someone like a book
  have someone's number

read me
  get me

read my lips
  fuck you
  get me

read the riot act
  chew out
  clamp down
  kick ass

the ready
  dough

ready to drop
  pooped

the real George
  humdinger

real guy
  the McCoy

really into it
  with it

really-truly
  honest-to-God

the real McCoy
  the McCoy

real money
  bundle

ream
  bugger
  chew out
  con
  fuck

reamer
  cock

reaming
  scam

ream out
  chew out

rear
  ass

recap
  rehash

receipts
  take

recommendation
  plug

red
  doll
  horse
  pot

red ass
  the blues

red-assed
  pissed off

red-carpet
  classy

a red cent
  zilch

red chicken
  horse

Red Cross
  M

Red Devil
  doll

redeye
  panther piss

red gunyon
  pot

redhanded
  dead to rights

red-head
  brick-top

red-hot
  antsy

red Lebanese
  hash

red-light
  hustle

redneck
  cracker
  hick
  redneck, "bigoted person"

red-necked
  pissed off

red oil
  hash

red rock
  horse

red up
  fix up

reefer
  dope
  joint
  junkie
  pot
  pothead

reefer hound
  pothead

reeling
  plastered

ref
  Blind Tom

reform
  go straight

register
  shoot up

regular
  fucking
  great
  honest-to-God

regular guy
  good guy

rehash, "review"

rehaul
  rejigger

reject
  dope
  nix

rejigger, "readjust"

relax
  kick back

relaxed
  laid-back

religionist
  Bible-banger

reltney
  cock

remain in place
  sit tight

remarkable
  a hell of a

remarkable person or thing
  humdinger

remote regions
  the boondocks

renege
  back out

reorganization
  house-cleaning

repeat
  come again

repeaters
  crooked dice

reprimand
  catch hell
  chew out

repulsive place
  dump

respond excitedly
  flip

restaurant
  greasy spoon

rest one's jaw
  shut up

retard
  dope

retool
  rejigger

return the compliment
  get even

Reuben
  hick

revamp
  rejigger

reveal
  go public

revenge
  get even

review
  brush up
  rehash

rev up
  jazz up

revved-up
  jazzed-up

RF
  asshole
  bum rap

RF session
  schmooz

rhubarb
  donnybrook
  flak
  free-for-all
  hassle

the rhubarbs
  the boondocks

rhythms
  bennies

rib
  broad
  bug
  knock

ribs
  chow

rib-tickler
  crack
  a howl

rice-belly
  Chink

Richard Roe
  Joe Blow

ricky-tick
  corn
  corny

ride
  ass
  bug
  fuck
  a fuck
  gut course
  jalopy
  knock

ride it out
  hang tough

ride old Sparky
  fry

ride shank's mare
  toddle

ride shotgun for
  go to bat for

ride the arm, "collect
    unmetered taxi fare"

riding the witch's broom
  hooked

riff
  act
  joint

a riffle
  a crack

rig
  rig, "prearrange
    dishonestly"
  works

rigged fight
  put-up job

right
 get me
 OK

righteous
 great

righteous bush
 pot

righteous dealer
 dealer

righteous egg
 good guy

right guy
 good guy

right-handed
 straight

right in there
 in there

righto
 OK

right on
 bet your ass
 OK
 on the nose
 way to go

the right stuff
 the McCoy

right there
 in there
 with it

right you are
 OK

rigmatick
 can of worms

rig-out
 threads

rig up
 doll up
 whomp up

rile
 bug
 piss someone off

riled up
 pissed off

ring
 buzz

ring-a ding
 razzle-dazzle

ring someone's bell
 wow

ring-ding
 dope

ringding-do
 can of worms

ring down the curtain
 wrap up

ringer
 double

ring in
 show up

ring off
 shut up

ringtail
 asshole
 jerk

ringtailed snorter
 humdinger

ring the bell
 come on strong
 hack it

rinky-dink
 corny
 crap
 crummy
 piddly

riot
 donnybrook
 free-for-all
 a hit

a riot
 a howl
 a laugh

rip
 bad-mouth
 binge
 a crack
 knock

rip-ass
 barrel

ripe
 dirty
 plastered

rip into
 blast
 chew out

ripoff
 heist
 scam

rip off
 con
 heist
 split

rip on
 knock

ripped
 high
 plastered

rippers
 bennies

ripping
 great

a ripple
 a crack

riproaring
 rootin'-tootin'

riproaring drunk
 plastered

ripsnorter
 a hit
 humdinger

risk
 stick one's neck out

risk all
  go for it

risky business
  a gamble

ritz
  swank

ritz it
  put on the ritz

ritz up
  doll up

ritzy
  classy
  great

rivets
  dough

roach
  butt
  joint

roach bender
  pothead

roach holder
  roach clip

road dog
  pal

road dope
  bennies

roaring drunk
  plastered

roast
  bad-mouth
  blast
  chew out
  fry
  knock

robbery
  caper
  heist

rock
  buck
  coke

horse
sock

rock and sock
  sock

rock 'em–sock 'em
  rootin'-tootin'

rocket
  pot

rocket fuel
  angel dust

rockhead
  dope

rocks
  balls

rock the boat
  make a scene

rocky
  green around the gills
  plastered
  rocky, "dazed"

rod
  cock
  hit man
  hot rod
  rod, "firearm"

rod boy
  hit man

rodded
  heeled

rodman
  hit man

Roger
  OK

rolf
  barf

roll
  ass
  con
  fuck
  a fuck
  heist

roller
  heist man

rollers
  crooked dice

roll in
  show up
  snooze

rolling in
  up to one's ass

rolling in it
  loaded

roll in the hay
  ass
  a fuck

roll over
  clobber

rolls
  ass

Romeo
  ladies' man

romp over
  clobber

the roof caves in
  hell breaks loose

rook
  con
  rookie

rooker
  con man

rookie
  greenhorn
  rookie, "neophyte"

rooking
  scam

room
  night spot

rooming house
  flophouse

roost
  pad

rooster
  stud
rooster brand
  big O
root
  butt
  cock
  joint
rooter
  fan
root for
  back
rootin'-tootin', "boisterous"
root tonic
  big O
rooty
  horny
rooty-toot
  corn
rope in
  con
  snow
roscoe
  rod
rosebud
  asshole
rose garden
  fruit salad
roses
  bennies
rosewood
  billy club
rosy
  cool
  plastered
rot
  bullshit
  suck
rotchy
  yucky

rotgut
  panther piss
rotten
  crummy
  yucky
rotten deal
  bum rap
  the shaft
rotten egg
  asshole
  bad man
rotter
  asshole
rough
  dirty
  hairy
rough-and-tumble
  rootin'-tootin'
rough as a cob
  hairy
rough-ass
  tough
rough customer
  goon
roughneck
  goon
rough stuff
  dirty tricks
  porn
rough up
  clobber
  rough up, "pummel"
round brown
  asshole
roundheels
  floozy
roundhouse
  sock
round the bend
  crazy

round up
  grab
rouser
  a hit
roust
  bug
  bulldoze
  bust
  roust, "harass"
  rumble
routine
  act
  line
Rover
  pooch
row
  donnybrook
  free-for-all
  hassle
row-de-dow
  donnybrook
rowdy-dowdy
  rootin'-tootin'
rowing with one oar in the
    water
  crazy
a row of pins
  zilch
royal
  great
royal blues
  acid
royal fucking
  bum rap
  the shaft
rub
  feel
  snuff
rubber
  hit man
  rubber, "condom"
  rubberneck

rubber boots
 rubber
rubber heel
 cop
 dick
rubberneck, "stare"
rubber room
 booby hatch
rubbish
 bullshit
rube
 greenhorn
 hick
rub off
 jack off
rub out
 clobber
 snuff
rub parlor
 whorehouse
rub one the wrong way
 give someone a pain in the
   ass
ruckus
 donnybrook
 flak
 free-for-all
 hassle
 hoopla
 wingding
ruction
 donnybrook
 free-for-all
 hassle
ruddy
 damn
rude
 cheeky
ruffian
 goon
 goon squad

rug, "wig"
rug ape
 kid
rugged
 hairy
ruined
 finished
 kaput
rule the roost
 boss
rum
 booze
rumbag
 lush
rumble
 donnybrook
 free-for-all
 heist
 rumble, "fight"
 rumble, "raid"
rum customer
 oddball
rum-dum
 crazy
 dope
 dumb
rumhound
 lush
rummage
 crap
rummed up
 plastered
rummy
 dumb
 lush
rum one
 oddball
rump
 ass

rumpot
 lush
rumpus
 donnybrook
 flak
 free-for-all
 hassle
 hoopla
 wingding
run
 boss
run after
 play up to
run a number
 snow
run a number on
 clobber
 con
runaround
 scam
run circles around
 beat
run down
 bad-mouth
 knock
 spell out
run in
 bust
run-in
 free-for-all
 hassle
run into the ground
 blow up
run it by again
 come again
run it up the flagpole and
   see if anybody salutes
 run it up the flagpole
running amok

run off at the
   mouth
 blow off
 bullshit
 gab
 shoot the breeze
run-of-the-mill
 bush
run on empty
 flop
run out
 break out
run out of gas
 fold
run out on
 walk out on
run ragged
 pooped
the runs
 the shits
runt
 shorty
runty
 little bitty
 piddly
run wide open
 barrel
rupture oneself
 bust one's ass
rural person
 hick
rush
 high
 a kick
rustle
 heist
 rustle up
rustle one's bustle
 get the lead out

rustler
 heist man
rustle up, "produce"
rusty-dusty
 ass
rutabaga
 buck
s
 pot
sack
 bag
 clobber
 deck
 fire
 sack time
the sack
 the axe
sack artist
 goof-off
sack drill
 sack time
 a snooze
sack out
 snooze
sack time
 sack time, "sleep"
 a snooze
sad
 crummy
sad apple
 jerk
 lightweight
 loser
 wimp
Sadie Thompson
 hooker
sad sack
 lightweight
 loser
 wimp

safe
 rubber
safecracker
 heist man
safety
 play it safe
 rubber
 works
sagebrusher
 horse opera
sail into
 blast
 chew out
sailor
 swabby
sakes alive
 Jeez
saleslady
 hooker
saloon
 gin mill
salt
 horse
salt and pepper
 pot
salty
 dirty
 feisty
salve
 dough
 soft soap
sam
 cop
sam how
 big O
sandbag
 bulldoze
 clobber
Sandoz
 acid

sandwich
  hero

san lo
  big O

San Quentin quail
  jail bait

Santa Claus
  sugar daddy

Santa Maria gold
  pot

sao
  asshole

sap
  dope
  jerk

sapfu
  snafu

saphead
  dope
  jerk

sapheaded
  dumb

sapperoo
  dope

sappo
  dope

sappy
  corny
  crazy
  dumb

sardine can
  mob scene

sashay
  toddle

sass, "impudence"

sassy
  cheeky
  smart-ass

satch
  blabbermouth

satch cotton
  works

satchel
  rig

satchelmouth
  bigmouth
  blabbermouth

satchelmouthed
  gabby

satiated
  fed-up

satisfactory
  cool

sativa
  pot

saturated
  plastered

Saturday night special
  rod

sauce
  sass

the sauce
  booze

sauced
  plastered

sausage
  cock
  dope
  pot

save your breath
  shut up

savvy
  dig
  get me
  smarts

saw
  sawbuck

sawbones, "physician"

sawbuck
  both hands
  sawbuck, "ten dollars"

sawed-off runt
  shorty

saw logs
  snooze

say amen to
  buy

says which
  come again
  izzatso

says who
  izzatso

say uncle
  fold

scab, "nonunion worker"

scads
  bundle
  scads, "large quantity"

scaffle
  angel dust

scag
  horse
  jerk

scale down
  shave

scalp
  clobber

scalper, "ticket seller"

scam
  con
  racket
  scam, "swindle"

the scam
  the straight dope

scammer
  con man

scanky
  crummy

scar
  horse

scarecrow, "ugly person"

scared stiff
 scared shitless

scaredy-cat
 chicken
 wimp

scare shitless
 scare the shit out of
 spook

scare stiff
 scare the shit out of
 spook

scare up
 grab
 rustle up

scarf
 chow
 chuck
 heist
 scarf, "eat"

scarf out
 pig out

scarf up
 scarf

scarper
 break out
 split

scary
 creepy

scat
 barrel
 horse

scatter
 hideaway

scatterbrain
 ditz

scatterbrained
 ditsy

scatty
 crazy
 ditsy

scene
 bag

schizo
 crazy

schiz out
 go crazy

schlechts
 horse

schlemazel
 lightweight

schlemiel
 dope
 jerk
 loser
 wimp

schlep
 butterfingers
 cart
 dope
 jerk

schlepper
 jerk
 nudnik

schleppy
 dumb
 ham-handed

schlock
 crap
 crummy
 horse

schlocky
 crummy
 schlocky, "inferior"

schloomp
 butterfingers
 dope
 goof off

schloomp around
 goof off

schmack
 horse

schmaltz
 corn

schmaltzy
 corny

schmear
 clobber
 soft-soap

the schmear
 the whole shebang

schmeck
 horse

schmegeggy
 bullshit
 dope

schmendrick
 dope
 loser
 wimp

schmo
 dope
 guy
 jerk
 loser
 wimp

schmooz
 schmooz, "conversation"
 shoot the breeze

schmuck
 asshole
 cock

schneider
 clobber

schnockered
 plastered

schnook
 jerk
 loser
 patsy

schnorrer
 moocher

schnozzola
 schnozz

schtoonk
 jerk

schvartze
 nigger

scissorbill
 scab

scoff
 chow
 heist
 scarf

sconce
 bean

scooch
 scrunch

scoop
 heist
 the poop
 snort

the scoop
 the poop

scoot
 barrel
 buck
 split

scope on
 check out

scope out
 check out

scorch
 barrel
 blast

score
 bite
 fuck
 hack it
 heist
 pay dirt
 score, "buy narcotics"
 score, "loot"
 take

the score
 the bottom line
 the damage

score with
 fuck

Scotch
 chintzy

Scotsman
 tightwad

scott
 horse

scout
 guy

scrag
 clobber
 fuck
 scarecrow
 snuff

scram
 break out
 split

scramble-brained
 dumb

scrap
 chuck
 free-for-all
 hassle
 scrub

scrape by
 get by

scrape up
 grab
 rustle up

scrap-heap
 chuck

scrap iron
 panther piss

scrappy
 feisty

scratch
 dough
 scrub

scratch someone's back
 soft-soap

scratch house
 flophouse

scraunch
 clobber

a scream
 a howl
 a laugh

the screaming meemies
 the jitters
 the shakes

screech
 panther piss

screw
 ass
 con
 cop
 fuck
 a fuck
 split

screw around
 goof off

screw around with
 fool around with

screwball
 crazy
 nut
 oddball

screwed over
 screwed

screwed-up
 fucked-up

screwing
 ass

a screwing
 the shaft

screw-loose
  glitch
  nut
  oddball
screw off
  goof off
  jack off
screw-off
  goof-off
screw over
  fuck
screw the pooch
  goof off
screw up
  fuck up
  goof
  screw up, "spoil"
screw-up
  boner
  fuck-up
  snafu
screw with
  fool around with
screwy
  cockeyed
  crazy
  flaky
  fucked-up
  plastered
screw you
  fuck you
  kiss my ass
scrimmage
  free-for-all
scrip
  buck
scrog
  fuck
scronched
  plastered

scrooch
  scrunch
Scrooge
  tightwad
scrounge
  bum
  rustle up
scrounger
  moocher
scrounge up
  bum
  rustle up
scroungy
  yucky
scrub
  bush
  duffer
  gofer
  scrub
scrub the slate clean
  go back to square one
scruff
  get by
scruff along
  get by
scruffy
  crummy
scrump
  fuck
scrumptious
  great
scrunch up
  scrunch
scrunge
  mung
scud
  scut work
scuffle
  free-for-all
  get by

scuffle along
  get by
scum
  asshole
  cum
  sleazebag
scumbag
  asshole
  rubber
  sleazebag
scum of the earth
  asshole
scumsucker
  asshole
  cocksucker
  sleazebag
scumsucking
  yucky
scunge
  mung
scurve
  asshole
  sleazebag
scut
  scut work
  sleazebag
scuttle
  nigger
scuttlebutt
  dirt
  the poop
scut work, "tedious work"
scuzz
  asshole
  mung
  scarecrow
scuzzbag
  asshole
  sleazebag
scuzzy
  yucky

seagoing bellhop
  leatherneck
sea lawyer
  latrine lawyer
sealing wax
  big O
  hash
search
  frisk
seat
  ass
seat-man
  shill
a sec
  a jiffy
second fiddle
  gofer
second job
  moonlight
second-rater
  duffer
second-story man
  heist man
second-stringer
  gofer
  lightweight
secret
  on the QT
secret associate
  shill
section eight
  nut
secure
  knock off
security blanket, "source of
  emotional security"
see a man about a dog
  check the plumbing
seed
  butt

seedy
  beat-up
  green around the gills
seeing pink elephants
  plastered
see red
  blow one's top
see Steve
  snort
see where one is coming
    from
  dig
seguro que
  bet your ass
self-interest
  take care of numero uno
self-starter
  eager beaver
sell
  con
  scam
  talk someone into
sell a bill of goods
  con
  snow
sell down the river
  fuck
sell on
  talk someone into
sell out
  fuck
  squeal
sell-out
  double cross
semen
  cum
seminude
  cheesecake
semolia
  dope

send
  blow grass
  wow
send away with a flea in his
    (or her) ear
  take someone down a peg
send it home
  shoot up
send to hell in a handbasket
  screw up
send to kingdom come
  snuff
send to the showers
  fire
send up
  blow grass
  spoof
send west
  snuff
sensaysh
  a hit
sent
  high
sentimental
  corny
sentimentality
  corn
  tear-jerker
sent to the showers
  finished
sergeant
  top-kick
serious
  great
serious money
  bundle
seriousness
  get down to brass tacks
  no fooling
  play hardball

service stripe
  hash mark
sesky
  sexy
sess
  pot
session
  stanza
set
  a fix
  schmooz
  works
set someone back, "cost"
set in concrete
  carved in stone
set in one's ways
  bullheaded
set of threads
  threads
set of wheels
  hot rod
  jalopy
set on one's ass
  high
set over
  snuff
set sail
  split
set the world on fire
  come on strong
settle
  snuff
settle accounts
  get even
settle someone's hash
  clobber
  fix someone
  kick ass
  snuff
  take someone down a peg

settle the score
  get even
set-to
  free-for-all
  hassle
set to rights
  fix up
setup
  cinch
  gut course
  pad
  patsy
  put-up job
set up
  frame
  rig
severe
  tough
sewed up
  cinched
sewer
  shoot up
sew up
  clinch
  wrap up
sex
  AC-DC
  ass
  balls
  basket
  beaver
  blow
  blow job
  bugger
  cheat
  cherry
  clit
  cock
  cocksucker
  cock-teaser
  come
  come out
  cruise

cum
cunt
cunt-lapper
dyke
feel
fingerfuck
floozy
French kiss
fuck
fur pie
gang bang
gay
grab-ass
hard-on
have hot pants
hooker
horny
hot pants
hung
jack off
jail bait
kinky
neck
pop someone's cherry
porn
proposition
quickie
rubber
sexy
sleep around
straight
stud
swing
whorehouse
sex act
  a fuck
sex job
  dish
  floozy
sex pot
  dish
  hunk
sexual arouser
  cock-teaser

439

sexual desire
  hot pants
sexually attractive
  sexy
sexually promiscuous male
  stud
sexual promiscuity
  sleep around
sexual search
  cruise
sex wagon
  pimpmobile
sexy
  great
  horny
  sexy, "sexually attractive"
shabby
  dirty
shackup
  floozy
shack up
  swing
shade
  nigger
shades, "sunglasses"
shadow
  nigger
  tail
shady
  dumb
shady business
  dirty tricks
shaft
  fuck
the shaft
  bum rap
  the shaft, "unfair
    treatment"
shafted
  screwed

shag
  bug
  fuck
  a fuck
  great
  split
  toddle
shag ass
  split
shagger
  tail
shake
  cop out
  frisk
a shake
  a jiffy
shake a leg
  get the lead out
shakedown
  scam
shake down
  bum
  con
  frisk
  put the bite on
shake hands on
  buy
shake it
  get the lead out
the shakes
  the jitters
  the shakes, "delirium
    tremens"
shake the money tree
  clean up
shake-up
  house-cleaning
shaky
  green around the gills
shallow-brained
  dumb

shamus
  cop
  snitch
shank it
  toddle
shanks
  pins
shape
  build
shape up
  clean up one's act
share
  bite
  piece
shark
  card sharp
  con man
sharp
  card sharp
  con man
  cool
  great
  with it
  works
sharpen up
  brush up
sharper
  con man
sharpie
  card sharp
  con man
  dude
sharpster
  card sharp
shat on
  screwed
shatting on one's uppers
  broke
shave, "decrease"
shaved
  plastered

shaver
  guy
shebang
  dive
the shebang
  the whole shebang
shee-it
  Jeez
sheen
  jalopy
sheeny
  kike
sheep-dip
  panther piss
sheesh
  hash
  Jeez
sheets
  angel dust
sheik
  dude
  ladies' man
shekels
  dough
shell
  cough up
shellac
  clobber
  panther piss
shell game
  scam
shell out
  blow
  cough up
  kick in
  pick up the tab
shemale
  broad
shemozzle
  donnybrook
  flak

hoopla
  split
shenanigans
  horseplay
Sherlock
  dick
she-she
  broad
shiever
  snitch
shikker
  lush
  plastered
shill
  billy club
  flack
  shill, "secret associate"
shiller
  shill
shim
  square
shindig
  wingding
shindy
  binge
  donnybrook
  free-for-all
  hassle
  hoopla
  wingding
shine
  cop out
  cut
  panther piss
shiner
  black eye
shine up
  brush up
shine up to
  brown-nose
  play up to

shirker
  goof-off
shirty
  feisty
  pissed off
shishi
  hash
shit
  asshole
  bullshit
  crap
  dope
  horse
  Jeez
  pot
  shit, "defecate"
  shit, "excrement"
  zilch
a shit, "defecation"
shit a brick
  blow one's top
  make a scene
shitass
  asshole
  jerk
shit bricks
  blow one's top
shit bullets
  panic
shitcan
  can
  chuck
shit-can
  scrub
the shit end of the stick
  the shaft
shitface
  asshole
shitfaced
  plastered
shit-for-brains
  dope

shit for the birds
  bullshit
  chickenshit

shit green
  panic

shithead
  asshole

shitheaded
  dumb

shitheel
  asshole

the shit hits the fan
  hell breaks loose

shithole
  dump

shithook
  asshole

shithouse
  can
  dump

shit in high cotton
  eat high on the hog

shit in your hat
  fuck you

shitkicker
  hick

shitkickers
  boondockers

shit-kicking
  tough

shit list, "undesired
    persons"

shit-list
  blackball

shit on
  screwed

shit on wheels
  hot damn
  hot shot

shit on you
  fuck you

shit or get off the pot
  fish or cut bait

shit out of luck
  kaput
  out of luck

shit one's pants
  panic

the shits, "diarrhea"

shitstick
  asshole

shitstorm
  snafu

shitsure
  bet your ass
  for sure

shitter
  asshole
  can

shitting one's pants
  scared shitless

shitty
  crummy
  yucky

the shitty end of the stick
  the shaft

shitwork
  scut work

shivery
  creepy

shlong
  cock

shoe
  cop
  white shoe

shoe polish
  panther piss

shoes
  boondockers
  kicks
  sneakers

shoo-in
  cinch

shook up
  jittery

shoot
  blow
  come
  Jeez
  plug
  shoot up

shoot someone a line
  soft-soap

shoot one's cookies
  barf

shoot down
  clobber
  screw up

shoot from the hip
  go off half-cocked

shoot gravy
  shoot up

shooting gallery, "narcotics
    venue"

shooting iron
  rod

the shooting match
  the whole shebang

shoot oneself in the foot
  cut one's own throat

shoot one's load
  come

shoot one's lunch
  barf

shoot off one's mouth
  blow off
  gab

shoot on
  knock

shoot the breeze, "chat"

shoot the bull
  blow off

gab
shoot the breeze

shoot the crap
blow off
shoot the breeze

shoot the works
bust one's ass
go for it

shoot up, "inject
narcotics"

shoot one's wad
come
go for it

shopping bag lady
bum

shopping list
laundry list

short
bag
broke
deck
jalopy
snort

short arm
cock

the short end of the stick
the shaft

short heist
heist

short order
a fix

short person
shorty

short piece
bag
deck

the shorts, "lack of
money"

short time
a jiffy

short-witted
dumb

shorty, "short person"

shot
bag
big shot
a fix
kaput
knock
on the blink
plastered
pooped
snort
sock

a shot
a clip
a crack

shot down
finished

shot down in flames
kaput
out of luck

shot in the arm
pick-me-up

shot up
high

shout
stick out like a sore thumb

shouter
broad

shout up
spotlight

shove it
fuck you
kiss my ass
stick it

shovelhead
dope

shoveling the black stuff
hooked

shovel it in
pig out

shovel the shit
bullshit

shove off
split

show
show up

show a leg
get the lead out

showboat
grandstand
grandstander

shower cap
rubber

showoff
grandstander

show off
grandstand

show the gate
fire

show up
beat
blow
show up, "arrive"

shpilkes
the jitters

shriek
horse

shrimp
jerk
shorty

shrink, "psychiatrist"

shrinker
shrink

shtarker
goon

shtick
act

shtoonk
asshole

shtup
  ass
  fuck
shuck
  bluff
  bullshit
  chuck
  con
  goof off
  kid
  kid around
  wing it
shuffle
  toddle
shuffle along
  split
shuffler
  con man
shush your mouth
  shut up
shut down
  crash
shuteye
  sack time
  a snooze
shut one's face
  shut up
shut out
  clobber
shut up, "command to stop
    talking"
shut up, "stop talking"
shut up shop
  knock off
shuzit
  pot
shvantz
  cock
shylock
  loan shark

shyster
  asshole
  con man
  shyster, "lawyer"
sick
  crazy
  weird
  yucky
sick as a dog
  green around the gills
sickie
  nut
  oddball
sick in the head
  crazy
sicko
  crazy
  nut
  oddball
  weird
  yucky
sick of
  fed-up
sickroom
  weird
sicksicksick
  crazy
  weird
  yucky
sick up
  barf
sidekick
  pal
side-splitter
  belly laugh
  a howl
sidestep
  weasel
sidetrack
  bust
sidewalk susie
  hooker

sidewheeler
  southpaw
sidewinder
  goon
sight
  scarecrow
sign in
  show up
sign off
  shut up
sign off on
  buy
sigoggling
  cockeyed
silk
  whitey
silk-stocking
  classy
Silly Billy
  ditz
simmer
  blow one's top
simmer down
  cool it
simoleons
  buck
  dough
simon-pure
  honest-to-God
simp
  dope
  jerk
simple as ABC
  easy as pie
since Hector was a pup
  ages
sing
  open one's yap
  squeal
  warble

sing another tune
  come down a peg

singer
  snitch

singing
  high

singing the blues
  down

single
  buck

single out
  zero in

sing out
  open one's yap
  squeal

sink
  clobber
  screw up

sinsemilla
  pot

sip
  blow grass

sis
  broad
  sissy

sissified
  chicken
  wimpish

sissy
  broad
  chicken
  gay
  sissy, "effeminate male"

sissy-pants
  sissy

sister
  blood
  broad
  M

sit in the catbird seat
  eat high on the hog

sit on one's hands
  goof off

sit pretty
  eat high on the hog

sit still for
  buy

sit tight
  hide out
  sit tight, "remain in place"
  sit tight, "wait"

sitting duck
  patsy

sitting pretty
  eat high on the hog
  in the driver's seat

situation
  a fix

Siwash
  cow college

six feet up a bull's ass
  loaded

sixgun
  rod

six of one and half a dozen
    of the other
  standoff

sixteenth
  bag

six ways to Sunday
  cockeyed
  flat-out

size up
  check out

sizzle
  blow one's top
  fry

SK
  hick

skag
  butt

jerk
scarecrow

skank
  hooker
  scarecrow

skanky
  yucky

skate
  goof off
  split

skedaddle
  break out
  split

skeezer
  broad
  hooker

skell
  bum

skewgee
  cockeyed
  fucked-up
  half-assed

skid
  horse

skiddoo
  split

Skid Row bum
  bum

skillet
  nigger

skimble-skamble
  fucked-up

skin
  beat
  buck
  cheesecake
  clobber
  con
  rubber

skin alive
  blast
  clobber

fix someone
  kick ass

skin along
  barrel

skinch
  smidgen

skin-diver
  cocksucker

skin flick
  blue movie

skinflint
  chintzy

skin flute
  cock

skin game
  scam

skinhead
  baldie

skin lesion
  zit

skinner
  con man

skinning
  scam

the **skinny**
  the poop
  the straight dope

skinny down
  shave

skin out
  break out
  split

skin pop
  a fix
  shoot up

skins
  dough

skin-search
  frisk

skint
  broke

skin through
  get by

skip
  break out
  cut
  give a miss
  split

skip out on
  walk out on

skipper
  boss

Skipper
  Jack

skirt
  broad

skirt-chaser
  ladies' man
  stud

ski-trip
  a fix

skivvies
  undies

skoofus
  joint

skookum
  great

skosh
  smidgen

skullduggery
  dirty tricks
  monkey business

skunk
  asshole
  beat
  clobber
  scarecrow

skunk out of
  con

skygodlin
  cockeyed

sky out
  split

sky rockets
  bennies

sky rug
  rug

sky up
  split

sky-west
  fucked-up

slab
  buck

slack
  goof off

slacker
  goof-off

slag
  bad-mouth
  horse
  knock

slam
  bad-mouth
  do
  knock
  sock

the **slam**
  the slammer

slam-bang
  half-assed
  rootin'-tootin'

the **slammer, "jail"**

slanging match
  hassle

slant
  the once-over

slant-eye
  gook

slant-eyes
  Chink**

slap
  knock
  smack
slap and tickle
  grab-ass
slap-bang
  smack
slapdash
  half-assed
slap five
  give five
slap-happy
  punch-drunk
slap in the face
  knock
slap on
  on the nose
slash
  broad
  dish
slash-and-gash film
  chiller
slasher
  chiller
  kid
slaughter them
  go over with a bang
slay
  break someone up
  clobber
  wow
sleaze
  bum
  crap
  sleazebag
sleazeball
  asshole
  sleazebag
  yucky

sleazy
  dirty
  yucky
sled
  bike
sleep
  coke
  sack time
  sleep around, "be sexually
    promiscuous"
  snooze
  a snooze
sleep around
  swing
sleeper
  doll
  horse
  long shot
sleep with someone
  fuck
Sleepy Town
  Philly
sleighrider
  junkie
sleighriding
  high
sleuthhound
  dick
slewed
  plastered
slice
  bite
  piece
slice-and-dice film
  chiller
slice of the melon
  piece
slick
  great
slick chick
  dish

slicker
  con
  con man
  dude
  smoothie
  snow
slicker game
  scam
slick up
  doll up
slide
  split
slim
  butt
slimeball
  sleazebag
sling the bull
  blow off
  bullshit
slinky
  sexy
slip
  kick in
slip someone
  stake someone to
slip a cog
  crack up
  goof
slip one's cable
  croak
slipper
  clean up one's act
  go straight
slip the info
  fill someone in
slip one's trolley
  go crazy
slip-up
  boner
  glitch

447

slit
 cunt
slob
 butterfingers
 fuck-up
 jerk
 lightweight
 loser
 sleazebag
slonchwise
 cockeyed
slop
 corn
slop chute
 asshole
slope
 gook
 split
slope-out
 cinch
sloppy
 corny
 fucked-up
 half-assed
sloppy Joe's
 greasy spoon
sloshed
 plastered
slot
 cunt
slow coach
 dope
sludge
 goo
sludgeball
 sleazebag
sluff
 goof off
sluff course
 gut course

slug
 clobber
 snort
 sock
a slug
 a clip
slug down
 guzzle
slugfest
 donnybrook
slugged
 plastered
slug it out
 hassle
slug-nutty
 punch-drunk
slurp
 blow
 guzzle
 snort
slurpy
 great
slush
 corn
slushy
 corny
slut's wool
 dust bunny
slutty
 sexy
smack
 horse
 pow
 smack, "exactly"
 sock
a smack
 a clip
 a crack
smack dab
 smack

smacker
 buck
smackhead
 junkie
smacko
 pow
smack up
 total
small
 little bitty
small amount
 smidgen
small beer
 chicken feed
 chickenshit
small-beer
 bush
 piddly
small change
 chicken feed
 chickenshit
 piddly
small potatoes
 chicken feed
 chickenshit
 lightweight
small-time
 bush
 piddly
the small time
 the bush leagues
small-timer
 lightweight
small town
 jerk town
smart aleck
 smart-ass
smart-alecky
 cheeky
 smart-ass

smart-ass
  cheeky
smart-ass, "impudent"
smart-ass, "impudent
    person"
smarten
  fill someone in
smarten up
  brush up
  fill someone in
  wise up
the smart money, "wise
    prediction"
smart piece
  a country mile
smarts, "intelligence"
the smart set
  the upper crust
a smart spell
  ages
smarty
  smart-ass
smartypants
  smart-ass
smash
  crash
  hash
  a hit
  sock
smashed
  high
  plastered
smashing
  great
smash mouth
  neck
smashup
  crash
smash up
  total

smear
  beat
  clobber
  sock
the smear
  the whole shebang
smeck
  horse
smecker
  junkie
smell
  suck
smeller
  schnozz
smitch
  smidgen
smoke
  barrel
  blow one's top
  bullshit
  butt
  clobber
  dope
  nigger
  plug
  pot
a smoke, "act of smoking"
smoke and joke
  goof off
smoke and mirrors
  razzle-dazzle
smoke marijuana
  blow grass
smoke out, "discover"
Smokey the Bear
  cop
the smoky seat
  the chair
smolder
  blow one's top

smooch
  heist
  neck
smooth
  great
smoothie
  dude
  hunk
  ladies' man
smoothie, "sophisticated
    person"
smother
  clobber
smuck
  con
  fuck
snaffle
  heist
snafu
  boner
  fucked-up
  on the blink
  screw up
  snafu, "confusion"
snag
  catch
  grab
snake
  floozy
  scarecrow
snakebit
  kaput
snake-bitten
  kaput
snake poison
  panther piss
snap
  cinch
  clout
  go crazy
  pizzazz

snap one's cookies
  barf

snap it up
  get the lead out

snapper
  dish
  punch line

snappers
  choppers

snappy
  full of piss and vinegar
  snappy, "stylish"
  zingy

snap to it
  get the lead out

snarf
  jerk

snarky
  feisty

snarl up
  screw up

snatch
  broad
  cunt
  heist

snatch defeat from the jaws
    of victory
  cut one's own throat

snazz
  swank

snazz up
  doll up

snazzy
  classy
  great
  snappy

sneaks
  sneakers

sniff
  snort

sniff out
  smoke out

sniffy
  snooty

snifter
  snort

snipe
  butt

snit
  swivet

snitch
  heist
  snitch, "informer"
  squeal

snitzy
  classy

snobbish
  snooty

snooker
  con
  snow

snooks
  honey

snookums
  honey

snoop
  kibitzer

snoot
  cut
  give the cold shoulder
  schnozz

snooty, "snobbish"

snooze, "sleep"

a snooze, "sleep"

snop
  pot

snorbs
  tits

snorf
  scarf

snort
  coke
  snort, "drink"
  snort, "inhalation"

snorter
  a hit
  humdinger

snotnose
  kid
  rookie
  young squirt

snottiness
  chutzpa

snotty
  cheeky
  snooty

snout
  schnozz

snow
  coke
  horse
  snow, "deceive"

snowball
  bulldoze
  coke

a snowball's chance in hell
  a fat chance

snowbird
  junkie

snowed
  high

snowed under
  up to one's ass

snow flakes
  coke

snow job
  line
  scam
  snow

snowmobile
  snort

snozzle
  schnozz
  snort
snozzled
  plastered
the snozzlewobblies
  the shakes
snub
  the cold shoulder
  cut
  give the cold shoulder
snubby
  rod
snuff
  buck
  clobber
  snuff, "kill"
snuff film
  chiller
snuff out
  clobber
  snuff
snuffy
  plastered
snug
  rod
snuggy
  dish
snurge
  goof off
soak
  binge
  lush
  sock
soaked
  plastered
so-and-so
  asshole
  blankety-blank
soap
  lude

soap opera
  soft soap
S O B
  asshole
sob story
  tear-jerker
sob stuff
  corn
  tear-jerker
social club
  blind pig
social prestige
  classy
sock
  blast
  clobber
  clout
  knock
  sock, "punch" (v and n)
sock away
  stash
sockeroo
  a hit
  humdinger
sock it to
  blast
  fix someone
sock line
  punch line
socko
  great
  pow
sodbuster
  hick
sodomize
  bugger
sod you
  fuck you
  kiss my ass

soft
  dumb
  easy as pie
soft-ass
  wimpish
softball
  bush
  doll
  piddly
softie, "compliant person"
soft in the head
  dumb
soft-pedal, "de-emphasize"
soft soap
  soft soap, "flattery"
  stroke
soft-soap, "flatter"
soft touch
  softie
softy
  sissy
sol
  cooler
S O L
  kaput
  out of luck
solar plexus
  belly
soldier
  buck private
  button man
  gangster
  goof off
sole
  hash
solid
  great
  honest-to-God
  with it
some
  a hell of a

some skin
 mitt

something
 humdinger

something else
 great
 a hit
 humdinger
 the most

something fierce
 flat-out
 like hell

something in the sock
 case dough

something on the ball
 smarts

something screwy
 glitch

something to write home
   about
 a hit
 humdinger

song
 line

song and dance
 flack
 line

son lo tar
 big O

son of a bee
 guy

son of a bitch
 asshole
 back-breaker
 a bitch
 guy

son of a gun
 guy

son of one
 hash

sophisticated person
 smoothie

soppy
 corny

sore
 pissed off

sorehead
 kvetch

soreheaded
 feisty

sorry
 half-assed

a sort of a
 bush

sort out
 fix up
 spell out
 work out

so-so
 bush

so's your old man
 fuck you

sot
 lush

soul brother
 blood

soul kiss
 French kiss

soul sister
 blood

sound
 the bird
 bug

sound off
 gab
 shoot the breeze

sound the horn
 honk

soupbone
 wing

souped-up
 jazzed-up

souped-up job
 hot rod

soupy
 corny

sourpuss
 kvetch
 scarecrow

souse
 guzzle
 lush

soused
 plastered

Southerner
 cracker

south of the border
 kaput
 schlocky

southpaw, "left-handed
   person"

south side
 ass

so what else is new
 so what
 that's the way the cookie
   crumbles

sozzled
 plastered

space bandit
 flack

space cadet
 junkie
 nut
 oddball

spaced
 high
 in a fog

spaced out
 crazy

in a fog

space-out
nut
oddball

spacey
high
in a fog

spade
nigger

spaghetti
wop

spang
smack

Spanish athlete
bigmouth

spank
tan

spanking
great

spar
hassle

spare tire
potbelly
spare tire, "fat waist"

sparkle plenties
bennies

spark plug
eager beaver

spastic
dope
dumb
oddball

spat
hassle

spazz
dope
dumb
oddball

spazzy
dumb
weird

speak
open one's yap

speakeasy
blind pig

speak for itself
stick out like a sore thumb

speak nonsense
bullshit

spear-carrier
gofer

specimen
cookie

speck bum
bum

speckled birds
bennies

specs, "eyeglasses"

speed
barrel
bennies
lickety-split

speedball
coke
junkie

spell out, "explain"

spend extravagantly
blow

spicy
dirty

spiel
flack
gab
line

spieler
blabbermouth

spiff
swank

spiffed
plastered

spiff up
doll up

spiffy
classy
great

spike
scrub
works

spiked
high

spike up
shoot up

spill
blow
lay it on the line

spill one's guts
blow
lay it on the line
let it all hang out
squeal

spill the beans
squeal

spinach
bullshit
crap

spin one's wheels
goof off

spit
zilch

spit and image
double

spitball
knock

spit it out
let it all hang out

spit tacks
blow one's top
make a scene

spitting image
 double

spiv
 moocher

spizzerinctum
 guts
 pizzazz

splash
 bennies
 high
 shoot up

splashy
 glitzy

splice the main brace
 guzzle

splint
 joint

split
 bite
 break out
 split, "depart"

split a gut
 break up
 bust one's ass

split hairs
 nit-pick

split some buns
 bugger

split the scene
 split

splivins
 bennies

splurgy
 glitzy

spoil
 screw up
 snuff

spoiling
 antsy

spondulics
 dough

sponge
 lush
 moocher

spoof
 kid
 snow
 spoof, "lampoon"

a spoof
 a put-on

spook
 nigger
 oddball
 scare the shit out of
 spook, "frighten"

spooked
 scared shitless

spoon
 bag
 deck
 neck
 works

spoony
 ditz

sport
 bingle
 Blind Tom
 bug
 chapter
 dude
 guy
 Jack
 ladies' man
 playboy
 stanza

sporting house
 whorehouse

sporting proposition
 a gamble

sports
 homer
 jock

sports official
 Blind Tom

spot
 bind
 bit
 dive
 snort
 zero in

spot someone
 stake someone to

spot as
 peg

spotlight
 spotlight, "emphasize"
 zero in

spouter
 blabbermouth

spout off
 blow off
 gab

spread
 a feed
 fuck

spread oneself
 bust one's ass

spread it on thick
 bullshit
 soft-soap

spree
 binge

springbutt
 eager beaver

spring for
 pick up the tab

sprout
 kid

sproutsy
 flaky

sprout wings
 clean up one's act

spruce up
 doll up

sprung
  high
  plastered
spudge around
  get on the ball
  get the lead out
spunk
  clout
  come
  cum
  guts
  pizzazz
spunky
  gutsy
spurt
  come
squab
  broad
square
  on the level
  smack
  square, "conformist"
  square, "conformistic"
  straight
square accounts
  get even
square apple
  straight
square deal, "fair
    treatment"
square dealer
  good guy
squarehead
  kraut
square John
  good guy
  Joe Blow
square joint
  butt
square one
  it's a new ball game

square peg
  excess baggage
square shooter
  good guy
squaresville
  square
squat
  pad
  shit
  zilch
a squat
a shit
squat hot
  fry
squaw
  broad
  old woman
squawk
  beef
  snitch
  squeal
squawk box
  bitch box
squeak by
  get by
squeaker
  cliffhanger
  snitch
squeak through
  get by
squeaky clean
  clean
  square
squeal
  snitch
  squeal, "tattle"
squeal like a stuck
    pig
  beef

squeeze
  scrunch
squeezebox, "accordion"
squiffed
  plastered
squiffy-eyed
  plastered
squint
  the once-over
squirrel
  acid
  banger
  cunt
  nut
  oddball
  stash
squirrel away
  stash
squirrel-food
  nut
squirrely
  crazy
  flaky
squirt
  guy
  jerk
  kid
  shorty
  young squirt
  zilch
squish
  softie
squishy
  corny
a stab
  a crack
stabber
  works
stack
  joint
  rig

stack asses
  kick ass

stacked
  built

stack some Zs
  snooze

stack the cards
  play dirty
  rig

stack up
  figure
  rack up
  total

stage a walkout
  walk

staggerer
  a hit

stake
  case dough

staker
  angel

stake someone to, "give"

stall around
  goof off
  stall

stallion
  dish
  stud

stand
  set someone back

stand someone
  stake someone to

stand behind
  back
  go to bat for

stand for it
  take it

stand one's ground
  sit tight

standoff, "deadlock"

standoffish
  snooty

standout
  a hit

stand pat
  sit tight

stand still for
  buy
  eat up
  play ball

stand the gaff
  hang tough
  take it

stand-up
  gutsy

stand up and be counted
  take it

stand up and take it
  bite the bullet

stand up for
  go to bat for

stand up to
  take on

stanza
  chapter
  stanza, "division of a
    game"

star
  ace

starch
  clout
  pizzazz

starchy
  full of piss and vinegar

star dust
  angel dust

stare
  rubberneck

stare one in the face
  stick out like a sore thumb

star-fucker
  groupie

starker
  goon

starkers
  bare-ass

start from scratch
  go back to square one

stash
  bag
  park
  stash, "conceal"

stash away
  stash

state
  swivet

state of the art
  with it

the state pen
  the slammer

static
  flak

stats
  the book

stay loose
  cool it

stay put
  sit tight

stay the course
  take it

steal
  heist

steam
  blow one's top
  clout
  piss someone off
  pizzazz

steamed
  horny
  pissed off

steamed up
  antsy
  pissed off

steamroller
  bulldoze
  clobber

steamy
  dirty
  sexy

steer
  tip

steerer
  shill

stem
  works

stems
  pins

stemwinder
  eager beaver
  humdinger

stemwinding
  high-powered

stencil
  joint

step on one's dick
  fuck up
  goof

step on it
  barrel
  fuck up
  get the lead out

step on the gas
  barrel

step out on someone
  cheat

stepped-up job
  hot rod

step up
  hike

stern
  ass

Stetson
  lid

stew
  binge
  blow one's top
  blowup
  flak
  lush
  piss-off
  snafu
  sweat
  swivet

stewbum
  bum
  lush

stewed
  plastered

stick
  beanpole
  con
  fogy
  hang tough
  jerk
  joint
  shill

stick country
  the boondocks

stick for
  bum

stick in the mud
  fogy

stick in there
  hang tough

stick it
  fuck you
  kiss my ass
  stick it, "expression of
    defiance"

stick it out
  hang tough
  take it

stick it to
  fix someone

hold someone's feet to the
  fire

stick man
  cop

stick one's neck out, "risk"

stick one's nose into
  butt in

stick of tea
  joint

stick out a mile
  stick out like a sore thumb

sticks
  pins

the sticks
  the boondocks

stick to one's guns
  sit tight

stick to one's knitting, "not
  meddle"

stick to your knitting
  lay off

stickum
  goo

stickup
  heist

stick up for
  back
  go to bat for

stickup man
  heist man

stick with it
  take it

sticky
  corny
  hairy

sticky-fingered, "thievish"

sticky wicket
  bad news
  bind

stiff
  bum
  bust
  con
  flop
  fuck
  guy
  jerk
  phony
  plastered
  rough up
  stiff, "corpse"
  working stiff
stiff-arm
  rough up
stiffen
  knock out
stiffneck
  mule
stiffnecked
  bullheaded
stiff one
  hard-on
stimulant
  pick-me-up
sting
  con
  heist
  scam
stinger
  catch
  con man
stingy
  chintzy
stink
  beef
  flak
  suck
stinker
  asshole
stinking
  crummy

  damn
  loaded
  plastered
  yucky
stinking drunk
  plastered
stinking rich
  loaded
stinking with
  filthy with
stink-list
  blackball
stinko
  crummy
  plastered
stink to high heaven
  suck
stinkweed
  pot
the stir
  the slammer
stir around
  get on the ball
stir bird
  con
stir-bugs
  stir-crazy
stir one's stumps
  get the lead out
a stitch
  a howl
  a laugh
stitched
  plastered
stoked
  tickled
stoke up
  scarf
stoking
  great

stomach
  belly
  potbelly
stomach Steinway
  squeezebox
stomp
  clobber
  rough up
stompass
  tough
stompers
  boondockers
stone
  fucking
  honest-to-God
  stone, "totally"
stone broke
  broke
stoned
  high
  plastered
stone fox
  dish
stoner
  junkie
stonies
  hot pants
stony
  broke
stooge
  brown-nose
  gofer
  shill
stooge around
  stall
stool
  snitch
  squeal
stop functioning
  go kerflooey

stop talking
  shut up

stop the show
  go over with a bang

storch
  guy
  patsy

Storch
  Joe Blow

storm
  barrel

the story
  the bottom line

stow it
  fuck you
  knock off
  shut up
  stick it

STP
  bennies

strafe
  kick ass

straight
  butt
  high
  honest-to-God
  square
  straight, "heterosexual"
  straight, "heterosexual male"
  straight, "honest"
  straight, "legitimate"
  straight, "narcotics-free"

straight-arrow
  square
  straight

the straight dope, "truth"

straighten out
  blow grass
  fly right

straighten someone out
  spell out

straighten up
  fly right

straighten up and fly right
  clean up one's act
  fly right

straight face
  poker face

straight from the shoulder
  straight

the straight scoop
  the straight dope

straight-shooting
  straight

straight talk
  the straight dope

strange
  weird

strangioso
  kinky
  weird

strap
  jock

strapped
  broke
  heeled

straw
  pot

strawberry fields
  acid

streak
  barrel

street job
  hot rod

stretch
  bit

stretch one's luck
  stick one's neck out

stretch some jeans
  bugger

stretch the rules
  play dirty

strictly between us
  on the QT

strike
  sock
  walk

strike oil
  go over with a bang
  hack it

strike out
  fuck up

striker
  eager beaver

string along
  snow

string along with
  buy

string bean
  beanpole

string with
  hang out with

stripper, "strip-tease dancer"

strip-search
  frisk

strip-tease dancer
  stripper

strive
  bust one's ass

stroke
  jack off
  stroke, "flatter"
  stroke, "flattery"

stroke book
  fuck book

stroker
  hot rod

strong-arm
  bulldoze
  goon
  rough up

459

strong-arm man
  goon

strong-arm squad
  goon squad

strongbox
  pete

stronger than pig-shit
  high-powered

struggle
  wingding

strugglebuggy
  jalopy

strung out
  high
  hooked

stubborn as an ox
  bullheaded

stuck on oneself
  stuck-up

stuck-up
  snooty
  stuck-up, "conceited"

stud
  dude
  guy
  ladies' man
  stud, "sexually
    promiscuous male"

student
  grind
  junkie

studhammer
  ladies' man
  stud

Studley
  hunky

stuff
  ass
  booze
  broad
  coke
  cunt

dope
fuck
guts
pot

stuff oneself
  pig out

the stuff
  clout
  dough
  humdinger
  smarts

stuffed
  fed-up

stuffings
  innards

stuff it
  fuck you
  kiss my ass
  stick it

stuffy
  pissed off
  square

stuka
  bennies

stumblebum
  bum

stumbler
  doll

stump for
  go to bat for

stump it
  toddle

stump-jumper
  hick

stump liquor
  panther piss

stumps
  pins

stunner
  dish

  a hit
  humdinger

stunning
  great

stupe
  dope

stupid
  dumb
  have a hole in one's head

stupid person
  dope

stupper
  doll

style
  grandstand

stylish
  snappy

stylishness
  swank

stymied
  up the creek

sub
  hero

submachine gun
  Tommy gun

submarine sandwich
  hero

subordinate
  gofer

succeed
  go over with a bang
  hack it
  work

success
  a hit

successful
  have a field day
  in

suck
  blow
  blow job

brown-nose
  clout
snort
suck, "be disgusting"
suck air
  panic
suck around
  brown-nose
  goof off
suck eggs
  suck
sucker
  con
  guy
  jerk
  patsy
  snow
  sucker, "thing"
suckered
  screwed
sucker game
  scam
sucker-punch
  blind-side
suck face
  neck
suck hind tit
  play second fiddle
suck-in
  scam
sucking canal water
  up the creek
suck it up
  bust one's ass
  clean up one's act
suck off
  blow
suck-off
  brown-nose
  yucky

suck rope
  suck
suck up to
  brown-nose
  play up to
suck wind
  fuck up
suction
  blow job
  clout
suds
  brew
sudser
  soap opera
suds scenario
  soap opera
suedehead
  baldie
suffering cats
  Jeez
sugar
  acid
  coke
  dough
  honey
  horse
  M
sugar-bun
  honey
sugar cube
  acid
sugar daddy
  angel
sugar daddy, "keeper of
    mistress"
sugar stick
  cock
sugar tit
  security blanket
suicide
  do the Dutch

suit
  pro
sultry
  sexy
sumbitch
  asshole
  back-breaker
  guy
Sunday best
  glad rags
Sunday punch, "hard blow"
sunglasses
  shades
sunk
  kaput
  out of luck
sunshades
  shades
sunshine
  acid
sunshine girl
  grind
super
  great
super blow
  coke
super-duper
  great
supergopher
  good guy
super grass
  angel dust
a supergroove
  a ball
superior
  the most
super Kools
  angel dust
super soaper
  lude

support
  back
support one's claims
  put up or shut up
supremo
  pot
sure
  bet your ass
  for sure
  have it both ways
sure as shootin'
  for sure
sure bet
  cinch
sure enough
  honest-to-God
  OK
sure shot
  cinch
sure success
  have something cinched
sure thing
  cinch
  for sure
  honest-to-God
  OK
surfeit
  up to one's ass
  up to here
surfer
  angel dust
surpass
  beat
surprise
  I'll be damned
surveillance
  tail
susfu
  fucked-up
suspense
  cliffhanger

suss out
  dig
  smoke out
swabby, "sailor"
swack
  sock
swacked
  plastered
swag
  pay dirt
  score
swallow
  bite
  buy
  eat up
  snort
swallow the apple
  choke up
  freeze up
swallow whole
  bite
swallow with a glass of
      water
  clobber
swamp
  clobber
swank
  classy
swank, "stylishness"
swank it
  doll up
  put on the ritz
swank up
  doll up
swanky
  classy
swap spit
  neck
swat
  sock

sweat
  blow one's top
  blowup
  sweat, "worry"
sweat bullets
  panic
sweat hog
  floozy
  scarecrow
sweep
  beat
  grand slam
sweet
  great
sweet baby
  broad
sweeten someone up
  soft-soap
sweet Fanny Adams
  zilch
sweetheart
  broad
  doll
  honey
  humdinger
  the McCoy
sweetie-pie
  honey
sweet Jesus
  M
sweet Mary
  pot
sweet momma
  broad
sweet Morpheus
  M
sweet patootie
  broad
  dish
  honey

sweet talk
 bullshit
 soft soap
 stroke
sweet thing
 broad
swell
 dude
 great
 swell, "aristocrat"
swelled up
 stuck-up
swell-elegant
 great
swellheaded
 stuck-up
the swells
 the upper crust
swift
 dumb
swig
 guzzle
 snort
swill
 guzzle
swim
 work
swimming in
 up to one's ass
swindle
 con
 scam
swindler
 con man
swing
 fuck
 sleep around
 swing, "be promiscuous"
swinge
 tan

swinger
 floozy
swingin'
 square
swinging both ways
 AC-DC
swing man
 dealer
swipe
 heist
 knock
 panther piss
 sock
swish
 classy
 gay
Swiss purple
 acid
switched on
 high
 with it
switch on
 goose
swivet, "angry fit"
swizzled
 plastered
swoop
 barrel
swozzled
 plastered
sycophant
 brown-nose
syrup
 horse
T
 pot
T A
 cheesecake
tab
 a fix
 M

pasteboard
 peg
 tab, "acknowledgment of
  debt"
the tab
 the damage
table finisher
 pig
table grade
 dish
tabs
 acid
 bennies
tackhead
 dope
tacky
 bush
 crummy
 schlocky
 yucky
taco
 bean-eater
tad
 smidgen
tag
 monicker
 sock
tail
 ass
 broad
 tail, "surveiller"
one's tail is dragging
 pooped
tailormade
 butt
tail peddler
 hooker
take
 buy
 clobber
 con
 pay dirt

score
take, "receipts"

take a back seat
play second fiddle

take a bath
fuck up
go broke
take a beating

take a bow
way to go

take a brace
clean up one's act

take a break
kick back
knock off

take a breather
kick back

take a bye
give a miss

take a chill spill
cool it

take a crack at
give something a shot
plug
take a crack at, "try"

take a crap
shit

take action
fish or cut bait

take a D
do the Dutch

take a dekko at
check out

take a dig at
bad-mouth
knock

take a dive
flop
take a dive, "lose
intentionally"

take a douche
split

take a dump
shit

take a fall
fall

take a flyer
stick one's neck out

take a flying fuck
fuck you

take a gander
rubberneck

take a gander at
check out

take a hike
split

take a hinge at
check out

take a leak
piss

take a lick at
give something a shot
take a crack at

take a load off
kick back

take a pop at
plug

take a potshot at
knock
plug

take a powder
break out
split

take a power nap
snooze

take a rain check
give a miss

take a reading
check out

take a riffle at
give something a shot

take a run at
take on

take a runout powder
break out
split

take a scunner at
hate someone's guts

take a shit
shit

take a shot at
give something a shot

take a squint at
check out

take a swipe at
bad-mouth
knock

take a walk
lay off
walk
walk out on

take a whack at
give something a shot

take a whizz
piss

take care of
fix someone
snuff

take care of business
ace

take care of number one
take care of numero uno

take-charge guy
eager beaver

take down a notch
take someone down a peg

take downtown
clobber

take fire
work

take five
  kick back
  knock off
take for a ride
  snow
  snuff
take someone for a ride
  con
take forty winks
  snooze
take French leave
  go over the hill
take heat
  take it
take in
  snow
take into camp
  clobber
take it
  bite the bullet
  eat dirt
  hang tough
  take it, "endure"
take it all
  beat
take it easy
  cool it
  kick back
  pussyfoot
take it in the ear
  fuck you
take it on the chin
  hang tough
  take a beating
  take it
take it on the lam
  break out
  split
take it out of someone's
    hide
  tan

take it standing up
  take it
take it to the street
  go public
take one's medicine
  bite the bullet
  take it
taken
  screwed
taken to the cleaners
  screwed
takeoff
  act
take off
  heist
  shoot up
  snuff
  split
  work
take off one's hat to
  hand it to someone
take off one's high hat
  come down a peg
take on
  buck
  roust
  take on, "challenge"
take one step at a time
  pussyfoot
takeout
  bite
take out
  clobber
  snuff
take shit
  eat dirt
take one's stand
  sit tight
take ten
  kick back
  knock off

take the bait
  bite
take the cake
  beat
take the gas
  fuck up
take the heat off
  cool it
take the pipe
  choke up
  freeze up
  fuck up
take the rap
  bite the bullet
  take it
take the starch out of
  take someone down a peg
take the strop to
  tan
take the wind out of
    someone's sails
  take someone down a peg
take time out
  kick back
take to the cleaners
  clobber
take to the woodshed
  tan
tale of woe
  beef
  tear-jerker
talk
  bat around
  bigmouth
  blabbermouth
  bullshit
  chitchat
  dirt
  double-talk
  gab
  gabby
  get down to brass tacks

open one's yap
  sass
  schmooz
  shoot the breeze
  shut up
  squeal
talkative
  gabby
talk big
  blow off
  bullshit
talk someone's ear off
  gab
talkfest
  schmooz
talk someone into,
  "persuade"
talk is cheap
  put up or shut up
talk straight from the
  shoulder
  lay it on the line
talk-talk
  gab
talk through one's hat
  bullshit
talk to the big white phone
  barf
talk-trap
  yap
talk turkey
  get down to brass tacks
  lay it on the line
talk up a storm
  gab
talky
  gabby
talky-talk
  gab
tall
  high

tall person
  beanpole
the tall timbers
  the boondocks
tambourine man
  dealer
tamper
  doctor
tamper with
  fool around with
tan
  sock
  tan, "spank"
T and A
  cheesecake
tangle
  hassle
tangle-foot
  panther piss
tangle-footed
  plastered
tan someone's hide
  tan
tank
  flop
  guzzle
  rig
  take a dive
the tank
  the slammer
tanked
  plastered
tank job
  put-up job
tank town
  jerk town
tank up
  guzzle
tanky
  plastered

tantrum
  blowup
tap
  broke
  put the bite on
  shoot up
Tap City
  broke
tap dance
  cop out
  pussyfoot
  stall
  weasel
taped
  cinched
  in the bag
tap out
  flop
  go broke
  go kerflooey
  take a beating
tapped
  broke
tapped out
  broke
  kaput
  pooped
taps
  curtains
tard
  dope
tarfu
  fucked-up
the tariff
  the damage
tart
  broad
tart up
  doll up
taste
  bite
  blow grass

a fix
  piece

tater
  bingle

tater trap
  yap

tats
  crooked dice

tattle
  blow
  squeal

tatty
  bush
  crummy
  schlocky

tawny
  great

taxi fare
  ride the arm

TCB
  ace

t'd off
  pissed off

tea
  joint
  pot

tea'd up
  high

teahead
  pothead

team up
  buddy up

team up with
  hang out with

tea party
  cinch

tear
  barrel
  hinge
  paint the town red

tear around
  hell around

tearing mad
  pissed off

tearing up the pea patch
  full of piss and vinegar

tear into
  blast
  chew out

tear-jerker, "sentimental
    story"

tear off a piece
  fuck

tear off a strip
  chew out

tear up the peapatch
  make a scene

teary
  corny

tease
  cock-teaser

tea-stick
  joint

tec
  dick

techie
  tech

tedious person
  jerk

tedious work
  scut work

tee'd off
  pissed off

teen
  teenybopper

teenager
  teenybopper

teentsy
  little bitty

teenybopper, "teenager"

tee someone off
  piss someone off

tee off on
  chew out

teeth
  choppers

teetotally
  stone

telephone
  give someone a ring

telephone call
  buzz

television
  the tube

tell all
  blow

tell a thing or two
  chew out

tell it like it is
  lay it on the line
  let it all hang out

tell it to the Marines
  izzatso

tell off
  chew out

tell tales out of school
  squeal

tell where to get off
  take someone down a peg

telly
  the tube

temple bells
  hash

ten
  dish

tenderfoot
  greenhorn
  rookie

ten dollars
  sawbuck

tenner
 both hands
 sawbuck

Tennessee blue
 pot

tennies
 sneakers

tens
 bag

tense up
 choke up

ten-spot
 both hands
 sawbuck

ten yards
 grand

teo
 pothead

terrific
 great

terrifying
 creepy

testicles
 balls

test the water
 run it up the flagpole

tetched
 crazy

tetchy
 crazy
 feisty
 goosy

Texas tea
 pot

Thai weed
 pot

that'll do it
 way to go

that's life
 that's the way the cookie
 crumbles

that's my boy
 way to go

that's the way the ball
 bounces
 that's the way the cookie
 crumbles

that way
 knocked up

there
 high
 with it

there's no way
 like hell

there you go
 that's the way the cookie
 crumbles

they are a dime a dozen
 the woods are full of
 something

thick
 dumb
 palsy-walsy

thickbrain
 dope

thickskull
 dope

thickskulled
 dumb

thief
 heist man

thievish
 sticky-fingered

thin
 broke

a thin dime
 zilch

thing
 bag
 joint
 sucker

a thing
 a bee in one's bonnet

the thing
 hot

thingamajig
 gadget

things come unstuck
 hell breaks loose

thin in the upper crust
 dumb

thinker
 egghead

thin-skinned
 goosy

third leg
 cock

third rail
 panther piss

third-rater
 lightweight

third-stringer
 gofer

third wheel
 excess baggage

thirteen
 joint

those in the know
 the in group

thou
 grand

thousand dollars
 grand

thrashing
 great

threads, "clothing"

three bricks shy of a load
 dumb

three-letter man
 gay

three sheets to the wind
  plastered

thrill
  high

thriller
  joint

thrill pill
  doll

throat
  grind

throne
  can

throw
  peg

a throw
  a clip

throw
  take a dive

throw a bird
  give someone the finger

throw a curve
  snow

throw someone a curve
  con

throw a fit
  blow one's top

throw a fuck into
  fuck

throw a hyper
  blow one's top

throw a pass
  proposition

throw a scare into
  scare the shit out of

throw away
  blow
  chuck

throw bouquets at
  hand it to someone

throw curves
  snow

throw in the towel
  cop out
  fold

throw in with
  buy
  hang out with

throw leather
  hassle

throw out on one's ear
  bounce

throw over
  walk out on

throw overboard
  walk out on

throw something together
  knock something out

throw the book at
  clamp down
  kick ass

throw the bull
  blow off
  bullshit
  gab

throw the hooks into
    someone
  con

thrusters
  bennies

thumb
  hitchhike
  joint

thumb down
  blackball
  nix

thumbs up
  the go-ahead
  the OK

thump
  hassle
  sock

thumping
  great
  high-powered

thunderbox radio
  ghetto box

Thunder weed
  pot

thwack
  sock

a tick
  a jiffy

ticked off
  pissed off

ticker, "heart"

the ticket
  great

ticket of admission
  pasteboard

ticket seller
  scalper

tickety-boo
  great

tickled pink
  tickled

tick someone off
  piss someone off

tickytacky
  crummy

tiddly
  plastered

tidy sum
  bundle

tie
  works

tie a can to
  fire

tied up
 in the bag

tie into
 blast
 plug into

tie off
 shoot up

tie one on
 clobber

tie one's shoes
 clean up one's act
 fly right
 get on the ball
 wise up

tie up
 shoot up
 wrap up

tiff
 hassle

tiger sweat
 panther piss

tight
 broke
 chintzy

tight as a drum
 chintzy

tight as a tick
 plastered

tight as Kelsey's nuts
 chintzy

tighten one's wig
 blow grass

the tights
 the shorts

tight spot
 bind

tightwad, "miser"

till one can taste it
 up to here

till hell freezes over
 for keeps

till one is blue in the face
 flat-out

till the cows come home
 for keeps

time
 ages
 bit
 a jiffy

time in
 show up

timidity
 chicken out

tin
 bag
 chicken feed
 deck
 dough
 tin, "police badge"

tin-can
 blackball

tingle
 high

tinhorn
 bush
 crummy
 lightweight
 piddly

tinik
 horse

tinkle
 buzz
 piss

a tinkle
 a piss

tinpot
 piddly
 schlocky

tin star
 private eye

tipoff
 tip

tipover
 rumble

tip over
 heist

tipster
 snitch

tipsy
 plastered

tip the elbow
 guzzle

tiptoe
 pussyfoot

tip-top
 great

tired
 pooped

tit art
 cheesecake

titivate
 doll up

tits
 great
 tits, "breasts"

tits and ass
 cheesecake

titties
 tits

tittle-tattle
 chitchat
 dirt

tizzy
 blowup
 flak
 swivet

TL
 brown-nose

T-man
 pothead

TNT
 horse

toad skin
  buck

toady
  brown-nose

to a fare-thee-well
  flat-out

toast
  cool
  fry
  great
  kaput

tobacco
  a smoke

to beat the band
  flat-out
  lickety-split
  like hell

toddle, "walk"

toddle off
  split

toddler
  kid

to-do
  flak
  hoopla

toe the mark
  clean up one's act
  fly right

toff
  swell

together
  cool

tog out
  doll up

togs
  threads

to hell and gone
  flat-out

toilet
  can
  check the plumbing

piss
  a piss
shit
  a shit
  the shits

toke
  blow grass
  butt
  toke, "inhalation"

toker
  pothead

toke up
  blow grass

tokus
  ass

tokus-licker
  brown-nose

Tom
  fink

tomato
  broad
  dish

tomcat
  ladies' man

tom-cat
  stud

tom-cat around
  hell around

tomfool
  crazy

Tommy gun, "submachine
  gun"

tommyrot
  bullshit

tongue
  shyster

tongue job
  blow job

tongue-wag
  schmooz

tongue-wagger
  blabbermouth

tongue-wagging
  gab

too big for one's britches
  stuck-up

tooie
  doll

tool
  barrel
  cock
  grind
  patsy

toole
  doll

toolie
  tech

tool in
  show up

tools
  works

too much
  great
  the most

toot
  binge
  coke
  honk
  a kick
  snort

tootie fruity
  sissy
  wimp

tootonium
  coke

toot one's own horn
  blow off

tootsie
  broad
  honey

Tootsie Roll
  horse

tootsie-wootsies
  tootsies

toot sweet
  on the double

top
  top-kick

top brass
  the brass

top dog
  boss

top-drawer
  classy
  great

top-hat
  snooty

top-kick, "sergeant"

top-notch
  great

topple
  clobber

the tops
  great
  humdinger
  the McCoy
  the most

top sawyer
  boss

top sergeant
  dyke
  top-kick

top-shelf
  classy

topsider
  big shot
  boss

top story
  bean

torch
  joint

torch up
  blow grass

torment
  Dutch rub

torn up
  high

torpedo
  hero
  hit man
  joint

torqued
  pissed off

tosh
  bullshit

to spare
  up to here

toss
  frisk
  standoff

a toss
  a clip

toss around
  bat around

toss one's cookies
  barf

toss in the towel
  fold

toss off
  guzzle
  jack off

toss out
  fire

toss overboard
  chuck

toss up
  walk out on

toss-up
  standoff

tot
  snort

total, "wreck"

totaled
  high
  kaput

total loss
  loser

totally
  stone

totally bitchen
  great

tote
  blow grass
  cart

to the max
  as shit
  flat-out
  like hell

touch
  bum
  caper
  put the bite on

touch-and-go
  iffy

touch up
  bum
  put the bite on

touchy
  goosy
  have a hair up one's ass

tough
  goon
  great
  hairy
  tough, "severe"

tough break
  tough shit

tough grind
  back-breaker

tough guy
  goon
tough it out
  hang tough
  take it
tough luck
  tough shit
tough noogies
  tough shit
tough shit
  bad news
  one couldn't care less
  tough shit, "expression of
    bad luck"
tough spot
  bind
tough stuff
  bad news
tough titty
  tough shit
tout
  flack
town
  jerk town
town bike
  floozy
town pump
  floozy
track record
  the book
trade
  ass
  cruise
trade punches
  hassle
tragic magic
  horse
train
  gang bang
train with
  hang out with

traipse
  toddle
traitor
  fink
tramp
  floozy
tranqued
  high
trans
  jalopy
transport
  cart
transportation
  jalopy
trap
  night spot
  yap
trappings
  threads
trash
  bullshit
  clobber
  knock
  total
trashy
  crummy
  schlocky
travel
  floor it
travel agent
  acid
  dealer
tree-hugger
  duck-squeezer
trendy
  snappy
  trendy, "au courant"
  with it
trick
  bit

caper
  fuck
  squeal
trick out
  doll up
  fuck
tricky
  hairy
trigger
  blow grass
  hit man
trigger man
  hit man
trim
  ass
  clobber
  con
  cunt
trip
  clobber
  fall
  high
tripe
  bullshit
  crap
tripes
  guts
  innards
triple whammy
  whammy
tripped out
  high
trips
  acid
trip up
  goof
trite story
  chestnut
trivial
  piddly

trivial person
 lightweight

troll
 cruise
 dope

trot
 split

the trots
 the shits

trotters
 pins
 tootsies

trouble
 bad news
 bind
 flak
 make a scene
 up the creek

trouble and strife
 old woman

trouble-shoot
 rejigger

trounce
 clobber

truck
 crap
 split

truck along
 split

truck drivers
 bennies
 doll

truly
 honest-to-God

trumpet
 schnozz

trun
 peg

truth
 the straight dope

try
 give something a shot
 take a crack at

a try
 a crack

try out
 run it up the flagpole

TS
 tough shit

tsuris
 bad news

tub
 fatty
 jalopy

tube
 floozy
 joint

the tube, "television"

tube it
 flunk

Tubesville
 kaput

tub of lard
 fatty

tubular
 great

tuck
 chow

tuck away
 scarf

tuckered out
 pooped

tuck in
 scarf

tuck one's tail
 come down a peg

tuifu
 snafu

tum
 belly

tumble
 fall

tumble for
 buy

tumble to
 dig

tummy
 belly

tum-tum
 belly

tuna
 cunt

tuna wagon
 jalopy

tuned
 plastered

tuned in
 on someone's wavelength

tunnel
 hide out

turd
 asshole
 shit

turf
 bag

turista
 the shits

turkey
 blow grass
 coke
 dope
 flop
 jerk
 loser
 wimp

turkey-shit
 chickenshit

turkey-shoot
 cinch

turnabouts
 bennies

turn chicken
  chicken out

turn down cold
  nix

turned off
  clean
  fed-up

turned on
  cool
  flip
  high
  horny
  with it

turn in
  snooze

turn-off
  gloomy Gus

turn off someone's water
  take someone down a peg

turn on
  blow grass
  goose

turn someone on
  wow

turn on the afterburners
  barrel

turn on the heat
  come on strong

turnout
  threads

turn out
  bounce

turn purple
  blow one's top

turn the cold shoulder
  cut
  give the cold shoulder

turn the trick
  hack it

turn thumbs down
  blackball
  nix

turn tricks
  hustle

turn up
  show up

turn up one's nose
  give the cold shoulder

turn up one's toes
  croak

turn yellow
  chicken out

tush
  ass

tusker
  scarecrow

tusks
  choppers

tussle
  free-for-all

twat
  ass
  cunt

tweenager
  teenybopper

twenty-five
  acid

twerp
  jerk

twiddle-twaddle
  bullshit

twig
  dig

twimble
  dope

twink
  oddball

a twink
  a jiffy

a twinkling
  a jiffy

twist
  broad
  joint

twist someone's arm
  lean on someone
  talk someone into

twisted
  high

twister
  binge
  pothead

twisty
  sexy

twit
  jerk

two-bagger
  scarecrow

two-bit
  bush
  crummy
  piddly
  schlocky

two-by-four
  little bitty
  piddly

two-fisted
  he-man

two hoops and a holler
  a jiffy

two hoots in hell
  zilch

two shakes of a lamb's tail
  a jiffy

two-time
  cheat
  double cross

two-timer
  con man

two-way hit
  acid
two whoops in hell
  zilch
typewriter
  Tommy gun
U
  collitch
U B B
  bet your ass
ugh
  yuck
ugly
  piss-ugly
ugly customer
  cowboy
  goon
ugly person
  scarecrow
uh uh
  nope
ump
  Blind Tom
umph
  clout
umptieth
  umpty-umpth
unadorned
  vanilla
uncertain
  iffy
unchangeable
  carved in stone
uncle
  cop
  M
Uncle Sugar
  Uncle Sam
Uncle Tom
  fink

unconscious
  knock out
  out
uncool
  square
undercover man
  dick
under one's hat
  on the QT
underpinnings
  pins
under the gun
  up the creek
under the influence
  plastered
under the table
  plastered
under the weather
  green around the gills
  off one's feed
underwear
  long johns
  undies
under wraps
  on the QT
undesired persons
  shit list
undies, "underwear"
unethical practice
  play dirty
unfair treatment
  the shaft
unfortunate
  out of luck
ungodly
  crummy
unhep
  square
unholy mess
  bind
  snafu

unidentified person
  what's-his-name
unidentified things
  glob
  goo
  Mickey Finn
  mish-mash
  mung
  sucker
  umpty-umpth
uninhibited
  let oneself go
unintelligible language
  double-talk
unkink
  kick back
unkjay
  crap
  junkie
unlax
  kick back
unlikely winner
  long shot
unload
  chuck
  let it all hang out
unmentionables
  undies
unnecessary person
  excess baggage
unreal
  great
unrestrainedly
  flat-out
untogether
  fucked-up
unwind
  kick back
up
  high

hike
a kick

up against it
hooked
out of luck
up the creek

up against the wall
fuck you

up-and-up
honest-to-God
straight

upchuck
barf

up front
straight

up front, "in advance"

up gefucked
fucked-up

uphills
crooked dice

upmarket
classy

upper
a kick

the upper crust,
    "aristocracy"

upper-cruster
swell

upper-crusty
classy

uppers
bennies

upper story
bean

uppity
snooty
stuck-up

ups
bennies

upscale
classy
great

up shit creek
up the creek

upstage
give the cold shoulder

upstairs, "mentally"

up stakes
split

up the creek, "in trouble"

up the kazoo
up to here

up the river
in stir

up the spout
kaput

up the wall
crazy

uptick
hike

uptight
jittery

up to one's ass, "surfeited"

up-to-datey
trendy

up to here
fed-up
up to one's ass
up to here, "surfeited"

up to here with
filthy with

up to scratch
cool

up to snuff
cool

up to the ears
plastered

up to the eyeballs
filthy with
plastered
up to here

up to the gills
plastered

up to the mark
cool

uptown
coke

up yours
fuck you
kiss my ass

urinate
piss

urination
a piss

urp
barf

use
do

use one's bean
wise up

useless reward
win the porcelain hairnet

use smoke and mirrors
snow

US Government
Uncle Sam

usurer
loan shark

utility infielder
gofer

vagrant
bum

vamoose
break out
split

vamp
bluff

clobber
  wing it

vamp till ready
  wing it

vanilla
  straight
  vanilla, "unadorned"
  whitey

varmint
  bad man

varnish remover
  panther piss

varoom
  barrel

varsity
  collitch

va-va-voom
  sexy

veg
  goof off

vegetable
  dope

vegetable garden
  fruit salad

veg out
  goof off

vehicle
  banger
  bike

vein shooter
  junkie

velvet
  gravy
  pay dirt

the veritable cack
  the straight dope

verse
  stanza

vert
  oddball

very
  as shit

vestpocket
  little bitty

vet
  check out
  jalopy

vetting
  the once-over

vials
  acid

vibrations
  vibes

vic
  con
  patsy

vicious
  great

victim
  patsy

victory
  grand slam

video
  the tube

viewpoint
  where one is at

villain
  bad man

vinegar-puss
  scarecrow

vines
  threads

VIP
  big shot

viper
  dealer

viper weed
  pot

virgin
  cherry

virginity
  pop someone's cherry

virtuous person
  goody-goody

viscera
  guts
  innards

viscous fluid
  goo

visit
  schmooz

vittles
  chow

vomit
  barf

vomity
  yucky

vonce
  joint

voomy
  sexy

vote for
  go for

vroom
  barrel

vulnerable arm
  glass arm

vulnerable chin
  glass jaw

vulva
  cunt

wacko
  crazy
  flaky
  oddball
  weird

wacky
  crazy
  flaky
  weird

wacky weed
  pot
wad
  bundle
wade into
  blast
  chew out
waffle
  clobber
  cop out
  stall
  weasel
wafflestompers
  boondockers
wagering
  crooked dice
  make a killing
wag the tongue
  gab
  shoot the breeze
Wahegan
  pot
wail
  warble
wailing
  great
wait
  sit tight
wake-ups
  bennies
walk
  toddle
  walk, "discontinue
    something"
  walk, "strike"
walkaway
  cinch
walkboy
  pal
walk cool
  kick back

walk heavy
  carry a lot of weight
one's walking papers
  the axe
walk on eggs
  pussyfoot
walk out
  walk
walk out on, "abandon"
walkover
  cinch
walk the straight and
    narrow
  go straight
wall banger
  lude
wallop
  clobber
  clout
  a kick
  sock
walloping
  monster
wall-to-wall
  stone
walrus
  fatty
waltz
  chapter
  cinch
  stanza
  toddle
waltz off
  split
waltz out on
  walk out on
walyo
  guy
  wop
wamper-jawed
  cockeyed

wampum
  dough
wang
  cock
wank off
  jack off
want list
  laundry list
warble
  open one's yap
  warble, "sing"
warm body, "any person"
warm someone's ear
  gab
warmed-over cabbage
  chestnut
warm fuzzies
  stroke
warm man
  moneybags
warm someone's seat
  tan
warning
  jiggers
  lay off
warp out
  split
warts and all
  the straight dope
wash
  figure
  standoff
washed up
  kaput
washout
  flop
wash out
  flop
  go broke
  scrub

479

washtub weeper
  soap opera
wash-up
  crash
waste
  blow grass
  clobber
  snuff
  total
wastebasket
  the circular file
wasted
  broke
  high
  kaput
watering hole
  dive
  gin mill
watermelonhead
  dope
wax
  blowup
  clobber
  swivet
waxed
  plastered
waxy
  pissed off
way out
  cool
  great
  high
  weird
way to go, "congratulation"
way to hell and gone
  a country mile
wazoo
  ass
  asshole
weak
  wimpish

weak in the head
  dumb
weak-kneed
  chicken
weakling
  wimp
weak sister
  chicken
  sissy
  wimp
wealth
  bundle
wealthy
  loaded
wealthy person
  moneybags
weapons
  carry
  rod
wearing her apron high
  knocked up
wear the pants
  boss
weary Willy
  bum
weasel
  snitch
  squeal
  weasel, "evade"
weasel out
  back out
  cop out
web-foot
  duck-squeezer
wedding bells
  acid
wedges
  acid
wee bit
  smidgen

weed
  butt
  joint
  pot
weedhead
  junkie
  pothead
weeds
  threads
ween
  grind
weenchy
  little bitty
weenie
  cock
  grind
  jerk
weentsy
  little bitty
weeper
  tear-jerker
weewaw
  cockeyed
wee-wee
  piss
weigh in
  butt in
  show up
weigh in with
  kick in
weinie
  cock
weird
  cool
  crazy
  flaky
  great
  kinky
  weird, "strange"
weirded out

weirdo
  nut
  oddball
  sleazebag
welcome to the club
  that's the way the cookie
    crumbles
well-built
  built
well-endowed
  hung
well-heeled
  loaded
well-hung
  hung
well-upholstered
  built
welsh
  back out
wench
  broad
West Coast turnabouts
  bennies
wet blanket
  drag
  gloomy Gus
wet-nose
  rookie
wetware
  bean
wet one's whistle
  guzzle
whack
  bite
  pow
  sock
a whack
  a clip
  a crack
whacking
  monster

whack off
  jack off
whack wack
  angel dust
whale
  ace
  blast
  bruiser
  clobber
  fatty
  tan
whale into
  blast
wham
  pow
  sock
wham-bam thank you
    ma'am
  quickie
whambang
  monster
  pow
whammo
  pow
whammy, "curse"
whang
  sock
whatchamacallit
  gadget
what cooks
  what's up
what do you say
  what's up
what do you want from me
  one couldn't care less
what else is new
  so what
what gives
  what's up

what goes around comes
    around
  that's the way the cookie
    crumbles
what it takes
  clout
  smarts
what say
  what's up
what's cooking
  what's up
what's happening
  what's up
what's-his-face
  what's-his-name
whatsit
  gadget
what's the good word
  what's up
what turns you on
  kicks
wheat
  pot
wheel
  big shot
wheeler-dealer, "busy
    person"
wheels
  jalopy
  pins
when push comes to shove
  when the chips are down
when the eagle shits
  eagle day
where one's head is at
  where one is at
where one is coming from
  where one is at
where it's at
  the straight dope

where the rubber meets the
  road
 the bottom line

where the sun doesn't shine
 asshole

wherewithal
 dough

whiff
 coke
 fuck up
 snort

whip out
 give five
 whomp up

whip-out
 dough

whipped
 high
 kaput
 pussy-whipped

whipsaw
 clobber

whip the dog
 goof off

whistle-blower
 snitch

whistle stop
 jerk town

whistle tooter
 Blind Tom

white
 coke

whitebread
 square

white buck
 white shoe

white death
 coke
 M

white horse
 coke

white knuckle
 cliffhanger

white-knuckled
 scared shitless

white lady
 coke

white lightning
 acid
 panther piss

white linen
 M

white meat
 whitey

white merchandise
 M

white mosquito
 coke

white mule
 panther piss

white nurse
 horse
 M

white Owsley's
 acid

white paste
 coke

white person
 whitey

white powder
 coke
 M

whites
 bennies

white Sandoz
 acid

white shoe
 Joe College
 **white shoe, "college
  student"**

white silk
 M

white stuff
 coke
 horse
 M

white tape
 coke
 M

white tornado
 coke

white trash
 cracker

whitewash
 clobber

whitey, "white person"

whiz
 ace
 hot shot
 humdinger

whiz-bitch
 back-breaker

whiz kid
 ace
 hot shot

whizz
 piss

the whole ball of wax
 the whole shebang

the whole enchilada
 the whole shebang

the whole hog
 flat-out

the whole kit and caboodle
 the whole shebang

the whole megillah
 the whole shebang

the whole nine yards
 flat-out
 the whole shebang

the whole schmear
 the whole shebang

the whole shooting match
  the whole shebang

the whole show
  the whole shebang

the whole story
  the straight dope

the whole works
  the whole shebang

whomp
  clobber
  sock

whomp up
  cook up
  knock something out
  rustle up
  whomp up, "devise"

a whoop
  zilch

whoopdedoo
  wingding

whooper-dooper
  binge

whoop it up
  have a ball
  hell around

whoopla
  flack

whoops
  barf
  boner

whoozis
  gadget
  what's-his-name

whop
  clobber
  sock

a whop
  a crack

whopper-jawed
  cockeyed

whopping
  monster

whore
  floozy

whore around
  hell around

whorehouse, "brothel"

who you kidding
  izzatso

whup
  clobber

Wichita
  double cross

wicked
  great
  hairy

wide open
  flat-out
  lickety-split

wide place in the road
  jerk town

widget
  gadget

wienie
  cock

wife
  old woman

wig
  dig
  flip
  great
  rug

wigged out
  high
  weird

wiggle out
  back out

wiggy
  cool
  great

high
weird

wig out
  crack up
  flip
  go crazy

wild
  antsy
  cool
  great

wild-ass
  crazy

wild cat
  panther piss

wild weed
  pot

the willies
  the jitters

wimp
  chicken
  jerk
  wimp, "weakling"

wimpish, "weak"

wimpy
  wimpish

the wim-wams
  the jitters

win a few lose a few
  that's the way the cookie
    crumbles

windbag
  bigmouth
  blabbermouth

windbox
  squeezebox

wind down
  kick back

windjammer
  bigmouth
  blabbermouth

windows
 specs

wind up
 wrap up

windy
 gabby

wing
 bluff
 wing, "arm"
 wingding
 wing it

wingding
 binge
 swivet
 wingding, "party"

winging
 in the groove

wing it
 bluff
 wing it, "improvise"

wings
 coke
 M

wing-wang
 asshole

wingy
 high

wink
 a snooze

a wink
 a jiffy

winkie
 asshole

winkle out
 smoke out

winks
 sack time

winner
 a hit
 hot shot

humdinger
 long shot

wino
 bum
 lush

win one's wings
 go through the mill

win out
 hack it

winter rat
 jalopy

winter underwear
 long johns

win the fur-lined bathtub
 win the porcelain hairnet

wipe someone's ass
 brown-nose

wiped
 plastered

wiped out
 broke
 high
 kaput
 plastered

wipe one's nose
 fly right
 go straight

wipe out
 clobber
 fix someone
 fuck up
 screw up
 snuff
 total

wipe-out
 grand slam
 loser

wipe the slate clean
 go back to square one

wipe up the floor with
 clobber

wire
 heist man

wired
 antsy
 cinched
 high
 in the bag
 jittery

wired into
 into

wired job
 put-up job

wired up
 cinched
 in the bag

wire-puller
 wheeler-dealer

wise
 smart-ass
 with it

wise-ass
 cheeky
 smart-ass

wisecrack
 crack
 kid

wise guy
 smart-ass

wise-guy
 cheeky

wise me up, "request for
 information"

the wise money
 the smart money

wisenheimer
 smart-ass

wise prediction
 the smart money

wise to
 have someone's number

wise up
 fill someone in
 wise up, "become aware"

wish list
 laundry list

witch
 bitch
 broad
 coke
 horse
 M
 scarecrow

witch Hazel
 horse

with a bang
 with flying colors

with a smoking gun
 dead to rights

with bells on
 with flying colors

with one's hand in the till
 dead to rights

with it
 dig
 on the ball
 trendy
 with it, "cognizant"

with knobs on
 with flying colors

without a pot to piss in
 broke

without a red cent
 broke

without a sou
 broke

without a stitch
 bare-ass

without brain one
 dumb

without mussing a hair
 with flying colors

without one dollar to rub
  against another
 broke

with one's pants down
 dead to rights

with rocks in the head
 dumb

with the goods
 dead to rights

wiz
 ace
 hot shot

wobble weed
 angel dust

wolf
 angel dust
 ladies' man
 stud

woman
 broad
 dish
 Jane

womanizer
 ladies' man
 stud

wombat
 nut
 oddball

Wonder Bread
 square

wonk
 grind
 jerk

wonky
 cockeyed
 green around the gills

wood
 cracker
 whitey

woodchuck
 cracker

woodenhead
 dope

woodenheaded
 dumb

wooden-stake
 scrub

woodhead
 dope

woodhick
 hick

the woods are full of
  something, "something
  is plentiful"

woof
 blow off
 bullshit
 gab

woofer
 blabbermouth

wool
 broad

woolhat
 cracker

woolies
 long johns

woozy
 plastered
 rocky

wop, "Italian person"

woppitzer
 kibitzer

word
 bet your ass
 the poop

the word
 the poop

word-slinger
 blabbermouth

work
 goof off

moonlight
  work, "succeed"
work both sides of the
    street
  have it both ways
worked up
  antsy
worker
  scab
  working stiff
working girl
  hooker
working stiff, "worker"
work into the ground
  blow up
work on
  lean on someone
work
  back-breaker
work out
  fuck
  work
  work out, "repair"
work over
  clobber
  rough up
works
  basket
  cock
  works, "narcotics
    apparatus"
the works
  best shot
  the whole shebang
work up
  cook up
world-beater
  hot shot
world-class
  great

worm
  angel dust
  asshole
  jerk
worm-food
  stiff
worm out
  back out
  cop out
wormy
  yucky
worn to a frazzle
  pooped
worried stiff
  jittery
worry
  sweat
the worser half
  hubby
worthless
  not worth a damn
wow
  break someone up
  humdinger
  wow, "delight extremely"
wowser
  humdinger
wow them
  go over with a bang
wrangle
  hassle
wrap up
  clinch
  wrap up, "complete"
wreck
  clobber
  fix someone
  jalopy
  total
wrecked
  high

wren
  broad
wretched place
  the pits
wrinkle
  glitch
wristlets
  bracelets
wrongarmer
  southpaw
wrong number
  bad man
wrong 'un
  bad man
wussy
  wimp
wuzzup
  what's up
X-double-minus
  crummy
X-rated
  dirty
XX
  double cross
yackety-yack
  bullshit
  chitchat
  gab
  shoot the breeze
yack it up
  gab
yahoo
  dope
yakoo
  whitey
Yale
  works
yammer
  beef
  gab

yang
  cock
yank
  fuck
  roust
yank someone's chain
  bug
  kid
yantsy
  antsy
  jittery
yap
  beef
  bullshit
  dope
  gab
  hick
  jerk
  patsy
  yap, "mouth"
yapper
  blabbermouth
yapping
  gab
yappy
  gabby
yard
  a bill
  cheat
  cock
yardbird
  con
  rookie
yard bull
  cop
yard rat
  kid
yatata
  gab
yawner
  chestnut

yawny
  dullsville
yaw-ways
  cockeyed
yeah
  bet your ass
  OK
yecch
  yuck
yecchy
  yucky
yegg
  cowboy
  goon
  heist man
ye gods
  Jeez
yell bloody murder
  beef
yell blue murder
  beef
yell one's head off
  beef
yellow
  chicken
yellow fever
  acid
yellow jacket
  doll
yellow sunshine
  acid
yellow ticket
  bobtail
yen chee
  big O
yen chiang
  big O
yen pock
  big O

yenta
  blabbermouth
  kibitzer
yentz
  con
  fuck
yentzed
  screwed
yentzer
  con man
yep
  bet your ass
  OK
yerba
  pot
yesca
  pot
yes indeedy
  OK
yes man
  brown-nose
yes sirree
  OK
Yid
  kike
yield profit
  pay off
yikes
  Jeez
ying-yang
  asshole
  cock
yip
  gab
yipe
  Jeez
yodel
  warble
yoke
  heist

yokel
  hick
yokeldom
  the boondocks
yoker
  heist man
yold
  patsy
you ain't just whistling
    Dixie
  bet your ass
you betcha
  bet your ass
  OK
you better believe it
  bet your ass
  honest-to-God
you can't win them all
  that's the way the cookie
    crumbles
you-know-what
  blankety-blank
  gadget
you know what you can do
    with it
  fuck you
  kiss my ass
you name it
  the whole shebang
youngblood
  blood
young girl
  jail bait
young male
  young squirt
young punk
  kid
  young squirt
young Turk
  eager beaver

young 'un
  kid
your basic
  vanilla
you're damn tootin
  bet your ass
you're full of hops
  izzatso
you're full of shit
  izzatso
you're telling me
  bet your ass
your Uncle Dudley
  yours truly
you said a mouthful
  bet your ass
you wouldn't shit me
  izzatso
  no shit
  so what
yowzah
  OK
yo-yo
  dope
  jerk
yuck, "expression of
    disgust"
yucky
  crummy
  yucky, "disgusting"
yuk
  break up
a yuk
  a howl
yummy
  great
yup
  OK

z
  deck
Z
  snooze
Zacatecas purple
  pot
zap
  clobber
  pizzazz
  plug
  pow
  snuff
zappy
  full of piss and vinegar
  jazzy
  zingy
zazzed-up
  jazzed-up
zazz up
  jazz up
zazzy
  classy
  glitzy
  jazzy
zebra
  Blind Tom
Zee
  snooze
Zelda
  square
Zen
  acid
zerk
  dope
zerking
  ditsy
  flaky
  weird
zero
  zilch

zero cool
  cool
  great
zero in, "single out"
zetz
  sock
zhlub
  jerk
  sleazebag
zig
  nigger
zigaboo
  nigger
zig-zig
  ass
zilch
  Joe Blow
  zilch, "nothing"
  zit
zillionth
  umpty-umpth
zing
  barrel
  high
  a kick
  knock
  pizzazz
  snuff
zing along
  barrel
zinger
  punch line
zingy
  full of piss and vinegar
  jazzy
  zingy, "energetic"

zip
  barrel
  gook
  pizzazz
  zilch
zip gun
  rod
zip one's lip
  shut up
zipped
  high
zippo
  pizzazz
  zilch
zippy
  full of piss and vinegar
  jazzy
  zingy
zip top
  kike
zit, "skin lesion"
zizz
  pizzazz
  snooze
  a snooze
zod
  jerk
  oddball
zoid
  square
zol
  joint
zombie
  dope
  oddball

zombie buzz
  angel dust
zone
  junkie
  oddball
zoned out
  high
zoner
  junkie
  oddball
zonk
  clobber
  pass out
zonked
  high
  plastered
zooey
  yucky
zoom
  angel dust
  barrel
  pot
zoom buggy
  jalopy
zot
  zilch
zowie
  pizzazz
  pow
Zs
  sack time
zuch
  snitch
zup
  what's up